Global Communications

Series editors

Michael Brüggemann
Sven Engesser
Carola Richter

Merlyna Lim
Marie-Soleil Frère
Ingrid Bachmann

About the series

Global Communications is a book series that looks beyond national borders to examine current transformations in public communication, journalism and media. Books in this series will focus on the role of communication in the context of global ecological, social, political, economic, and technological challenges in order to help us understand the rapidly changing media environment. We encourage comparative studies but we also welcome single case studies, especially if they focus on regions other than Western Europe and North America, which have received the bulk of scholarly attention until now.

Empirical studies as well as textbooks are welcome. Books should remain concise and not exceed 300 pages but may offer online access to a wealth of additional material documenting the research process and providing access to the data. The series aspires to publish theoretically well-grounded, methodologically sound, relevant, novel research, presented in a readable and engaging way. Through peer review and careful support from the editors of the series and from the editorial team of Open Book Publishers, we strive to support our authors in achieving these goals.

Global Communications is the first Open Access book series in the field to combine the high editorial standards of professional publishing with the fair Open Access model offered by OBP. Copyrights stay where they belong, with the authors. Authors are encouraged to secure funding to offset the publication costs and thereby sustain the publishing model, but if no institutional funding is available, authors are not charged fees. Any publishing subvention secured will cover the actual costs of publishing and will not be taken as profit. In short: we support publishing that respects the authors and serves the public interest.

You can find more information about this series at:
https://www.openbookpublishers.com/section/100/1

Arab Media Systems

Edited by Carola Richter and
Claudia Kozman

https://www.openbookpublishers.com

© 2021 Carola Richter and Claudia Kozman. Copyright of individual chapters is maintained by the chapters' authors.

This work is licensed under a Creative Commons Attribution 4.0 International license (CC BY 4.0). This license allows you to share, copy, distribute and transmit the text; to adapt the text and to make commercial use of the text providing attribution is made to the authors (but not in any way that suggests that they endorse you or your use of the work). Attribution should include the following information:

Carola Richter and Claudia Kozman (eds), *Arab Media Systems*. Cambridge, UK: Open Book Publishers, 2021, https://doi.org/10.11647/OBP.0238

In order to access detailed and updated information on the license, please visit https://doi.org/10.11647/OBP.0238#copyright

Further details about CC BY licenses are available at https://creativecommons.org/licenses/by/4.0/

All external links were active at the time of publication unless otherwise stated and have been archived via the Internet Archive Wayback Machine at https://archive.org/web

Updated digital material and resources associated with this volume are available at https://doi.org/10.11647/OBP.0238#resources

Every effort has been made to identify and contact copyright holders and any omission or error will be corrected if notification is made to the publisher.

This project received support from the Arab-German Young Academy of Sciences and Humanities (AGYA) that has been funded under the German Ministry of Education and Research (BMBF) grant 01DL20003.

This publication was financed in part by the open access fund for monographs and edited volumes of the Freie Universität Berlin.

ISBN Paperback: 9781800640597

ISBN Hardback: 9781800640603

ISBN Digital (PDF): 9781800640610

ISBN Digital ebook (epub): 9781800640627

ISBN Digital ebook (mobi): 9781800640634

ISBN XML: 9781800640641

DOI: 10.11647/OBP.0238

Cover design by Anna Gatti based on a photo by Duangphorn Wiriya on Unsplash at https://unsplash.com/photos/KiMpFTtuuAk

Contents

Contributor Biographies		vii
Introduction *Carola Richter and Claudia Kozman*		xi
1.	Lebanon: A Faltering Mesh of Political and Commercial Interests *Sarah El-Richani*	1
2.	Syria: A Fragmented Media System *Yazan Badran*	19
3.	Palestine: Resilient Media Practices for National Liberation *Gretchen King*	37
4.	Jordan: Media's Sustainability during Hard Times *Basim Tweissi*	55
5.	Iraq: Media between Democratic Freedom and Security Pressures *Sahar Khalifa Salim*	73
6.	Saudi Arabia: From National Media to Global Player *Marwan M. Kraidy*	91
7.	United Arab Emirates: Media for Sustainable Development *Mohammad Ayish*	109
8.	Qatar: A Small Country with a Global Outlook *Ehab Galal*	127
9.	Bahrain: Media-Assisted Authoritarianism *Marc Owen Jones*	145
10.	Kuwait: From "Hollywood of the Gulf" to Social Media Diwaniyas *Fatima Alsalem*	163

11. Oman: Time for Fundamental Changes 181
   Abdullah K. Al-Kindi

12. Yemen: Unsettled Media for an Unsettled Country 197
   Abdulrahman M. Al-Shami

13. Egypt: A Divided and Restricted Media Landscape 215
   after the Transformation
   Hanan Badr

14. Sudan: Media under the Military–Democratic Pendulum 233
   Mahmoud M. Galander

15. Libya: From Jamahirization to Post-Revolutionary Chaos 249
   Carola Richter

16. Tunisia: The Transformative Media Landscape after 267
   the Revolution
   Noureddine Miladi

17. Algeria: The Costs of Clientelism 285
   Nacer-Eddine Layadi, translated by Abdelhak Bouifer

18. Morocco: Competitive Authoritarianism in 303
   Media Reforms
   Bouziane Zaid and Mohammed Ibahrine

Conclusion 323
Carola Richter and Claudia Kozman

Acknowledgements 343

Index 345

Contributor Biographies

Abdullah K. Al-Kindi, Ph.D., is Professor of Journalism and Electronic Publishing at Sultan Qaboos University, Oman. In his research, he focuses on media policies, media coverage of wars and crisis, and Omani media. He has authored and translated several books, and he recently co-authored a book entitled *Omani Pioneer Journalists* (2020).

Abdulrahman Al-Shami, Ph.D., is Associate Professor of Broadcast Journalism at Qatar University. In his research, he focuses on new media and social change, as well as on satellite channels. He is the co-founder of AREACORE, the Arab-European Association of Media and Communication Researchers, and a board member of AUSACE, the Arab-US Association of Communication Educators.

Fatima Alsalem, Ph.D., is Assistant Professor of Mass Communication at Kuwait University, College of Arts. In her research, she focuses on social media, public opinion and journalism, as well as on online extremism and radicalization.

Mohammad Ayish, Ph.D., is Professor and Head of the Department of Mass Communication at the American University of Sharjah, UAE. His research interests include Arab world satellite broadcasting, media ethics, social media and convergence, and digital storytelling. His most recent co-authored book, with Noha Mellor (2015), is titled *Reporting in the MENA region: cyber engagement and pan-Arab social media*. Previously, he served as Dean of the College of Communication at the University of Sharjah, UAE.

Hanan Badr, Ph.D., is Associate Professor in Mass Communication at the Gulf University for Science and Technology (GUST), Kuwait, Assistant Professor at Cairo University, and a long-time affiliate of

Freie Universität Berlin, Germany. Her research focuses on comparative media systems, Arab journalism, political communication and digital public spheres.

Yazan Badran is a Ph.D. fellow of the Research Council–Flanders (FWO) and a researcher at the Echo and imec-SMIT research centers at the Vrije Universiteit Brussel, Belgium. His research lies at the intersection of new journalism and political activism in the post-2011 Middle East and North Africa region (MENA).

Sarah El-Richani, Ph.D., is Assistant Professor of Communications at the American University in Cairo, Egypt. She was Visiting Fellow and Academic Visitor at the Centre for Lebanese Studies and St. Antony's College, University of Oxford during the academic year 2016–2017. Her research interests include political communication, contentious politics, media history, and comparative media studies.

Ehab Galal, Ph.D., is Associate Professor at the Department of Cross-Cultural and Regional Studies, Copenhagen University, Denmark. His research focuses on Arab media, Arab audiences, mediatized religion and politics, and Arab diaspora. Since 2018, he has been leading a research team working on the project "Mediatized Diaspora", which investigates transnational media use and contentious politics among Arab diaspora in Europe.

Mahmoud M. Galander, Ph.D., was Associate Professor in the Department of Mass Communication, Qatar University. Currently, he is a freelance Professor of Journalism and Mass Communication affiliated with several Sudanese universities. He was formerly the editor of a Sudanese newspaper, *Al-Quwat Al-Mussallaha*, and is a member of the Sudan Journalists' Union. He is the co-founder of the Arab-European Association of Media and Communication Researchers (AREACORE), and a member of the International Association of Media and Communication Researchers (IAMCR).

Mohammed Ibahrine, Ph.D., is Associate Professor of Integrated Marketing Communication at the American University of Sharjah, UAE. His research interests cover technology and marketing, entrepreneurship, innovation, and the technologies of the fourth industrial revolution.

Marc Owen Jones, Ph.D., is Assistant Professor of Middle East Studies at Hamad bin Khalifa University. His work focuses on social media, disinformation and propaganda in the Middle East. He has written extensively on the use of digital media as a tool of social control, and has an upcoming book on *Digital Authoritarianism in the Middle East* (2021) with Hurst/OUP.

Gretchen King, Ph.D., is Assistant Professor of Communication and Multimedia Journalism at the Lebanese American University in Beirut. She serves as the Director of Pedagogy and Curriculum Design at LAU's Institute for Media Research and Training. In her research, she focuses on alternative media and community radio in the regions of North America, North Africa, and West Asia.

Claudia Kozman, Ph.D., is Assistant Professor of Multimedia Journalism and the Research Director at the Institute of Media Research and Training at the Lebanese American University in Lebanon. Her research primarily focuses on news content and audience perceptions in the Arab world, in addition to comparative studies at the regional and international levels.

Marwan M. Kraidy, Ph.D., is Dean and CEO of Northwestern University in Qatar, and the Anthony Shadid Chair in Global Media, Politics and Culture at Northwestern University, Evanston, USA. He is a Fellow of the International Communication Association. Previously he was the founding director of the Center for Advanced Research in Global Communication, at the Annenberg School for Communication, University of Pennsylvania. He has published 130+ essays and 13 books.

Nacer-Eddine Layadi, Ph.D., is Professor of Communication Studies at Algiers 3 University. He has previously worked as a professor at Arab Gulf universities, and as a journalist. In his research, he focuses on media and cultural change in Algeria and the Arab world.

Noureddine Miladi, Ph.D., is Professor of Media and Communication and former Head of the Department of Mass Communication at Qatar University. His research interests include social media and social change, youth, identity and social media networks, media and democracy, media ethics, Al-Jazeera, and changes in the global media flow. He is the editor of *JAMMR*, an international peer-reviewed journal specializing in Arab and Middle Eastern media and society, and a founding member of the Arab Media and Communication Network (AMCN).

Carola Richter, Ph.D., is Professor of International Communication at Freie Universität Berlin, Germany. In her research, she focuses on Arab media, foreign news coverage, media and migration, and public diplomacy. She is the co-founder of AREACORE, the Arab-European Association of Media and Communication Researchers.

Sahar Khalifa Salim, Ph.D., is Professor at the Department of Journalism of the College of Media of Iraqia University in Baghdad, Iraq. Her research interests include digital media education, investigative journalism and propaganda. She is the Vice Chairperson of the Al-Baseera Society for Media Research and Development, a member of the Arab-European Association for Media and Communication Researchers (AREACORE), and a board member of the Advisory Committee of Arab Research Id (ARID).

Basim Tweissi, Ph.D., is Professor in Media Studies, former Dean of the Jordan Media Institute (JMI), and former Chairman of the Jordan Radio and Television Board of Directors. He has published six books on media, social development and political issues. He is a senior researcher in the national research project "Development of Quality and Professional Criteria for Media in Jordan".

Bouziane Zaid, Ph.D., is Associate Professor of Global Communication at the University of Sharjah, UAE. His research interests lie in the areas of media technologies, media law and policy, media advocacy, and corporate communication.

Introduction

Carola Richter and Claudia Kozman

> Building on extant scholarship about media systems, this chapter provides a set of criteria to examine the Arab countries, and by doing so, to allow a comparative analysis. Taking into account the various issues previous studies have had with such classifications, we designed the benchmarks of our analysis to reflect the various factors that intertwine to both draw similarities and highlight differences in the media among the Arab countries. As such, the aim of this chapter is to classify Arab media along a set of dimensions in order to better understand the overall systems that characterize media in the Arab region.

The Arab world has existed for thousands of years, but it has never received as much attention from the international community as it has during the last decade, where political unrest has resulted in changes to long-standing governing styles. At the heart of such changes were the media that played a significant role in supporting or resisting these transformations. To better understand how Arab media are situated at the intersection of politics, culture, and technology, we turn to media systems. Notwithstanding the similarities they share with one another, Arab media are not homogeneous. Therefore, to comprehend their collective power, we need first to understand their individual potential before we grasp their regional breadth.

Arab media matter globally. They matter because they reflect a range of often distinct but specific political approaches and understandings of publics and the public sphere. These approaches are potentially shaping media practices beyond the Arab world, incorporated by migrant audiences, transnational journalists or globally investing companies. They matter because they point us to economic media models that go beyond the Western notions of "public" and "private" with strong implications for the role media can play in societies. They matter because of the ways in which digital and, in particular, social media are incorporated in both regimes' and users' practices, providing us with an insight into the possible effects of digital media technologies on society, economy and politics globally.

With the term "Arab media," we refer to mass media in the Middle East and North Africa (MENA) region—a region that comprises more than 300 million people in over 20 states stretching from the Atlantic Ocean to the borders of Iran. People living in these states are of different ethnic origins and adhere to different religions. These states are shaped by different forms of governance, ranging from hereditary monarchies to federal republics. Some are considered the richest countries in the world, whereas others are the poorest. This vast region, which was once considered the cradle of humankind, boasting some of the oldest reminders of early civilization, has witnessed various historical forces that have rendered its current political structure a product of colonial dependencies, with some states being on the brink of collapse or disintegration. Thus, the "Arab world" is by no means a homogenous entity, nor are its media. As such, any attempts at examining it require a careful analysis that centers on the historical, political, social, and economic peculiarities of the different countries making up the region. Given this need to treat the Arab world as an area of varying political and cultural structures, the primary unit of our analysis will be the nation-state. Indeed, there is a common bond of history among the countries under investigation in this book, which started with the spread of Islam in the 600s, and was amplified by a century-long incorporation of most of what is today considered the MENA region into the Ottoman Empire. There are also shared experiences of colonialism, subsequent struggles for independence and the oftentimes ongoing search for a national identity. And, separating it from all other important world regions, such as Europe, sub-Saharan Africa, East Asia, or even Latin America, is a unifying language, Arabic, which creates a sense of belonging and togetherness—despite the different local dialects, the influence of colonial languages, and the multiplicity of indigenous languages such as Kurdish or Tamazight.

A common language, a shared history, and, often, mutual political interests led to the foundation of the Arab League, comprising 22 countries, in 1945. In the following chapters, we examine 18 of them, excluding only Somalia, Mauritania, and the microstates of Djibouti and the Comoros, as they belong geographically and culturally to sub-Saharan Africa.

One major argument for specifically considering the nation-state as our unit of analysis is the historically proven pattern of the non-simultaneity of the development of Arab media, which continues even today. While as early as the nineteenth century, Cairo, Beirut, and Baghdad had already established themselves as centers of intellectual media production with a lively press landscape, today's technologically-advanced Gulf states had no mass media at that time. Structural, economic, and political differences are also constitutive today, as can be observed, for example, in Internet connectivity, which ranges from almost 100% of the population in Kuwait to 22% in Libya (International Telecommunication Union, 2018). However, repeating the pattern from a century ago, highly mobile Arab journalists and media producers are once again driving forward intra-Arab and international exchange and media development. Whether the object of discussion is newspapers founded in Cairo in the 1800s by Syrian intellectuals from Beirut, a Tunisian-moderated talk show at the *Al-Arabiya* television station in the Emirates today, or a Palestinian newspaper in London financed by Qatari investors, Arab media must be understood in both their national and transnational contexts. This book aims to provide a picture of current Arab media systems, building on their past and predicting their future. To do so, it relies on new dimensions that create a framework for evaluating the media in each of the Arab countries, as they highlight the characteristics that render these media systems unique, while placing them within the larger Arab systems.

This introduction provides an overview of Arab media systems, putting forward a set of new criteria to examine media in the Arab countries and, in doing so, allowing a comparative analysis. The development of these criteria is guided by a de-westernizing approach that builds on a critical review of extant scholarship about media systems. It thus speaks to an audience of media and communication scholars, or students who are interested in expanding their knowledge in international and comparative political communication. In addition, the emphasis the book puts on the historical and current complexities of the Arab region allows for a deeper understanding of the shared yet distinct characteristics of Arab media in their political, economic and societal contexts. As such, the book is potentially interesting to a broader audience of political scientists, media workers, and even politicians or NGOs.

Following the introduction, the subsequent country chapters offer a more nuanced understanding of Arab media through the insights of authors who are mostly, with the exception of a few experts, natives of the countries about which they are writing. It is worth mentioning that the task of providing a comprehensive overview of the historical formation, current status quo, and future challenges faced by the media systems in a short chapter is impossible. We therefore aimed to focus on the broader picture, opting to refrain from presenting a plethora of facts and figures.

To sum up the information on individual countries, the conclusion identifies common themes gleaned from individual chapters, classifying Arab media according to a spectrum that features the specific characteristics of media in the Arab region.

Comparison of Media Systems as an Analytical Perspective

We use the term "media system", although not everyone is content with this term (see Jakubowicz, 2010, p. 9). Dennis McQuail (2010) has defined media systems as "the actual set of mass media in a given national society" (p. 220), which points out the problem of thinking of media systems as hermetic, national "containers." We instead follow the notion of systems advanced by Andrew Chadwick (2013), who contends that systems should be seen as being constitutive of structure-actor relationships; thus the term "system may often connote flexibility, adaptability, and evolutionary change emerging from the sum of social interaction" (p. 16). Building on these concepts and applying such a perspective, we will take a closer look at structures that shape practices that, in turn, shape structures in both national and transnational contexts.

Scholars have contended that media systems reflect the historical trajectories of a society and the political and legal systems, economic system, and social composition of the country in which they are located. In this realm, a comparative approach to media systems appears to be a useful way to explain different patterns of media governance and performance. The past decades of comparative research have revealed that this approach has not been driven purely by scholarly motivation but has been used as a means to normatively evaluate media systems as free/ unfree or developed/underdeveloped and to draw political conclusions from this typology. Beyond their political instrumentalization, these typologies can also help researchers to grasp major differences and similarities in media organization and performance quickly—but they must be established with care.

However, comparative media system analysis has predominantly focused on criteria related to the historical, political, and economic aspects, often neglecting the social aspect. One of the few authors to consider this latter aspect is John Downing (1996), who proposed analyzing media systems according to factors such as political power, economic crisis, dramatic social transitions, and small-scale media. The field of comparing media systems was first conceptualized via the publication of the *Four Theories of the Press* by Fred Siebert, Theodore Peterson, and Wilbur Schramm (1963). In this book, the authors identified four types of media system logics according to the media's "chief purpose" (Siebert et al., 1963, p. 7): 1) an authoritarian model in which media advance and support the policies of the government and are thus strongly controlled by it; 2) a libertarian model in which media are meant to inform and entertain and can be owned by whoever has the economic means to do so; 3) a social responsibility model in which media are also meant to inform and entertain but with the purpose of discussing and solving societal conflicts; 4) a Soviet totalitarian model in which the chief purpose of the media is to propagate the ideas of the ruling party, and the media is therefore almost exclusively state-owned.

The book, which arose from the investigation Siebert and his colleagues conducted at the request of the Hutchins Commission on Freedom of the Press, was strongly driven by a Cold War impulse to highlight Western media systems as superior to those influenced by the Soviet Union. For instance, while model 1 seems to mark the early state of a society, which can be overcome by democratic developments and eventually leads to the models 2 or 3, model 4 is seen as deviant and undesirable. Perhaps, the most potent criticism of the four theories came from media historian John Nerone (1995), who contended that the book is essentially one theory with four examples.

Regardless, this typology of what role the media ought to play in society and how they are therefore organized has shaped generations of scholars. Some have tried to add models (or theories), such as James Carey's (1992) "ritual model", which depends on shared understandings between sender and receiver that help to maintain society; William Hachten's (1981) "revolutionary model", which emphasizes the mobilizing and propaganda role of media; Dennis McQuail's (1994) "developmental model", in which he referred to media as a contributor to positive national development; or James Curran's (1991) "radical democratic model", in which he proposed that media should be free of commercial interests and belong to the people. All of these models were clearly based on contemporary perspectives, reflecting the political and economic contexts in the particular world regions with which they engaged during a particular time.

Only in 2004 did a book of a truly comparative nature, *Comparing Media Systems* by Daniel Hallin and Paolo Mancini, set a new benchmark. Limiting their investigation to the 18 media systems of North America and Europe, and excluding Eastern Europe, the authors devised three types of media-politics relationships:

1) the liberal model, which is characterized by a market-driven understanding of the media, a low structural political parallelism, and little external regulation of the media, as is found in the US;

2) a democratic corporatist model, in which media are considered a public good and moderately regulated, as in Sweden;

3) a polarized pluralist model, in which political parallelism is strong and media are often seen as instruments used by either the state, political parties, or business tycoons, as we see in Greece.

This seemingly ready-to-use typology of media systems has drawn much attention and been heavily quoted in subsequent studies, but it has also been strongly criticized. One of the major criticisms against it is that the ideal types outlined above are too general and not applicable beyond the Western hemisphere (Hallin & Mancini, 2012). Both criticisms indicate a misunderstanding of Hallin and Mancini's intentions. The authors made it clear from the very beginning that their typology should be understood as a possible range of ideal types with many overlaps and grey zones in between, implying that none of the countries analyzed in their study fitted exactly into any single one of the types. Furthermore, the authors never intended to apply these models or types to examples outside the Western world. Thus, the polarized pluralist, which has often been labeled as some kind of "catchall category" (Voltmer, 2012, p. 225) for media systems of the Global South, would have to be reshaped or reconceptualised for use as a starting point to look beyond the Western world.

Taking into consideration the above thoughts on Hallin and Mancini's work, and in line with demands raised in the context of the debate on de-westernizing communication studies (Waisbord & Mellado, 2014), we find it necessary to reflect on the criteria Hallin and Mancini devised to form the conceptual base of their three types and their applicability to non-Western media systems. These criteria are related to both the political and media systems and are integral to each model. With regard to the political system, Hallin and Mancini emphasized the importance of the political history of a country, i.e. whether it is a consensus or majoritarian government, and whether it operates within the context of political pluralism.

With regard to the media system, they emphasized the significance of factors such as the development of the newspaper industry, the presence of political parallelism in media organizations, and the level of professionalization among journalists, as well as the role of the state in regulating the media. Thus, their models focussed strongly on history, media-politics relationships, legal aspects, and journalistic role perception, but ignored many other elements, such as technological and social aspects. Perhaps even more importantly, a rather static application of the derived criteria to the analysis of a media system misses out less explicit and non-codified practices in the realm of media policies. Waisbord and Mellado highlight that "de-westernization demands a shift in the analytical mindset" (2014, p. 364), in particular with regard to the "body of evidence" (p. 364). Still, many scholars have continued to rely on the same limited focus on politics-media relations, such as Roger Blum (2014) who built on Hallin and Mancini's criteria to develop a typology for the entire world. He proposed 11 dimensions that mirror these very same foci (p. 295). According to Blum, each of the dimensions, for example, media freedom or political parallelism, can unfold in three ways—liberal, middle, or regulated. As a result, six models are possible: the liberal model (represented by the US) at one end of the spectrum and the command model (represented by North Korea) at the other, with mixed models in between these two poles, such as the public service model (represented by Germany), the clientelist model (represented by Italy), the shock model (represented by Russia), and lastly, the patriot model (represented by Iran). Yet again, the applicability and adequacy of these labels—in particular in relation to non-Western countries—need to be reviewed. Examining the ubiquitous and uncritical use of the media system models brought forth by Siebert, Peterson and Schramm, as well as by Hallin and Mancini, we conclude that such limiting labeling should be avoided in order to give credit to the various features of media systems beyond a static analysis of media-politics relations. In the following section, we focus on the kinds of dimensions and criteria that are particularly helpful in thoroughly analyzing Arab media systems.

Comparative Media Systems in the Arab World: The Status Quo

Until recently, there have been only a few attempts to classify Arab media systems. What exist are a number of case studies of a single Arab country, or comparisons of two states (e.g. El-Richani, 2016; Webb, 2015; Kraidy, 2012; Khamis, 2009). Often, these studies refer to one of the abovementioned classification systems and speak about the "authoritarian" or—to a lesser degree—the "polarized pluralist" character of the respective media system. Blum, for instance, analyzed three Arab states—Syria, Egypt, and Lebanon—and categorized them unsurprisingly in the command model, the patriot model, and the clientelist model, respectively. By taking into consideration the typical dimensions outlined earlier (history, media-politics relationships, and journalistic performance), only rather general conceptualizations seem to be possible.

For a long time, the only, and probably most widely read, attempt to classify Arab media systems has been the work of William Rugh, *The Arab Press*, published as early as 1979, and updated in 2004 under the new title of *The Arab Mass Media*. According to this latest version, there are four main models by which Arab media systems may be classified. The first is the mobilization press, which represents a model stemming from the era of modernization, when republican regimes had the vision of awakening and educating their people through strongly controlled media. While in 1979 most republics were classified by Rugh as corresponding to this model, by 2004, only Syria, pre-2003 Iraq, Libya, and Sudan remained in this category. His second model is the loyalist press, whose main characteristic is its loyalty to and general support of the ruling elites, despite the fact that it consists of private media conglomerates. Rugh placed Palestine and all the countries surrounding the Persian or Arabian Gulf, with the exception of Kuwait, in this category. A third model is the diverse (print) media where media—or at least the print media sector—are characterized by a plurality of political opinions, most often indicating a strong political parallelism in the countries that are loosely (or not at all) controlled by a central government. Among the countries that Rugh believes to belong to this model are Lebanon, Kuwait, Morocco, and Yemen. The fourth model, which Rugh offered in order to reflect changes in many countries at the beginning of the 2000s, is the transitional system of (print) media. In 2004, Algeria, Egypt, Jordan, and Tunisia were featured as examples of this model because they had introduced privatization measures in the media sector that had started to unfold with different yet "unsettled" effects (Rugh, 2004, p. 121). Since his book was published, major political developments (e.g. the uprisings well known as the "Arab Spring", and their aftermaths), as well as intra-regional and international military interventions (e.g. the US-led invasion of Iraq in 2003, the NATO mission in Libya in 2011, or the war in Yemen since 2015) over the past two decades have shaken up the classifications of certain countries in terms of Rugh's models. The mobilization press model, for instance, is slowly vanishing. On the other hand, the loyalist media model persists and needs further elaboration. With this model of the media,

Rugh has significantly contributed to Arab media system comparisons by taking into account the important category of ownership. In most previous typologies, from Siebert, Peterson, and Schramm (1963) to Blum (2014), only a simple distinction had been made between state-owned, public-owned, and privately-owned media. This distinction is predicated on an unspoken assessment of state-owned media as "bad" (because of government control) and privately-owned media as being "good" (because they guarantee pluralism and watchdog attitudes). While Rugh did not dig too deeply into the role of ownership, he did show, with regard to the loyalist press, that privately-owned media do not necessarily equate to independent or free media. Instead, private ownership can be used as a means to control media output even more effectively. Thus, a critical review of the specific features of the political economy of media governance and ownership in the MENA region will be very important in our analysis.

Certain other authors have made insightful contributions to further differentiate the types of media systems and the dimensions of analysis. Examining the early era of satellite television proliferation in the Arab world, Mohammad Ayish (2002) put forward a new type of classification system, distinguishing three types of patterns of government control and media purpose: 1) traditional government-controlled television; 2) reformist government-controlled television; and 3) liberal commercial television. He took a closer look at which kind of content was being processed in the media and asked whether typical "red lines" of reporting, such as political, security, and moral concerns, were being pushed by journalists in their reporting (Ayish, 2002, p. 141). Similarly, and by analyzing news content in 16 Arab countries, Noha Mellor (2005) developed her own classification criteria, mainly with regard to the content of the news and considering "the commercial purposes that these media serve, whether it is to generate as large a profit as possible or to contribute to building a new image and hence goodwill for a particular country or media outlet" (p. 73). While the purpose or philosophy of media and their functions had previously been established as categories by Siebert et al. (1963), Mellor's introduction of content classification indeed represented a new and empirical category for analysis.

Another, still preliminary, attempt to classify Arab media systems has come from Mahmoud Galander (2016) in a working paper. He distinguished between four types: 1) the socially focused media system, 2) the modernist monarchies media system, 3) the modernist republics media system, and 4) the socially liberal media system. Using a distinction based on the form of governance (in particular monarchies vs. republics)—similar to other typologies—he introduced additional dimensions in order to avoid "the inaccurate and—sometimes faulty—interpretation of politics as the key constituent of media-government relationship in the region" (Galander, 2016, p. 3). Galander argued that the sociopolitical aspects of public decision-making and organization, such as the degree of tribalism or collectivism, along with religious fragmentation, need to be considered in the analysis of Arab media. According to him, the Gulf states, excluding Kuwait, feature in the first type—the socially focused—while modernist monarchies such as Kuwait, Morocco, and Jordan have more in common with one another and make up the second type. Sudan, Syria, and Algeria belong to the modernist republics, while Egypt, Tunisia, Yemen, Libya, Iraq, and Lebanon belong to the socially liberal category. While, again, the allocation of countries to a certain type can only provide a snapshot, due to ever-changing dynamics in the MENA region, Galander has made us aware of the importance of taking into consideration aspects of a country's social composition—a factor that has been inexcusably neglected by many comparative approaches.

Others analyzing Arab media have not used typologies, but have instead either described the different developments of media systems by providing contemporary snapshots of country cases (Guaaybess, 2013), discussed a certain media genre such as television or film in a comparative perspective (Sakr, 2007; Mellor, Ayish, Dajani, & Rinnawi, 2011), or considered specific dimensions of media systems, such as the economy or audiences (Hafez, 2008; Della Ratta, Sakr, & Skovgaard-Petersen, 2015). Reasons for this hesitation to classify Arab media systems include the above described heterogeneity in so many of the key categories of comparison, the highly dynamic developments in the region, which create major ruptures and changes in opposition to the persistence of European countries, and the lack of available empirical data to permit a solid comparison of multiple categories.

Towards a Conceptual Approach to Arab Media Systems Comparison

Building on this review of extant scholarship about media systems, this section attempts to provide a set of criteria to examine media systems of Arab countries, and by doing so, to allow a comparative analysis. To achieve our goal, we carefully weighed the different approaches outlined above to ensure that the respective dimensions would help us grasp both the heterogeneity and commonalities of the media in the MENA region. This also led us to consider characteristics that might distinguish some or all countries in the region from those specified in the typologies in the West. Our investigation led us to analyze the media in each country according to the following dimensions:

1. Historical Developments

All media system classifications consider historical developments, because they have strongly shaped the patterns of current media structures, production, and consumption. However, different scholars have defined "history" differently: Siebert et al. (1963), for example, tended to relate history to a specific cultural influence that they tried to grasp by looking at certain philosophical writings of the time as reflective of a specific mentality, such as "Russian thinking" (p. 7). Blum (2014), on the other hand, considered whether the historical development of a country had been somewhat linear, or shaped strongly by ruptures. Hallin and Mancini (2004) viewed history mainly in relation to the introduction of newspapers and the size of their reception by a national readership. All Arab countries, however, have experienced strong ruptures in their historic development. Therefore, it is not the question of *whether* that needs to be answered here, but rather the question of *how* these countries have dealt with these changes. Arab countries have depended on and been strongly influenced by foreign powers; thus a closer look at the ways in which their historical development has been shaped by transnational influences will emphasize the effect of such political trajectories on these media systems. Taking these trajectories into consideration may also help to explain political decision-making or societal conceptions of media far more thoroughly than a simple reflection on cultural mentalities, as found in Siebert et al. (1963).

Let us take, for instance, the geographical history of the region. At the beginning of the twentieth century, hardly any of the Arab countries existed in their current forms. Colonial powers (in particular France and Great Britain, but also Spain and Italy) strongly determined the MENA region's fate up until the 1960s. Some countries, such as Algeria, only gained independence after bloody wars. In the Mashriq—that is, the eastern part of the MENA region—and also in Libya, numerous ethnically or religiously disparate populations were "thrown" into state structures, leading to political and social tensions that remain to this day. Iraq, Syria, and Lebanon are prime examples of colonial restructuring. On the positive side, the encounters and confrontations with European colonizers and the subsequent end of the centuries of Ottoman domination in the region triggered many developments in the media sector, including the importation of new technologies and formats (Skovgaard-Petersen, Harbsmeier, & Simonsen, 1997).

After World War II, the Arab region served as a playing field for the new superpowers, the Soviet Union and the US. The contest to determine their respective spheres of influence resulted in numerous conflicts and proxy wars that repeatedly set back the region's development. Examples of this may be observed in the Arab-Israeli conflict with major wars in 1948, 1967, and 1973, and many other conflicts, including the Iran-Iraq war in the 1980s and the Iraq wars of 1990 and 2003. During these times, the superpowers also supported authoritarian rulers who guaranteed internal stability and showed loyalty to them, with the aim of maintaining a balance of political power during the Cold War (Turner, 2012). The main beneficiaries of such political arrangements were hereditary royal houses, as seen in Saudi Arabia, Jordan, Oman, Kuwait, Qatar, the United Arab Emirates, and Morocco, as well as nationalist republican regimes, which often developed a strong cult of leadership, as seen in Egypt, Libya, Syria, Algeria, Tunisia, Sudan, and Iraq.

Such historic dependence on Western actors is not the only transnational development to consider. Marwan Kraidy (2012) has also reminded us of the strong pan-Arab connections. Due to a common language, the MENA region has been, and continues to be, a hub of mobility for media producers and journalists. Media has been an instrument of both rivalries and coalitions between Arab countries. For instance, Egypt's Nasser targeted Saudi Arabia with his pan-Arab ideology in the 1960s via transnational radio production, which was in turn a major motivator for the Saudi regime in fostering their own infrastructure (Boyd, 1975).

A major, more recent rupture has been the Arab uprisings—often labeled as the "Arab Spring"—which started in 2011 in Tunisia, Egypt, Libya, Yemen, Syria, and Bahrain, with another wave taking place in Algeria, Sudan, Lebanon, and Iraq in 2019. In particular, young and educated people have taken to the streets and the Internet to revolt against authoritarian structures, economic hardships, and social exclusion, and to advocate for respecting the dignity of citizens and their rights in political decision-making (Howard & Hussain, 2013). While in some countries, such as Egypt and Bahrain, authoritarian rule has been restored, other countries, such as Libya, Syria, and Yemen, witnessed a major disaggregation of state structures. And others still, such as Tunisia, Lebanon, Iraq, and Sudan, seem to have succeeded, at least partly, in forcing a change of their structures of government.

As a result, anyone looking into historical developments must also consider changing transnational influences and their effects on the media market and production in a given country.

2. Background: Social Composition, Languages and Geography

Contextual information on the social composition of a country, with regard to gender and age equality and ethnic, religious, and linguistic diversity, is often neglected in comparative media system analyses. This oversight downplays the importance of such information for our understanding of media and culture's role in their production and usage. These social factors raise questions about appropriate representation in the public sphere, or question of how, through the media, they shape struggles for hegemony over discourse, and thus provide fertile ground for social conflicts. Sarah El-Richani (2016), in her analysis of the Lebanese media system, introduced "crisis" as a salient factor that has been neglected by Hallin and Mancini, and most other authors (p. 181). In the case of Lebanon, the crisis stems from a decades-long confessional conflict that influences the media market, media governance, and media content. Hallin and Mancini (2004) indicated there might be some value to analyzing this aspect more closely when they referred to "patterns of conflict and consensus", and discussed whether a polarized or a moderate pluralism shapes party politics (pp. 59–61). Blum (2014) similarly referred to a dimension that he called "political culture" (p. 295) and considered whether there is a polarized or a consensus-oriented political culture of negotiation. But the reduction of such complex contextual factors to a single category seems to overlook the relevance of any culture as a shared space of meaning-making.

Religion, for example, has become a main driver for conflict along distinct understandings of a cultural identity. The Arab world is often falsely generalized as "Muslim." We say falsely because the region is also the cradle of Judaism and Christianity, with dozens of denominations, such as Orthodox or Coptic Christians, living in several countries. The word "Muslim" in itself is not unidimensional; it comprises a heterogeneity of groups stemming from the major division in Sunni and Shi'ite Muslims, which are themselves distinguished through various subdivisions. In particular, Lebanon—but also Iraq, Egypt, and Syria—has built a fragile confessional model of representation of these diverse groups in its media. Bahrain, where a Sunni minority politically dominates a Shi'ite majority, is another example of these divisions. We must also not forget the heated debates on religiously inspired Islamic groups, such as the Muslim Brotherhood and their parties, indicating that there is no unified interpretation of "Islam" or "Muslim" in the region (Nawawy & Elmasry, 2018).

Ethnicity is a further significant aspect of culture. Substantial numbers of Imazighen (or Berber) people in Morocco and Algeria, as well as Tuareg in Libya, or Kurds in Iraq and Syria, do not consider themselves as being of Arab ethnicity and demand official acknowledgement of their own language and traditions (Fischer-Tahir, 2013; Pfeifer, 2015). The Kurds' struggle for recognition is a longstanding campaign that has eventually led to autonomy for Kurds in Iraq, and is on the brink of achieving the same for Kurds in Syria as well. The secession of South Sudan from Sudan in 2011 is yet another case in point that shows the possible power of such struggles. Besides the citizens, one should also consider the enormous foreign work force—particularly in the Gulf countries—representing different ethnicities and/or religions from India, Pakistan, Bangladesh, and the Philippines, among others. Media production, as well as media content, is influenced by this cultural diversity of languages, religions, and ethnicities.

There are other factors, such as demographics, to consider. The population in the Arab world is very *young*: 15–41% of the people are younger than 15 years of age, with Sudan, Yemen, Iraq, and Palestine having the highest share. These young Arabs are growing up as digital natives using mobile phones, the Internet, and digital media, which consequently throws the legitimacy of traditional media into question, especially if the youth do not feel represented in a restricted media environment (Gertel & Hexel, 2018).

Struggles about *gender* equality also should not be neglected—both with regard to physical and content-related representation in the media. The spectrum of female appearance in the media ranges from extremely popular Lebanese media personalities to the nonexistence of anchorwomen on Saudi national television, with the exception of one female anchor in 2019, thus reflecting different notions of paternalism (Sakr, 2007). In general, women are still a minority among journalists and media producers in the MENA region.

Finally, *education*, a strong indicator for class differences, needs to be considered. While the Arab world has paved its way from a largely illiterate region to acceptable rates of around 70–98% of the population being literate, there are still strata of society that cannot read and write. In Morocco, 31% of the population are still considered to be illiterate. Yemen represents the lowest rate of literacy with 66% of its population unable to read and write, a situation that is predicted will deteriorate even further due to the ongoing war there. In addition, other war-ravaged countries, such as Syria, Iraq, and Libya, will likely continue to witness the decline of general education and literacy levels (UNICEF, 2015).

These elements of a cultural and social context are constitutive of the Arab uprisings and thus intricately connected with other major factors, namely the political system, legal framework, and economy, which have strongly shaped crises in the region.

Another often neglected aspect that shapes media systems is the *geography and size of a country* as well as the size of its population. El-Richani (2016) introduced this concept as the "state size" factor (p. 180). It has implications for the media system that may be observed through each of the major dimensions we will go on to discuss. With regards to infrastructure and technology, these are of course more difficult to implement if, as in Sudan, there is a vast landmass to be covered by radio waves and Internet fiber cables, rather than a tiny island like Bahrain. As for the political economy of the media, it is important that the size of a possible target audience is known. Licensing nine national television stations for a population of under five million, as is the case in Lebanon, might jeopardize the prospect of any meaningful business model for each of the separate stations. In the case of the MENA region and the common language it shares, this often fosters a transnational pan-Arab orientation, as seen with *Al-Jazeera*, which broadcasts from the tiny emirate of Qatar (Zayani, 2005). In the European context, where many small states such as Belgium, Denmark, or Austria exist, a substantial amount of literature has been produced on the "giant neighbor" problem, in which national markets become dominated by more potent neighboring countries, as seen, for instance, in Germany's effect on Austria or France's impact on Belgium (Puppis, 2009). These smaller markets often develop strategies to avoid being overtaken by their "giant neighbor", such as establishing a quota for national production or—as in the case of Denmark, with the help of state subsidies—investing strongly in niche markets such as crime series production in order to have a unique selling point (Lund & Berg, 2009). The UAE or Jordan's media cities could be seen as embodying such strategies as a result of the diminutive size of their markets (Khalil, 2013). Finally, and with regard to the political dimension, Kraidy (2012) argued that *Al-Jazeera* and other "transnational media institutions can shape national politics in specific countries, in addition to pan-Arab politics" (p. 180). Indeed, Qatar's *Al-Jazeera* has created conflicts with almost every Arab state due to its coverage, and it has been cited as a main reason for the ongoing Saudi-Qatari diplomatic crisis (Al-Jaber, 2018). Therefore, state size will also be considered in our analysis.

3. Political System and Legal Framework

The main focus of all media system typologies is the political environment behind a given system, which follows the guiding principle of Siebert et al. (1963) that media take on the "form and coloration of the social and political structure" (p. 1) in which they operate. While the social composition of a country is often overlooked as a factor in analyses of its media, political structures are always taken into consideration. The kind of governing system, the definition of media functions in society, how the media are controlled, and the kind of state intervention that regulates the media, are all important cornerstones of analyses in all typologies. However, the degrees used to measure these categories are often highly normative. The "democracy bias" often means that, hybrid regimes are seen through the lens of democratization and thus categorized as flawed, incomplete, or "transitional" democracies (Levitsky & Way, 2002), when in fact they are not transitioning anywhere, or at least not towards becoming democracies. In fact, acknowledging the broad range of political authoritarianisms and the different mechanisms of control and regulation could be more helpful than applying abstract ideas and norms of democratic governance.

In "How Far Can Media Systems Travel?", Katrin Voltmer (2012) pointed to the fact that the dimensions used by Hallin and Mancini might suit comparisons of media systems in established democracies, but are not useful in comparisons of those outside the West (pp. 227–29). Basing our analysis on Voltmer's argument, we contend that the question of whether there is a "high" or "low" degree of state intervention in the media system does not adequately explain what takes place in Arab media systems. Using the values designed by Hallin and Mancini for Western systems would, in almost all cases, lead to the diagnosis of a comparatively "high" degree of state intervention, or of a "not free" system (as evident in other comparative approaches used by such groups as Freedom House, Reporters Without Borders, etc.). Notwithstanding the importance of the state intervention criterion used by Hallin and Mancini, perhaps the more interesting questions are *how* does state intervention manifest, and *how* can these mechanisms be classified, as opposed simply to whether or to which degree they exist. Indeed, political scientists have diagnosed the MENA region as a "persistence of authoritarianism" (Albrecht & Schlumberger, 2004, p. 371), indicating that different and dynamic strategies are employed by the incumbents in order to maintain the status quo. Heydemann and Reenders even speak of an "authoritarian learning" of regimes throughout the region and characterize the resulting strategies as aiming "to affect the strategic calculus of citizens, allies, and adversaries, even while constantly updating their own probabilities" (2011, p. 649).

It is therefore important to take a closer look at the objectives of state interventions with regard to the media, which precise means are used to intervene, and if and how "authoritarian learning" has shaped these processes.

For example, the idea, propagated in the 1950s and 1960s, that mass media use has a strong and direct effect on people's will was ultimately internalized by rulers in almost all Arab countries. As a result, regime control of the media was and still is ubiquitous. Each ruler has claimed to know best what is good for the population and what information it should receive, relying on emphatic moral, religious, or security arguments. Typically, media outlets were first seen as instruments for the education and development of society, but often this instrumentalization has resulted in their being degraded to mere propaganda tools (Rugh, 1979). As a rule, information ministries that granted licenses for all types of media and made or reviewed personnel decisions served to implement this logic and the associated censorship. While state control through ministries of information has declined, other institutions have been set up to regulate the media, and these are rarely independent of state or government influence, as we can observe in the long struggle for independence in Tunisia since 2011 (Farmanfarmaian, 2014). By comparing regulation laws and procedures in 11 Arab countries, Zaid (2018) came to the conclusion that media regulations "are tools of authoritarian upgrading rather than genuine attempts to liberalize the broadcast sector and enhance pluralism and diversity" (p. 4415). Indeed, the official and internationally well-received abolition of ministries of information like those in Jordan or Qatar would, in fact, appear to be a form of window-dressing, rather than any real attempt at reform.

From a European perspective, the litmus test of precisely how independent media can be in a given country is the introduction of public service media that are intended to serve public interests, represent all sections of society, and are governed independently of the state. Yet, while some attempts have been made to foster public service broadcasting in the MENA region, none of the "public" television channels in the Arab region fulfils these criteria (Dabbous, 2015; Guaaybess, 2013).

Another objective for strong state intervention can also be detected in articulated visions of state-led development that are the result of attempts to respond to the forces of economic and technological globalization. In particular, the UAE, Saudi Arabia, Bahrain, and Oman have pushed forward ambitious plans of modernization that link welfare and stability for its populations with political control. Since this framing of state intervention resonates well with their societies, it has become a frequently used tool in the MENA region.

A further reason for strong state control is the above described crisis mode that is a constitutive element of many states in the region. This could be due to ongoing conflicts in countries such as Iraq, Libya, or Lebanon, or conflicts with other countries as seen in Yemen or Syria. Even the frequent claim by incumbent elites of being subject to terrorist threats can strongly shape the objectives and means of state intervention in the media. The plethora of cybercrime laws that were introduced in the past couple of years in most Arab countries are an indicator that securitization is a frequent strategy of state intervention in the media. Thus, we need to analyze carefully the political context, including the (legal) measures taken and the motivations behind them when analyzing media systems.

Finally, we want to note that, as we delve into an analysis of the nature of the respective political systems, we will use the term "regime"—in accordance with political science terminology—to describe a political institution as a set of rules and norms for regulating government–society interactions without imposing any specific connotation on the term.

4. Economy and Ownership Patterns

Categories relating to the economy and ownership of the media have frequently been included in media system comparisons. Sparks and Splichal (1988) even distinguished between a "commercial" and a "paternal" model of media systems, thus indicating the important role of the economic approach and respective financial sources. Blum

(2014) echoed this in his "funding of media" (p. 295) category, and also distinguished between the state and the market. Blum (2014), as well as Siebert et al. (1963), went further, differentiating between private and public ownership in their consideration of "media ownership".

The often implicit and simplified line of argumentation is as follows: public ownership equals government influence, which equals state control and is thus considered paternalistic, whereas private ownership equals a liberal market, which equals commercial approaches and is thus considered an example of free media. However, this argument is misleading especially when it comes to the Arab countries.

As a result, a critical examination of the political economy of the media is indispensable. Many Arab countries can be considered rent-seeking economies (Nour, 2016), that is, economies based on revenues not generated by the production of goods or services. For example, finances might come from the sale of raw materials, such as crude oil (as in all Gulf countries, Algeria, Iraq, Sudan, and Libya), from state-owned stable sources of income (such as the Suez Canal in Egypt), or from non-state-owned resources (for instance as remittances of migration), as is the case in Morocco, as well as Palestine, Lebanon, Algeria, and other countries. Rent-seeking economies are therefore heavily dependent on only a few sources of income, and their economies usually have a very low degree of diversification. This affects their media systems because the limited domestic revenue sources and the resulting distribution of wealth could dictate who is powerful enough to own media. Moreover, the degree of dependence on such income has an impact on the level of taxation (and indeed whether or not taxes are being imposed on the population at all), which can ultimately result in popular demands for representation in the media. So far, many regimes have rejected demands for representation with the claim that without taxes, (media and political) representation does not need to be guaranteed (Anderson, 1987).

In all MENA countries, the state elites have secured their stakes in the relevant economic sectors. Anyone who wants to profit from this status quo must be loyal to the ruling elites (Roll, 2013). As a result, in most of these countries, patronage networks have frequently emerged, focusing on the ruling elites, who consolidate their position of influence through their control of political institutions and the economy. In this context, the media are of particular importance, both as economic enterprises and political instruments (Richter & Gräf, 2015). For example, during the 1990s and 2000s, and mostly due to political or economic legitimization crises, several Arab regimes such as Tunisia, Morocco, and Egypt introduced "liberalization measures" in the media market (Guaaybess, 2013). In the Gulf, particularly in Saudi Arabia and the UAE, investment in media was seen as a strategy to diversify a rent-based economy. In all these cases, the alleged privatization of media has rarely been more than a transfer of ownership to the regime's close associates from among the business elite. "Private" thus should not be misunderstood as "independent." Instead, and in accordance with the dictum "divide and rule," a limited amount of the "privatized" media's critical reporting is accepted, as long as it does not attack the cornerstones of the regime's rule. Other means of securing loyalty from "private" media have already been described in detail by Rugh (1979), in his chapter on the "loyalist press." These include guaranteed government advertisements and subsidies, or threatened withdrawals of newspaper copies. Commercially successful financing models for independent press, radio, or television media, on the other hand, are rare in the Arab world.

In this context, the often-used category of "political parallelism" is given a new twist. Hallin and Mancini (2004) and Blum (2014) made it one of their four key categories. The concept of political parallelism was first proposed by Seymour-Ure (1974) as "party-press parallelism," which he argues is characterized by close associations between political parties and media, thus entailing a culture of journalism that openly promotes political parties and their positions. Hallin and Mancini (2004) developed this concept further, adapting it to the realities of the early twenty-first century in the Western hemisphere and disconnecting it from the party-as-organization notion. They argued that, in countries with high political parallelism, "media are still differentiated politically, [although] they more often are associated not with particular parties, but with general political tendencies" (Hallin & Mancini, 2004, p. 28). However, De Albuquerque (2012) criticized the term "political parallelism" as an arbitrary coinage. He emphasized that, in order to distinguish between simply politically engaged media or media advocacy and "real" political parallelism, one must identify whether there are clear or unclear relationships between actors in the media and the political system (De Albuquerque, 2012, p. 93). Taking this suggestion seriously, we can see that the political involvement of media owners is a major driver of political parallelism. Thus, ownership patterns, in addition to the funding of media outlets by political actors, are the essential aspects that must be investigated in order to ascertain the nature and degree of political parallelism.

In most Arab countries, political actors are commonly involved in the media business, and vice versa. In addition, Kraidy (2012) has pointed to the fact that there are transnational structures of political parallelism and media instrumentalization (pp. 194–95). He discussed the case of Saudi investment in the Lebanese market, which had clear political interests behind it. It is also obvious that political actors from Saudi Arabia, the UAE, and Qatar finance media in war-torn Libya, in order to play out their rivalries and secure zones of influence (Wollenberg & Richter, 2020).

Yet there are also other models of ownership and funding beyond these dominant state-funded or loyalist models. Local or community media have long been marginalized, but have recently gained ground in manifold ways, as evidenced by small local radio stations in Jordan, Tunisia, and Libya, or by hyper-local online, or even print, media in Iraq, Palestine, and Egypt (Sakr, 2016). The potential for decentralized and less costly production via the Internet has been a major driver for new forms of media production situated on the border between journalism and activism. Often, these media can be categorised as "alternative media" (Atton, 2001), i.e. media that are not only organized differently, but also aim to disseminate content differently from the mainstream media. Nonetheless, the financial sustainability of these models is always in question.

5. Technology and Infrastructure

None of the well-known media system typologies focuses on the role of infrastructure and technology. In fact, one of the major criticisms Hallin and Mancini faced was their neglect of the Internet as a technological and transnational factor (Norris, 2009). Although they acknowledged the role of technology as a "force [or] limit of homogenization" (p.

251) in their original book in 2004, they did not see it as a particular factor to be considered separately, but rather as inherent in social practices that shape the market, the professionalization of journalists, or political parallelism. Indeed, technology should not be treated in such a way as to foster a technological deterministic viewpoint. However, it is to be considered as both a specific outcome of and influence on social practices, or, as Andrew Chadwick (2013) described it, a driver of hybridity. This "notion of a hybrid system," he argued, "draws attention to change and flux, the passing of an older set of cultural and institutional norms, and the gradual emergence of new norms" (Chadwick, 2013, p. 10). The notion of convergence of media should also be considered in this discussion. Convergence refers to both the changes of media technologies themselves and the implications for how we create, consume and distribute media within these converging technologies. The questions of how, when, and why new technologies have been included in a media system, and with what effect, are thus important factors in the analysis of media systems.

With regard to the spread of technologies, a strong culture of oral communication in the MENA region, which persists due to continued widespread illiteracy in some regions, might explain the spectacular success of radio and, later, television (Armbrust, 1996; Fahmy, 2011). Print media such as newspapers have been consumed by the educated elite since their inception, and thus have a limited readership. In contrast to broadcasting, they have usually been less strongly regulated by the state. Internet-based media now provide a hybridization of oral, visual, and written elements.

To place this in a political context, it is important to ask how and why the different regimes did, or did not, upgrade their media technologies. Most likely, they were seeking a balance between connection to technological modernity, which was important for their own legitimacy, and the closest possible control of new media discourses. Modernization ideology and the interest of spreading education through technology, on the one hand, stood in opposition to the fear of threats to national unity or challenges to moral values, on the other hand. These factors have undeniably influenced the support of technological advancement in the media sector (Abdulla, 2007).

The first major advancement in this realm was made during the 1980s. The 22 states of the Arab League decided to invest in their own satellite system called *ArabSat* (the first satellite was launched in 1985). The costs for this project, which at the time totaled around USD 500 million, were distributed proportionately among the different countries according to their financial power: Saudi Arabia therefore paid 36.6%, Kuwait 14.5%; Libya 11.2%; Qatar 9.8%; the United Arab Emirates 4.6%; Jordan 4.0%; Lebanon 3.8%; Bahrain 2.4%; Syria 2.0%; Iraq 1.9%; Algeria 1.7%; Yemen 1.6%; Egypt 1.5%; Oman 1.2%; Tunisia 0.7%; Morocco 0.6%; Mauritania, Sudan, Palestine and Somalia 0.2% each; and Djibouti 0.1% of the costs (ArabSat, 2019). Although *ArabSat* carried most of the Arab national television channels, it was dominated by huge media consortia, such as *MBC*, *ART*, *Orbit*, and *Rotana*, which were backed by Saudi investors. Egypt invested in its own system, *NileSat* (launched in 1998), as did the UAE with *YahSat* (launched in 2011). Qatar, with its *Al-Jazeera* consortium, also started its own system, *Es'hailSat* (launched in 2014), so as to become independent from its rival Saudi Arabia.

Mobile telephony has been another technology that has leapfrogged the poor landline infrastructure in almost all of the Arab world since the beginning of the 2000s. As a rule, statistics show that, by 2010, at least half of the Arab population had their own mobile phone—albeit with strong asymmetries in distribution: the Gulf states were again early and strong adopters, while Yemen, Syria, and Palestine came in at a much lower level. Mobile phone use is closely connected to the upgrading of the Internet infrastructure, since the Internet is overwhelmingly accessed through mobile devices (Salem, 2017). Those countries in which the Internet had been propagated as a symbol of modernity and education had a particularly rapid growth in the number of users. Besides the Gulf states, during the 2000s the regimes in Egypt, Morocco, and Tunisia, despite their fear of the Internet as a hub for oppositional political activism, enlarged their DSL infrastructures and enormously expanded access for a large part of the population, with campaigns promoting "A computer for every household."

However, at that point, the race had only just begun, and given the manifold effects of Internet communication on all areas of life (even beyond the decidedly political ones), social change seemed unstoppable. The networking of formerly marginalized political groups

(Kopty, 2018), the challenge to religious and political authorities (Faris, 2013), new communication spaces for gender discourse (Al-Rawi, 2014; Antonakis, 2018), and resurgent connections between population groups and their relatives in the diaspora (Khamis, 2017) all owe their existence to the public spaces created by the new media technologies and must consequently be considered in a media system analysis. In particular, the convergence of media use and production across platforms can stimulate extremely dynamic political and social practices in relation to media. On the other hand, the dominance of a few giant (Western) technology companies in this convergent media environment may also create "algorithmic harms," as Zeynep Tufekci (2015, p. 207) has put it, meaning that there might be a lack of visibility of certain strata of society and an information asymmetry due to a digital divide and a kind of algorithmic gatekeeping. In addition to taking these companies into consideration, one must take into account the ownership and control of such an infrastructure in the countries analyzed. The proprietorship of Internet service providers and telecommunications companies in many cases already resembles the cronyistic ownership structures described in the section on political parallelism—with major regime-loyal businessmen, such as Egypt's Naguib Sawiris, being at the forefront (Sakr, 2015). This raises the question of what this means for the shape of the respective media systems.

Other dimensions that have often been discussed—such as the self-perception or professionalization of journalists and the role of audiences—will not feature as separate categories in our analysis. We do not consider them unimportant, but in not defining them as separate categories, we acknowledge that, in a digitally shaped media system, the role of journalists can no longer be distinguished so clearly from that of audiences (Chadwick, 2013). Furthermore, the question of who can talk in the media, and the role that he or she is able to play, is in our country cases not a matter of professionalization, but rather one of social composition, legal framework, economic realities, and technological possibilities of the system. As such, we incorporate the discussion of the roles of journalists into these separate categories.

Book Structure

In the following chapters, we provide insights into the different media systems in the MENA region. The book is structured according to geographic groupings of countries, starting in the east with the Levante or Mashriq region, which comprises Lebanon, Syria, Palestine, Jordan, and Iraq, and followed by the Gulf and the Arabian Peninsula, which consists of Saudi Arabia, the UAE, Qatar, Bahrain, Kuwait, Oman, and Yemen. We then continue with Egypt and Sudan, and end with the west of the MENA region, the Maghreb, which includes Libya, Tunisia, Algeria, and Morocco. This regional grouping specifically highlights the relationships between neighboring countries that often share a common (colonial) experience, as in the case of the Levante and the Maghreb. Some also face similar challenges, such as the incorporation of ethnic minorities, or the response to the post-oil boom era.

To allow for a systematic comparison of the different media systems, each country chapter follows the dimensions outlined above through an analysis of the specific characteristics of each media system within its political, social, cultural and economic contexts. Adhering to these criteria does not overshadow the uniqueness of each media system, but is rather an approach that examines the specific features and developments of a particular media system, while allowing for comparative analyses across the countries. Finally, the conclusion highlights major themes that can be identified from the in-depth studies provided in the country chapters.

References

Abdulla, R. A. (2007). The Internet in the Arab world: Egypt and beyond. New York: Peter Lang.

Albrecht, H. & Schlumberger, O. (2004). "Waiting for Godot": Regime change without democratization in the Middle East. *International Political Science Review*, 25(4), 371–92. https://doi.org/10.1177/0192512104045085

Al-Jaber, K. (2018). The war of manufacturing consent and public mobilization. In K. Al-Jaber & S. Neubauer (Eds.), *The Gulf Crisis: Reshaping alliances in the Middle East* (pp. 89–108). Washington: Gulf International Forum.

Al-Rawi, A. (2014). Framing the online women's movements in the Arab world. *Information, Communication & Society*, 17(9), 1147–61.

Anderson, L. (1987). The state in the Middle East and North Africa. *Comparative Politics*, *20*(1), 1–18. https://doi.org/10.2307/421917

Antonakis, A. (2018). Feminist networks in times of multi-layered transformations: Perspectives from Tunisia. In C. Richter, A. Antonakis, & C. Harders (Eds.), *Digital media and the politics of transformation in the Arab World and Asia* (pp. 137–59). Wiesbaden: Springer VS. https://doi.org/10.1007/978-3-658-20700-7_7

ArabSat (2019). *About us*. https://www.arabsat.com/english/about

Armbrust, W. (1996). *Mass culture and modernism in Egypt*. New York: Cambridge University Press.

Atton, C. (2001). *Alternative media*. London: Sage.

Ayish, M. I. (2002). Political communication on Arab world television: Evolving patterns. *Political Communication*, *19*(2), 137–54. https://doi.org/10.1080/10584600252907416

Blum, R. (2014). *Speakers & opponents: An approach to comparing media systems* [in German]. Köln: Herbert von Halem.

Boyd, D. (1975). Development of Egypt's radio: 'Voice of the Arabs' under Nasser. *Journalism Quarterly*, *52*(4), 645–53. https://doi.org/10.1177/107769907505200406

Carey, J. W. (1992). A cultural approach to communication. In J.W. Carey (Ed.), *Communication as Culture. Essays on Media and Society* (pp. 13–36). London: Routledge.

Chadwick, A. (2013). *The hybrid media system: Politics and power*. Oxford: Oxford University Press.

Curran, J. (1991). Rethinking the media as a public sphere. In P. Dahlgren & C. Sparks (Eds.), *Communication and citizenship: Journalism and the public sphere in the new media age* (pp. 27–57). London: Routledge.

Dabbous, D. (2015). *Assessment of public service broadcasting in the southern Mediterranean region*. http://stmjo.com/wp-content/uploads/2015/10/MedMedia-PSB-report.pdf

De Albuquerque, A. (2012). On models and margins: Comparative media models viewed from a Brazilian perspective. In D. C. Hallin & P. Mancini (Eds.), *Comparing media systems beyond the western world* (pp. 72–95). Cambridge, New York: Cambridge University Press.

Della Ratta, D., Sakr, N., & Skovgaard-Petersen, J. (Eds.). (2015). *Arab media moguls*. London: I.B. Tauris.

Downing, J. (1996). *Internationalizing media theory: Transition, power, culture; Reflections on media in Russia, Poland, and Hungary, 1980–1995*. London: Sage.

El-Richani, S. (2016). *The Lebanese media system: Anatomy of a system in perpetual crisis*. New York: Palgrave Macmillan.

Fahmy, Z. (2011). *Ordinary Egyptians: Creating the modern nation through popular culture, 1870–1919*. Stanford: Stanford University Press.

Faris, D. (2013). *Dissent and revolution in a digital age: Social media, blogging and activism in Egypt*. London: I.B. Tauris.

Farmanfarmaian, R. (2014). What is private, what is public, and who exercises media power in Tunisia? A hybrid-functional perspective on Tunisia's media sector. *The Journal of North African Studies*, 19(5), 656–78. https://doi.org/10.1080/13629387.2014.975663

Fischer-Tahir, A. (2013). Science-based truth as news: Knowledge production and media in Iraqi Kurdistan. *Kurdish Studies*, 1(1), 28–43. https://doi.org/10.33182/ks.v1i1.384

Galander, M. (2016). *Towards a new classification of Arab media-government relationship*. http://www.areacore.org/ims/overview-3/classification-of-arab-media-systems/classification-of-arab-media-systems-script-en/

Gertel, J., & Hexel, R. (Eds.). (2018). *Coping with uncertainty: Youth in the Middle East and North Africa*. London: Saqi.

Guaaybess, T. (2013). *National broadcasting and state policy in Arab countries*. Houndmills: Palgrave Macmillan.

Hachten, W. A. (1981). *The world news prism: Changing media, clashing ideologies*. Ames: The Iowa State University Press.

Hafez, K. (2008). *Arab media: Power and weakness*. New York: Continuum.

Hallin, D. C., & Mancini, P. (2004). *Comparing media systems*. Cambridge: Cambridge University Press.

———. (Eds.). (2012). *Comparing media systems beyond the western world*. Cambridge, New York: Cambridge University Press.

Heydemann, S. & Leenders, R. (2011). Authoritarian learning and authoritarian resilience: Regime responses to the 'Arab Awakening'. *Globalizations*, 8(5), 647–53. https://doi.org/10.1080/14747731.2011.621274

Howard, P. N., & Hussain, M. M. (2013). *Democracy's fourth wave? Digital media and the Arab Spring*. Oxford: Oxford University Press.

International Telecommunication Union (2018). *Percentage of individuals using the Internet 2018*. https://www.itu.int/en/ITU-D/Statistics/Documents/statistics/2019/Individuals_Internet_2000-2018_Jun2019.xls

Jakubowicz, K. (2010). Introduction — media systems research: An overview. In B. Dobek-Ostrowska, M. Gtowacki, K. Jakubowicz, & M. Sükösd (Eds.), *Comparative media systems: European and global perspectives* (pp. 1–22). Budapest: Central European University Press.

Khalil, J. (2013). Towards a supranational analysis of Arab media: The role of cities. In T. Guaaybess (Ed.), *National broadcasting and state policy in Arab countries* (pp. 188–208). Houndmills: Palgrave Macmillan.

Khamis, S. (2009). Modern Egyptian media: Transformations, paradoxes, debates and comparative perspectives. *Journal of Arab & Muslim Media Research*, 1(3), 259–77. https://doi.org/10.1386/jammr.1.3.259_1

——. (2017). The Internet and new communication dynamics among diasporic Muslims: Opportunities, challenges and paradoxes. In M. R. Kayikci & L. D'Haenens (Eds.), *European Muslims and new media* (pp. 35–52). Leuven: Leuven University Press.

Kopty, A. (2018). Power dynamics in online communities: The Palestinian case. In C. Richter, A. Antonakis, & C. Harders (Eds.), *Digital media and the politics of transformation in the Arab World and Asia* (pp. 61–84). Wiesbaden: Springer VS.

Kraidy, M. (2012). The rise of transnational media systems: Implications of pan-Arab media for comparative research. In D. C. Hallin & P. Mancini (Eds.), *Comparing media systems beyond the western world* (pp. 177–200). Cambridge, New York: Cambridge University Press.

Levitsky, S., & Way, L. (2002). Elections without democracy: The rise of competitive authoritarianism. *Journal of Democracy*, 13(2), 51–65.

Lund, A. B., & Berg, C. E. (2009). Denmark, Sweden and Norway: Television diversity by duopolistic competition and co-regulation. *The International Communication Gazette*, 71(1–2), 19–37. https://doi.org/10.1177/1748048508097928

McQuail, D. (1994). *Mass communication theory: An introduction* (3rd ed.). London: Sage.

——. (2010). *McQuail's mass communication theory* (6th ed.). London: Sage.

Mellor, N. (2005). *The making of Arab news*. Lanham: Rowman & Littlefield.

Mellor, N., Ayish, M., Dajani, N., & Rinnawi, K. (2011). *Arab media: Globalizing and emerging media industries*. Cambridge: Polity Press.

Nawawy, M., & Elmasry, M. H. (2018). *Revolutionary Egypt in the eyes of the Muslim brotherhood: A framing analysis of Ikhwanweb*. Lanham: Rowman & Littlefield.

Nerone, J. (1995). *Last rights: Revisiting Four Theories of the Press*. Urbana: University of Illinois Press.

Norris, P. (2009). Comparative political communications: Common frameworks or Babylonian confusion? *Government and Opposition*, 44(3), 321–40. https://doi.org/10.1111/j.1477-7053.2009.01290.x

Nour, S. M. (2016). *Economic systems of innovation in the Arab region*. Basingstoke: Palgrave Macmillan.

Pfeifer, K. (2015). *"We are not Arabs!" Amazigh identity construction in Morocco* [in German]. Bielefeld: transcript.

Puppis, M. (2009). Introduction: Media regulation in small states. *The International Communication Gazette*, *71*(1–2), 7–17.

Richter, C., & Gräf, B. (2015). The political economy of media: An introduction. In N.-C. Schneider & C. Richter (Eds.), *New media configurations and socio-cultural dynamics in Asia and the Arab World* (pp. 25–36). Baden-Baden: Nomos. https://doi.org/10.5771/9783845253923-22

Roll, S. (2013). Egypt's business elite after Mubarak: A powerful player between generals and brotherhood. *German Institute for International and Security Affairs (SWP)*. https://www.swp-berlin.org/fileadmin/contents/products/research_papers/2013_RP08_rll.pdf

Rugh, W. A. (1979). *The Arab press: News media and political process in the Arab world*. New York: Syracuse University Press.

———. (2004). *Arab mass media: Newspapers, radio, and television in Arab politics*. Westport: Praeger.

Sakr, N. (2007). *Arab television today*. London: I.B. Tauris.

———. (2015). Naguib Sawiris: Global capitalist, Egyptian media investor. In D. Della Ratta, N. Sakr, & J. Skovgaard-Petersen (Eds.), *Arab media moguls* (pp. 147–64). London: I.B. Tauris.

———. (2016). Survival or sustainability? Contributions of innovatively managed news ventures to the future of Egyptian journalism. *Journal of Media Business Studies*, *13*(1), 45–59. https://doi.org/10.1080/16522354.2015.1125608

Salem, F. (2017). The Arab social media report 2017: Social media and the Internet of Things: Towards data-driven policymaking in the Arab world. *MBR School of Government*. https://www.mbrsg.ae/getattachment/1383b88a-6eb9-476a-bae4-61903688099b/Arab-Social-Media-Report-2017.aspx

Seymour-Ure, C. (1974). *The political impact of mass media*. London: Constable.

Siebert, F. S., Peterson, T., & Schramm, W. (1963). *Four theories of the press*. Urbana: University of Illinois Press.

Skovgaard-Petersen, J., Harbsmeier, M., & Simonsen, J. B. (1997). The introduction of printing in the Middle East. *Culture and History*, *16*, 73–88.

Sparks, C., & Splichal, S. (1988). *Journalistic education and professional socialization*. Paper presented at the 16th IAMCR Conference, Barcelona, Spain.

Tufekci, Z. (2015). Algorithmic harms beyond Facebook and Google: Emergent challenges of computational agency. *Journal on Telecommunications and High Technology Law*, *13*(2), 203–18.

Turner, J. (2012). Great powers as client states in a Middle East Cold war. *Middle East Policy*, *XIX*(3), 124–34.

UNICEF (2015). *Education under fire*. https://www.unicef.org/mena/media/2276/file/EducationUnderFire-September2015-AR.pdf.pdf

Voltmer, K. (2012). How far can media systems travel? Applying Hallin & Mancini's comparative framework outside the western world. In D. C. Hallin & P. Mancini (Eds.), *Comparing media systems beyond the western world* (pp. 224–45). Cambridge, New York: Cambridge University Press. https://doi.org/10.1017/CBO9781139005098.013

Waisbord, S., & Mellado, C. (2014). De-westernizing communication studies: A reassessment. *Communication Theory, 24,* 361–72. https://doi.org/10.1111/comt.12044

Webb, E. (2015). *Media in Egypt and Tunisia: From control to transition?* New York: Palgrave MacMillan.

Wollenberg, A., & Richter, C. (2020). Political parallelism in transitional media systems: The case of Libya. *International Journal of Communication, 14,* 1173–93.

Zaid, B. (2018). A normative study of broadcast regulators in the Arab world. *International Journal of Communication, 12,* 4401–20.

Zayani, M. (Ed.). (2005). *The Al-Jazeera phenomenon*. Boulder: Paradigm.

Country	Population[1] (2018, in Mio.)	GDP[2] (per capita, 2018, in USD)	Age under 15 years[3] (2018, in %)	Literacy rate[4] (2005-2016)	Internet users[5] (2017, in %)	mobile-cellular subscriptions[6] in 2018 in %	Rank Press Freedom Index[7] (2019)
Algeria	42.2	$4,279	30%	75.1%	47.7%	121.9%	141
Bahrain	1.6	$24,051	19%	94.6%	95.9%	133.3%	167
Egypt	98.4	$2,549	34%	75.1%	45.0%	95.3%	163
Iraq	38.4	$5,878	38%	79.0%[8]	49.4%	94.9%	156
Jordan	10.0	$4,248	34%	97.9%	66.8%	87.6%	130
Kuwait	4.1	$34,244	22%	95.7%	100.0%	178.6%	108
Lebanon	6.8	$8,270	26%	91.2%	78.2%	64.5%	101
Libya	6.7	$7,235	28%	89.9%[8]	21.8%	91.5%	162
Morocco	36.0	$3,238	27%	69.4%	61.8%	124.2%	135
Oman	4.8	$16,419	22%	93.0%	80.2%	133.4%	132
Palestine	4.6	$3,199	39%	96.9%	65.2%	89.5%	137
Qatar	2.8	$69,027	14%	96.7%	97.4%	141.9%	128
Saudi Arabia	33.7	$23,219	25%	97.7%	82.1%	122.6%	172
Sudan	41.8	$977	41%	73.4%[8]	30.9%	72.0%	175
Syria	16.9	$2,033	31%	85.1%[8]	34.3%	98.4%[9]	174
Tunisia	11.6	$3,447	24%	79.0%	64.2%	127.7%	72
United Arab Emirates	9.6	$43,005	15%	90.0%	94.8%	208.5%	133
Yemen	28.5	$944	40%	66.4%	26.7%	55.2%	168

Table 1 Data on each country included in the study.

[1] World Bank, "Population, total". https://data.worldbank.org/indicator/sp.pop.totl
[2] World Bank, "GDP per capita (current US$). https://data.worldbank.org/indicator/ny.gdp.pcap.cd
[3] World Bank, "Population ages 0-14 (% of total population)". https://data.worldbank.org/indicator/SP.POP.0014.TO.ZS
[4] United Nations Development Programme, "Literacy rate, adult (% ages 15 and older)". http://hdr.undp.org/en/indicators/101406#a
[5] International Telecommunication Union, "Percentage of Individuals using the Internet". www.itu.int/en/ITU-D/Statistics/Pages/stat/default.aspx Definition: "This is the proportion of individuals who used the Internet from any location in the last three months.", https://www.itu.int/dms_pub/itu-d/opb/ind/D-IND-ITCMEAS-2014-PDF-E.pdf, p. 54
[6] International Telecommunication Union, "Mobile-cellular subscriptions". www.itu.int/en/ITU-D/Statistics/Pages/stat/default.aspx
[7] Reporters Without Borders, "Ranking 2019". https://rsf.org/en/ranking/2019
[8] Unicef, "Literacy rate (2009-2013)".
[9] In 2017.

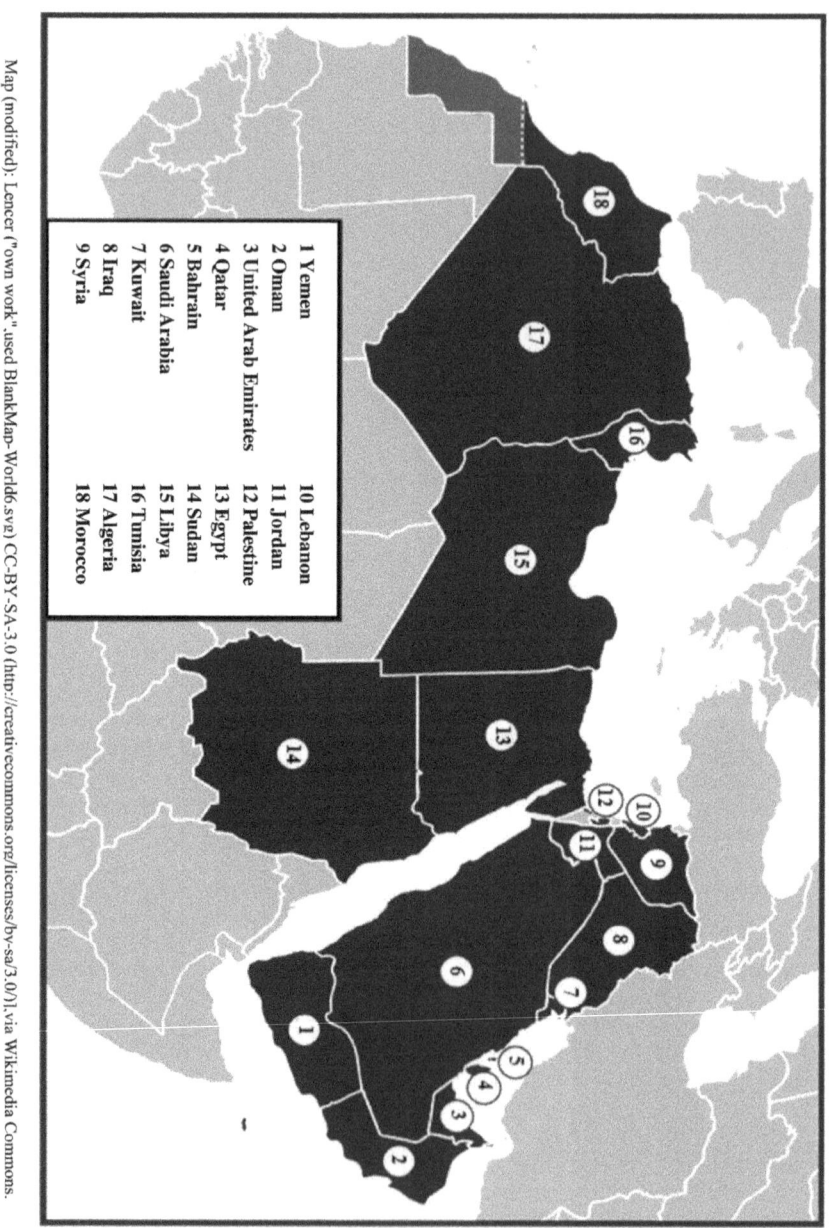

Map (modified): Lencer ("own work" used BlankMap-World6.svg) CC-BY-SA-3.0 (http://creativecommons.org/licenses/by-sa/3.0/), via Wikimedia Commons.

1. Lebanon: A Faltering Mesh of Political and Commercial Interests

Sarah El-Richani

> The Lebanese media, much like Lebanon itself, are boisterous and colorful. The pluralism that characterizes Lebanese society is reflected in its Babelesque media. In addition to the gamut of voices represented, freedom of expression is generally respected with the occasional transgressions. This chapter assesses the state of the Lebanese media from its inception to the present day, taking stock of the legal and political framework and the challenges encountered as well as the prospects for media in Lebanon.

Background

Lebanon, which was carved out by colonial powers from its Syrian hinterland in 1943, is among the smallest nations in the Arab world in terms of size and population. The Mediterranean country of approximately five million citizens also comprises a sizeable number of Syrian and Palestinian refugees. According to United Nation (UN) agencies, there are 910,256 registered Syrian refugees in Lebanon and just under 470,000 registered Palestinian refugees who fled to Lebanon after the establishment of Israel in 1948. The government, however, estimates that 1.5 million Syrian refugees are present in the country (UNHCR, 2020), making Lebanon the country with the highest number of refugees in relation to its size: 173 per 1,000 inhabitants (UNHCR, 2017).

Another characteristic of Lebanon is its diversity. While it is the only country in the Arab world that does not have an official religion, religion plays a dominant role in public life. Lebanon has 18 recognized Muslim and Christian religious groups, which have been given the prerogative over family status affairs. This pluralism is also reflected in parliament and political and state offices where positions are divided between the Christian and Muslim sects.

The manner in which this pluralism is organized in Lebanon has been contentious and is regarded as one of several factors that spurred the Lebanese Civil War, which began in 1975 and lasted approximately 15 years. The war claimed nearly 120,000 lives and resulted in the mass emigration of Lebanese citizens. The Ta'if Accord, which eventually brought an end to the war in the early 1990s, rearranged the division of power in a more proportional manner and effectively gave Syria the role of oversight. Syrian armed forces were already on Lebanese soil at the start of the civil war in a failed bid to end the war, and their influence on Lebanese political life would grow in strength in the post-war period.

Even in the post-war era, the power-sharing system, the weakness of the state, and the strength of the political and sectarian groups that are often supported by external regional players have made governance in this precarious nation a challenge. Additionally, it has made competition within each group difficult. The recurring conflicts, whether the devastating wars with Israel and the Israeli occupation of South Lebanon, which lasted from 1982 to 2000, or internal political, security, and economic crises, have further crippled the country, thereby impacting its media.

Indeed, the media reflect the political and social architecture of Lebanon. To begin with, most religious and political groups are represented on some level of the media system in one form or another. This makes the Lebanese media stand out in a region where free expression and pluralism are limited.

Historical Developments

The Lebanese media were pioneers in the region in terms of both publishing and broadcasting. The first Arabic newspaper to be published by Arabs, *Hadikat Al-Akhbar*, was launched in 1858 in what today is modern Lebanon. This was followed by several other newspapers published by the *nahda* literati. *Nahda* refers to the cultural renaissance that took place in the Levant and Egypt at the turn of the twentieth century. Indeed, on the eve of World War I, there were 168 publications published in Beirut alone.

As the Ottoman Empire, dubbed the "sick man of Europe", faltered, its grip over the provinces it controlled tightened before its ultimate collapse. As a result, some of these intellectuals and journalists fled to the more autonomous Egypt where they would establish prominent newspapers. Among these was the renowned *Al-Ahram* daily, which had been established by the Taqla brothers. Other publishers and writers, however, opted to stay put and agitate for freedom at a heavy cost—death. On 6 May 1916, a cohort of intrepid leaders, including 16 journalists, was sent to the gallows by the brutal Ottoman Wali Jamal Pasha, "the bloodshedder," in what would later be named Martyrs' Square (El-Richani, 2020).

Following the fall of the Ottoman Empire in 1918, Lebanon fell under French Mandate and witnessed strict controls on free expression. Nevertheless, the vibrancy of newspapers born out of individual effort would continue. After Lebanon's declaration of independence from France in 1943, the Lebanese press would enjoy even more freedom. In fact, their coverage of corruption in the first government was partially credited with the 1952 resignation of the republic's first president, Bechara El-Khuri.

The period between independence and the start of the Lebanese civil war in 1975 also witnessed the launch of Lebanese television, which, unlike in other countries in the region, began as a private and commercial enterprise offering regular programming. In 1959, the *Compagnie Libanaise de Télévision* (*CLT*) was launched and was followed in 1962 by *Tele Orient*, another commercial broadcaster. Despite the broadcast of advertisements, the two channels failed to yield profits. Their financial troubles were further exacerbated by the start of the civil war. Therefore, in 1977, the government intervened and bailed them out by merging the two companies to form *Télé Liban* (*TL*) of which it owned 50% of the shares. The remaining private sector shares were later purchased by Rafik Hariri, a future Lebanese premier who was later assassinated in 2005. Hariri eventually sold his shares in *TL* to the state and set up a privately-owned television station and media empire.

With the start of the Israeli-Palestinian conflict, and unlike the Arab press which embodied the slogan "no voice rises above the voice of the battle," the diversity of views in Lebanon would remain extant. The liberal *An-Nahar* daily was critical of Egypt's president and Pan-Arab leader Gamal Abdel Nasser, whereas others were more sympathetic to the Pan-Arab cause. For instance, the popular and now defunct *As-Safir* published daily Abdel Nasser quotes on the back page throughout the decades and labeled itself the "newspaper of Lebanon in the Arab world and the paper of the Arab World in Lebanon."

The polarization of the press, though a welcome manifestation of free expression and pluralism, reflected the increased divisions in the Lebanese polity and eventually resulted in conflict. In 1975, a number of factors caused the rupture including gross inequalities and the regional crises afflicting the country, which saw the influx of the Palestinian *feda'yeen* or armed groups into Lebanon. The civil war, which spanned nearly 15 years, witnessed the emergence of militia tabloids alongside newspapers representing the entire political spectrum. In 1977, an amendment to the press law was passed in an effort to stifle the press seen by then President Elias Sarkis as inciting strife (Khazaal, 2018, p. 72). The amendment was, however, difficult to implement in this Hobbesian "war of all against all". Meanwhile, in the 1980s, pirate television and radio stations would emerge challenging the national broadcaster *TL*, which sought to sanitize coverage of the war and further what Khazaal (2018) termed "the peace bubble" (p. 68). One of these television stations, *LBC*, managed to attract a wide audience despite its flagrant affiliation to the right-wing Christian militia at the time. Following the end of the war, the channel severed its links to the disbanded party, whose leader was imprisoned. Yet, the channel still remains prominent to this day (El-Richani, 2015, pp. 49–50).

After 1990, during the post-war years, newspapers and media in general benefitted from the return of commercial activity despite the limitations on free expression imposed by the Syrian caretakers. Live coverage of protests was banned (Rugh, 2004, pp. 202–04), censors were implanted in television stations, and journalists were often closely monitored. In 2002, *MTV*, a popular broadcaster was accused of violating Article 68 of the electoral law, although even the Minister of Information at the time admitted that this was just a pretense and the closure was on "purely political" grounds (Kraidy & Khalil, 2009, pp. 129–32).

The next rupture was the assassination of former Prime Minister Rafik Hariri along with several other politicians and journalists in 2005. This led to major protests and the emergence of the March 8 and March 14 political camps, with the former consisting of pro-Syria parties and groups and the latter of a coalition of parties and politicians who were against Syria's long-standing interference in Lebanon. The massive protests and international pressure eventually forced the Syrian troops to leave and effectively ended Syrian tutelage over Lebanon. Shortly after the withdrawal of Syrian troops and the weakening of Syria's influence in 2005, the decree to close *MTV* was reversed, and the station eventually relaunched in 2009.

In July 2006, a devastating war between Israel and Lebanon erupted causing vast destruction. Rising from the ashes was the *Al-Akhbar* newspaper, which, despite its close links to Hezbollah and the Syrian regime, as the coverage of the Syrian civil war would later reveal, offered a refreshing and brazen approach to news and a break with protocol news. In May 2008, civil unrest flared up between the two polarized groups: March 8 and March 14. During this period, the Hariri-affiliated *Future Media* empire, belonging to the March 14 coalition, were forced off the air for four days by armed gangs affiliated with the powerful March 8 coalition. 'This is Lebanon. We were not protected, as we should have been. And, nothing will or can stop them from doing it again as simple as this', lamented a *Future TV* executive (El-Richani, 2016, p. 80). Lebanon today, though politically stable, is in dire economic and financial straits that have resulted in the closure of many businesses including a series of media outlets such as *Future TV* and the *Al-Safir* daily.

Political System and Legal Framework

The Lebanese political system is characterized by power-sharing, which for all intents and purposes has rendered the state weak. Political power is shared among political and sectarian patrons commonly referred to as *zu'ama* (or *za'im* in singular). Denigrated as "les fromagistes" by President Fu'ad Chehab, who attempted to strengthen the state during his tenure in the late 1950s, this political and sectarian elite is only interested in their share of the proverbial pie and has subsequently benefitted from the system of patronage and clientelism (AbuKhalil, 1998, p. 197). As mentioned earlier, the 18 officially recognized religious groups are proportionally represented in parliament and government. The National Pact, an oral agreement among the independence leaders, has traditionally allotted the position of president of the republic to a Maronite Christian, the premiership to a Sunni Muslim, and the position of speaker of parliament to a Shi'a Muslim.

Despite this attempt at sharing power among the groups, the strength of some *zu'ama* and parties has resulted in a series of impasses, leaving key posts vacant for several years. The current president, Michel Aoun, was elected in October 2016, nearly two and a half years after his predecessor left office. His predecessor, Michel Suleiman, was elected president also after a vacancy in the presidency and after regional players intervened to end scuffles that erupted in May 2008 between the two dominant camps in Lebanon, March 14 and March 8. The tussle over influence and profit also delayed civil servant appointments including the post of director of the state television *TL* and, more importantly, delayed the agreement over the electoral law leading to the postponement of parliamentary elections, which finally took place in May 2018—nine years after the May 2009 elections. Although the postponement of the elections was allegedly for security reasons relating to the ongoing Syrian civil war, some observers believe it was due to a squabble over the electoral law. The formation of the cabinet has also usually been a matter of contention. Following the parliamentary elections in May 2018, it took nine months to finally establish a council of ministers after much wrangling over cabinet portfolios, veto power, and the number of portfolios each party and religious group would get. Less than a year later, the prime minister would resign in light of an unprecedented economic and financial crisis and rampant protests. After three months of political wrangling, a new council of ministers was formed to face the crippling economic crisis, an issue further exacerbated by the COVID-19 pandemic. The government, however, resigned in August 2020 following the harrowing explosion in the Beirut port that claimed 200 lives and billions of dollars in damages. The blast, much like the economic crisis, appears to be a result of mismanagement, corruption and criminal negligence.

In addition to the corruption and clientelism that exist, the size of the state, which is small by all measures, has also greatly impacted both the political and media system and augmented Lebanon's financial woes. This reality is reflected in the media system to a large extent, characterized by a high degree of political parallelism or media partisanship. In terms of structural pluralism or media ownership, the political and sectarian groups are all, more or less, represented on the level of the media system whether by direct ownership or indirect affiliation. While the broadcasting licensing system, to be described below, paved the way for external pluralism where each religious group or political entity would own its own channel, there are a number of successful outlets such as *LBCI* and *Al-Jadeed* that have been pluralized internally both in terms of content and staff.

Meanwhile, the state broadcaster *TL*, which also reflects the state in terms of its weakness and lackluster output, is unable to compete with the privately-owned media. The representative rationing that has arguably crippled governance is also practiced within the station with sharp political divisions among departments and disagreements, leaving the position of director vacant for years on end. This and its limited annual budget, which is equivalent to what the popular privately-owned television networks spend in a month, have meant that any aspirations for the channel to fulfil its promise, serve the public, and sow national unity remain naïve at best (Buccianti & El-Richani, 2015, pp. 24–26).

Before delving into a discussion of the legal framework, it is worth noting that, paradoxically, the level of freedom extant in the country is largely due to state weakness rather than liberal laws. The weak state cannot always impose its harsh laws, particularly against media outlets that are supported by powerful owners or backers.

The laws currently on the books include the press law, which dates back to 1962 and the audio-visual media law which was passed in 1994. The press law has remained largely unchanged, save for some amendments including the 1977 decree 104, which penalizes journalists for offending the president, religious groups, or foreign leaders. The press law also proposes sanctions for impersonating a journalist, which on paper applies to anyone who is not on the Press Association registry. Today, the majority of media practitioners are not enrolled in the Press Association's registry and therefore fall afoul of this article. For this reason, it could be regarded as a boon for the media that the laws are not strictly observed. Other contentious articles that are rarely enforced are articles 16, 20 to 23, and 25 of the Lebanese press laws that stipulate the imprisonment of journalists for press offenses such as defamation and libel.

Another contentious law relevant to the print media is decree number 74 that was issued by President Camille Chamoun in 1953, which states that no further political publications other than the 110 extant ones can be licensed until the number drops to 25. The decree tasked the ineffective Ministry of Information with withdrawing licenses from dormant publications. The Ministry, however, never fulfilled this role, therefore rendering these licenses assets that could be sold to wealthy entrepreneurs who were keen on starting a newspaper. The advent of the Internet and the move towards digital publications, however, has thoroughly weakened this monopoly on the public sphere and rendered the licenses more or less worthless.

Another oversight duty the Ministry of Information has refrained from exercising is its monitoring of the finances of media outlets to ensure they remain independent. As the media largely rely on political money to sustain themselves, the Ministry's neglect of this role has allowed the media to sustain themselves through financial subsidies from philanthropists, politicians, and foreign governments seeking to play an influential political role, such as Saudi Arabia, Iran, Qatar, the USA, and the like. At the same time, broadcasting is regulated by audio-visual media law 382/94, which came about after the civil war to organize and regulate the audio-visual sector and effectively end the already challenged monopoly of *TL* over the airwaves. The law stipulated the formation of the National Audio-Visual Council (NAVC), which was tasked with approving applications for licensing television stations. The NAVC members were selected by parliament and the government in equal measure, rendering them politically captive to those parties and the politicians who selected them. Licenses were therefore granted to the *de facto* powers and along sectarian lines rather than to worthy applicants. For instance, *Al-Jadeed TV*, owned by an adversary of the then PM Rafik Hariri, was forced to shut down after having its application rejected for dubious reasons. After four years of litigation, the State Council arbitrated in its favor, and *Al-Jadeed* was granted a license in 2000. Meanwhile *NBN*, often jokingly referred to as the Nabih Berri Network in reference to its effective owner, the Speaker of Parliament, received its license despite not meeting the requirements. Other licensees included the now defunct *Future TV* owned by the influential Hariri family, *Murr Television (MTV)*, owned by the influential Greek Orthodox Al-Murr family, and the *Lebanese Broadcasting Corporation (LBC)*, formerly owned by the Lebanese Forces militia, whose members were persecuted in the post-war period. Later, Hezbollah's *Al-Manar*, which began broadcasting in 1991, was also granted a license. Meanwhile, *Télé Lumière*, set up by the Assembly of Catholic Patriarchs and Bishops in Lebanon as a non-profit television station, continues to broadcast without a license. In 2006, the Free Patriotic Movement was also granted a license to establish *OTV* following the return of current President Michel Aoun from exile. According to one of *OTV*'s executives, the license would not have been granted easily "had there been no political side behind this station" (El-Richani, 2016, p. 76).

In addition to licensing, the NAVC was also tasked with monitoring broadcast media to ensure they upheld the laws, although this was done in an *ad hoc* fashion. The few instances where they would censure a station for violating the law were often at the behest of political actors.

The Ministry's task to monitor the finances of television outlets to ensure their revenue streams stem from legitimate sources, such as advertising and production enterprises, has also been suspended. This is evidenced by a cursory look at the media market which is simply inadequate to sustain the media outlets extant in Lebanon (El-Richani, 2016, p. 123). In an interview with the author, the then Minister of Information recalled how the NAVC cynically told him not to bother with the laws because of the entanglement of politics and the media (El-Richani, 2016, p. 75).

It is important to note here that this state of affairs does not mean that all the media laws have been suspended. On the contrary, issues relating to defamation and spreading false news, for example, often result in time-consuming litigation. Still, there have been calls by media professionals and advocacy groups to modernize the media laws, in part because they are outdated and do not take into consideration technological advancement and its impact on the media, but also because the current laws are difficult to implement with vague articles and expressions that run against the spirit of the Lebanese constitution. One example is the harsh sanctions for violations of the elusive ideal of objectivity, which again has luckily been overlooked.

Although these initiatives have been discussed by the communications committee in parliament, they remain dormant for now and are yet to be passed. The advocacy groups that deliberated media rights and regulations within organized meetings also know full well that the final piece of legislation would also be far from ideal as it would be drafted and passed by parliamentarians who have a large stake in the media. Until new laws are passed, however, it is important to take stock of the *de facto* situation in Lebanon in addition to that which is *de jure*.

Economy and Ownership Patterns

Lebanon is a small state in every sense of the word. This means that, particularly in terms of political communication, which has limited regional traction and is highly competitive, the market is saturated and subscription and circulation rates woefully inadequate to sustain the media. Furthermore, the unprecedented economic and financial crisis in which the country has found itself since 2019 has also exacerbated matters with advertising expenditures being cut by approximately 70%–90% (Arab Ad, 2020).

Many media outlets have therefore had to rely on political subsidies from their political backers, which, as recent closures have revealed, is not sustainable, particularly in light of the serious economic problems facing the country. In October 2018, *An-Nahar* issued a blank copy to raise the alarm about the financial woes facing the Lebanese media and spur politicians to form a cabinet and confront these challenges. In December 2019, the newspaper started a campaign to collect donations that would ensure its survival.

Political parallelism is therefore high with many of the media outlets subsidized or owned in part or full by political actors. On the level of broadcasting, external pluralism, where each party or religious group is represented, is rather high. Alongside the national broadcaster, which toes the government line, the Shi'ite power brokers are represented by two television stations: *NBN* is owned by long-serving speaker of parliament and a *za'im*, Nabih Berri, who heads the Amal Movement, whereas Hezbollah owns *Al-Manar* through affiliated shareholders. Also, the influential Sunni Hariri family owned *Future TV* until it shut down in 2019. Striking a sectarian balance, *MTV* is owned by the influential Greek Orthodox Al-Murr family, *LBCI* is owned by the Maronite Christian Pierre Daher, and other shareholders have also been licensed. After a long legal battle, *New TV*, which was rebranded as *Al-Jadeed* and is owned by a then-Hariri rival, also obtained its license. The party of the current president, the Free Patriotic Movement, also launched its own television after its members returned from exile. Finally, the Catholic Church also continues to run a non-profit television station *Télé Lumière* (El-Richani, 2013, p. 71).

The print industry is not much different and also includes a series of partisan newspapers, such as *Al-Anba'* run by the Progressive Socialist Party, *Al-Bina'* run by the Syrian Socialist Nationalist Party, and *Al-Mustakbal* run by Hariri's Future Movement. Other newspapers are supported in part or full by a variety of political shareholders or contributors: *An-Nahar* is owned by several political shareholders, including at one point the Hariri family, *Al-Akhbar* is owned by investors close to Hezbollah, and *Al-Diyar* is owned and run by the eccentric publisher Charles Ayoub, who, in 2011, openly wrote an editorial about the "gifts" and broken promises he had received from Saudi Arabia, Syria, and Hariri, among others (El-Richani, 2016, p. 152). The newspapers *Al-Liwa'* and *El-Sharq* are both close to Hariri and Saudi Arabia with the latter owned by the head of the editor's association, Awni Al-Kaaki, and his sibling, whereas *Al-Liwa'* is owned by the Salam family. Other newspapers in the March 14 camp include *Al-Jumhouriyya*, which is owned by the former Minister of Defence Elias Murr, the francophone *L'Orient le Jour*, which is owned by the wealthy Edde, Chouieri, and Pharaon families, and the anglophone *The Daily Star*, founded by prominent journalist Kamel Mroueh but currently owned by Hariri associates as well as Qatari associates. *The Daily Star* decided in early 2020 to suspend its print edition and continue only with digital distribution. Meanwhile in October 2020, the French daily *L'Orient le Jour* launched its English-language edition *L'Orient Today*.

Other newspapers include the now defunct, once prominent leftist Pan-Arab daily *Al-Safir*, owned by Talal Salman and funded by a variety of regional stakeholders, including the wealthy investor and philanthropist Jamal Daniel in 2014. After 42 years of uninterrupted publishing, the newspaper folded in 2016. Another newspaper that folded in 2018 was the catchall commercial newspaper *Al-Balad*, owned by the Kuwaiti Al-Wataniya company, which, for a number of reasons, failed to capture the interests of Lebanese readers. Despite this wave of closures, one newspaper, *Nida' Al-Watan*, and two recent digital platforms, *Daraj* and *Megaphone* have emerged in recent years. While *Nida' Al-Watan* champions the March 14 camp, *Daraj* and *Megaphone* are independent in so far that they are not linked to parties or officials in the country. The two digital platforms, however, both rely on grants from European donors, which raises questions about long-term sustainability.

This ownership structure prompted media scholar Nabil Dajani (2013) to claim that media freedom in Lebanon is a myth, citing restrictions imposed by financiers on the media they support. While this may be true to a certain extent, in so far as one rarely finds criticism of Saudi Arabia on Hariri-affiliated media or of Iran in Hezbollah-affiliated media, critical and strident views about all political actors and regional and international players are prevalent in the Lebanese media and readily accessible to all.

Nevertheless, following the rise of Rafik Hariri to the premiership and the consolidation of ownership over several media outlets, there was a serious concern that pluralism might be limited and criticism of his policies could be snuffed. The sprawling Hariri conglomerate across several industries from banking and contracting to real estate and insurance included at one point a considerable media portfolio. The Hariri media empire acquired shares in a number of publications, such as the liberal *An-Nahar* and *Al-Liwa'*, and it also owned entire media outlets, including two television channels, one newspaper, and one radio station, *Radio Orient*. This moguldom has been largely undone by Rafik Hariri's son and former Prime Minister Saad Hariri who is now facing financial difficulties (Nötzold, 2015, p. 80). Indeed, *Future News* satellite channel ceased operations in 2012, five years after its launch, followed by the closure of *Future TV* in September 2019, the *Future Media* empire's flagship, after years of stagnation and unpaid salaries. The *Al-Mustakbal* daily also discontinued its print edition in June 2019, 20 years after its launch.

Meanwhile, *LBC*, one of the leading television stations in Lebanon, also flirted with the idea of conglomeration, and for a period of five years, it merged with Saudi Mogul Al-Waleed bin Talal's *Rotana* media empire. This union, however, ended in acrimony with a series of lawsuits; *Rotana* retained *LBCSat*, and *LBC* had to launch a new satellite channel called *LDC* in 2012 (El-Richani, 2015, pp. 52–55).

Undoubtedly, there is a high level of political parallelism in the Lebanese media. The politics and media nexus, though sometimes lamented, can also be regarded as a boon in that all groups are more or less represented and have a platform, whereas attempts at mainstreaming might result in the further marginalizing of vulnerable communities. On the other hand, it is also worth noting that the most successful media outlets, such as *LBCI* and *Al-Jadeed*, are internally pluralistic and offer solid professional content. These media outlets have managed to reach viewers from beyond their traditional built-in partisan audiences. While echo chambers certainly exist, highly critical views of the Lebanese political and sectarian elites are readily available on the level of the media system.

Technology and Infrastructure

The Lebanese state has a monopoly on the lucrative telecommunications sector, which is the highest revenue generator for the government (Hodali, 2019). Mobile telecom services are provided by two privately-owned companies, *Alfa* and *MTC Touch*, managed by the Egyptian telecom company *Orascom Telecom, Media and Technology* (*OTMT*) and the Kuwaiti *Zain*, respectively. According to the statistics by the

International Telecommunication Union (ITU) (2019), approximately 65% of the population subscribe to mobile cellular phone services.

Despite Lebanon's pioneering role in terms of publishing and broadcasting, embracing the Internet was a slightly slower affair due to slow connections offered at exorbitant prices. While DSL Internet was launched in Lebanon in 2007, the Internet, which falls entirely under the Ministry of Telecommunications and is overseen by the state-owned Ogero Company, remained slow for nearly a decade, so much so that people referred to it as *ontornet* (*ontor* being Arabic for wait). Until 2017, Internet speeds were kept low and costs high for a variety of reasons including corruption. Allegations of corruption, including the discovery of illegal parallel networks, resulted in the sacking of the director of Ogero who also occupied a high post in the relevant ministry. In recent years, the instalment of 6,000 kilometers of fiber instead of copper cables has also helped improve speeds and decrease the digital divide between urban and rural areas (Executive (Middle East), 2017). The drop in prices following the change of leadership has also increased Internet penetration in Lebanon, which, in 2018, was estimated at 78% by the ITU.

In a testament to the weakness of state structures, the filtering or blocking of websites—though limited in scope—is carried out on an *ad hoc* basis by the Ministry of Telecommunications. Currently, there are blocked websites relating to pornography, homosexuality, copyright breaches, and gambling. Meanwhile, cybercrimes are usually investigated by the Cybercrimes Bureau at the behest of the public prosecutor. The Cybercrimes Bureau was established in 2006 "without a legislative decree" (Freedom House, 2017). In 2018, there were 38 summonses for posts written online that resulted in forcing citizens to apologize or remove the content, whereas there were 63 reported cases in 2019 according to the Muhal Observatory for Free Expression.[1]

While Internet penetration is on the rise, 99% of Lebanese still watch television with 94% believing that it is an important source of news (Dennis, Martin, & Hassan, 2019). Nevertheless, due to the rise in the use of smartphones to receive news from 76% in 2017 to 92% in

---

1   The Muhal Observatory for Freedom of Expression has documented all 2019 cases on their website which can be accessed on the following link https://muhal.org/en/cases/

2018, most media outlets have now established much followed social media accounts as well as apps (Dennis et al., 2019). *LBC*, *MTV* and *Al-Jadeed* have also introduced paywalls for full access to their online content in an attempt to generate more revenue. Meanwhile, content by the alternative news platform *Megaphone*, which began on *Facebook*, is primarily designed to be disseminated on social media platforms and to target the ever-growing number of Lebanese people who get their news from social media sites. The most popular social media application according to a survey is *WhatsApp* with 92% users, followed by *Facebook* with 78%, *YouTube* 68%, and *Instagram* at 45% (Dennis et al., 2019).

In a bid to raise revenue in October 2019, the council of ministers adopted the infamous and now revoked "*WhatsApp* tax" proposal, which intended to levy a monthly USD 6 tax for the use of *WhatsApp*. This led to mass protests across the country with demonstrators displaying their anger at the government's incompetence in dealing with the deep economic crisis, eventually leading to its resignation.

Challenges

The Lebanese media system currently faces three key challenges. Like most media around the world, the heightened fragmentation of audiences due to the infinite choices made available via the Internet has led to the scattering of "eyeballs" and, therefore, advertising revenue. While in terms of political communication and due to political and economic crises, there is an unquenchable thirst for local news, the saturated market cannot continue as it stands. Staff redundancies, media closures, and cost reduction have been regular occurrences over the past years. At the same time, political money funneled into media outlets to serve political actors in their contentions over the control of Lebanon is expected to continue even if that, too, will diminish due to the economic strain impacting the country. Still, partisan media may indeed look at more cost-effective ways of reaching their built-in audiences. The series of media outlets folding and closing, though lamentable in terms of job losses, is also an expected byproduct of the marketplace model. Thus, the commercially viable media need to orchestrate ways to remain relevant, be it by introducing paywalls or investing in enticing programs.

Another key challenge facing the Lebanese media is the absence of current laws that take stock of technological advancements and the new realities created by them. Although the codified laws are currently only loosely applied, they still need to be updated to safeguard freedom of expression and the rights of journalists and citizens alike. Recently, there has been an increase in the number of summonses and arrests made against social media users, which clearly indicates the need for a new law that addresses the online media and clarifies the job description of the Cybercrimes Bureau.

The third and final challenge relates to the state television, *Télé Liban*. While a public service broadcaster would help to overcome the problems of rampant commercialization and unabashed polarization in Lebanon, *TL* in its current form does not and cannot meet those expectations. The government will, therefore, need to decide whether it can afford to inject the ailing station with more funds and thereby support it, or to cease its operations altogether thereby limiting losses.

Outlook

As outlined above, the Lebanese media, much like the country itself, are in dire straits. As audiences continue to fragment, political stakeholders who had traditionally sustained the Lebanese media are finding more efficient and effective platforms. Meanwhile, the commercially viable channels are struggling to produce content that they hope will retain their audiences. While more austerity measures in the media are expected, possibly including further closures, it is believed that the remaining outlets will continue due to the demand for local content. The successful television stations are those that have, to some degree, pluralized internally, particularly in terms of content and staff composition. It is therefore expected that this pluralism, which is a central feature of the Lebanese media, will remain intact. Moreover, the ever-diminishing digital divide has also ensured that even the most marginal of voices would be able to connect with their audiences to varying degrees and in varying ways, such as through social media.

The main concern for the Lebanese media in the coming months and years as it grapples with an unprecedented economic crisis, however, is not the invisible hand resulting in the closure of non-profitable endeavors, but the visible and forceful hand clamping down on free expression.

References

AbuKhalil (1998). Historical dictionary of Lebanon. Asian Historical Dictionaries: Vol. 30. Lanham: Scarecrow Press.

Arab Ad (2020, February 18). Lebanon: Advertising in times of crisis. http://arabadonline.com/en/details/advertising/lebanon-advertising-in-a-time-of-crisis

Buccianti, A., & El-Richani, S. (2015). After the Arab uprisings: The prospects for a media that serves the public. BBC Media Action Policy Briefing, 14. http://downloads.bbc.co.uk/mediaaction/pdf/policybriefing/after-the-arab-uprisings-sept-2015.pdf

Dajani, N. (2013). The myth of media freedom in Lebanon. Arab Media and Society, 18. https://www.arabmediasociety.com/the-myth-of-media-freedom-in-lebanon/

Dennis, E. E., Martin, J. D., & Hassan, F. (2019). Media use in the Middle East, 2019: A seven-nation survey by Northwestern University in Qatar. www.mideastmedia.org/survey/2019

El-Richani, S. (2013). The Lebanese broadcasting system: A battle between political parallelism, commercialism and de-facto liberalism. In T. Guaaybess (Ed.), National broadcasting and state policy in Arab countries (pp. 69–82). London: Palgrave Macmillan.

———. (2015). Pierre Daher: Sheikh, baron, and mogul of LBC. In D. Della Ratta, N. Sakr, & J. Skovgaard-Petersen (Eds.), Arab media moguls (pp. 49–62). London, New York: I. B. Tauris.

———. (2016). The Lebanese media: Anatomy of a system in perpetual crisis. New York: Palgrave Macmillan.

———. (2020). Whither the Lebanese Press? The trials and tribulations facing the Lebanese press. In N. Mellor & N. Miladi (Eds.), Handbook for Arab media. London: Routledge.

Executive (Middle East) (2017, May 11). Unleash the speed. Gale General Onefile. https://go.gale.com/ps/i.do?p=ITOF&u=aucairo&id=GALE|A496403834&v=2.1&it=r&sid=ITOF&asid=02d91840

Freedom House (2017, November 20). Freedom on the net 2017: Lebanon. https://www.justice.gov/eoir/page/file/1180896/download

Hodali, D. (2019, May 7). Lebanon–Telecommunication in government hands. Deutsche Welle. https://www.dw.com/en/lebanon-telecommunication-in-government-hands/a-48634796-0

International Telecommunication Union (2019). ICT Data. https://www.itu.int/en/ITU-D/Statistics/Documents/statistics/2019/Individuals_Internet_2000-2018_Jun2019.xls

Khazaal, N. (2018). Pretty liar: Television, language, and gender in wartime Lebanon. New York: Syracuse University Press.

Kraidy, M., & Khalil, J. (2009). Arab television industries. Basingstoke: Palgrave Macmillan.

Nötzold, K. (2015). The Hariris, father and son: The making and unmaking of moguldom? In D. Della Ratta, N. Sakr, & J. Skovgaard-Petersen (Eds.), Arab media moguls (pp. 63–80). London, New York: I. B. Tauris.

Rugh, W. A. (2004). Arab mass media: Newspapers, radio, and television in Arab politics. London: Praeger.

UNHCR (2017). Mid-year trends 2016. https://www.unhcr.org/dach/wp-content/uploads/sites/27/2017/04/midyeartrends_2016.pdf

——. (2020). Lebanon fact sheet. https://reliefweb.int/sites/reliefweb.int/files/resources/UNHCR%20Lebanon%20COVID-19%20Update%20-%2016APR20_0_0.pdf

2. Syria: A Fragmented Media System

Yazan Badran

The nine-year-long conflict in Syria has had a ruinous impact on the country's social fabric, economic life, and territorial integrity. The territorial fragmentation, in particular, has led to the dissolution of the tightly controlled information environment which existed before the conflict. While the regions that remained under the control of the central government reflect, more or less, a continuation of the authoritarian logics of the Syrian regime from pre-2011, the regions controlled by Kurdish forces and opposition-linked rebel forces developed radically different, albeit unstable, media environments. Additionally, the substantial Syrian refugee population in neighboring countries and beyond has given impetus to the development of exilic and diasporic media outlets. These fundamental changes, and contradictions, in the Syrian media landscape will need to be reconciled and negotiated in any future settlement of the conflict.

Background

As the Ottoman provinces in the east were redrawn following World War I, the modern state of Syria emerged as the largest entity of the former Bilad Al-Sham, or Greater Syria. In the interwar period, Syria was placed under French occupation in accordance with a League of Nations mandate. Since gaining independence from France in 1946, Syria has been at the heart of the strategic competition among the surrounding regional hegemons (Turkey, Iran, Egypt, Saudi Arabia, and Israel), as well as between the

USSR and the US during the Cold War. Being at the forefront of the Arab-Israeli conflict also meant that investment in the military took priority immediately after independence, and that the military establishment had an outsized role in Syria's national politics. The politics of Syria were also very much intertwined with and shaped by the ideology of Arab nationalism. Indeed, Damascus was the seat of the earliest Arab nationalist government (1918–1920), and Syria's different post-independence regimes have been oriented towards Arab nationalism in one way or another. The strength of the Arab nationalist ideology notwithstanding, Syria has been, since its modern borders emerged, a multiethnic and multireligious state. The tension between the dominant ideology among the ruling elite and ethno-religious heterogeneity of Syrian society, especially as Arab nationalism hardened its ethnolinguistic borders under the Ba'ath Party regime, is most visible in the state's troubled relationship with the sizable Kurdish minority in northeastern Syria. The almost two million Syrian Kurds, many of whom were stripped of their Syrian citizenship following a controversial census in 1962 (Albarazi, 2013), have been the subject of sustained state discrimination against their culture and, in particular, the Kurdish language for decades (Hassanpour, Skutnabb-Kangas, & Chyet, 1996). When the northeastern regions of the country proclaimed autonomy following the Syrian conflict, reclaiming the Kurdish language and culture was placed at the heart of that political project (Badran & De Angelis, 2016).

Several other factors have had a significant impact on Syria's politics and society throughout its modern history. These factors include the urban-rural and class divisions and sectarian and religious differences—all of which are often overlapping and intermeshed. Syrian politics have long been dominated by the landowning urban elites of the large cities—Damascus, Aleppo, and Homs—a class that was almost entirely made up of Sunni Muslims and, to a much lesser extent, Christians. This dominance began to unravel as rural regions became more developed. Moreover, while the army was long shunned by the urban Sunni elites, it was seen by the peasantry, as well as the religious minorities such as Alawites,[1] as an opportunity for social mobility and economic

---

1   Alawites, a minority sect of Shi'a Islam, represent about 12% of Syria's population, while Sunni Islam is practiced by an estimated 75%. As a syncretic sect, Alawites are considered a distinct branch of mainstream Twelver Shi'a Islam practiced in Iran.

advancement. As the role of the army in the country's politics expanded, so did the fortunes of these groups. The Ba'ath Party's *coup d'état* in 1963 finally ended the dominance of the urban bourgeoisie and brought about a new ruling class from the cohorts of the army. Specifically, the regime of Hafez Al-Assad (1970–2000), with its reliance on clan and family members, mostly of Alawite origin, in key positions in the state and the army, established a new structure of elite power in Syria "which draws strength simultaneously, but in decreasing intensity, from a tribe, a sect-class, and an ecologic-cultural division of the people" (Batatu, 1981, p. 331).

The popular uprising of 2011, and the subsequent protracted military conflict, brought into sharp relief all of these overlapping factors. It also reignited the regional and international competition over the future and orientation of the Syrian polity. The more direct and immediate consequence of the war was the devastating impact it had on Syrian society and economy. Syria's pre-war population, which was estimated at 21 million by 2011, has been decimated. By February 2020, the United Nations High Commissioner for Refugees (UNHCR) estimated that more than half have been displaced—with over 5.6 million fleeing to neighboring countries, such as Turkey, Lebanon, Jordan, and beyond, and a further 6.1 million having been internally displaced. Additionally, large swathes of the country's urban infrastructure have been destroyed by shelling, aerial bombardment, and clashes, and estimates for the cost of post-war reconstruction range from USD 350–400 billion. Finally, the Syrian exodus following 2011, coupled with the territorial and political disintegration and polarization, fractured the former unitary media system in the country and led to a fragmentation in audiences, media, and regulatory regimes.

Historical Developments

The earliest attempts to establish a popular press in what is now Syria had to contend with the highly restrictive laws of the Ottoman Empire. Indeed, since the earliest recorded paper *Al-Shahba*, published by Hashem El-Attar and Abdul Rahman Al-Kawakibi in Aleppo in 1877, the 91 different publications that emerged under the Ottomans were subject to "suspension, confiscation, or seizure" according to Dajani and

Najjar (2003, p. 303). This highly restricted environment ended with the demise of the Ottoman Empire following its defeat in World War I. The new political horizon of Arab nationalism, in ascendance since before the war, was reflected in the popular press in the tumultuous period of self-governance from 1918 until 1920 when France took over as the colonial hegemon in Syria and Lebanon. During the period of the French Mandate, press regulation came under the direct authority of the office of the French High Commissioner of the Levant. The period also witnessed the emergence of strong journalistic figures who commanded a nationwide audience. For instance, Najib Al-Rayyes, the so-called dean of Syrian journalism, was a nationalist writer and newspaper publisher, and his paper, *Al-Qabas*, enjoyed wide readership because of its support of Syrian independence. Other important publications included the nationalist daily *Al-Ayyam*, published by Najib Al-Armanazi, and the satirical weekly *Al-Mudhik Al-Mubki*, published by Habib Kahaleh (Rafai, 1969). Moreover, the antecedent to Syrian radio was established in 1941 by the French authorities with 15 employees and used short- and medium-wave transmission. In 1945, the radio stopped broadcasting after its Syrian staff resigned in protest of French policies in the country. It returned to the air on Independence Day, 17 April 1946, and became a full-fledged state broadcaster (Dajani & Najjar, 2003, p. 305).

The period immediately following independence was marked by political instability with power changing hands between civilian and military regimes. The 1948 Arab-Israeli war resulted in the arrival of over 80,000 Palestinian refugees in Syria (Said, 2003). The war also saw a series of military setbacks for the newly formed Syrian Army for which the officers held the politicians responsible. The social and political tensions in the aftermath of the conflict heralded a succession of military coups (1949–1954), which resulted in several highly restrictive press laws. From 1954–1958, parliamentary democracy was restored and, with it, the more liberal Press Law of 1949. These so-called democratic years ushered in a golden age of journalism in the country. Public and private dailies, weeklies, and specialized periodicals proliferated with a minimal censorship regime and a politically competitive environment (Martin, 2015; Rugh, 2004).

The major breaking point in the history of Syrian media came with the Arab Socialist Ba'ath Party *coup d'état* on 8 March 1963. One of the first steps taken by the new revolutionary leadership on that day was to ban all but three (Ba'ath-affiliated) newspapers, *Al-Ba'ath*, *Al-Wahda*, and *Barada*. Legislative decree No. 48 in 1963 took further steps by centralizing all legal publishing in one state-owned organization, the Al-Wahda Foundation for Printing and Publishing (Dajani & Najjar, 2003). In 1965, the Journalism Syndicate was brought under the government's authority. By the end of that year, only two national and three regional dailies, and a handful of local periodicals, were left, all of which were published by the state or Ba'ath Party organs. The 1963 coup ushered in an era of "mobilization press" where the media's main function was the promotion of the regime's interests and the mobilization of public support (Rugh, 2004). The Ba'ath Party instilled a socialist planned economy that promoted nationalization and state ownership and control of most of its sectors. It established a *de facto* state monopoly of all media organs, including the press, publishing and distribution, radio, television, and audiovisual production sectors that remained largely undisturbed until the late 1990s. Furthermore, from 1962 onward, following a failed coup attempt by Nasserists, Syria was placed under the provisions of emergency law (partially modified in the mid-2000s and officially lifted in 2011), which gave broad discretion to the executive authority and allowed it to bypass the constitution. The regime of Hafez Al-Assad invested heavily in state media and towards perpetuating a strong cult of personality revolving around Assad and his immediate family (Wedeen, 1999).

The tenets of the Ba'ath Party's dominance of the economy were severely challenged by the economic crisis of the late 1980s, the collapse of the Soviet Union, and the emergence of the US as the global hegemon. These developments pushed the regime to take some tentative steps towards economic liberalization (*infitah*) culminating in Law No. 10 of 1991, which opened some sectors of the economy to private investment. In the media sector, this was only realized in the field of audiovisual production where private investment, starting in 1988, initiated a significant development of the television drama (*musalsalat*) industry (Blecher, 2002).

The death of Hafez Al-Assad in 2000 and the succession of his son Bashar Al-Assad brought a reinvigoration of economic liberalization processes. The process of authoritarian upgrading under the regime of

Bashar Al-Assad included a considerable opening of Syria's economy to world markets, privatization of state assets, gradual withdrawal of state subsidies, shrinking of the public sector, and the growth of a new class of businessmen loyal to the regime. Steps were also taken towards limited easing of restrictions on freedom of expression, but very little in respect to structural political reform (Hinnebusch, 2012). In 2001, the government adopted a new publications law that, while still very restrictive, opened the door for private ownership of print media. *Al-Domari*, a satirical newspaper, was one of the first to be established under the new law in February 2001. However, persistent government censorship and economic pressures led to its closure in 2003. Many of the licenses for private media went to Al-Assad crony businessmen, such as Rami Makhlouf, Mayzar Nizam Al-Din, and Majd Suleiman. The Internet also emerged as an important medium during the early 2000s. Syrian news websites, many of which were also owned by crony businessmen, were notable for providing a more open space for the discussion of Syrian politics than what was available in traditional media (De Angelis, 2011; Brownlee, 2020).

Political System and Legal Framework

The political and territorial fragmentation brought about by the Syrian conflict since 2011 is reflected in the fragmented Syrian media environment. This fragmentation has led to the development of parallel political economies within the country, in which radically different media exist. In particular, we can discern three separate media environments. The first comprises regions that have remained under the control of the central government (in particular, the coastal regions of Latakia and Tartus, the cities of Homs and Hama, and the capital Damascus) reflect, more or less, a continuation of the authoritarian logics of the Syrian regime from pre-2011 with only limited attempts at upgrading and reforming the system.

A second separate media environment emerged in the regions that came under the control of rebel groups characterized by the proliferation of completely new small- and medium-sized media initiatives, most of which were later to follow the Syrian exodus to neighboring countries (Turkey and Lebanon) or further afield to Europe where they have been operating as *exilic* media. In northeastern Syria, Kurdish forces, led by the Democratic Union Party (PYD), established a *de facto* autonomous region—Rojava—with its own largely independent institutional and regulatory frameworks and media, which comprises the third media environment.

Starting in 2011, the Syrian regime initiated several legal and constitutional reforms in an attempt to placate the protest movement. These reforms included abolishing Article 8 of the constitution which granted the Ba'ath Party a guaranteed leadership role in the Syrian government, as well as abolishing presidential plebiscites in favor of elections with multiple candidates. These legal and constitutional changes, however, did not fundamentally alter the *de facto* political system in the country, nor address the existing power bases of the regime in the state security agencies. The presidential election of 2014, dismissed as a sham, resulted in the reelection of Bashar Al-Assad to a new term of seven years with a plurality of 88.7% of the vote in a contest against two largely unknown candidates.

As for the media, the most important legislative change came with Decree No. 108 of 2011, which replaced preceding legislation as the regulatory framework governing the media sector. The law introduced several liberalizing provisions, including articles banning monopolies in the media sector and facilitating and regulating private investment in news agencies and broadcast, print, and Internet-based media (Article 35). It also included provisions protecting freedom of speech and the right to access public information (Article 3), as well as eliminating prior censorship of content "if the media does not fail its responsibilities" (Article 6). Under the law, the Ministry of Information is responsible for evaluating applications, issuing and revoking licenses to private media organizations, monitoring the operations of media outlets, and issuing accreditation and press credentials to non-Syrian journalists who wish to operate in the country (Article 22). The law, however, keeps in place the broad restrictions on content that "harms national unity," "incites sectarian or confessional strife," and "harms state symbols," and all unauthorized content on the armed forces (Article 12). Notwithstanding their more liberal leanings, these provisions are rarely applied in practice, especially articles relating to freedom of expression, access to information, and protection of journalists. Access to information is still subject to the whims of regime officials and to broad restrictions on the basis of national security. Control and intimidation of journalists persists through an arbitrary and broad interpretation of Article 12 and the extant penal code, which criminalizes defamation of the president, the courts, and the military, as well as through extralegal means.[2] In addition, while the state of emergency, in place since 1962, was officially rescinded with Legislative Decree No. 161 of 2011, many of the provisions allowing arbitrary detention were reincorporated in the Counterterrorism Laws of 2012. For example, provisions of this new law were used to prosecute journalists, lawyers, and human rights defenders, such as Mazen Darwish and Hussein Ghrer who were charged with "publicizing terrorist acts" and "promoting terrorist activities."

Institutionally, the domestic broadcasting sector remains dominated by the state broadcaster: The Organization of Syrian Arab Radio and Television (ORTAS) that is an entirely state-owned entity and accountable directly to the Council of Ministers. The television section of the entity is responsible for three terrestrial and five satellite channels. The satellite offerings include channels dedicated to news, entertainment, and television dramas, as well as a newly launched religious channel aimed at promoting the regime's narrative within Syrian conservative circles. The radio broadcasts are carried on seven dedicated channels, including broadcasts over FM, AM, online, and satellite radio.

As previously noted, the collapse of the regime's territorial control during the Syrian conflict has also provided spaces for new actors to emerge within the media environment. The northeastern regions of Syria, with substantive Kurdish populations, fell from direct regime control in 2012. The area—encompassing parts of the governorates of Raqqa, Deir ez-Zor, Aleppo, and the whole of Hasakah—has remained relatively stable and been spared the mass destruction seen in other areas that fell from government control. Media activity within the region is regulated by the Information Law of 2015 which was passed by the autonomous administration's government. The law contains provisions to guarantee freedom of expression and the right to establish media organizations. The law also has a general provision guaranteeing access to public information with exceptions for national security and

---

2   See for example this report from Reporters Without Borders: https://rsf.org/en/news/harassment-pro-government-journalists-growing-syria

international relations. The law additionally established the Higher Council for Media, which is tasked with regulating the media sector in Rojava. The Council's 15 members are elected by the media professionals, outlets, and professional syndicates active in Rojava. It has the right to grant and revoke licenses to operate in the region for local and foreign media, as well as freelance journalists.

The media scene in Rojava is largely dominated by the autonomous administration-owned state media organ *Ronahi*. The organization runs the main satellite television station that broadcasts from the region, as well as the main semi-daily print newspaper of the same name. It broadcasts mostly in Kurdish, with special programming in Arabic and English. *Ronahi*'s coverage leans heavily in favor of the PYD as the most dominant political force in Rojava. At the same time, most other political parties publish their own political newspapers, albeit with limited distribution. This includes parties affiliated with the Kurdish National Council, the main anti-PYD coalition in the region. Furthermore, a significant number of media outlets exist that are not officially linked to political parties. These media are mostly small community radio stations, print magazines, and news websites linked to civil society organizations and are dependent on media development aid and the limited advertising market for survival. The exception is *Arta FM*, which started as a community radio based in Amouda with support from European and US media development organizations and has become the largest independent media active in Rojava. This station broadcasts over the whole region and runs a sister station in Raqqa aimed at the mostly Arab population (Badran & De Angelis, 2016).

Another notable development was the opposition-affiliated media activists and collectives that sprang up early on in the protest movement in an attempt to circumvent the regime's control over the media sphere. Their work during the early years of the conflict was instrumental in providing a different narrative of the events to that of the regime's official version, especially because foreign journalists were not allowed access to the country (Halasa, Omareen & Mahfoud, 2014). As the conflict grew more protracted, and more areas fell out of regime control, the early media activism efforts began to coalesce into new media outlets, providing a different narrative to that of the regime-affiliated media. This development was further empowered by the influx of foreign media development funding and support channeled to these actors from Western and regional governments and agencies (Della Ratta, 2018). In 2014, there were more than 93 Syrian media outlets operating inside opposition-controlled areas, not counting the official media of oppositional military and political groups. This new sphere of media was unified only by its staunch anti-regime orientation and was otherwise extremely heterogeneous in terms of ideology (from Islamist to staunchly secular leftist) and covered a variety of media, including broadcast and online radio stations, print and online news journals, magazines, and web-based news agencies (Badran & Smets, 2018).

As the conflict conditions inside Syria worsened, a process of consolidation and relocation commenced. Most of these media outlets had to move their core editorial and administrative operations to neighboring countries (in particular Turkey), while retaining a network of reporters inside the country. Since 2016, the structural conditions within which these media outlets must operate have become increasingly more difficult, in particular with regard to the Turkish policies towards Syrians in the country and the shifting priorities in donors' funding. Thus, only the most consolidated of these initiatives remain today. An example of these new media initiatives is *Enab Baladi*, which started in 2011 as a small pamphlet in the town of Darayya, south of Damascus, and has become a major news website and print weekly. Within this sphere of oppositional media, we can also include *Syria TV*, which was established in 2018 in Istanbul and is managed and run by Syrian media professionals who defected from regime control. The television station is part of the Qatar-based *Fadaat Media Group*, which manages other Syrian and regional media outlets such as *Zaman Al-Wasl* and *The New Arab*. Another important broadcaster is *Orient News TV* which is based in Dubai and owned by Syrian businessman Ghassan Aboud. There have also been several attempts to develop sector-wide institutions within this media sphere in an attempt to create a credible alternative to the regime-controlled media ecosystem. For example, the Syrian Journalists Association, based in Paris, was established as an independent professional journalists' union with the aim of offering an alternative body to the regime-controlled Syrian Journalists Union. It is now a recognized associate member of the International Federation of Journalists.

Economy and Ownership Patterns

In the areas controlled by the central government, licensing for private media (broadcast and print) remains at the discretion of the Prime Minister's office. This largely means that private media ownership is the domain of businessmen loyal to the regime. The largest media owner in the country by far was, until fairly recently, Rami Makhlouf, the maternal cousin of President Bashar Al-Assad, and one of the wealthiest men in Syria. Makhlouf's spectacular and highly-publicized fallout with Al-Assad in mid-2020 leaves a question mark around how his media and telecommunications interests (which, alongside the rest of his wealth, are currently under state custody) will be distributed. Makhlouf, along with Mohammad Hamsho, a businessman close to Assad's brother Maher Al-Assad, controls the only private news television station, *Sama TV* (formerly *Addounia TV*). Makhlouf also owns outright *Ninar FM*, an entertainment and music radio station, and *Sham FM*, a news radio station in addition to the largest private daily newspaper, *Al-Watan*, and its financial sister weekly, *Al-Iqtissadiya*. Samer Foz, another business tycoon with close links to the Syrian regime, owns the entertainment television station *Lana TV*, and one of the largest media production houses, Sama Al-Fan (SAPI). The United Group (UG), a media publishing and advertising company, which previously published the only other private political daily, *Baladna*, along with an assortment of other entertainment and specialist magazines, is owned by Majd Suleiman, the son of Bahjat Suleiman, a former director in the state security apparatus and current ambassador to Jordan. Other private media outlets, mostly entertainment-focused radio stations, are also controlled by the regime-crony businessmen nexus.

The Syrian economy has been severely damaged by the ongoing war, declining by more than 70% since 2011. This, along with European and US sanctions on the Syrian regime and individuals and businesses linked to it—both Makhlouf and Foz are on the US Treasury Department's sanctions list—has led to an exodus of Syrian capital to neighboring countries. The UG media conglomerate, for example, moved most of its regional operations, which include the weekly classified paper *Al-Waseet* and the Lebanese daily *Al-Balad*, to the Dubai-based AWI Company. This was also the case for Syrian television drama production, a substantial sector before the war, which moved much of its productions to other countries, such as the UAE, Egypt, and Lebanon. For instance, Foz's SAPI production company, one of the largest television drama producers, moved its operations to Dubai.

The flight of Syrian capital has led to stagnation in media production within the country. Additionally, the collapse in the living standards of ordinary Syrians, both within and outside the country, has meant that the advertisement market for media outlets is extremely limited. Syrian media, in all three different spheres, are dependent on outside funding for their operations. In the case of regime-oriented media, this funding is usually funneled through well-connected, wealthy owners. In the case of oppositional and Kurdish media, such as *Enab Baladi* and *Arta FM*, this funding sometimes comes from European and US development aid which is usually more transparent and is managed by specialized intermediary media development organizations. Less transparent, however, is the direct funding from foreign governments to media outlets such as *Syria TV* (with funds from Qatar) or new radio stations in former ISIS territories (with funds from France and the US). This lack of sustainable business models for Syrian media outlets means they are heavily dependent on their wealthy backers, or the priorities and policies of donor bodies and governments. This makes for an extremely precarious condition for the organizations and the media workers and limits their scope for professionalization or institutionalization.

On the other hand, the emergence of relatively more independent new spaces within the oppositional media sphere created novel opportunities and avenues for a new generation of Syrian journalists, artists, and media makers to establish themselves. These new actors were able to benefit from generous funding for professional and technical skill building, especially in the early years of the Syrian conflict, as well as from the global interest in the Syrian conflict. This is most evident in fields such as independent film production. For example, a number of new Syrian filmmakers have emerged who have accrued critical acclaim for their work. Indeed, several Syrian-directed documentary films have been nominated for Academy Awards in recent years.[3] Furthermore, several independent production houses and film collectives, such as Bidayyat and Abounaddara, have been established since 2011 (Wessels, 2019).

Technology and Infrastructure

The ongoing military conflict has also had a devastating effect on the country's telecommunications infrastructure, especially in the opposition-controlled regions where most of the military operations have taken place. Even in government-controlled regions, the infrastructure has deteriorated through years of underinvestment, and the frequent electricity shortages mean that access to communication services has been greatly curtailed. The Syrian Telecommunication Establishment (STE) remains the sole regulatory agency tasked with the supervision of the telecommunications infrastructure in the country. The STE also authorizes private Internet service providers (ISPs) to deliver their services inside Syria, but in practice, its authority only extends to government-controlled areas. More than 20 different ISPs operate within the government-controlled regions of the country. According the International Telecommunication Union (based on STE estimates), Internet penetration stood at 34% with 7.8 fixed broadband subscriptions per 100 inhabitants in 2018, while mobile cellular subscriptions stood at 98 per 100 inhabitants. The mobile cellular network is operated by two companies, *Syriatel*, owned by Rami Makhlouf, and *MTN Syria*, a subsidiary of the South African multinational MTN Group Ltd. Outside of what was under regime control, however, the extant telecommunications infrastructure was largely destroyed and has been replaced with *ad hoc* solutions. Internet connections in this area are dependent on either satellite Internet receivers or, as in the border regions, cable links with neighboring countries—Turkey in the Idlib and Aleppo region and Iraqi Kurdistan in the Kurdish regions.

---

3   *Last Men in Aleppo* (2017, directed by Feras Fayyad), *Of Fathers and Sons* (2018, directed by Talal Derki), *The Cave* (2019, directed by Feras Fayyad), and *For Sama* (2019, directed by Waad Al-Kateab and Edward Watts).

Despite the aforementioned conditions, it is the Internet-based media that have seen the most fundamental changes. The regime's early steps in 2011 to lift the blocking of *Facebook* and other social media websites allowed it to cultivate a strong partisan, loyalist constituency that can challenge the opposition's more established online presence. Indeed, social media platforms, in particular *Facebook*, have become a major site of contestation in the ongoing conflict. *Facebook* penetration in Syria climbed from 1% in 2010 to 37% in 2017 (Salem, 2017). Since 2011, there has been an explosion of local community media pages—largely based on *Facebook*—that cater to the loyalist communities in regions that have remained under government control. This development mirrors a similar phenomenon seen in opposition communities, especially during the early years of the Syrian conflict. These media are often concerned with local development in the city or region and are staunchly pro-government, particularly with regard to the Syrian Army and the military conflict with armed opposition groups. Nevertheless, they also contain some modicum of criticism of government policies, in particular with regard to widespread lawlessness, corruption, and the deterioration of services (Issa, 2016). As the military conflict winds down, there are signs the regime is attempting to bring this section of the media in line and to restrict its relative independence. In 2019 alone, there were several cases of detention by state security agencies of high-profile loyalist journalists who had covered the conflict on the side of the Syrian regime (e.g., Raif Salamah was arrested and held for more than a month in May 2019; Wissam Al-Tayr, a journalist from the Damascus Now network, was arrested in December 2018 and released only nine months later in August 2019). In terms of the legal framework within which these media have to operate, the Cybercrime Law of 2012, which regulates information access online, has important implications for their operation. The law provides a legal framework for online censorship, content, and user monitoring by ISPs who are required to retain records of Internet traffic. Moreover, website owners and providers are instructed to divulge their names and contact information under the provisions of this law.[4]

---

4   For more details see the Internet Legislation Atlas: https://Internetlegislationatlas.org/data/summaries/syria.pdf

Challenges

The territorial and political fragmentation brought about by the war since 2011 has meant that Syrian audiences are now divided across at least three different media spheres. Each of these spheres has developed its own logics, discourses, and *modus operandi*. There is very little interaction among these different spheres. Only rarely do media outlets acknowledge or reference media content from the other segments, and this usually comes with accusations of fabrication and bias. Thus, polarization among these different spheres is extremely high as they engage in a three-sided "war of narratives." In a sense, this accurately reflects the highly polarized political environment, as well as the deep societal divisions that have existed since 2011. Such polarization, however, is often manifested in the proliferation of hate speech in much of the media content coming from Syria.[5] Moreover, this polarization is certainly reinforced by the fact that journalists from loyalist media cannot operate openly in opposition-held regions, and vice versa. Conditions for the work of journalists, especially international journalists, are much more favorable in the Kurdish-controlled regions, but certain restrictions still apply with regard to criticism of the PYD and in covering the conflict with ISIS.

The resurgence of the Syrian regime of Bashar Al-Assad and its emergence as the victor in the military conflict also means that the fundamental rules governing Syria's media system—at least in the regions claimed by the regime—will remain unchanged in the foreseeable future. The regime's control over the media sector leaves very little space for dissenting voices within the state-controlled media. Since 2011, oligarchs and crony businessmen have further entrenched their control over wide sectors of the economy and especially the privately-owned media sector. The media conglomerate of Rami Makhlouf includes interests in all sectors of the media business, including press, television, and radio, as well as media production businesses and telecommunication. Furthermore, there has been increasing evidence of the regime reasserting closer control over loyalist social media groups and Internet websites that have had, until recently, broader margins in their reporting.

---

5   See for example this report from the Syrian Center for Media and Freedom of Expression: https://scm.bz/en/en-studies/hate-speech-and-incitement-to-violence-in-syrian-media-research-study

Outlook

The future of Syria's media system will be deeply linked to how the later stages of the Syrian conflict evolve. It will be one of the fundamental elements of negotiations for any future compromise settlement over the shape of Syria's post-war polity. The latest steps of the Syrian regime to bring even loyal media that are mildly critical under control can be seen as an effort to reassert its legal position as sovereign over the whole of the Syrian state and to create a legal framework for any future reintegration of other regions that will be favorable for its continuity. Nevertheless, in practice, the Syrian regime does not have enough power to assert this sovereignty over large swathes of the country that are either under direct military control by regional and international actors or their local proxies. Furthermore, the emergence of oppositional, exilic, and Kurdish media in areas outside of regime control have ushered in fundamental changes in terms of the informational environment that Syrians now have access to. These new realities will be extremely difficult to simply reverse, and any future settlement will have to consider ways to reintegrate them. Finally, the sheer number of Syrian refugees who have fled the country, around 25% of Syria's pre-war population, suggests that exilic and diasporic media will come to play an increasingly significant role in the future. Independent media makers who have developed their skills and know-how in Turkey, Lebanon, and Europe over the past years, as well as larger media producers who have moved their productions to Dubai and Egypt, can be expected to perpetuate this trend.

References

Albarazi, Z. (2013). *The stateless Syrians* (Research Paper No. 011/2013). Tilburg: Tilburg Law School. https://ssrn.com/abstract=2269700

Badran, Y., & De Angelis, E. (2016). 'Independent' Kurdish media in Syria: Conflicting identities in the transition. *Middle East Journal of Culture and Communication*, 9(3), 334–51. https://doi.org/10.1163/18739865-00903001

Badran, Y., & Smets, K. (2018). Heterogeneity in alternative media spheres: Oppositional media and the framing of sectarianism in the Syrian conflict. *International Journal of Communication*, 12, 4229–47.

Batatu, H. (1981). Some observations on the social roots of Syria's ruling, military group and the causes for its dominance. *Middle East Journal, 35*(3), 331–44.

Blecher, R. (2002). When television is mandatory: Syrian television drama in the 1990s. In N. Méouchy (Ed.), *France, Syrie et Liban 1918–1946: Les ambiguïtés et les dynamiques de la relation mandataire* [*France, Syria and Lebanon 1918–1946: Ambiguities and dynamics of a mandatory relationship*] (pp. 169–79). Damas: Presses de l'Ifpo, Institut français d'études arabes de Damas. https://doi.org/10.4000/books.ifpo.3177

Brownlee, B. J. (2020). *New Media and Revolution: Resistance and Dissent in Pre-uprising Syria*. Montreal: McGill-Queen's University Press.

Dajani, N. H., & Najjar, O. A. (2003). Syria, Lebanon, and Jordan, Status of media in. In D. H. Johnston (Ed.), *Encyclopedia of International Media and Communications* (pp. 301–15). Cambridge: Academic Press.

De Angelis, E. (2011). Syrian news websites: A negotiated identity. *Oriente Moderno, 91*(1), 105–24. https://doi.org/10.1163/22138617-09101010

Della Ratta, D. (2018). *Shooting a revolution: Visual media and warfare in Syria*. London: Pluto Press. https://doi.org/10.2307/j.ctv7vct7t

Halasa, M., Omareen, Z., & Mahfoud, N. (Eds.). (2014). *Syria Speaks: Art and Culture from the Frontline*. London: Saqi Books.

Hassanpour, A., Skutnabb-Kangas, T., & Chyet, M. (1996). The non-education of Kurds: A Kurdish perspective. *International Review of Education, 42*(4), 367–79. https://doi.org/10.1007/bf00601097

Hinnebusch, R. (2012). Syria: From 'authoritarian upgrading' to revolution? *International Affairs, 88*(1), 95–113.

Issa, A. (2016). *Syria's new media landscape: Independent media born out of war* (MEI Policy Paper No. 2016–9). Washington, DC: The Middle East Institute. https://www.mei.edu/sites/default/files/publications/PP9_Issa_Syrianmedia_web_0.pdf

Martin, K. W. (2015). *Syria's democratic years: Citizens, experts, and media in the 1950s*. Bloomington, IN: Indiana University Press.

Rafai, S. A. (1969). *Tārīkh al-ṣaḥāfah al-Sūrīyyah* [*History of Syrian journalism*]. Cairo: Dar Al-Ma'arif.

Rugh, W. A. (2004). *Arab mass media: Newspapers, radio, and television in Arab politics*. Westport: Praeger.

Said, W. E. (2003). Palestinian refugees: Host countries, legal status and the right of return. *Refuge: Canada's Journal on Refugees, 21*(2), 89–95. https://doi.org/10.25071/1920-7336.21293

Salamandra, C., & Stenberg, L. (Eds.). (2015). *Syria from Reform to Revolt: Vol. 2, Culture, Society, and Religion*. Syracuse, NY: Syracuse University Press.

Salem, F. (2017). *The Arab social media report 2017: Social media and the Internet of Things: Towards data-driven policymaking in the Arab World*. Dubai: MBR School of Government https://www.mbrsg.ae/getattachment/1383b88a-6eb9-476a-bae4-61903688099b/Arab-Social-Media-Report-2017

Wedeen, L. (1999). *Ambiguities of domination: Politics, rhetoric, and symbols in contemporary Syria*. Chicago, IL: University of Chicago Press. https://doi.org/10.7208/chicago/9780226345536.001.0001

Wessels, J. (2019). *Documenting Syria: Film-making, video activism and revolution*. London: I.B. Tauris.

3. Palestine: Resilient Media Practices for National Liberation

Gretchen King[1]

> This chapter provides an overview of Palestinian media practices in historic Palestine and in the diaspora. Since the printing press arrived in the region, the Palestinian people have used media for national liberation and self-determination. However, the Israeli regime's ongoing occupation and displacement of the Palestinian people produces major challenges for the development and sustainability of the media system in Palestine.

Background

Historic Palestine is geographically situated between the Jordan River and the Mediterranean Sea. Before 1922, when the League of Nations imposed the British Mandate that enshrined the Balfour Declaration's Zionist intentions, the region of historic Palestine had been organized under the Ottoman administration for four centuries. Under Ottoman rule and throughout the British Mandate period, Palestinians organized for independence and self-determination. However, in 1947, the United Nations General Assembly passed a non-binding vote proposing a partition plan for historic Palestine under UN Resolution 181 (II). The resolution, opposed by the Palestinians, suggested that Jews, who were one-third of the population and only occupied 6% of land, could carve out a "Jewish state" on nearly 60% of the land. Immediately after

---

1 With research assistance from Ghiwa Haidar Ahmad, Ayman Lezzeik, and Fatima Takash.

the British withdrawal, Zionist militias attacked the largely unarmed Palestinians. In 1948 and after ethnically purging more than 700,000 Palestinians, or half the indigenous population of the land, Israel declared itself in control of 78% of historic Palestine. These events are known as the Palestinian *nakba* (or catastrophe). Later, the remainder of historic Palestine was divided into the Gaza Strip and the West Bank, annexed by Egypt and Jordan, respectively, until occupied by the Israeli military in 1967 after the Six-Day War (Alshaer, 2012, p. 237).

Today, Palestinians make up the world's largest refugee population, despite their right to return to their land in Palestine being officially declared by the UN since 1948 (Resolution 194). Approximately 13 million Palestinians are spread throughout the world with the largest population outside of Palestine residing in Jordan and outside of the Arab region in Chile (Palestinian Central Bureau of Statistics, 2019). There are 1.5 million Palestinians residing in the territory of what was declared as Israel in 1948, who are also known as the '48 Palestinians. Additionally, there are 5.4 million Palestinian refugees registered with the United Nations Relief and Works Agency (or UNRWA), approximately one-third of whom reside in refugee camps located inside of Palestine and neighboring countries such as Jordan, Lebanon, and Syria. Due to war, occupation, the blockade of the Gaza Strip, and social and economic exclusion, a majority of Palestinian refugees live in poverty (UNRWA, 2019).

The state of Palestine, recognized by the UN in 1988 (Resolution 43/177), comprises the Gaza Strip and the West Bank, including Jerusalem, with a population of nearly five million (Palestinian Central Bureau of Statistics, 2019). The official language in Palestine is Arabic. The state of Palestine is characterized by its majority Muslim population (only 1% are Christian), high youth population (nearly 40% are under fifteen years of age), high population density in the Gaza Strip (826 people per square kilometer), high birth rate (the average family has four or more children), high unemployment (more than one-third of the labor force), low illiteracy rate (less than 3%), high smart phone use (almost 90% of households own one or more), and increasing Internet access at home (nearly 75% in West Bank homes and over 50% in Gaza) (Palestinian Central Bureau of Statistics, 2019).

Since the declaration of the independent state of Palestine followed by the designation of the Palestinian National Authority and the Palestinian Legislative Council, the occupation by Israel has become further entrenched. The Israeli regime perpetuates the ongoing forced displacement of Palestinians through continuous wars and attacks waged by the Israeli military that target civilians and infrastructure. This includes Israeli airstrikes that leveled the Gaza Strip's only power plant in 2014, disrupting power and cutting off drinking water for millions of people. Additionally, the Israeli military closed the Gaza Strip for nearly a year in 1996 and today maintains an air, land, and sea blockade that makes the area, according to some, the world's largest "open-air prison." In the West Bank, Israel illegally built an eight-meter-high concrete wall around the territory, and the Israeli military maintains hundreds of checkpoints and obstacles that prevent Palestinians from accessing school, work, healthcare, each other, and the rest of the world. This history of colonialism and the worsening occupation of Palestine led the UN's Economic and Social Commission for West Asia (UN-ESCWA) to declare that Israel maintains and imposes an "apartheid regime" (UN-ESCWA, 2017).

Historical Developments

Media development in Palestine has been distinguished by several phases, beginning with the period of the Ottoman administration, followed by the British Mandate period, the period after 1948 that saw the occupation of Palestine by Israel, and the most recent period that included two intifadas, the introduction of a Palestinian state and media governance systems, and the ongoing Israeli wars (Omer, 2015). By the 1850s, multiple printing presses were operating in Palestine, and in 1876, the Ottoman representative in Jerusalem began publishing the newspaper *Al-Quds Al-Sharif* in Turkish and Arabic. When constitutional reforms were introduced after the Young Turk Revolution in 1908, the first privately-owned newspaper, *Al-Quds*, was published in Arabic. During this time, dozens of newspapers began to circulate, and, in spite of censorship and penalties, the press covered politics and criticized the Zionist movement as well as Ottoman rule. This included *Falastin*, a newspaper founded in 1911 that was eventually shut down by the Ottomans and later re-opened, continuing today as one of the oldest publications in Palestine (Omer, 2015, p. 111). Scholars have documented how the first phase of media development in Palestine during the Ottoman period contributed to the linking of Palestinian journalism with the struggle for national liberation (Najjar, 2005).

Before the end of the First World War, Britain and France divided the territories of the defeated Ottoman empire under the Sykes-Picot Agreement of 1916. The agreement was kept secret from the Palestinians, in part because no newspapers were permitted to be published during the war (Omer, 2015). During the British Mandate period in which Britain occupied and colonized Palestine, newspaper publishing was renewed and increased. While the Ottoman laws concerning printing and publications were still in effect under British rule, newspapers in Palestine began to connect to and disseminate news from around the globe through telegraph systems that crisscrossed the British Empire. The launch of even more newspapers during the 1920s and 1930s, swelling to over 40 publications by 1939 (Najjar, 2005), coincided with the growth of the Palestinian National Movement and the direct involvement of newspaper editors and journalists in the struggle to liberate Palestine, regardless of Britain's attempts to silence them through shutdowns, arrests, or exile (Omer, 2015).

To better compete with the politicized printed press, British authorities initiated the *Palestine Broadcasting Service (PBS)* as the first radio station serving the region. The station went on-air in 1936 through studios maintained in Jerusalem with a transmitter and tower located in Ramallah. The *PBS* aired broadcasts in English, Arabic, and Hebrew, including programming from the *BBC's Empire Service* (Boyd, 1999). Soon after, small-scale broadcasting also took to the airwaves as early as 1938 with radio stations operated by Zionist organizations, such as the Irgun, and Palestinians broadcasting on *Sawt Al-Falestin* (King, 2017).

During the war of 1948, Zionist forces took over the *PBS* studios in Jerusalem while the Jordanian military claimed the transmitter and tower in Ramallah. Subsequently, a studio was added to the equipment acquired by Jordan to relaunch *PBS* as the *Hashemite Broadcasting System (HBS)*. The *HBS* operated from the West Bank under the Jordanian Ministry of Information until 1967 when Israel occupied the Gaza Strip and the West Bank (Boyd, 1999). All broadcasting was banned by the

Israeli government in the Occupied Palestinian Territories (Somiry-Batrawi, 2004), leaving Palestinians without a national radio or television station until the 1990s.

Jamal (2009) described the period after the *nakba* of 1948 as a "communication vacuum" (p. 40) in which all media came under Israeli military censors (p. 62). The vibrant Palestinian newspaper industry was displaced and destroyed, with owners and journalists expelled along with many Palestinian women who lost their jobs in radio (Somiry-Batrawi, 2004). The first Palestinian newspaper to continue publishing after 1948 was *Al-Ittihad*, but the publication was closed several times by Israeli forces (Jamal, 2009). After the occupation of Gaza and the West Bank in 1967, Palestinians attempted to establish new or reopen publications, but Israeli forces continued to censor all press and forced multiple Palestinian publications to close (Jamal, 2009). However, by 1990, more than 40 newspapers were circulating in the Occupied Palestinian Territories (Nossek & Rinnawi, 2003).

Beginning in the 1950s, audiences in historic Palestine had access to state radio from the Arab region, and later, Arab state television broadcasts began in the 1970s. In addition, Palestinians in exile "assembled their media world" (Bishara, 2009, p. 15) by broadcasting on other states' media systems. During this period, Palestinian-produced broadcast media moved into the transnational sphere. Palestinian programming was initially aired from studios provided by state-owned radio broadcasters in Syria, Iraq, Egypt, Tunisia, Jordan, and Algeria (Boyd, 1999; Browne, 1975). Later, in 1965, the Palestinian Liberation Organization (PLO) acquired its own transmitter and began broadcasting programming across the region of Palestine from Syria (Browne, 1975). Another station was set up in 1988 in Lebanon, and although initially destroyed by Lebanese militias and, later, by Israeli airstrikes, the station was rebuilt to broadcast in support of the First Intifada (Bookmiller & Bookmiller, 1990).

During the First Intifada, a youth- and student-led Palestinian uprising against the Israeli occupation that began in December 1987 and lasted until September 1993, the Israeli military imposed dangerous conditions for media workers by injuring and killing a number of reporters. As a result, international media organizations recruited local Palestinians, effectively growing the media and journalism sector in

Palestine. This resulted in increasing the number of Palestinian women working in media due to the international media relying on their gender to overcome "social restrictions" (Somiry-Batrawi, 2004, p. 111). Just before the Oslo process granted the state of Palestine the right to use broadcasting frequencies, Palestinians could tune into television news programming produced by Palestinians in Palestine for the first time. This came with the launch of experimental television news programming in early 1993 produced by the Institute of Modern Media (IMM) based at Al-Quds University. After several successful broadcasts, IMM secured a license in 1996 from the Palestinian Ministry of Information for *Al-Quds Education TV (AETV)* (Somiry-Batrawi, 2004).

After the Six-Day War that Israel waged against Egypt, Syria, and Jordan in 1967, the First Intifada by Palestinians against the Israeli occupation in 1987, and the declaration by the PLO of the independent state of Palestine in 1988, the Oslo Accords between the Israeli government and the PLO began in 1993. The negotiations immediately addressed and resulted in tangible media gains for the Palestinian people. This included the allocation of one medium wave and 10 FM frequencies granted to the Palestinian Authority (PA), as the designated government of the state of Palestine (Boyd, 1999). The PA rushed to establish a Ministry of Information to develop media policy and draft a press law. These changes allowed, for the first time, the licensing of television and radio stations broadcasting from Palestine (Boyd, 1999). Immediately following the negotiations, the Palestinian Broadcasting Company (PBC) was launched in 1993 as a publicly funded state-owned media organization, airing programming that focused on state actors and followed government agendas (Sakr, 2007). As part of the PBC, the *Voice of Palestine*, a state-owned radio station, went on-air in July 1994 and was well-received among Palestinian audiences as it aired popular programs such as *Good Morning Palestine* and a prison radio show that connected on-air the families of the detained with their loved ones listening from Israeli jails (Boyd, 1999). *Voice of Palestine* also suspended regular programming to provide live coverage of the Second Intifada, which began in 2000 and lasted until 2005 (Salama, 2006).

The launch of *Voice of Palestine* was followed by that of the newspaper *Al-Hayat Al-Jadida*, which was published with funding from the PA (Saraste, 2010). Beginning circulation in November 1994, *Al-Hayat*

Al-Jadida became the first daily newspaper published in Palestine that promoted the positions of the PA (Jamal, 2000). By 1996, the PBC television station was broadcasting Palestinian-produced television programming from a control room located in the PA president's compound in Gaza with the transmission facilities in Ramallah. After the death of the PA president Yasser Arafat in 2004, oversight of the station was transferred to the Ministry of Information, a move that provided mechanisms for public accountability over station budgets and appointments. Soon after that, Hamas won a majority in the Palestinian Legislative Council elections in 2006, and the acting PA president Mahmoud Abbas from Fatah designated that all state media, including the PBC, would be under the authority of the president's office (Sakr, 2007).

During this time, satellite television was introduced in the state of Palestine, and by 2002, 78% of Palestinians had access to it (Rugh, 2004, p. 220). The PBC would soon establish the *Palestinian Satellite Channel*, which reached transnational audiences. With the rise of satellite and private channels after the Oslo Accords, audiences in Palestine had access to national and transnational content from privately-owned stations in Palestine that broadcast satellite content from other stations, typically without legal authorization (Somiry-Batrawi, 2004). Palestinian audiences could tune into programming from hundreds of Arabic media channels, but little content was produced by Palestinians. However, some satellite channels, such as *Al-Jazeera*, hired Palestinian journalists to work on the ground. Local journalists reporting for satellite networks played a crucial role covering the Second Intifada and the repeated wars and attacks waged by the Israeli military during that time (Saraste, 2010). This coverage not only informed Palestinian audiences in the state of Palestine, but also Palestinians in the diaspora and audiences across the Arab region.

After the success of Hamas in the 2006 elections, *Al-Aqsa TV* was launched from Gaza as a satellite television channel that complemented Hamas's bi-weekly newspaper *Al-Risalah* and its radio station *Sawt Al-Aqsa*, which began broadcasting in 2003 (Alshaer, 2012, p. 239). With a mandate to serve the Islamic movement in Palestine, the station does not air any programming that contravenes Islamic traditions or laws. Positioned as independent of Hamas, these various media represent the views of the Islamic movement similar to how PBC's programming represents the views of Fatah. Programming focuses on the activities of the Hamas government, criticizes the PA, Fatah, and Israel, and covers religion, culture, and politics (Alshaer, 2012, pp. 241–42). After the Israeli military destroyed the station and equipment of *Al-Aqsa* during the 2009 war on Gaza, the broadcast studios moved to a secret location, and the station is available today throughout the state of Palestine.

Internet-based media from Palestine did not exist before Oslo as there was no Internet access due to the widespread effects of the Israeli regime's occupation. In fact, Internet access was illegal until the negotiations granted the PA the right to build a telecommunications infrastructure. With the expansion of access through privatized development, Internet usage among Palestinians quickly became one of the highest per capita rates in the region (Tawil-Souri & Aouragh, 2014). As a result, Palestinians in Palestine could more easily report on local events to a global audience through a growing number of Internet news websites based in Palestine and abroad. Both *The Palestine Chronicle*, founded in 1999, and *The Electronic Intifada*, founded in 2001, operate from the United States as non-profit, independent news and opinion multimedia websites providing Palestinian perspectives on events in Palestine and abroad. The *International Middle East Media Center* was launched from the West Bank in 2008 to provide news produced by Palestinians from across Palestine in English and in multimedia formats for an international audience. Additionally, the popular *Quds News Network* founded in 2013 provides independent news in Arabic for mostly younger Palestinians and in English for global audiences from its online and social media platforms, attracting millions of followers.

Political System and Legal Framework

Today *WAFA*, the official Palestinian news and information agency, reports that there are over 50 newspapers printed and published online on a daily, weekly, and monthly basis in Palestine, covering a variety of topics from politics to entertainment. Publications in Palestine today include over 150 magazines that also target children, tourists, human rights advocates, and academics. There are currently over 30 television and radio stations broadcasting in Palestine, airing a variety of entertainment and cultural programming, including sports, religion, and music as well as news. According to a recent national survey, the majority of audiences 15 years of age or older in the state of Palestine watch television daily, followed by one-third of audiences who listen to radio and who access the Internet daily. The same survey also reported fewer than 10% of audiences surveyed in Palestine reported reading "at least one daily [newspaper] yesterday" (Ipsos, 2013, p. 17).

Today, three overlapping policy regimes regulate the media system in Palestine: Israeli military rule, various laws enacted by the PA, and policies of Hamas for Palestinians residing in the Gaza Strip. In addition, the increasing use of social media by Palestinians means that censorship policies of social media companies (mostly US-based monopolies) also impact online media practices in Palestine. However, beginning in the last decades of the Ottoman Empire, laws were used to incriminate Palestinian journalists for criticizing imperial figures and policies or to even shut down newspapers, as in the case of *Falastin* (Omer, 2015). With the imposition of the British Mandate in Palestine, the new imperial authorities' practices towards media workers did not change. In fact, the British maintained the same repressive laws used by the Ottomans, adding the discriminatory legal requirement of a university degree for any newspaper editor-in-chief (Omer, 2015).

The Israeli government enforces the 1933 Press Ordinance and the 1945 Emergency Regulations, both continued from the British Mandate period, and both are still applied today across historic Palestine, meaning that multiple generations of Palestinian media makers living in the state of Palestine have experienced sustained military censorship (7amleh, 2016). Under these measures, a license from the Israeli military is required to publish a newspaper. In occupied Jerusalem, licenses for publishing are required from Israel's Ministry of the Interior. Additionally, all content intended for publication must be approved by Israeli military censors, who require material to be submitted twice for censorship before publication (Nossek & Rinnawi, 2003). According to some scholars, this mechanism of prior censorship has resulted in 25% of newspaper content being deleted (Najjar, 1992, as cited in Bishara, 2009). In fact, during the First Intifada, some newspapers had their licenses revoked all together by Israel for nearly two months, and some journalists were jailed and others deported (Bishara, 2009). The policies maintained by the Israeli regime provide Palestinians no "space for freedom of expression or representation" (Jamal, 2009, p. 127). These practices impact offline and online media practices in Palestine.

Under the PA, the Basic Law was enacted and amended in 2003 along with the 1995 Press and Publications Law, both of which supplemented Israeli military laws that are still in effect. The Basic Law, under the draft constitution (revised on 4 May 2003), guarantees freedom of expression (Article 37), declares the right to own media and receive information (Articles 38 and 40), and provides for a free press (Article 39). However, the Press and Publications Law contravenes the Basic Law by relying on vague language to describe crimes of the press. The Press and Publications Law requires licensing for print media, sets conditions and capital requirements for who can own media and act as editor-in-chief, and includes vague content restrictions concerning morals and a ban on any content that may "harm the national unity" (Article 37). Finally, the law sanctions any media violations, and fines and jail time can be levied against media workers and organizations (Mendel & Khashan, 2006). Such restrictions have resulted in rampant self-censorship among Palestinian journalists, and there is no independent body to apply these regulations because the authority to apply the law is directly in the hands of the government (UNESCO, 2014). The Press and Publications Law has been used to limit freedom of expression and the press. As a result, there have been multiple incidences of the PA closing private cable television stations and arresting journalists under the provisions of the Press and Publications Law. This includes the jamming of *AETV*'s signal and detention of its director after the station broadcast sessions of the Palestinian Legislative Council in 1997 (Jamal, 2000).

It is worth noting that, after the intimidation of *AETV*, the Palestinian government under President Arafat was pressured to create a 13-member committee made up of several ministers and representatives of various ministries as well as legal and technical experts to regulate private television and radio under the 1995 Press Law. Eventually, the Ministry of Information proposed creating an independent body, whose members would be appointed based on experience, to regulate media. However, the proposed revisions to the broadcast law remained in draft form after the 2006 elections crisis, which included Israel's mass arrest of members of the Palestinian government (Sakr, 2007). A new broadcasting law has been drafted, revising many of the concerns raised above, but it has yet to be implemented due to the ongoing governance crisis in Palestine.

In 2016, PA president Mahmoud Abbas signed the Declaration on Media Freedom in the Arab World and designated 1 August as Freedom of Opinion and Expression Day in Palestine (Melhem, 2016). However, a year later, the president also signed the Electronic Crimes Law that violated the Basic Law provisions that guarantee freedom of expression and freedom from censorship. The new law imposed fines and imprisonment, raising concerns for Palestinians publishing media or communicating online (Fatafta, 2018). Just weeks before signing the bill, dozens of popular news websites, including the *Quds News Network*, were blocked by the PA's Attorney General (Fatafta, 2018). Both journalists and activists in the West Bank have been targeted with arrests and charged under the new law for posting content online. In the Gaza Strip, a similar amendment to Law 3 was passed in 2009 which, in intentionally vague terms, criminalized the misuse of technology, which could also be used to censor online media practices (Fatafta, 2018).

Economy and Ownership Patterns

Media ownership in Palestine has a varied history of private, political party, and state ownership. While non-governmental organizations (NGOs) under the current regulations are allowed to operate broadcast media, there is no distinct category of licensing for community-owned, non-profit media. With the influence of neo-liberalization and privatization underpinning the Oslo Accords process, privately-owned media increased greatly in Palestine. Private media in Palestine are largely sustained by commercial income. However, poverty, high unemployment, and economic exclusion impact the media economy and create a small advertising market (UNESCO, 2014). State media accept commercial sponsorships, but mainly operate on funds granted by the government. In the telecommunications sector, the private company *PALTEL* maintains a near monopoly, and as a result, its revenues from subscriber fees contribute 10% of the state of Palestine's economic activity, providing 30% of the PA's annual tax revenues (Tawil-Souri, 2015).

In general, the Palestinian Ministry of Information maintains a welcoming strategy that "freely issue[s] 'no objection' notices or 'temporary licenses'" (Sakr, 2007, p. 25) to broadcasting license applicants. The practice of granting most licensing requests aims to create "facts on the ground" (Sakr, 2007, p. 25) in Palestine to use in future negotiations concerning the Israeli occupation. The Ministry also believes a plethora of broadcasters are necessary, not only for promoting freedom of expression, but also to ensure Palestinian broadcasting continues regardless of any Israeli attack on the media system. This practice resulted in dozens of stations being on-air, some even operating without a license, by the late 1990s. This policy contrasted with the majority of Arab media systems at the time that were still monopolized by state broadcasters (Sakr, 2007). While the PA licensed dozens of privately-owned radio and cable television stations, much of the programming offered was related to entertainment and therefore sought to monetize audiences. Thus, stations were unstable, opening and closing regularly because they were not profitable (Jamal, 2000).

Some privately-owned media in Palestine have sustained their organizations through blending social entrepreneurship with commercial practices, such as *Radio Nisaa FM*, launched in 2009, as the only commercial radio station and multimedia website for Palestinian women that is also run by women. *Radio Nisaa* receives financial support through a mix of corporate sponsorships and advertising as well as donations and funds from international organizations, the Ministry of Women Affairs in Palestine, and the Palestinian Business Women Forum. The prioritization of women in media management and production at *Radio Nisaa* addresses a gender gap in Palestinian media. A study released by Women Media and Development (TAM) reported that media in Palestine marginalizes women in their participation as media workers as well as in their representation in media content. The study found that a stereotypical image of women is perpetuated in Palestinian media largely due to the fact that media organizations include about 10% of female employees, and very few of these are in media production or management roles (TAM, 2017).

Technology and Infrastructure

Where the Oslo Accords granted Palestinians the right to independent communication systems, the greatest restriction on the development of media technology and infrastructure in Palestine is the Israeli occupation. Israel restricts the ability of Palestinian media and telecommunications companies to import the technology needed to maintain and modernize the media system. The Israeli government also constrains access to frequencies for transmitting broadcasts (Jamal, 2000) and restricts telecommunications companies to 2 or 3G because of limits imposed on spectrum allocation (Fatafta, 2018). The PBC maintains no television broadcasting equipment or studios in the Gaza Strip. Field equipment is also limited in availability, and as a result, television programming largely consists of pre-recorded programs or footage of community events.

Repeated Israeli military aggressions have targeted Palestinian media offices, studios, and infrastructure, resulting in millions of dollars in damages and, in some cases, closures. In January 2002, during the Second Intifada, the Israeli military blew up the 5-storey building that housed the *Voice of Palestine* in Ramallah and destroyed the station's transmitters. *Voice of Palestine* continued broadcasting from a secret location and over privately-owned radio stations but was unable to rebuild its transmitters due to a lack of resources (Saraste, 2010). Other Palestinian media faced similar destruction at the hands of the Israeli military, such as in November 2018 when Israeli air strikes on the Gaza Strip repeatedly targeted and eventually leveled the building that housed *Al-Aqsa TV*. As a result of the unending targeting of media infrastructure by the Israeli military, Palestinian broadcasters are increasingly moving their equipment and operations to covert locations.

With regard to the Internet in Palestine, all connections to the World Wide Web flow through Israel, which conducts regular shutdowns and destruction of Palestinian-owned telecommunications infrastructure. Additionally, advocacy groups such as 7amleh have noted that Israeli regime agencies collaborate with private technology companies to censor and shut down Palestinian accounts. This includes Israel maintaining agreements with several social media companies to remove Palestinian content, including posts on *Facebook* and content on *Google* (7amleh, 2016).

Yet, Internet penetration is very high in Palestine. This is also amplified in the spread of social media in Palestine, with one in three Palestinians active on various platforms (Fatafta, 2018, p. 8). Palestine maintains the largest concentration of *Facebook* users per capita in the Arab region (Tawil-Souri & Aouragh, 2014). Newspapers, television, and radio stations in Palestine also connect with the world through the Internet. Traditional media not only use the Internet as an extension of their media practice, but also as an innovative media tactic to connect with audiences worldwide. For example, *Radio Free Palestine* is an international and collaborative 24-hour radio broadcast that commemorates the *nakba* on 15 May. The live programming is hosted and shared by stations in Palestine and beyond, which broadcast live to audiences online and on FM radio stations across five continents (King & Marouf, 2018). These practices indicate that social media and the Internet have become tools that Palestinians use to facilitate mass communication locally and transnationally.

Challenges

Throughout the occupation of Palestine, Israeli authorities have censored, detained, deported, and killed Palestinian journalists. Actions by the PA and Hamas have also shut down Palestinian stations and websites, and they have arrested Palestinian journalists who cover oppositional politics. However, since 1948 the Israeli regime has repressed media freedom in Palestine through various agencies. Regularly, the Israeli Press Office refuses to renew the press cards of Palestinian journalists, and this limits their ability to travel and work in Palestine. Beyond this, mass restrictions on the movement of all Palestinians limit the ability of Palestinian journalists to access and cover news events (Saraste, 2010). In 2018, the violent targeting of media workers in Palestine by the Israeli military continued with the murder of two Palestinian journalists while they were reporting on news events in the Gaza Strip. After an independent investigation, the United Nations and the Committee to Protect Journalists reported that Israeli military snipers deliberately shot the two journalists, concluding that the Israeli's killing of Palestinian journalists has become "part of a pattern" (CPJ, 2019).

Recently, Palestinians have been increasingly arrested for social media activity by Israel, the PA, and Hamas. The majority of arrests have been made by Israeli police forces for "incitement through social media" (7amleh, 2016, p. 113), and Palestinians have been sentenced to a year or more in prison. For example, Palestinian poet Dareen Tatour posted her poem 'Resist, My People, Resist Them' on *Facebook* in 2015 and was afterwards confined to almost three years of house arrest before being sentenced to five months in prison for "incitement" and "support for terror" with her post (IMEMC, 2018). Notably, Israeli police have applied the charge of inciting violence online only against Palestinians (7amleh, 2016).

The danger facing Palestinian journalists and media workers, the criminalization and censorship of Palestinian political communication online, and the regular destruction of media infrastructure and the limits imposed on technology present major challenges for the development of the media system. In addition, the economic sustainability of the media system in Palestine is threatened by the PA's regulatory push towards privatization. As a result, the small and impoverished media market is saturated with commercial and for-profit interests. Further, there is no specific license or funding made available by the Palestinian Ministry of Information for non-profit or community-owned media that operate with little or no advertising and provide a complement to commercial, privately-owned, state-run, and political party-affiliated media in the system. However, where NGOs are increasingly participating in the facilitation of not-for-profit media production in Palestine, the reliance of NGOs on project funding from international sources makes such media unsustainable and often limits it to serving the foreign interests of donors.

Outlook

Palestinians in historic Palestine and in the diaspora have always used media for national liberation and self-determination. The resilience of Palestinian media is complemented by various media tactics that continue to defy and circumvent the Israeli occupation. Today, the Israeli regime oppresses the Palestinian people politically, economically, and socially with policies that also impoverish the media system in Palestine. Therefore, the media economy in Palestine is made unsustainable by the Israeli regime's ongoing occupation of electromagnetic spectrum, destruction of infrastructure, sanctions on media technology, and attacks on Palestinian media workers and activists. Additionally, the governance crisis in Palestine since the 2006 elections has resulted in overlapping policies of the regimes that target journalists and political speech online further negatively impacting the media system. Yet, innovation in media practices, including the creative use of the Internet and social media by news websites, traditional media, and media activists, is connecting Palestinians in occupied Palestine with the world. For Palestinian and non-Palestinian media makers globally, the diaspora and transnational media projects in solidarity with the Palestinian people provide a rich opportunity to embolden the Palestinian media space. The aforementioned IMEMC and *Radio Free Palestine* are just two of many examples of the ways Palestinians in Palestine are connecting with media makers and audiences across the globe, through and beyond the Internet.

References

7amleh – Arab Center for Social Media Advancement. (2016). Hashtag Palestine– Palestinian social media activity during 2015. *Jerusalem Quarterly, 68*, 111–18.

Alshaer, A. (2012). Hamas broadcasting: Al-Aqsa channel in Gaza. In K. Hroub (Ed.), *Religious broadcasting in the Middle East* (pp. 237–61). London: C. Hurst & Co Publishers Ltd.

Bishara, A. (2009). *New media and political change: The case of the two Palestinian Intifadas*. Working Paper, EUI RSCAS, 2009/21, Mediterranean Programme Series. http://hdl.handle.net/1814/11487

Bookmiller, K. N., & Bookmiller, R. J. (1990). Palestinian radio and the intifada. *Journal of Palestine Studies, 19*(4), 96–105. https://doi.org/10.2307/2537391

Boyd, D. A. (1999). *Broadcasting in the Arab world: A survey of the electronic media in the Middle East* (3rd ed.). Ames: Iowa State University Press

Browne, D. R. (1975). The voices of Palestine: A broadcasting house divided. *Middle East Journal, 29*(2), 133–50.

Committee to Protect Journalists. (2019, February 28). *UN commission: Israeli snipers 'intentionally shot' Palestinian journalists in 2018, killing 2*. Committee to

Protect Journalists, https://cpj.org/2019/02/un-commission-israeli-snipers-intentionally-shot-p.php

Fatafta, M. (2018). *Internet freedoms in Palestine: Mapping of digital rights violations and threats.* https://www.apc.org/en/pubs/internet-freedoms-palestine-mapping-digital-rights-violations-and-threats

IMEMC (2018, May 4). *Convicted for poetry: Dareen Tatour.* https://imemc.org/article/convicted-for-poetry-dareen-tatour/

Ipsos. (2013). Top Line Results–Palestine: National Media Analysis (NMA) Study Nov–Dec.

Jamal, A. (2000). The Palestinian media: An obedient servant or a vanguard of democracy? *Journal of Palestine Studies, 29*(3), 45–59. https://doi.org/10.2307/2676455

——. (2009). *The Arab public sphere in Israel: Media space and cultural resistance.* Bloomington: Indiana University Press

King, G. (2017). History of struggle: The global story of community broadcasting practices, or a brief history of community radio. *Westminster Papers in Communication and Culture, 12*(2), 18–36. https://doi.org/10.16997/wpcc.227

King, G., & Marouf, L. (2018). *Radio Free Palestine: A model for cross-border solidarity broadcasting.* https://www.ritimo.org/Radio-Free-Palestine-A-Model-for-Cross-Border-Solidarity-Broadcasting

Melhem, A. (2016, August 22). *Freedom of the press: Palestine's journalists call for action.* https://www.al-monitor.com/pulse/originals/2016/08/palestine-journalists-arrests-freedom-of-the-press-opinion.html

Mendel, T., & Khashan, A. (2006). *The legal framework for media in Palestine and under international law.* https://www.article19.org/data/files/pdfs/analysis/palestine-media-framework.pdf

Najjar, A. (2005). *Palestinian press and national movement 1900–1948* [in Arabic]. Amman: The Arab Institute for Research and Publishing.

Nossek, H., & Rinnawi, K. (2003). Censorship and freedom of the press under changing political regimes: Palestinian media from Israeli occupation to the Palestinian authority. *International Communication Gazette, 65*(2), 183–202.

Omer, M. (2015). Against all odds: Media survive in Palestine. *Global Media Journal–African Edition, 9*(2), 105–33.

Palestinian Central Bureau of Statistics. (2019, July 10). *About 13 million Palestinians in the historical Palestine and diaspora.* http://www.pcbs.gov.ps/post.aspx?lang=en&ItemID=3503

Rugh, W. A. (2004). *Arab mass media: Newspapers, radio, and television in Arab politics.* Westport: Praeger.

Sakr, N. (2007). *Arab television today.* London: I.B. Tauris. https://doi.org/10.5040/9780755610075

Salama, V. (2006, June 1). Hamas TV: Palestinian media in transition. *Arab Media & Society*. https://www.arabmediasociety.com/hamas-tv-palestinian-media-in-transition/

Saraste, A. (2010). *Media regulation and censorship in occupied Palestine*. https://icahd.fi/wp-content/uploads/2010/05/media_regulation_and_censorship_in_palestine.pdf

Somiry-Batrawi, B. (2004). Echoes: Gender and media challenges in Palestine. In N. Sakr (Ed.), *Women and media in the Middle East: Power through self-expression* (pp. 109–19). London: I.B. Tauris. https://doi.org/10.5040/9780755604838.ch-007

TAM. (2017). *Media monitoring of Palestinian women's image and representation in news related to peace and security*. http://tam.ps/en/wp-content/uploads/2018/02/media-monitoring-report-english-FINAL.pdf

Tawil-Souri, H. (2015). *Occupation apps*. https://www.jacobinmag.com/2015/03/occupation-apps-souri-palestine/

Tawil-Souri, H., & Aouragh, M. (2014). Intifada 3.0? Cyber colonialism and Palestinian resistance. *The Arab Studies Journal*, 22(1), 102–33.

UNESCO. (2014). *Assessment of media development in Palestine based on UNESCO's media development indicators*. http://unesdoc.unesco.org/images/0022/002277/227784E.pdf

UN-ESCWA. (2017, March). *Israeli practices toward the Palestinian people and the question of Apartheid*. https://electronicintifada.net/sites/default/files/2017-03/un_apartheid_report_15_march_english_final_.pdf

UNRWA. (2019). *Occupied Palestinian territory emergency appeal 2019*. https://www.unrwa.org/resources/emergency-appeals/occupied-palestinian-territory-emergency-appeal-2019

4. Jordan: Media's Sustainability during Hard Times

Basim Tweissi

> This article will shed light on the main features of the Jordanian media system and how it relates to the political, economic, and legal systems. It focuses on the efforts to develop a sustainable media industry under difficult circumstances. For many decades, Jordan navigated the turbulent waters of the Middle East, the scene of devastating regional wars, civil wars, uprisings, and political instability, all of which undermined the efforts for political reform and the development of a healthy, robust media.

Background

Jordan is strategically located in a region that rarely escapes news headlines. Bordered by Saudi Arabia, Iraq, Syria, Palestine, and Israel, it is landlocked with the exception of 26 kilometers on the Red Sea. Its 89,200 square kilometers are predominantly desert in the south and east. Its capital, Amman, is the center of political, cultural, and media activities. With limited agriculture and natural resources, it struggles economically.

Jordan boasts a rich history within its borders, which were established in 1946. Islamic, Byzantine, Roman, and Nabatean monuments and archaeological sites stand witness to past civilizations that flourished there. The most critical battles of the Arab Revolt in 1916 and 1917, which ended the Turkish-Ottoman occupation of the Arab World, were fought out on its lands. The collapse of the Ottoman Empire culminated in the Sykes-Picot Agreement between Britain and France. An outcome of the agreement was the establishment of the Emirate of Transjordan in 1921 under the British Mandate.

In 1946, Jordan became a constitutional monarchy called the Hashemite Kingdom of Jordan. Following the Arab-Israeli war in 1948, the West Bank of the River Jordan, including parts of Jerusalem, was annexed, but in June 1967, after the second Arab-Israeli war, Israel occupied the West Bank and East Jerusalem. In 1988, Jordan relinquished its sovereignty over the West Bank to the Palestinian Liberation Organization (PLO), and in 1994, the Jordanian-Israeli peace treaty, ending the state of war between the two countries, was signed. Over the decades, however, the flight of waves of Palestinians from violence, occupation, and economic hardship have altered the demographic structure of Jordan's population, as well as integrating the Palestinian cause into its politics.

Jordan's geopolitical position has given it strategic and political significance as a regional player. It shouldered the responsibility of receiving waves of Arab refugees fleeing regional conflicts. In addition to the significant influx of Palestinian refugees during the wars of 1948 and 1967, thousands of Lebanese sought refuge during the mid-seventies, fleeing the civil war that had erupted in their country. The situation was further exacerbated in 1990 when Iraq occupied Kuwait, leading to the expulsion or departure of tens of thousands of Palestinian and Jordanian guest workers to their country of residence, Jordan. More waves were to follow with Iraqis escaping the hardships of the UN sanctions and the post-2003 occupation of their country. From 2011, a huge number of Syrian refugees streamed over Jordan's northern frontiers as the civil war raged in Syria. More than 1.3 million refugees fled to Jordan, of which 640,000 were registered with the UN and settled in camps (Department of Statistics, 2015). Thus, in the 55 years since independence, Jordan's population has more than doubled to 10.6 million today. Non-Jordanians constitute 30% of the total population, of whom 15% are Syrians, and the remainder are Palestinians. Young people constitute the majority of the population, with 34% being under 16 years of age.

Jordan's economy prospered for some decades. However, since 2010, Jordan's economy has suffered due to cost of energy, water, poor agricultural unemployment, and the burden of hosting Syrian refugees. Media have nonetheless flourished and responded to the fast-changing pace of events. The rapid population growth has presented new opportunities to the media.

Jordan adapted to the new circumstances. In 1989, it embarked on a program of democratic reform marked by the suspension of martial law, the resumption of parliamentary life, and the formation of political parties. The democratic transformation made significant strides before regressing in the 2000s. Although parliamentary elections continued to be held regularly, they were designed in a manner that limited their power. Following the 2011 Arab uprisings, known as the Hirak Protests in Jordan, the Jordanian government once more undertook a series of reforms through the introduction of broad constitutional amendments and the establishment of an Independent Electoral Commission and Constitutional Court. Historical Developments

The birth of journalism in Jordan coincided with the birth of the state more than nine decades ago, when it began to play a significant role in the construction of national institutions and the formation of a Jordanian identity, by underscoring positive achievements. Currently, the media is still undergoing a massive transformation that is proportional to the country's slow political reform.

Historically, the Jordanian media has evolved in three phases: the Emirate years from 1921 to 1946, the Kingdom years from 1946 to 1970, and the current phase, which can be divided into two periods. The first period (from 1970 to 1989) was marked by financial stability and the adoption of modern technologies. The second period began in 1989, when Jordan underwent a democratic transformation (Al-Moussa, 1998).

The first Jordanian newspaper, *Al-Haqq Ya'alu*, was published in 1921 in the city of Ma'an. When printing was introduced in 1923, the official weekly and sometimes biweekly *Al-Sharq Al-Arabi* newspaper was published. In 1926, the newspaper's name was changed to *The Official Gazette of the Government of Trans Jordan*. It was later changed again to *The Official Gazette of the Hashemite Kingdom of Jordan* (Al-Moussa, 1998, p. 261). It is still being published today.

In 1927, several privately-owned newspapers were published: *The Arab Peninsula, The Arab Echo,* and *Al-Urdun* which ceased printing in 1982. In the 1930s, there were short-lived attempts to publish newspapers and magazines, such as *Al-Hikma, Al-Mithaq,* and *Al-Wafa'a*, but none survived (Al-Moussa, 1998, p. 261). During this period, Jordanian journalism could be described as unsettled, financially poor, and lacking a clear identity. Party-affiliated newspapers began to emerge. Their content was predominantly political and literary.

The second phase began in 1946 when Jordan gained independence and became a constitutional monarchy. The West Bank of Palestine was annexed, and the 1952 constitution was enacted, guaranteeing political and civil freedoms and freedom of the press for the first time. This phase continued until 1967 when the second Arab-Israeli War broke out, resulting in Jordan's loss of the West Bank. The Palestinian resistance movements set up training camps in Jordan, and Israeli fighter jets patrolled the skies over Jordan unchallenged. The coverage, content, and quality of newspapers representing all political parties improved at the beginning of this period and readership was wide. However, in 1959, there was a marked decline in quality when democracy was put on hold. The 1960s were characterized by a polarized political climate in the Arab world. Newspapers became more partisan, and the government stepped in to micromanage media; some papers were suspended, others were banned altogether. With the rise of Gamal Abdel Nasser, Egypt's charismatic leader—who captivated Arab masses with his message of Pan-Arabism supported by his fiery rhetoric, which was widely broadcast with his country's powerful radio transmitters—Jordan's monarchy felt threatened and tried to counter the tide of Nasserism. Jordan launched, in 1956, a national radio station from Amman as its first national public media outlet, and shared the allocated frequency with its then primary radio station, which broadcast its programs from Ramallah in the West Bank.

Jordan's government also felt that Jordanian newspapers published in Jerusalem were not helpful in countering Nasserism associated with Palestinian patriotism. The government, headed by Premier Wasfi Al-Tel, believed that media which advocated Arab nationalist movements countenanced Nasserism. Against this backdrop, in 1967, the government introduced a new publications law (replacing the 1955 law) to enable governmental control of newspapers. The law was known as "the Merger Law" because several newspapers were forced to merge as a result of it. *Palestine* and *Al-Manar* merged into the *Addustour* newspaper, which later moved from Jerusalem to Amman, where it is still being published today. Similarly, *Al-Difa'a* and *Al-Jihad* merged into the *Al-Quds* newspaper, which is still published in Palestine (Sakkijha, 1998, p. 45). On 13 May 1971, the government issued a decree for the establishment of a cultural institute and a state-owned newspaper capable of analyzing the political scene. In due course, the Jordan Press Foundation was established and published the *Al-Rai* newspaper, which later became a public shareholding company (Hijazi, Al-Fank, & Kharob, 1995, p. 11).

The third phase (1970–1989) was characterized by stability and modernization. The government restructured the ownership of Jordanian newspapers, turning them into publicly-owned corporations. A total of 35% of the shares were retained by the original owners, 25% by shareholders, 15% by independent public enterprises (i.e. Jordan's Social Security Corporation and the Postal Savings Fund), 20% by traders on the stock market, and 5% by newspaper employees. During this period, a new generation of qualified Jordanian journalists emerged, raising professional standards, and on the business side, new financially and administratively independent corporations emerged.

In addition, HBS radio underwent further expansion in the 1970s and 1980s and began transmissions on different wavelengths and frequencies; its short-wave transmissions reached audiences worldwide. Today, it boasts five radio stations with different programs, along with regional radio stations in Irbid in northern Jordan. In 1968, *Jordan TV* (*JTV*) was launched as a state-owned station. By the 1970s and 1980s, the *JTV* staff had the know-how and editorial skills needed to be regarded as pioneers and helped with the process of setting up other television stations in the region. However, they also carried with them the values that had been instilled in them, such as the notion that the image of the state was paramount.

The fourth phase (1989–present) was characterized by the democratic transformation process, in which the Press and Publication Law of 1993 was introduced. The new law contributed to the growth of media; the number of dailies rose to nine, and weeklies jumped to 32 in 1995. In 1997, the number of newspapers reached 17; however, following amendments to the law, that number dwindled to seven. It was also a time in which new media started to emerge.

Ammon News, the first news website, was launched in 1997. The new broadcasting era that shaped the Arab region from the late 1990s onwards was reason enough for Jordan's parliament to approve the Audiovisual Media Law in 2002, thereby ending the government's monopoly over radio and television broadcasting rights. The private sector and civil society were granted the right to own and manage radio and television stations.

In 2019, Jordan's media landscape included 39 licensed satellite television channels, representing 16 Jordanian and 23 foreign channels, and 40 radio stations, including slide show (a televised form of radio) channels. Print outlets numbered 19 (including seven daily, nine weekly, and three monthly newspapers). Furthermore, the number of licensed news websites and so-called "electronic publications" reached 122.

Political System and Legal Framework

The Hashemite Kingdom of Jordan is a constitutional monarchy made up of three branches—the executive, legislative, and the judiciary—in accordance with the 1952 constitution, with ministerial portfolios that should reflect the various political and social components of society.

The constitutional amendment of 2011 protects the freedom of the press. Article 15 stipulates: "The State shall guarantee freedom of expression and every Jordanian shall be free to express his/her opinion in speech, in writing, or visual representation and other forms of expression provided that such expression does not violate the law." The amendment also stipulates that "the State shall guarantee the freedom of the media and publishing within the limits of the law." The same article states that "newspapers and information media may not be suspended nor license thereof revoked except by a court order in accordance with the provisions of the law." However, the ensuing relevant laws have limited these freedoms (Shukeir, 2011).

Jordan ratified the International Covenant on Civil and Political Rights in 2006, which states in Article 19 that "everyone shall have the right to freedom of expression," and the Arab Charter on Human Rights in 2004, which guarantees the right to information and freedom of opinion. Moreover, Jordan is a signatory to the United Nations Convention for the Rights of the Child, which ensures a child's right to freedom of expression, and the Euro-Mediterranean Partnership (EuroMed) agreement between Jordan and the European Union, which supports media freedom and the rights stipulated in international conventions, and which was signed in 1999 (Shukeir, 2011, pp. 19–26).

Media regulation remained volatile during the democratic transformation process, although, since 1989, the Kingdom has moved towards a more pluralistic political structure, lifting martial laws and guaranteeing freedom of expression through the Press and Publication Law No. 10 of 1993 and the multiparty system which was established through the Law for Political Parties No. 32 of 1993. Starting these reforms required substantial effort because, until that point, media management and control were the legacy of the Cold War in a region that sought to use the press as a weapon. In the 1970s, William Rugh (1979) categorized the Jordanian press as "loyalist" with a heavy influence from the government (pp. 25–29). Rugh also described the content of Jordanian press as featuring limited diversity, touting the government's point of view, failing to report accountability, and always supporting the status quo. He also said that it was slow in responding to events (pp. 79–80). Rugh's findings were still valid a decade later, as evidenced in Issam Moussa's (1989) content analysis of the *Al-Rai* daily newspaper, where he found that international content featured a degree of variety, while there was limited coverage of domestic issues, with a focus instead on official and domestic political topics (p. 98).

Since the mid-1990s, Jordanian media has seen important positive changes: a movement towards pluralism and editorial independence driven by a competitive spirit among newspapers (Al-Kilani, 2002). Another factor for the improved coverage was the emergence of weeklies, which proliferated following the enactment of the Publication Law of 1993 (Jones, 2002), but eventually decreased in number.

Yet media reforms kept taking one step backward for every step forward (Sakr, 2002). In 2001, for example, the government opted for the dissolution of the Ministry of Information and reassigned some of its roles to other public institutions, such as the Audiovisual Commission and the Department of Press and Publications. With these steps, Jordan's media regulation displayed more openness and tolerance compared with its neighboring countries (Armijo, 2009). On the other hand, growing official dissatisfaction with the media's performance led to allegations that it was harming Jordan's image, and consequently, the Press and Publication Law was amended five times between 1997 and 2012. Some of these amendments represented a step forward, while others represented a step backwards. For example, daily newspapers still needed to be licensed through a decision of the Cabinet of Ministers. Moreover, although Jordan is considered the first Arab country to enact a law upholding the right to access information (the Access to Information Law No. 47 of 2007), the application of this law did not result in a noticeable change on the ground. Most surveys showed that a lack of access to information was just the first of many challenges to improving media professionalism.

The Internet, on the other hand, was not officially regulated until December 2010 when the Court of Cassation, the highest civil judicial authority, issued a ruling stating that all websites shall be subject to the Press and Publication Law. In 2012, parliament passed new amendments to the law that required news websites to register with the Jordan Media Commission in order to be licensed to operate.

Despite the positive legislative changes introduced during the last decade, progress has been slow and limited. The overlapping laws in various parts of the legislation render the media law complex. There are 12 effective laws that restrict the freedom of the press within the 24 bills pertaining to the press and media. Chief among these are: the Penal Code, Protection of State Secrets and Documents Law, the State Security Court Law, the Press Association Law, Law on the Contempt of Court Proceedings, the law governing municipalities, the Code of Criminal Procedure, and the Public Assemblies Law.

Against the backdrop of the Hirak Protests in 2011, allegations were made on social media by non-governmental organizations (NGOs) and civil society activists against the authorities, accusing them of exploiting poor media professionalism and poor content as a pretext to curtail media freedom (Hawatmeh & Pies, 2011). Amendments to the Cybercrime Law were proposed by the government using hate speech as an excuse and claiming it was spreading on social media networks. The draft law is still being debated.

The progress of media freedom since the start of the reform era can thus be best described as teetering within the context of other public liberties. 1993 was characterized by sweeping political reforms (Freedom

House, 1994), and as such is also regarded as a liberal year for the media. Similarly, freedom of expression improved during the Hirak Protests but has regressed again as a consequence of the war on terrorism, especially since 2013. New laws, including the Anti-Terrorism Law, were created, and online activities were closely monitored. Further ambiguities in the legal framework have hampered the pluralistic development of the media: although journalists enjoy the privilege of protection of their sources by law, the legal and political systems continue to justify practices which do not comply with international media standards (UNESCO Office Amman, 2015). In addition, there is the problem of the limited independence of the Jordan Media Commission, a regulatory body whose head is appointed by the prime minister and charged with licensing media channels and services and addressing complaints. The commission thus gives the government the final say in licensing radio and television channels or newspapers.

In the meantime, despite a climate of rampant social media abuses and distortion of news, the public has expressed concern for media independence. Public opinion surveys revealed that respondents believe the freedoms of movement, ownership, worship, and belief are more protected than the freedom of the press and freedom of expression (Center for Strategic Studies, 2011).

Another problem is that the compulsory membership of journalists in the Jordan Press Association is used as a tool of control—only those who are members of the association are considered journalists and thus protected by the laws. But broadcast or online journalists are not included under the umbrella of the Jordan Press Association. Membership is restricted to editors and anchors of news bulletins. Therefore, some journalists advocate the establishment of multiple associations (UNESCO Office Amman, 2015).

Finally, although the Jordan Radio and Television Corporation Law describes *JTV* as a public entity that enjoys administrative and financial independence, the reality is different. An evaluation study carried out by the UNESCO Office Amman (2015) concluded that *JTV* tends to act as a mouthpiece for the government instead of focusing on its role as a public service broadcaster. An important development in this context was the Independent Public Service Broadcasting Channel Bylaw of 2016, which paved the way for setting up *Al-Mamlaka TV* as a new public service channel. The station, a 24-hour news and information television channel, has developed its own editorial policies and uses focus groups to shape them. The Board of Directors is appointed by the King, and the government has no say in the appointment of its staff in contrast to *JTV*. *Al-Mamlaka TV*, which is state-funded, faces challenges such as drastic cuts in budget support and its dwindling ability to protect its editorial mandate in the face of official pressure.

Economy and Ownership Patterns

Jordan's economy is relatively small and has endemic problems. External debt levels constituted 94% of Jordan's GDP in 2019 and this figure is growing due to the impact of the COVID-19 pandemic on the economy. Although poor in natural resources, the Kingdom's human resources, competitive investment environment, and openness to world markets are major positive attributes. These factors have helped to boost growth and expansion of the media industry despite the modest advertising expenditure of USD 220 million in 2018, a small proportion of what has been spent in neighboring oil-producing countries.

The Audiovisual Media Law of 2002 put an end to the government's monopoly on radio and television ownership. Although the law allows both public and private ownership of media, there is no explicit reference to the status of ownership of community service media that are owned and run by civil society. Despite this lack of regulation, community service media have started to make their presence felt, albeit on a small scale, since 2005, namely through the initiative *AmmanNet*, which includes *Radio Al-Balad*. Moreover, public institutions, such as universities and municipalities, own ten smaller radio stations which serve their local communities.

The government has a stake in various sectors of the media industry and owns, along with Jordan Radio and Television (JRTV), the only two land-based terrestrial channels, in addition to three satellite channels and the national news agency *Petra*, a public entity. The private sector, on the other hand, owns seven satellite channels, including *Roya TV*, *Amman TV*, and *Jo TV*, and with the government co-owns two Arabic-language and one English-language newspaper out of a total of seven. The state holds, through its Social Security Corporation, 55% of *Al-Rai* shares and 33% of *Addustour* shares, while the balance is held by the public. JRTV also owns five public radio stations. The private sector, however, owns 25 radio stations. Statistics show that private media ownership is expanding, with businessmen owning most media outlets; for example, *Roya TV* is owned by the Al-Sayegh Family, and the *Al-Ghad* newspaper is owned by Mohammad Olayan.

Article 9 of the Competition Law, which regulates the market concentration, stipulates that a written ministerial approval is required if 40% of the shares of a media enterprise are to be traded, which reflects a reluctance on the part of the government to relinquish control of the media (UNESCO Office Amman, 2015).

Since 2011, print media in Jordan have struggled as the economic crisis has deepened. The decline of print media is due to the contraction of its advertising revenue share. The print media's failure to adapt to the digital publishing technologies is one of the main reasons for this crisis (Economic and Social Council, 2018). The two major Arabic dailies, *Al-Rai* and *Addustour*, began to hemorrhage financially and were forced to take drastic cost-cutting measures. In 2011, *Addustour* had to lay off 77 of 700 employees, and closed down its weekly English edition. Three years later, it adopted further drastic measures, reducing its staff to 320. The government had to intervene when the newspaper failed to pay staff salaries and committed advertising funds for government legal notices as support (Economic and Social Council, 2018). *Al-Rai* daily, for its part, stopped giving annual salary increases to employees as of March 2011, and reduced the number of columnists it employed from 53 to eight. In March 2015, it closed down some of its offices outside the capital. Another newspaper, *Al-Arab Al-Yawm*, also became a casualty of the crisis and had to close down completely in 2015.

The fear of a runaway media has slowed down the emergence of a professional class of journalists able to produce commercially sought-after content. The relaxed implementation of copyright laws is also a stifling disincentive. On the other hand, *Google* and *Facebook* have an unfair competitive advantage since they dominate the limited advertising market available to local media.

Technology and Infrastructure

Jordan's media infrastructure is considered adequate compared with that of other developing countries. JRTV is one of the biggest Arab media corporations with advanced technical capabilities and know-how, which were acquired when *BBC* engineers and production staff assisted with setting it up. In the early 1970s, JRTV provided essential engineering and production staff to Arabian Gulf countries who set up national television and radio stations. JRTV became a national flagship during this period. It helped found the Arab States Broadcasting Union and became an active member of the European Broadcasting Union. Since 1972, it has contributed news coverage from Jordan, and has produced international scoops, such as the first pictures of Syrian tanks capturing the Golan Heights in October 1973, because it was the only television station at the time with access to a satellite ground station. In 2001, Jordan agreed to set up a tax-free zone, the Jordan Media City (JMC), to provide regional and international broadcasting services, production facilities, satellite uplinks, and television channel streaming. An agreement was signed with the Arab Media Corporation, which invested USD 15 million with its activities to be overseen by the media regulator in accordance with the laws of the Jordan Media Authority (UNESCO Office Amman, 2015). JMC currently uplinks and turns around 450 television channels and provides Jordan's first commercial television station, *Roya TV*, with studios and transmission facilities (Jordan Media City, 2020). During the COVID-19 pandemic, *Roya TV* encountered state intervention due to their broadcast of a video of protesting citizens who had suffered a loss of income due to the lockdown.

Despite the expansion of Internet coverage in Jordan over the last decade, the printing and book publishing industry have also seen a remarkable development. The number of small printing houses based in Amman grew to 439 in 2019. The number of advertising companies stood at 384 (Jordan Media Commission, 2019). Similarly, the media production industry flourished. *Al-Rai* and *Al-Ghad* newspapers borrowed heavily to invest in enormous printing plants, in the belief that print media would last forever, disregarding the impact of the inevitable advance of electronic publishing. As the flow of advertising revenue migrated from traditional print media to the new media, there were serious financial shockwaves and massive debts to be reckoned with. Since the lockdown in March 2020 due to the COVID-19 pandemic and the suspension of all print media, the future of Jordan's print media remains in doubt.

Startups in the field of video production have played an increasingly important role in creating a significant change in content and form. An example is *Kharabeesh*, a platform for digital creativity founded in 2007, which focuses on entertainment, humor, and satire, and publishes its animated cartoons widely on the Internet. *7iber* is another example, which describes its role as "producing and publishing original multimedia journalism and analysis, and providing a platform for critical conversation", and frequently publishes daring videos and investigative reports which have caused discomfort and elicited retaliation in the form of suspensions by the authorities.

The Internet was introduced to Jordan in the mid-1990s (Shukeir, 2009). As a result, the telecommunications market grew and became more competitive over the following two decades. Three communication companies currently dominate the market: *Zain*, *Orange*, and *Umniah*. Two of them, *Zain* and *Orange*, are international operators, and *Umniah* is Jordanian. Their services encompass ADSL, 3G, and 4G Internet access technologies. Fiber-based broadband is also being rolled out in the capital and most governorates.

The 3G and WiMAX technologies were introduced in Jordan in 2010. At the time, 38% of the population was estimated to have access to the Internet. Since then, news websites have begun to grow on the web, delivering news at a faster pace than conventional newspapers.

The 2017 statistics show that the spread of computers, smartphones, and tablets had increased, and 67% of the population now have access to the Internet. A similar rise has occurred in the use of social networks, specifically *Facebook*. The figures also show that 88% of people had mobile phone subscriptions in 2018, while 38% of households had a computer. 89% of households had Internet access, while 7% of the total population subscribed to the WiMAX service (Telecommunications Regulatory Commission, 2017).

The digitization of newsrooms in Jordanian newspapers began with the advent of ADSL and 2G Internet technologies at the turn of the century. In 2006, *Ammon News* became the first news website to go online, challenged only by conventional dailies and weeklies. By 2019, the number of news websites officially registered in Jordan stood at 167 (Tweissi, 2019). Recent developments in ICT also indicate a stronger engagement of local communities, as users are allowed to post their comments and feedback on news websites. However, amendments to the Press and Publications Law of 2011 stipulate that website owners are held personally liable for any opinions published through their outlets. The measures were brought about due to the tense climates generated by the Hirak Protests and the protests that raged across the Arab world. News websites were launched with the specific mission of toppling the government with what were regarded as hearsay, rumors, and fake news. The choice laid before the government was either chaos or closure of websites which could not be held accountable in a court of law. Nonetheless, the Internet had already changed Jordan's media landscape, enabling the use of multimedia and ICT, which helped to enrich the content produced and consumed (UNESCO Office Amman, 2015). Additionally, all of Jordan's six dailies embraced the technology and launched online versions with varying degrees of coverage and quality.

Challenges

Jordan's media system reflects a state of "frazzled stability" as any progress made has been offset by setbacks and restrictions. Media reforms and political reforms are interdependent. Recognizing the importance of free, independent, and diverse media on the political level will be crucial to pushing the media reform agenda forward. Although Jordan went through a prolonged transitional period since the launch of political reforms and the return to parliamentary life, the reforms undertaken from 1989 to 2019 were lacking. Regional instability, on the other hand, still poses the biggest challenge to Jordan's media system, given that Jordan is dependent on the Arab Gulf states support, and specifically Saudi Arabia, which opposes the rise of any Arab media system that upholds values or a philosophy different from its own. Thus, fear of the independent media has generated pressure on the government to create laws that have seriously undermined the media's capacity to be the watchdog and guardian of public interest. In all, 22 laws have been introduced to curb the freedom and independence of the media.

Furthermore, the comparatively modest size of the advertising market restricts its expansion and provides little incentive to investors, unless they are politically motivated or partisan. While new media offer economically viable models, traditional media have failed to follow in their footsteps to adapt to new technologies, for which they have paid a hefty price. Traditional media outlets have been in regression of late and face capacity-building challenges. They have failed to fully embrace digital transformation, and many dailies are plagued with acute financial difficulties and the mounting costs of paper combined with a recession of readership. Unionization is another problem too since it remains weak, and Jordan's Press Association Law does not meet international standards.

Codes of conduct are also still new to the media community, while previous attempts to appoint a media ombudsman have failed. Efforts are also needed to address the gap between journalism schools' curricula and media market needs. Media education is mostly theoretical, with little or no field training. Textbooks and teaching methods are outdated. Furthermore, the lack of access to information remains a major hurdle that impedes the media's capacity to gain the trust of society, despite the fact that Jordan was the first country to adopt a freedom of access to information law in 2007.

Outlook

The degree of media freedom is not likely to change in the next few years. However, modest progress might still be realized in the area of freedom of speech and the independence of media institutions. Jordan, in the meantime, will try to maintain a reasonable level of Internet freedom. The government believes that advancing the promising ICT sector depends on providing a favorable legal environment, which would positively affect digital media platforms and Internet freedom.

In recent years, the government has paid a great deal of attention to entrepreneurship and startups. It has also launched digital startup accelerators. New media startups that embrace digital technology have also begun to surface. These developments provide a vast window of opportunity for the growth of digital media, which will likely have an impact on the future of the media in Jordan and in the region.

Public broadcasting also took a positive step by enacting the Independent Public Service Broadcasting Channel Bylaw, which established *Al-Mamlaka* news station. Moreover, *JRTV* has developed and begun implementing a series of plans to enhance performance and to enforce the public broadcasting standards. The COVID-19 pandemic has reversed some of these modest achievements and the fear of what is to come has stifled the will of policy makers. Furthermore, recent regional developments and the political landscape of Arab-Israeli relations has required the media to restrain its reaction to events. This move was driven by fear of offending fellow Arab countries who do not separate media attitudes from official government stances on an issue. A complex series of factors unique to Jordan's position in the Middle East are always in play, hampering and slowing down the development of the media, and its ability to break free.

References

Al-Kilani, S. (2002). *Press freedoms in Jordan*. Copenhagen: Euro-Mediterranean Human Rights Network.

Al-Moussa, I. (1998). *Media development in Jordan 1920–1970: A publication of the Higher Committee for Writing about history of Jordan* [in Arabic]. Amman.

Armijo, E. (2009). Building Open Societies: Freedom of the Press in Jordan and Rwanda. *International Journal of Communications Law & Policy, 13*(Winter).

Badran, B. (1988). Press-government relations in Jordan: A case study. *Journalism & Mass Communication Quarterly, 65*(2), 335–46.

Center for Strategic Studies (2011). *Democracy poll* [in Arabic]. Amman: University of Jordan.

Department of Statistics (2015). *General population and housing census* [in Arabic].

Economic and Social Council (2018). *Country report* [in Arabic]. http://dosweb.dos.gov.jo/ar/population/population-2/

Freedom House (1994). *Freedom in the World. The Annual Survey of Political Rights and Civil Liberties, 1993–1994.* https://freedomhouse.org/sites/default/files/2020-02/Freedom_in_the_World_1993-1994_complete_book.pdf

Hawatmeh, G., & Pies, J. (2011). Jordan: Media accountability under the patronage of the regime. In T. Eberwein, S. Fengler, E. Lauk, & T. Leppik-Bork

(Eds.), *Mapping media accountability in Europe and beyond* (pp. 101–13). Köln: Herbert Von Halem Verlag.

Hijazi, A., Al-Fank. F., & Kharob, M. (1995). *The Jordan Massage to the Arab world* [in Arabic]. Amman: Jordan Press Foundation.

Jones, A. (2002). *The press in transition: A comparative study of Nicaragua, South Africa, Jordan and Russia.* Hamburg: Deutsches Übersee-Institut.

Jordan Media City (2020). *Welcome to Jordan Media City.* http://www.jordanmediacity.com/en/

Jordan Media Commission (2019). *Report on the audiovisual media map in Jordan for the year 2019* [in Arabic]. http://mc.gov.jo/Pages/viewpage?pageID=34

Rugh, W. A. (1979). *The Arab press: News media and political process in the Arab world.* New York: Syracuse University Press.

Sakkijha, B. (1998). Development of journalism in Jordan [in Arabic]. In H. Houranic (Ed.), *Media and freedom of the press in Jordan* [in Arabic] (pp. 23–34). Amman: Dar Sinbad.

Sakr, N. (2002). Media reform in Jordan: The stop-go transition. In M. E. Price, B. Rozumilowicz, & S. G. Verhulst (Eds.), *Media reform: Democratizing the media, democratizing the state* (pp. 107–32). London, New York: Routledge.

Shukeir, Y. (2009). Jordan. *Global Information Society Watch.* https://giswatch.org/sites/default/files/jordan.pdf

——. (2011). *Introduction to News Media Law and Policy in Jordan. A primer compiled as part of the Jordan Media Strengthening Program.* Jordan Media Strengthening Program and Center for Global Communication Studies (CGCS). https://repository.upenn.edu/cgi/viewcontent.cgi?article=1001&context=jordan_program

Telecommunications Regulatory Commission (2017). *Annual report for 2017* [in Arabic]. Amman: TRC. https://trc.gov.jo/EchoBusV3.0/SystemAssets/%D8%A7%D9%84%D8%AA%D9%82%D8%B1%D9%8A%D8%B1%20%D8%A7%D9%84%D8%B3%D9%86%D9%88%D9%8A%202017.pdf

Tweissi, B. (2017). Transformations of Arab Public Media: Questions of Democracy and Public Service Standards [in Arabic]. *Al-Jazeera Center for Studies.* https://studies.aljazeera.net/ar/mediastudies/2017/09/170910094936081.html

——. (2019). Electronic Journalism in the Arab World: The Context of Development and Challenges [in Arabic]. *Al-Jazeera Center for Studies.* https://studies.aljazeera.net/ar/mediastudies/2019/02/190211075743953.html

UNESCO Office Amman (2015). *Assessment of media development in Jordan: Based on UNESCO's media development indicators.* https://unesdoc.unesco.org/ark:/48223/pf0000234425?posInSet=1&queryId=fc3a40cc-a1d7-4c45-8a1b-b9e07d394fa1

5. Iraq: Media between Democratic Freedom and Security Pressures

Sahar Khalifa Salim

> This chapter discusses the historical beginnings of the media in Iraq and how it has developed over time under Ottoman control and during the British occupation, which was followed by a dictatorial rule that has completely restricted the media. Since 2003, Iraq has entered a democratic era, which has fostered an openness and relative freedom in the media. However, because of deteriorating security conditions, widespread corruption, and the control exerted by political parties and religious movements over governance, freedom of the press in Iraq is globally ranked among the lowest in the index of press freedom.

Background

Iraq is considered the cradle of civilizations, where the earliest societies in the world were established, namely those of Mesopotamia. The most important of these were the Babylonian, Sumerian, Akkadian, Assyrian, and Chaldean. One of the most important accomplishments of the Mesopotamian civilizations was the Sumerians' invention of writing. The first written laws were also issued in Iraq.

Great kingdoms were established in what is now Iraq, and they rendered the region an important state. Iraq was an important part of the Persian, Greek, and Roman empires. In the seventh century, it became an essential and integrated part of the Islamic world. In the eighth century, Iraq contained the capital of the Abbasid State until the Ottomans took control of it. It remained under their control until the establishment of the new national state during the period of 1914–1918. After the First World War, and in light of a growing national awareness, the Iraqis enjoyed a kind of freedom, and newspapers tended to discuss politically controversial topics, but most of them were short-lived (Bakr, 1969).

In the twentieth century, the country experienced periods of stability and upheaval. The royal era from 1932–1958 is considered the most pluralistic one. During this period, many newspapers and magazines were issued that called for a free and independent state, and mobilized the citizens (Bakr, 1969). After a revolution in 1958, a republic was set up. The 1970s witnessed an improvement in the living conditions of Iraqis due to the nationalization of Iraq's oil resources in 1972, which had previously been run by a monopoly of foreign companies. In the 1980s, the Iraqi-Iranian war affected the economic and political conditions. It depleted the country's resources and created a schism among its citizens. The war ended in 1988, but it was followed by Iraq's invasion of Kuwait, an action that led to another war, a war on Iraq led by the US, which began on 17 January 1991. The coalition air raids attacked the infrastructure of all the Iraqi cities, which led to total destruction. Moreover, three northern cities united to form an autonomous region called Kurdistan that has its own language. International military and economic sanctions followed due to the losses caused by the Iraqi invasion of Kuwait. The embargo lasted for nearly 12 years and ended on 19 March 2003, when the US and the coalition states launched a war against Iraq under the pretext that it had weapons of mass destruction. The war ended with the US-led coalition's defeat of the Iraqi forces and the occupation of Iraq on 9 April 2003.

Iraq is a major connecting point between Europe, on the one hand, and Southeast Asia and Australia, on the other. The capital, Baghdad, is considered an important crossroads in the Middle East. Iraq is surrounded by Syria, Jordan, Saudi Arabia, Kuwait, Turkey, and Iran. The area of Iraq is nearly 438,446 km^2. There are 18 Iraqi governorates. The region of Kurdistan consists of three of these: Sulaimaniya, Erbil, and Duhok. Although there were neutral areas that separated Iraq from Jordan, Kuwait, and Saudi Arabia, in addition to Shat Al-Arab that separated Iraq from Iran, the change in the political system after 2003 affected Iraqi borders, and some areas were seized by neighboring countries such as Kuwait (Khalil, 2018). The population of Iraq amounts to more than 38 million. The capital, Baghdad, has the highest population with eight million people, representing 21% of the total population of the governorates. Nineveh comes second, with 10% of the total population, and is followed by Basra, with 8%. Those below 15 years of age represent 38% of the total population (Iraqi Ministry of Planning, 2018).

The Iraqi people are multiethnic, multilingual and multiconfessional, which strongly affects the diversity of its media landscape. Arabs and Kurds are the two major nationalities in Iraq. Arabs represent the majority of the population with nearly 75–80%, while the Kurds represent 12–18%. Other nationalities and ethnic groups represent 5%. Arabic and Kurdish are the official languages in Iraq. Arabic, however, is considered the primary language because 80% of the population speaks it. Kurds live in the northeastern regions, Sulaymaniya, Erbil, and Duhok, where they represent the majority. They also represent a small percentage of the population in Nineveh, Diyala, and Baghdad. Most of the Kurds are Sunnis. The most significant minority in Iraq are the Turkmen, who represent the third largest ethnic group. They live close to the Kurdish region in the cities of Kirkuk, Diyala, Nineveh, and Salahud-Din. The language of the Turkmen (a Turkish dialect) and Syriac are official languages in the administrative units where the Turkmen or Assyrians represent the majority of the population. There are other languages, including Mandean, Sureth, Armenian, and Gypsy, which are used by minorities (Al-Husseini, 2008).

Islam is the religion of 95% of the population. Muslims are divided into two main denominations, Sunni and Shi'ite, but there are no official statistics defining the precise ratio. Christians, Mandeans, and Yazidis represent 5%. The Iraqi law acknowledges 14 official Christian sects. They are spread over different Iraqi regions, mainly in Baghdad, Erbil (in Ankawa), and Mosul (Nineveh plain). Currently, they have their own religious and political representation. Before the US-led coalition occupation in 2003, they numbered nearly 1.4 million. This number, however, has decreseased due to continuous migration and the occupation by the Islamic State (ISIS) of Syria and Iraq, which also led to the displacement of the Christians. According to the estimations of

Christian organizations, between 250,000 and 300,000 Christians remain in the area. There are also the Zoroastrians, who had previously lived in Kurdistan and who belong to an ancient religion, Zoroastrianism, which had disappeared from Iraq, but reappeared after 2015 (Salloom, 2017).

Yazidis represent an ancient religious and ethnic group who lived mainly in northern Iraq, and specifically in the Sinjar mountain region northeast of Mosul on the Iraq-Syria border. Some of the Yazidis speak the Kurdish language, and some of them speak Arabic. During the rule of ISIS in this area, tens of thousands of Yazidis fled for their lives, and between 2000 and 5500 Yazidis were killed, and around 3000 kidnapped, by ISIS (Fidh, 2018).

Historical Developments

The beginnings of media in Iraq occurred with the publication of the first official newspaper in Baghdad. The first issue of *Al-Zawra'* was published in 1869, when Iraq was ruled by the Ottomans. It was established by Midhat Pasha, the Ottoman governor in Iraq. Issued in Arabic and Turkish, it was the Ottoman province's official mouthpiece. Soon after, *Al-Mosul*, a weekly newspaper, was issued in Mosul beginning in 1885. In 1889, *Al-Basra* weekly newspaper was first published in Basra. These newspapers continued to exist until the British occupation in 1917 after the fall of the Ottoman state at the end of World War I (Batti, 1961).

The British occupying forces controlled the press and journalism in Iraq. They achieved this by taking control of the public publishing houses and buying all of the private ones. They were then used for printing newspapers that promoted the consolidation of the British military rule. Consequently, all of the newspapers that had been published in the Ottoman era were closed, and new ones were established, the most famous of which was *Al-Awqaf Al-Basriyya*, which was followed by a two-page newspaper entitled *Al-Arab*. The content of these newspapers supported British policy in Iraq, which aimed to develop closer relationships with the Arabs and incite them against the Turks (Batti, 1985).

In 1918, Iraq was placed under the League of Nations mandate. According to the resolutions of San Remo, Iraq was placed under the British administration. Soon after that, the 1920 revolution began against the British occupation. Journalism was the most effective media used by the Iraqis in their political struggle to achieve success in the revolution. In that period, newspapers prospered, and several newspapers were publishing content and opinions that opposed the British occupation. During that period, several political parties were established. These parties employed the partisan press to express their ideologies of politics and reform. Thus, there was a relatively independent media environment at that time (Al-Mashhadani, 2013).

The beginnings of radio broadcasting in Iraq go back to 22 March 1932, when the Iraqi government conducted the first experimental radio broadcast from 8:30–10:30 p.m. On 26 January 1935, the first shortwave Iraqi radio broadcasting station was established. Its program was announced in the official newspapers of that time. It included songs, music, and lectures. The official broadcasting of *Baghdad Radio* started in 1936. The program included anthems, news, and lectures. That station was closed several times, until a new regulation for the Iraqi wireless broadcasting was issued in 1937. It was followed in 1938 by the Radio Tax Law. After that, daily broadcasting started, but it could hardly be heard outside of Iraq. The British Forces that were established in Iraq had a positive effect on the development of broadcasting, as they provided Iraq with new radio transmitters that allowed them to establish new radio stations, such as the Kurdish radio station in Kirkuk in 1952. New foreign-language radio stations were also established in 1952 (Al-Rawi, 1992).

These media developments were followed by the beginning of Iraqi television in 1954 when the British BAY Company, while conducting an exhibition for manufactured and commercial goods, built a mobile television station in the exhibition area in Baghdad. This station started broadcasting different programs, including ice skating, music, dancing, and singing performances, as well as programs for children. The BAY Company ultimately presented the station to the Iraqi government in return for a contract to import the required resources for operating the station and training its personnel. On 4 January 1956, the first experimental broadcast of *Baghdad TV* was conducted. Its programs supported the policy and decisions of the Iraqi government, in addition to supporting its objectives and activities.

A revolution in July 1958 ended the royal era in Iraq. It marked the beginning of the republican rule that also ended the British Forces' existence in Iraq. A wide range of newspapers representing several political and ethnic segments of society appeared. Radio and television broadcasting improved. In 1963, *Baghdad TV* witnessed new technical developments, especially the introduction of video tapes. In 1967, the station's broadcasting reached all the Iraqi territories. It can be considered the first television station in the Middle East. Its programs were in Arabic, Kurdish, Turkish, and Syriac languages (Radhi, 2010).

In 1968, when the Ba'ath party took over, the media were monopolized by the government. A newspaper was established to be the mouthpiece of the party, *Al-Thawra*. In 1975, Iraq witnessed television broadcasting in color for the first time. In 1979, Saddam Hussein became ruler in Iraq, and during his rule (1979–2003), the media were totally monopolized under his control.

The first satellite broadcasting of an Iraqi channel started in Iraq with the use of the Internet in 1998. Internet services were not freely accessible to everyone. At that time, they were controlled legally by the Iraqi government and were subject to high security measures. In addition, the infrastructure was not suitable for this service due to the international sanctions imposed after Iraq had occupied Kuwait in 1991. The subscribers amounted to 45,000 out of a total of 24 million Iraqis. Most of these subscribers were from official Iraqi institutions, and many were rich individuals because the subscription was very expensive. The State Company for Internet Services (SCIS), which belonged to the Ministry of Communication, managed that service. It designed the electronic sites for the Iraqi media, including the Iraqi News Agency and a number of the official newspapers. However, some electronic newspapers were poorly designed, and they concentrated only on essays and studies. On 27 July 2000, the first public Internet café was opened, but surfing was limited to the sites allowed by the Iraqi government.

The major change that occurred in Iraq and is considered a turning point in its political life was the establishment of a new political regime after the US-led occupation in 2003. The invasion turned the country upside down economically, politically, and socially. The new regime dismantled all military institutions and appointed a civilian governor.

New political and social institutions were established with a new system of election that led to a new governing regime based on a parliamentary system. A separation was established between the legislative and executive authorities. A new constitution was issued, most of which was derived from the Transitional Iraqi State Administration Law of 2004 that was set up under the so-called Coalition Provisional Authority (CPA) directed by the US-imposed Provisional Governor, Paul Bremer. Its articles mainly drew on Western experiences, neglecting Iraqi realities on the ground (Ali, 2018).

Because of the war with the US-led coalition that ended with the occupation of Iraq in 2003, Iraq has witnessed major and deeply pervasive political, security, social, and economic changes. The security conditions deteriorated dramatically after the order of Provisional Governor Bremer, which dismantled the public security institutions, the first of which was the Iraqi army. That order led to sectarian fighting that ultimately resulted in the deterioration of almost all public and health services. These consequences further led to a large brain drain due to assassinations, threats, and extortions, where significant numbers of qualified Iraqis left the country.

In 2014, the Islamic State in Iraq and Syria (ISIS), a terrorist organization, occupied three major Iraqi governorates—Mosul, Anbar, and Salahud-Din—and declared it to be an "Islamic state". It recruited militants from various countries all over the world to fight with it. A war against ISIS ensued, involving many international and regional powers until ISIS as an occupying entity was declared defeated in Iraq at the end of 2017. Still, during the fighting whole cities were destroyed and have not yet been rebuilt, and many people were killed or displaced.

After 2015, the economic condition of Iraq also deteriorated due to the decline in international oil prices, as well as pervasive political, economic, and administrative corruption in most of its public institutions (Transparency International, 2018). That corruption, nevertheless, has continued after oil prices have risen again. Moreover, according to the latest report issued by Transparency International in 2018, Iraq scored only 18 out of 100 points, ranking 168 out of 180 states, thus indicating an extremely high level of corruption.

Political System and Legal Framework

With the US-led occupation in 2003, a new political system was established in Iraq. The authoritarian regime of the dictator Saddam Hussein, who had ruled for 35 years, collapsed. The characteristics of the new Iraqi political system were enshrined in the articles of the Iraqi Republic's Constitution of 2005, namely, Articles 1, 5, 6, and 47. Article 1 states that "the Republic of Iraq is a single federal, independent and fully sovereign state in which the system of government is republican, representative, parliamentary, and democratic."

After 2003, Iraq gained the freedom to establish political parties and gatherings. While for decades there had only been one party allowed, in the parliamentary elections of 2018, almost 204 parties, entities, and political movements were registered (Independent High Electoral Commission of Iraq, 2017). The governing regime has also been renewed as Iraq has become a parliamentary democratic federal republic, a system of pluralism. The executive authority is executed by the prime minister as the chairman of the cabinet. There is also a president for the republic. The legislative authority is handled by the Iraqi parliament.

After 2003, the relationship between the political system and the media changed. At that time, the Provisional Governor immediately ordered all the media institutions to be dismantled and their staffs dismissed. He issued Order No. 6 in June 2003 to establish the Iraqi Media Network (IMN) as a replacement for the dismantled Ministry of Information. Orders No. 65 and 66 were drafted and issued in March 2004 to provide a suitable legal basis to organize the Iraqi media. In the introduction for Order No. 65, the National Communications and Media Commission was established to be responsible for granting licenses, organizing the telecommunications services, broadcasting, transmitting, and organizing information services and Iraqi media. Order No. 66 directed the establishment of the Iraqi Commission for Broadcasting and Transmitting Services.

The CPA initially hoped to establish the IMN as a copy of the BBC model, with the aim for it to become an independent professional and transparent commission. This model, however, was diverted from its independent path when the IMN started to adopt the government's positions. This occurred because the President of the IMN was appointed by the government or the governing party, and its board was appointed according to a sectarian quota. The public media, which Bremer had tried to set up to follow the BBC model, quickly turned into a state media organ par excellence. The current IMN has its own budget which is formulated by parliament. It is also financed by advertisements, programs, and artistic works it produces, sells, and broadcasts. The IMN comprises three television channels—*Al-Iraqiyya*, *IMN News*, *IMN Sports*—, three radio stations—*Republic of Iraq, Furqan*, and *Iraqiyya Radio*—, a Media Training Institute, and the *Al-Sabah* newspaper and *Al-Shabaka* magazine. The IMN employs more than 3,000 individuals.

All the previous constitutions from 1925, 1958, 1964, 1968, and 1970 notably included texts about freedom of expression and the press, although they were bound by a group of written laws. For instance, the Publications Law No. 206 of 1968 allowed the authorities to impose their sponsorship on all newspapers, magazines, and books, which required previous approval. There was also the modified Iraqi Penal Law No. 111 of 1969, which included more than 30 criminal defamation articles. According to this law, the penalty for expressing or publishing one's opinions may amount to capital punishment, life or temporary imprisonment, confiscation of movable and immovable property, etc.

Also, after 2003, several laws were issued to regulate the media in Iraq, such as Order No. 14, which was issued by the CPA. It defined limitations to the freedom of expression. For instance, the third section of this order states, under Detection of Prohibited Activities, that "the administrator may authorize on-site inspections of Iraqi media organizations' work without notice, in order to ascertain compliance with this order and to seize any prohibited materials and any production equipment and seal off any operating premises." In accordance with Order No. 65, the National Commission of Communication and Media was established to regulate radio broadcasting and to grant licenses for broadcasting. Notably, the order also granted the freedom to establish newspapers without the need for licenses by any entity; thus, anyone in Iraq could publish a newspaper (Al-Sarraj, 2017).

Nevertheless, the previous laws that restricted the freedom of the press, or posed dangers for that freedom in Iraq, are still valid in the judicial system. These laws subject journalists to arrest and excessive fines, especially in the present articles, such as those known as the

Defamation Articles in Law No. 111 of the Iraqi Penal Law of 1969. The latest law is the Rights of Journalists Law, issued in 2011, whose provisions include a number of contradictions with reality, and which allows for muzzling and politicization of the media.

Governmental or official institutions, especially the Media and Communication Commission, issued orders to temporarily restrict freedom of opinion and the media, especially during the large-scale protests in 2019. For instance, the letter issued by the Media and Communication Commission at the end of 2018 was addressed to all the press institutions in Iraq and informed them of the necessity to stop any abuses of national and religious symbols.

Some satellite channels were closed down, such as the *Baghdadiya*, *Al-Babiliya*, and Qatari *Al-Jazeera* channels in Iraq. The websites of the Qatari owned *Al-Araby Al-Jadeed*, and the Saudi-owned *Asharq Al-Awsat* newspapers, and a number of news agencies were blocked due to their criticisms of the performance of the Iraqi government.

Beyond the laws, there are security factors on the ground which affect the media more strongly. While doing their job, especially when covering demonstrations, protests, or acts of violence, journalists are exposed to security threats such as harassment and attack. According to a report issued by the Defending Freedom of Press in Iraq Society, 231 journalists were subjected to 207 acts of harassment during the period from 3 May 2018 to 3 May 2019. These included five arrests, 17 detainments, 30 assaults, various preventions and hindrances of coverage by government officials or their bodyguards, and nine armed attacks on journalists and media institutions. Some of these violations were against civil activists and political analysts; furthermore, a group of journalists was detained for criticizing the government (Sadoon & Tariq, 2019).

Economy and Ownership Patterns

Nearly 95% of the finances included in the state's general budget for the Iraqi economy depend on Iraqi crude oil revenues. The budget thus depends on how high or low oil prices are. Consequently, this affects the individual and national income. With the increase in oil exports in the period from 2004–2014, and the availability of enormous financial resources, many newspapers and media institutions became active.

They employed many journalists; however, they were often run by unqualified administrations and had no sustainable business plans.

Governmental subsidies offered to the media are limited to only the official IMN media. Most of the media in Iraq are financed by parties, political and religious movements, state officials, and businessmen, in addition to foreign entities which come from Arab, regional, or neighboring states, such as Iran, Turkey, and Saudi Arabia. The economic crisis hit Iraq in 2015 hard and heavily affected most media institutions. Several daily newspapers and some satellite television stations were forced to close down because of bankruptcy. Some others were forced to change from print publications to digital websites. Other groups downsized their staffs or reduced the number of publications.

With the beginning of the economic crisis in 2015, many international organizations and entities stopped supporting the media. The private sector, moreover, deteriorated, and there was a total dependency on importation. Consequently, local advertisements for products weakened. In addition, the state stopped encouraging investors to advertise. Thus, the media lost a major source of income. This crisis was also reflected in the journalistic content: it was employed as propaganda for powerful entities in the government and those political parties that financed the media. This has also affected the media genres that are currently being invested in.

At this point, there is no print medium with effective and wide circulation that can continue to exist solely on its revenues. Yet, there are some papers that have continued to be published despite the economic crises and bad security conditions that have affected Iraq since 2003. The *Al-Sabah* newspaper, which is financed by the state and which is the leading newspaper in Iraq, publishes fewer than 6,000 copies. There are other papers that publish from 1000–4000 copies. As for radio stations, their broadcast range is limited to the major cities, and they are ineffective in reaching the wider Iraqi community. In addition, most of them are financed by political and religious parties and movements. However, there is a significant number of nearly 55 satellite television channels with wide circulation inside Iraq. Yet, each channel has its own segment of viewers because they follow specific political and religious parties and movements, and thus they promote specific perspectives through ethnic and confessional lenses. Since 2003, Internet service has become available to all citizens. Consequently, electronic sites have become widespread. Most traditional Iraqi media have their own websites on the Internet. Moreover, social media sites, such as *Facebook*, *YouTube*, *Instagram*, and *Twitter*, have become widespread.

Ownership of Iraqi media can be divided into three types: public, private, and partisan. The public type is in fact controlled by the Iraqi government because the IMN is financed by the Iraqi parliament, and the government indirectly mandates the written policy decisions of the media controlled by this network. Private and individually owned channels, such as the very popular *Al-Sharqiya*, which is owned by the pressman Sa'ad Al-Bazzaz, *Huna Baghdad*, which is owned by the businessman Fadhil Al-Dabbas, *Ur*, which is owned by the businessman Ma'mool Al-Samarra'i, and *Al-Sumariyya*, which is owned by a Lebanese businessman, as well as the *Al-Mashriq* newspaper, represent their owners.

Freedom given to their employees, therefore, is restricted by the policies and orientations of their editors-in-chief and owners. The third type, the partisan, is the most common in the Iraqi media. Here, parties or political individuals own the media institutions. Partisan media are omnipresent, and they are generously financed. Such media, however, are known for giving editorial directions to their employees and publishing propaganda for the party or entity that owns them. In Iraq, there are 204 registered parties and political entities, and many of them have their own media. Everyone working at such an outlet has to abide by the written policy specified by the president of their network, who represents either a party or a political entity. The employees work in line with the written policies derived from the political orientations of these parties.

There are nearly 15 satellite channels owned by Shi'ite parties and entities, whereas Sunni parties or influential individuals own nearly 11 channels. For example, influential members of Shi'ite parties, such as the Islamic Dawa Party, own satellite channels, including *Afaq*, which is owned by ex-prime minister Noori Al-Maliki, *Al-Masar* which is owned by Abdul-Kareem Al-Inizi, and *Al-Rasid* which is owned by ex-prime minister Haydar Al-Abadi. There are also the satellite television channels including *Al-Furat*, owned by the Hikma Movement, and *Al-Ghadeer*, *Biladi*, *Al-Na'eem*, *Al-Ahd*, *Al-Nujaba'*, *Al-Ittijah*, and *Asia*.

All these satellite television channels represent political orientations close to Shi'ite interest groups in Iraq. A distinction between these satellite channels can be made according to affiliation, ownership and financing, and according to their discourses that closely correspond to the discourses of the influential parties behind them (Al-Ruwashdi et al., 2010; Iraqi Media House, 2015). There are, moreover, the satellite television channels *Karbala*, owned by the Shi'ite Endowment, *Al-Salam*, owned by the Shi'ite religious man Husayn Al-Sadr, *Ahl Al-Bayt*, owned by Shi'ite religious authority Hadi Al-Mudarrisi, and *Al-Wala'*, owned by the Popular Mobilization Forces.

TV channels that reflect a Sunni partisan orientation in Iraq are, for example, the satellite television channels *Baghdad*, owned by the Islamic party, *Al-Fallooja*, owned by the businessman and politician Khamees Al-Khanjar, head of the Arab Project, *Dijla*, owned by the Al-Hal movement headed by Jamal Al-Karbooli, and *Al-Rasheed*, owned by the businessman and politician Sa'ad Asim Al-Janabi.

There are, moreover, satellite television channels, such as *Al-Hadath*, owned by the religious man Abdul-Lateef Al-Hmayyim, who also supervises *Diwan*, which is owned by the Sunni Endowment, and *Al-Rafidayn*, which is owned by the Muslim Scholars Commission that opposes the Iraqi government.

In the region of Kurdistan, the Kurds own some other channels which work separately from the local Iraqi media because of their preference for the Kurdish language which is used in this region, unlike in the other Iraqi governorates. They are, however, no different from the other Iraqi media with regards to the freedom they are permitted. Influential Kurdish parties in Kurdistan own these media, and they are the ones who decide on their content, which most often identifies with their political ideologies and orientations. There are Kurdish satellite television channels, such as *NRT*, owned by Shiswar Abdul-Wahid—head of the New Generation Movement in Kurdistan—, *Zagros*, owned by the Kurdish Democratic Party, *Ruwudaw*, owned by Masood Barazani, and *Al-Mishraq*, owned by the Feili Kurds.

Furthermore, there are many radio stations that belong to these satellite television channels, are promoted by them, and are owned by the same owners. As for newspapers, they are the least popular medium, although they follow the orientations of the institutions that own them.

For instance, *Al-Sabah* newspaper and *Al-Shabaka* magazine belong to the public IMN; *Al-Zaman* newspaper is owned by the Al-Zaman Institution, which also owns the *Al-Sharqiya* satellite television channel. There are also other newspapers that are owned by political and religious parties and movements.

Technology and Infrastructure

As for technology, Iraq is still lagging behind compared with international standards. This can be attributed to several factors, including wars, political conflicts, and economic crises. Iraq is also lagging behind in comparison to other Arab states regarding the use of technology in its public institutions. The technology used is basically limited to various routine procedures.

According to a study conducted by Akamai, which is an institution specializing in the Internet, Internet services in Iraq are poor and very expensive (NRT, 2019). Internet speed in Iraq is only 0.75 megabytes per second. Yet, the demand is high—there were more than 19 million Internet subscribers in 2019, which is half of the population. They mostly use social media sites to access information, news, and analysis. Iraq does not have a state company for communications to control cyberspace in the country, so it is a largely unregulated and free space. At the end of 2019, however, and responding to massive anti-government protests in Baghdad and the southern provinces, the government cut off Internet connections completely to prevent the demonstrators from communicating with each other.

At the same time, the state also does not invest in infrastructure. In Iraq, there are three mobile communication companies, *Zain*, *Asia Cell*, and *Korek Telecom*, all of which are private companies, some with stakeholders from abroad. Mobile phone penetration is quite high, with 95% of the population subscribing to mobile phones.

The semiofficial media, such as the IMN, which owns television channels, radio stations, and newspapers, are technologically developed because they are sufficiently financed by the state. Some of the other media, which are owned either by parties, religious and political individuals, or businessmen, have developed technology and modern programs, while others work with comparably more modest capabilities.

Some media, moreover, have modern studios and cameras with HD broadcasting, sites on social media, and digital applications on smart phones.

Traditional techniques are still used in Iraqi media. These include more basic technology and working methods. Press coverage still employs traditional methods with audio and digital camera videos, while 3D technology is not in use. Drones and cloud computing, which are usually used to cover events in dangerous or critical areas, are also not used.

In covering the news, satellite television channels use traditional audio and video techniques with digital cameras, film cameras, editing, and photography programs. Modern techniques of virtual studios in news broadcasting, however, are employed by only one channel in Iraq, namely *Al-Furat*, which is owned by the National Hikma Movement headed by Ammar Al-Hakeem.

Progress is slow in the use of modern technologies in the media. This is because they are expensive, especially the virtual studios and the use of artificial intelligence for editing and presenting. In most of these media, the financing resources are weak.

Challenges

In Iraq, the political conflict among the parties and political and religious blocs, which is covertly motivated by Shi'ite-Sunni and Arab-Kurdish conflicts to acquire power, represents the main obstacle to the progress and sustainability of the media. This conflict hinders the media's professionalism and neutrality in in enhancing democracy and the values of coexisting, diversity, cultural and religious pluralism. This is negatively reflected in the content of these media, most of which have started to support and follow specific political ideologies or serve individual political or religious interests so that they have become arenas for political accusations, political overthrow, and incitement during sectarian crises. Most of the political entities have adopted media owned or financed by themselves as propaganda to promote their ideologies at the expense of free journalism. Thus, journalists cannot deviate from the policy adopted by their own institution for fear of losing their jobs. In addition, in Iraq, the capital is monopolized by the political and religious parties, which restricts the wider development of the media.

Yet the most severe challenge that hinders freedom of the media in Iraq is the state of security conditions. There are terrorist groups and organizations, such as ISIS, which have succeeded in occupying three major Iraqi governorates. Due to the deterioration of security conditions after 2003, journalists were killed simply for being present in fighting areas. After 2017 and the liberation of the cities, journalists faced further challenges, namely harassment, arrest and physical attack by security forces and militias in Iraq. Some political entities have tried to restrict freedom of expression because journalists covered demonstrations and protests against bad services and pervasive corruption, for instance in Basra and some other Iraqi cities. Thus, there are not enough guarantees for journalists to work free from political pressures. The legislative and executive authorities are unable to protect journalists. The constitutional articles are not enough to protect freedom of expression, unless followed by executable legislation.

Outlook

With the ongoing conflicts in the Middle East, the propaganda and media wars that surround Iraq—whether those between the USA and Iran and between Israel and Arab states, or those in Yemen or Syria—keep the Iraqi media controlled by political powers that direct the Iraqi authorities. Consequently, the media remain politicized and not neutral. Many of their arguments do not reflect the Iraqi people's suffering. These media cannot progress until they are freed of the politicians' control, and until the media are allowed to serve the public. The media have to be neutral to play an active and effective role in uncovering corruption and establishing the concepts dedicated to freedom. The rights of journalists must be guaranteed by law, and these laws need to be implemented. The professional administration of these media should be encouraged. Access to information needs to be guaranteed. The IMN and its media institutions must be freed from government control in order to realistically serve the public. This can be achieved by encouraging advertising, and requiring those companies investing in Iraq to advertise in the Iraqi media. Moreover, the local media inside the cities need to be better supported in order to be viable media alternatives capable of representing these cities and local regions.

References

Al-Husseini, A. (2008). *Iraq, in the past and present.* [in Arabic]. Baghdad: Maktaba Tariq al-Ilm.

Ali, W. H. (2018). *Modernism and stability in the political Iraqi system after 2003* [in Arabic]. Berlin: Arab Democratic Centre for Strategic, Political and Economic Studies. https://democraticac.de/?p=51243

Al-Mashhadani, S. S. (2013). *History of Iraqi media in Iraq* [in Arabic]. Amman: Dar Osama

Al-Rawi, K. H. (1992). *History of radio and television in Iraq* [in Arabic]. Baghdad: Dar Al-Hikma for Printing and Publishing.

Al-Ruwashdi, A., Al-Mahmud, A., & Adnan, A. (2010). Religious Satellite Channels in Iraq [in Arabic] *Haq News.* http://www.al-aqidah.com/dimofinf/contents/moxiemanager/sheechannels_haqnews.netl29-1-2010.pdf

Al-Sarraj, I. (2017, 26 December). *A year's total of violations against journalists in Iraq* [in Arabic]. https://arabic.sputniknews.com/arab_world/201712261028758112-/

Bakr, M. (1969). *The Iraqi Press and Its Political, Social and Cultural Trends (1869–1921).* Baghdad, Al-Rashad Press.

Batti, F. (1961). *Iraqi Press: Birth and development* [in Arabic]. Baghdad: Dar Al-Bilad.

Batti, S. R. (1985). *Iraq's press* [in Arabic]. Baghdad: Dar Al-Kindi.

Fidh (2018). *Iraq. Sexual and gender-based crimes Committed against the Yazidi community: The role of foreign fighters in organizing ISIS* [in Arabic]. https://www.fidh.org/IMG/pdf/sexual_violence_against_yazidis.pdf

Independent High Electoral Commission of Iraq (2017). *Parties Approved by The Independent High Electoral Commission in Iraq Until 25/12/2017* [in Arabic]. http://www.ihec.iq/HOME/IconFiles/pageC9.aspx

Iraqi Media House (2015). Promoters of Hate. The fourteenth media monitoring report [in Arabic]. https://www.imh-org.com/fourteenth-report-promoters-of-hate

Iraqi Ministry of Planning (2018). *Iraq statistical summary for 2018: Central Statistical Organization* [in Arabic]. http://cosit.gov.iq/ar/?option=com_content&view=article&layout=edit&id=1220

Khalil, S. (2018, February 24). Kuwait Seizes Iraqi Lands with Premeditation [in Arabic]. *Rawabet Center for Research and Strategic Studies.* https://rawabetcenter.com/archives/62986

NRT (2019). *Reports: Iraq is the most expensive Internet provider among Arab countries* [in Arabic]. https://www.nrttv.com/AR/News.aspx?id=14067&MapID=2

Radhi, W. F. (2010). *Radio and television in Iraq* [in Arabic]. Baghdad: Dar An-Nahrayn.

Sadoon, G., & Tariq, I. (2019). *Defending freedom of press in Iraq society: Report on monitoring indicators on violations against Iraqi journalists* [in Arabic]. https://pfaa-iq.com/?cat=5

Salloom, S. (2017). *Protections of religious, ethnic and linguistic minorities in Iraq: An analytic study within the international, regional and national frames* [in Arabic]. Baghdad: Koofa University.

Transparency International (2018). *Index 2018*. https://www.transparency.org/cpi2018

6. Saudi Arabia: From National Media to Global Player

Marwan M. Kraidy

A combination of geopolitics, religion, and economics have shaped the media of Saudi Arabia. The country's media structure began as a national broadcasting system in the 1960s, alongside a well-established privately-owned Arabic-language press, and had by the 1990s evolved into a regional system of Arabic- and English-language outlets. This made Saudi Arabia the media superpower of the Middle East. The ascent of Crown Prince Mohammed bin Salman in the 2010s ushered in an era of direct control of both news and entertainment media. As a result, Saudi government influence over Arab media has grown more expansive and more direct. The desire to clamp down on dissent globally led to the disastrous killing of Jamal Khashoggi and the resulting global uproar has affected the stature of Saudi Arabia. Nonetheless, Saudi Arabia's media face multiple challenges, including the difficult-to-control, burgeoning digital media environment, and the tensions arising between the kingdom's political and economic priorities.

Background

Located in West Asia, the Kingdom of Saudi Arabia occupies most of the Arabian Peninsula. The modern kingdom was founded in 1932 by King Abdulaziz Al-Sa'ud, known as Ibn Sa'ud. Because Saudi Arabia is a large country bordering other smaller states, including Qatar, the United Arab Emirates, Bahrain, Oman, and Yemen, and located across waterways from several other states, its geography grants it dominance in neighborly relations. Since the Islamic Revolution in Iran in 1979, Saudi Arabia has been locked in a battle with Iran for geopolitical influence over the Middle East, in which ideology and religion play an important role, with Saudi Arabia being a conservative monarchy and the cradle of Sunni Islam, and Iran being a revolutionary republic and the center of gravity of Shi'a Islam.

If geography appears to predestine Saudi Arabia for regional influence, geology provides the decisive elements of economic and geopolitical power that extend far beyond Saudi Arabia's borders: hydrocarbons and other minerals. With arable land making up 1.5% of the territory, and irrigated land a mere 16,300 square kilometers, agriculture is a relatively small contributor to the Saudi economy. However, the Saudi land is rich in hydrocarbons and minerals, chiefly natural gas, petroleum, iron ore, and gold. The abundance of underground mineral wealth has, since the 1930s, made Saudi Arabia one of the leading economies of the world, and provided it with geopolitical tools that have made it a great power in the Middle East, and the broader Islamic world. Mineral wealth is also the bloodline for Saudi's national media sector and its regional and global extensions.

Religion is another source of Saudi transnational power. Long before the discovery of oil, gas, and minerals, another force shaped the rise of Saudi statehood, society, and culture: Islam. Saudi Arabia is the birthplace of Islam, the world's second largest religion, with nearly two billion adherents across the globe, and remains closely associated with the religion. Mecca and Medina, the two holy cities central to Islamic history and Muslim identity, are located in Saudi territory, and millions of Muslims visit every year to perform the *hajj*, or pilgrimage, that is one of the pillars of their religion. Not only is Islam closely associated with Saudi Arabia, it is also foundational to the rise of the modern Saudi state, based on a politico-clerical regime. Saudi Arabia is the only country in the world to be named after a single family, the Al-Sa'uds, who forged a historical power-sharing agreement with the Al-Shaykh family. According to this ruling *quid pro quo*, the Al-Sa'uds have full power over domestic politics, defense, and security, and foreign policy, whereas the Al-Shaykhs control religious and educational institutions.

A combination of geography and demographics poses a national cohesion problem for Saudi rulers. Because of Saudi Arabia's large area, the country has a low population density of 15 inhabitants per square kilometer (Trading Economics, 2019). The population retains strong local and tribal identities; thus, ever since Ibn Sa'ud decided to establish a wireless network in the 1920s, Saudi rulers have regarded national media, particularly television, as a crucial instrument for creating and sustaining feelings of national belonging. In this context, it is important to recall that Saudi Arabia hosts a large community of (mostly Asian) foreign workers who, by some estimates, fill two thirds of all jobs in the kingdom. Since 2017, authorities have imposed taxes and labor restrictions on foreign workers, cutting their number by 20% from 2017 to 2019 (AsiaNews, 2019). Moreover, the country is a desert kingdom with only a few major cities connected by thoroughfares. Most of the population is concentrated in the middle of the Arabian Peninsula, in and around the metropolitan areas of Dhammam to the east, the capital, Riyadh, in the center, and the Mecca-Medina area to the west.

Saudi Arabia's history, as well as its media, has been shaped by geography, geology, and religion—the desert, oil, and Islam. In such a large, tribally fractured, and sparsely inhabited country, where mass communication historically plays a vital role in maintaining national identity, Islam is the connective belief system—the software—and the media system is the hardware that keeps Saudi Arabia cohesive. "Cohesion" is a relative term in this context, because the Saudi ruling bargain monopolizes power in the hands of Sunni Muslims, making the sizeable Shi'a minority (estimated at 15% to 25% of a total population of approximately 34 million) into second-class citizens. In fact, the Saudi version of Islam, known as *wahhabiyya*, is puritanical and excludes Shi'a Muslims and others who do not follow stringent Sunni-Salafi tenets. As such, a strict version of Sunni Islam is at the heart of Saudi nationalism and cultural identity. When one considers that media technologies, by exposing societies to foreign ideas and images, tend to be harbingers of cultural shifts and social change, and that *wahhabiyya* insists on a pure Sunni Islam unadulterated by alien values, it is not surprising that Saudi media have since the beginning been a battleground between modernization and change, on the one hand, and doctrinal purity and social homogeneity, on the other. Moreover, the rise of Crown Prince

Mohammed bin Salman in 2017, and his firm grip on all aspects of Saudi life, suggests a new authoritarian consolidation of power with the Al-Sa'ud.

Historical Developments

The beginning of Saudi media can be traced to 1908, when Lebanese, Syrian, and Turkish journalists operated the country's first newspapers in the Western province of Hijaz, the site of Islam's holy cities of Mecca and Medina (Rugh, 1980). Newspapers were critical of political leaders in the first three decades of the twentieth century, but when Ibn Sa'ud founded the kingdom in 1932, the press came under the sway of the Al-Sa'ud ruling family and turned its focus away from politics and towards poetry and literature. Since that time, newspapers have reflected the importance of royally dictated public consensus. As Saudi Arabia experienced the first oil boom and ensuing modernization of the state in the 1950s, newspapers prospered and grew more outspoken again, especially in Jeddah, the commercial center, and the most socially liberal city in the kingdom. The government cracked down in the late 1950s, shutting down the most critical dailies and merging others (Kraidy, 2010).

The so-called "Faisal Era," named after Ibn Sa'ud's son Faisal who ruled as the Saudi monarch from 1964 to 1975, is a significant historical period in the development of Saudi media, and ironically, Faisal's assassination was at least partly inspired by his introduction of television to Saudi Arabia (Kraidy, 2009). The reason lies in its coupling of expansion with repression. In 1962, Saudi Arabia had no magazines and only three newspapers, with a combined distribution of 25,000 copies (Rugh, 1980). In the 1960s, after several journalists were banned from writing in the country, the press grew more quiescent. In the 1970s, according to the Ministry of Information, the "common goal" of the government and the press was to develop the country, so Saudi journalists were "called upon" to write in support of that objective (Rugh, 1980, p. 85). With rising literacy rates and a growing economy, by 1976, Saudi Arabia had seven Arabic-, and two English-language, dailies (Rugh, 1980).

The siege of the Grand Mosque in Mecca by radical militants in 1979 led the royal family to consolidate its grip on the media, and prompted further repression of the press in the 1980s. Official Saudi media did not announce the incident on the day it occurred, and the government jammed the signal of *Radio Monte Carlo Middle East*, then a widely followed news source in the kingdom (Boyd, 2001). Later, Saudi television carried a speech by Prince Nayef bin Abdulaziz, Minister of the Interior, and showed footage of rebels who had been taken prisoner. In July 1981, a royal decree announced a new Higher Media Council and put Saudi media and information policy under the control of the Minister of the Interior (Boyd, 2001). Today, the Saudi press consists of more than a dozen daily newspapers, mostly concentrated in the capital Riyadh, which is home to *Al-Riyadh*, *Al-Sharq*, and *Al-Jazeera*, and in the Red Sea city of Jeddah, which hosts *Okaz* and the two English-language dailies, *Arab News* and *Saudi Gazette*.

Wireless and radio communications emerged from the nation-building imperative. In the mid-1920s, as Ibn Sa'ud was consolidating his grip over what would become the Saudi kingdom, he considered wireless communication crucial for his ability to control his growing dominion, so he commissioned the construction of radio facilities. The country's archconservative clerics expressed fierce opposition to wireless technology, fearing it would subvert religion. To persuade them that wireless communication would actually propagate God's word, the king had Qur'anic verses read aloud and transmitted between Riyadh and Mecca in both directions (Boyd, 1999, p. 145). Ibn Sa'ud, who believed that media and communications were central to the modernization of the desert kingdom, would go on to cunningly negotiate with the clerics every time a new media technology came on the scene. Ibn Sa'ud introduced radio into Saudi Arabia in May 1949, and installed his son Faisal as supervisor of the new station (Boyd, 1999, pp. 145–46).

Saudi authorities first tested a national television broadcasting service on 17 July 1965. Before then, the two television stations operating in the country were not Saudi: One, *AJL-TV*, had been run by the US Air Force since 1955 (Boyd, 1999), and another had been operated by the Arabian American Oil Company (ARAMCO) since 1957 (Rugh, 1980). The state-run *Al-Saudiyya* (Saudi Channel One) was originally launched in 1963 as the flagship Arabic-language channel, and it switched from black-and-white to color in 1976. The English-language *Saudi Channel 2* went on the air in 1983 (Kraidy, 2013). By 1975, Saudi television reached 1.5 million viewers (out of a population of around seven million) (Kraidy, 2013).

In 1991, as the Gulf War roared on, viewers in Saudi Arabia who had access to hotels tuned in to *CNN*, while Saudi soldiers on the front were exposed to both Saddam Hussein's propaganda and Egyptian government messaging through the Egypt Satellite Channel (Kraidy, 2010). In response, Saudi rulers allowed close family members and business associates to launch *MBC* from London in 1991, inaugurating the Arab satellite "revolution" (Kraidy & Khalil, 2009).

The mid-2000s witnessed important developments in Saudi media, particularly television. Since the beginning of satellite television in the early 1990s and the demonstrated success of channels such as Qatar's *Al-Jazeera* in news and Lebanon's *Lebanese Broadcasting Corporation* in entertainment, a recurrent preoccupation of Saudi officials has been to reform Saudi television to win back Saudi viewers from non-Saudi broadcasters. This entailed a "modernization" drive for Saudi television, resulting in the 2003 launch of *Al-Arabiya*, a pan-Arab news channel owned by the MBC Group and based in Dubai, and the 2004 launch of *Al-Ekhbariyya*, a Saudi national round-the-clock news channel (Kraidy, 2013), in the wake of terrorist attacks in the kingdom. As in the 1980s, changes in television policy reflected the government's desire to be able to provide coverage at a time of crisis.

In 2018, spurred by Prince Mohammed bin Salman's focus on media and entertainment in his Vision 2030 strategic framework, Saudi Arabia launched a new channel, *SBC*, both the acronym and the name of one channel within the Saudi Broadcasting Corporation, which was designed to "lure young viewers and project a modern image beyond the kingdom's borders" (Sanjar & Harissi, 2018). Daoud Al-Sherian, a renowned Saudi columnist and talk show host on *Al-Arabiya*, was recruited to head the new channel. He made it clear that the channel's objective was to fulfill components of Vision 2030, most notably to "complement the changes seen in the kingdom in the artistic, cultural and entertainment spheres" (Sanjar & Harissi, 2018). *SBC* was developed as the entertainment flagship channel to be added to a religious channel, an educational channel, and the news channel *Al-Ekhbariyya*, all under the aegis of the Saudi Broadcasting Corporation.

Political System and Legal Framework

The foundations for the current regulatory framework for Saudi media were established by Faisal, who became the king in 1964, and expanded Saudi media and regulatory institutions. These included the Ministry of Information in 1962 (renamed as the Ministry of Culture and Information in 2003, and as the Ministry of Media in 2018), a new Press Code in 1964, and the Saudi News Agency in 1971. However, these official institutions have never been the only forces shaping media policy. When they feel sidestepped by the royal family, Saudi clerics feel empowered enough to make public statements about the television industry (Kraidy, 2009). Every year during Ramadan, the holy month and most important season for the media market, several Saudi clerics are vocally critical of television programs that do not adhere to their strict standards (Kraidy & Khalil, 2009).

As such, the Saudi religious establishment constitutes an influential media policy institution that counteracts the "liberal" tendencies of media owners, journalists, and intellectuals, resulting in culture wars between the two camps. In exchange for their political support after the siege of the Great Mosque, clerics were allowed to severely limit the role of women in Saudi media. Their voices clamored for censorship in the name of religious morality during culture wars about literature, reality television, music video, and, more recently, social media.

Even with a clerical establishment capable of influencing media policy on social issues, Saudi media follow directives from the Ministry of Media on all political issues. The Ministry "works in an active role by identifying and preserving the Saudi identity, spreading Islamic values in the Saudi citizen's life, expressing the achievements of Saudi Arabia... [and contributing] to raise... awareness" (Ministry of Media, 2019). The Minister of Media, like other cabinet members, is appointed by royal decree. Among the Ministry's tasks, as laid out on its website, is the assurance that the media are a "strategic tool" that enables the kingdom to "deal with media attacks from abroad" and to "generate national belonging" domestically (Ministry of Media, 2019).

Television outlets are run by the Saudi Broadcasting Authority, whose head reports to the Ministry of Media. Relevant laws and regulations include the Regulation for the Protection of the Rights of Authors, or copyright law, the Regulation for Press Institutions, or the press law, the Regulation of Publications and Publishing, and the masterplan Media Policy of the Kingdom of Saudi Arabia, in addition to various regulations concerning legal implementation.

Since Saudi media, particularly television, is intricately connected with the larger pan-Arab media system, Saudi Arabia has actively tried to influence the transnational Arab political and regulatory environment. This was clearest when in 2008 Saudi Arabia and Egypt advocated the so-called Arab Satellite Television Charter, prompted by televised attacks on Saudi leaders during the 2006 war between Israel and Hezbollah, mainly by the *Al-Manar TV* channel, and the rise of pro-Muslim Brotherhood channels, such as Hamas's *Al-Aqsa TV*, which made the Egyptian government feel threatened. On 12 February 2008, in an emergency meeting of Arab Information Ministers in Cairo, the charter was officially adopted. Covering news, talk shows, entertainment, and sports, the charter gave Arab governments instruments to penalize satellite channels for criticizing leaders, harming the "national reputation," and disseminating morally undesirable content (Kraidy & Khalil, 2009).

After a decade of more or less business as usual, the Saudi media sector was poised for radical change once Mohammed bin Salman was named Crown Prince and quickly set out to develop Saudi Vision 2030. In that ambitious plan to wean the Saudi economy off of fossil fuels, media and entertainment figured prominently, but as instruments for economic growth and social pacification, and not as platforms of free expression. Indeed, in October 2018, the Saudi journalist Jamal Khashoggi walked into the Saudi Consulate in Istanbul to take care of some paperwork, and there he was brutally murdered. What followed was one of the biggest global media events of 2018. The Saudi government first denied any knowledge of what had transpired, but then admitted that Khashoggi died by accident in a fist fight, after Turkish intelligence agents leaked information to the media that Saudi agents dispatched from Riyadh had killed Khashoggi inside the consulate. Finally, in September 2019, Prince Mohammed bin Salman took "full responsibility" for the death, because "it happened under my watch," on a US television news show (Maxouris,

2019). The Saudi government has an unfortunate history of tracking, kidnapping, or liquidating dissident journalists and exiled princes worldwide, but for the US political elite, killing a journalist working for a US newspaper of record such as *The Washington Post* crossed a red line. This shocking killing has had a chilling effect on Saudi journalists.

Economy and Ownership Patterns

A peculiar political economy rules Saudi media. As an absolute monarchy, Saudi Arabia's media hew closely to the editorial line set by the palace. The royal family's grip on the media has shifted over the decades, but under King Salman and his son Crown Prince Mohammed, political autocracy has hardened, and the country's media have become little more than platforms for Saudi domestic and foreign policy. Historically, royal princes have also been media owners, sometimes indirectly, by association with non-royal businessmen, but often through direct ownership of newspapers and television channels. As such, Saudi public discourse, including those media outlets that express the viewpoints of various princes, has generally reflected a consensual view of the royal family. This changed drastically with the elevation of Mohammed bin Salman to the position of Crown Prince and *de facto* ruler of Saudi Arabia. Under his leadership, Saudi politics has undergone a radical narrowing of the margins of discourse, and Saudi media ownership has become increasingly consolidated in the Crown Prince's hands.

After this consolidation, the Saudi state is now the dominant media owner in the country, and whatever media the royal family does not own, it controls—the Saudi royal family *is* the Saudi state. The Saudi government owns and operates all terrestrial and satellite television channels based on Saudi territory. The state-run Broadcasting Service of the Kingdom of Saudi Arabia (BSKSA) is in charge of all television activities, and private television channels are prohibited from satellite broadcasting from Saudi soil unless they are fully controlled by the government, or partially owned by royal princes. Though the media ownership patterns of Saudi companies operating on Saudi soil remain rigid, the ownership of transnational Saudi media, such as *MBC*, *Rotana*, and *ART*, typically based outside of Saudi territory, initially reflected a shift from government ownership to government-controlled private ownership.

Recent changes notwithstanding, private Saudi media ownership is a well-established phenomenon. In 1975, the Saudi brothers Hisham and Mohammed Ali Hafez launched the Arab world's first English-language daily, *Arab News*. The sons of a Jeddah publisher, the two brothers would go on to establish the Saudi Research and Marketing Company as one of the largest Arab media conglomerates (Loqman, 1997). In late 1975, the Lebanese Civil War forced the Lebanese publisher Kamel Muruwwah to shut down the respected Beirut-based English-language newspaper *Daily Star*, leaving in its wake a group of unemployed journalists and editors experienced in publishing an English-language daily in the Middle East. *Arab News* recruited the group led by Jihad Al-Khazen (Lebling, 2005), who edited *Arab News* before going on to lead the two major Saudi-owned, London-based pan-Arab papers, *Asharq Al-Awsat* and *Al-Hayat*.

As always, the creation of Saudi media initiatives and institutions was driven by geopolitical threats. The Saudis stepped into the transnational realm as a reaction to external threats, starting with the media war against Egypt in the 1960s, and developed a formidable transnational media capacity through various companies that it controlled or influenced. An effective media system was also needed internally because inhabitants of the Eastern Province were watching television from Kuwait, Iran, Qatar, and the UAE (Rugh, 1980). These two factors—economics and security, the latter including rhetorical and military conflicts—continue to this day to shape the Saudi involvement in the pan-Arab media system, and most likely drove Mohammed bin Salman's inclusion of media moguls in his 2017 "economic purge" of the Saudi elite.

On 5 November 2017, authorities arrested dozens of the kingdom's royal, political, and business elite. In a series of choreographed moves, security forces sequestered members of the elite for various charges of corruption. Among the detainees were media moguls Prince Al-Waleed bin Talal (*Rotana*), Saleh Kamel (*ART*), and Walid Al-Ibrahim (*MBC*), three men who have shaped Saudi media and the Arab satellite boom (Kraidy, 2015). This move by the Crown Prince, who is himself considered a media mogul since his family owns one of the largest Arab media conglomerates, Saudi Research and Marketing Company, thus increased his control. As a result, contemporary Saudi rulers are increasingly exerting direct media control, politically and economically, in news and entertainment. Entertainment is central to the Crown Prince's Vision 2030 strategic framework. In 2016, a royal decree created the new General Entertainment Authority, and in 2017, the Public Investment Fund of Saudi Arabia announced that USD 2.7 billion had been earmarked for entertainment media. By putting pressure on the media moguls mentioned above, the Crown Prince is gaining financial leverage over some of Saudi Arabia's richest men, thereby concentrating an astonishing amount of Arab media power in his own hands, and positioning himself to control a nascent entertainment sector that is poised to grow explosively in the near future.

Technology and Infrastructure

A comprehensive media and telecommunications infrastructure was essential to transform a tribally fractured and geographically dispersed population into a national community ruled by the House of Sa'ud. This became all the more important when inhabitants of the Eastern Province started receiving television signals from Kuwait and Iran, and later from Qatar and the United Arab Emirates (Rugh, 1980). During the Gulf War in the early 1990s, inroads made by *CNN* and, later in the decade, by *Al-Jazeera*, spurred continuous infrastructural developments in Saudi Arabia.

Founded in 1926 as the Post, Telegraphs and Telephones Directorate by King Abdulaziz, who was conscious of the centrality of post and telecommunications for state building, "and the necessity of using modern inventions in this sector to link the vast and remote areas of the kingdom with each other," the Saudi Ministry of Communications and Information Technology has undergone several makeovers and name changes, and currently focuses on "Empowering Digital Saudi" (Ministry of Communications and Information Technology, 2019b).

Much of the kingdom's current telecommunications infrastructure that hosts most Saudi digital activity took shape in the mid-2000s, particularly in 2006 and 2007. The year 2006 was a watershed for the Ministry of Communications and Information Technology: it (1) launched a national 3G mobile telephone service, (2) restructured national Internet service provision, moving it from King Abdulaziz City for Science and Technology and placing it under the authority of the Communications and Information Technology Commission, and (3) finalized the Anti-Cyber Crime Law, and got it approved. The following year, 2007, saw (1) the adoption of the First National Communications and Information Technology Plan, (2) the approval of a National Spectrum Plan, and (3) the establishment of the Universal Service Fund, dedicated to financing information infrastructure that connects remote rural areas to the kingdom's national grid (Ministry of Communications and Information Technology, 2019b). Since Crown Prince Mohammed bin Salman ascended to the effective leadership of the country, the Ministry has focused on "Empowering Digital Saudi," as its motto claims on its official website, by organizing events and workshops to develop Saudi citizens' digital skills and instructing all Saudi companies and public services to do the same, as stipulated in the Framework to Empower Digital Skills of Saudi Youth, released in October 2019 (Ministry of Communications and Information Technology, 2019a).

The Saudi political economy of mobile telephony is a state-private hybrid. The leading operator, *Saudi Telecommunications Corporation (STC)*, is 70% state-owned and 30% privately-owned, and the second-, third- and fourth-largest companies (respectively, *Mobily*, *Zain*, and *Bravo*) feature owners or majority shareholders who are close to the Saudi, Kuwaiti, or UAE government. Though they are generally considered as Gulf-based, rather than strictly national companies, they have had global holdings since at least 2013, when *STC* operated in Turkey and Indonesia in addition to Bahrain and Kuwait (Rasooldeen, 2013).

Contemporary Saudi Arabia has some of the highest connectivity and social media use rates in the world. According to the latest available report by the Saudi Communications and Information Technology Commission, fixed broadband service penetration is 33.6%, while mobile broadband penetration is 93.5%, and Internet services penetration is 82% (Communications and Information Technology Commission, 2017). However, if all modalities of connectivity are taken into account, mobile and Internet penetration approached 100% in 2018, according to the General Authority for Statistics (Mubasher, 2019). Saudi Arabia also has a high penetration of social media. As of October 2019, Saudi

Arabia had more than ten million *Twitter* users, roughly one-third of the population (Statista, 2019).

Saudi Arabia indirectly controls one of the most valuable media and information infrastructures in the Middle East: *ArabSat* and its network of satellites. The Arab Satellite Organization was founded in 1976 by the 21 member-states of the Arab League. Reflecting the outsize Saudi role in bankrolling *ArabSat*'s expensive infrastructure, the organization was headquartered in Riyadh, the Saudi capital (Kraidy & Khalil, 2009). One of the largest satellite operators in the world and the Arab world's leader in that domain, *ArabSat* owns and operates six satellites that carry more than 500 television channels, 200 radio channels, several pay-television networks and more than 95 high definition channels and services.

In the 2000s, in order to make Saudi television the first choice for the Saudi viewer, Saudi media officials initiated a reform of media policy directed at invigorating programming, upgrading infrastructure and facilities, and training personnel. In 2007, a systematic modernization of Saudi television, the first since its founding in the 1960s, was guided by a committee of experts at the Ministry of Culture and Information. Officials took advantage of the *hajj* to introduce several innovations, including live news reporting, more exciting graphics, and new logos (Al-Khulayfy, 2007; Hawari, 2008). On-air presenters were instructed to be more informal, and live shots from iconic sites in the kingdom were shown (Al-Khulayfy, 2007). Ten new programs were introduced, including the very first program on Saudi state television that integrated viewer participation (Kraidy, 2013). Reforms continued to be implemented in 2009, when the Ministry announced it would build production and transmission facilities in all regions of the country, move all television transmission to high definition, gradually introduce digital broadcasting for terrestrial television, and create a broadcasting archive (Al-Khulayfy, 2007). There was a defined goal to "establish local media that serve all the regions of the country" (Al-Hamady, 2009). Funds were disbursed to set up radio and television production infrastructure in every province of the country (Kraidy, 2013). Existing channels got a face-lift: the logos and technical capacities of *Saudi Channels 1* and *2*, and *Al-Ekhbariyya*, were upgraded.

Challenges

The Saudi media system faces several challenges. First, the development of Saudi media institutions has followed a clearly *reactive* historical pattern. The 1979 siege of the Great Mosque in Mecca by radical armed Islamists led to a consolidation of the royal family's grip on the press and widespread repression in the 1980s. *MBC* was allowed to begin pan-Arab satellite broadcasting from London in 1991 to provide a Saudi-controlled alternative to *CNN*'s coverage of the first Gulf War. *Al-Arabiya* went on air in 2003 as a direct competitor to *Al-Jazeera*, and was tasked with fending off the Qatari channel's attacks on Saudi Arabia in the wake of the 11 September 2001 attacks, and their global repercussions. *Al-Ekhbariyya* was launched in 2004 for the government to be able to control, or at least contribute to, the news narrative following terrorist attacks inside the kingdom. Thus, the current phase, where an increasingly large share of Saudi national and transnational media is coming under the personal control, directly or indirectly, of Crown Prince Mohammed bin Salman, is the culmination of a half-century trend of consolidation and repression.

Second, media consolidation with growing authoritarianism, coupled with a desire to grow the economy based on the growth of the digital and entertainment sectors will create politico-economic tensions that media institutions and workers will feel most acutely. This will most likely lead to ever more media concentration under the direct control of the royal family, and make media that is nominally privately-owned increasingly beholden to political power. It remains to be seen whether the Khashoggi scandal will lead to decreased harassment of Saudi journalists and dissidents in the long term, but in the short term, international reactions have not had a tangible, positive impact on the rulers' behavior.

Third, the advent of globally networked digital media will continue to pose a challenge to royal family control. The rise of global streaming platforms, such as *Netflix*, and the wide popularity of social media platforms, such as *Twitter*, in the kingdom will continue to challenge official Saudi narratives. The Saudi government has tremendous economic tools to stave off these challenges, and it could invest in these platforms so as to be able to influence their policies, but the negative turn that Saudi economic growth took in 2019 may ultimately limit their capacity to counter information they cannot control. Social media also have the potential to fuel culture wars between conservatives and liberals, and to increase political polarization in the kingdom.

Outlook

As a result of the dynamics discussed above, the prospects for qualitative progress in Saudi Arabian media are dim, and the likelihood that the autonomy of Saudi media institutions will increase is low for the short to medium term. The Saudi media, paralyzed by direct government control, are heading towards more of the same in the foreseeable future. In their struggle for a different political system, and whether pushing for a more liberal or a more Islamist government, dissidents are likely to take advantage of emerging digital platforms that can be accessed inside and outside of Saudi Arabia. Despite this, the rise of digitization has not shaken the foundations of the system, since it has never been an entirely market-based system to begin with, but rather a system with strong dependency on princes, and in recent years, princes close to Crown Prince Mohammed bin Salman.

The new policy has focused on expanding entertainment venues, from cinema theaters to concert halls. For a while this may placate youths and liberals, many of whom have thrown their lot in with the Crown Prince, whom they see as a potent counterweight to conservative forces. However, it is too early to conclude whether this model combining political authoritarianism, social freedom, and economic concentration will move the country towards developing a more inclusive polity. The situation that Saudi media outlets find themselves in appears to offer limited opportunities for change outside of the space created and controlled by the rulers.

References

Al-Hamady, Y. (2009, October 29). Saudi Arabia consolidates local media by launching satellite channels for the regions [in Arabic]. *Asharq Al-Awsat*.

Al-Khulayfy, A. (2007, December 30). Saudi television wears a new 'robe': after executing biggest modernization of channels since inception [in Arabic]. *Asharq Al-Awsat*.

AsiaNews (2019, September 20). *Nearly 2 million foreign workers flee Saudi Arabia*. http://www.asianews.it/news-en/Nearly-2-million-foreign-workers-flee-Saudi-Arabia-48056.html

Boyd, D. A. (1999). *Broadcasting in the Arab world: A survey of the electronic media in the Middle East* (2nd ed.). Ames: Iowa State University Press.

———. (2001). Saudi Arabia's international media strategy: Influence through multinational ownership. In K. Hafez (Ed.), *Mass media, politics and society in the Middle East* (pp. 43–60). Cresskill: Hampton Press.

Communications and Information Technology Commission (2017). *Annual Report 2017*. [in Arabic]. Riyadh, Saudi Arabia.

Hawari, W. (2008, January 11). At long last, Saudi TV gets a bold makeover. *Arab News*. https://www.arabnews.com/node/307607

Kraidy, M. M. (2009). Reality television, gender and authenticity in Saudi Arabia. *Journal of Communication*, 59(2), 345–66. https://doi.org/10.1111/j.1460-2466.2009.01419.x

———. (2010). *Reality television and Arab politics: Contention in public life*. Cambridge, New York: Cambridge University Press.

———. (2013). Television reform in Saudi Arabia: The challenges of transnationalization and digitization, 1991–2011. In T. Guaaybess (Ed.), *National broadcasting and state policy in Arab countries* (pp. 21–48). London: Palgrave Macmillan. https://doi.org/10.1057/9781137301932_3

———. (2015). Prince Al-Waleed Bin Talal, media mogul. In D. Della Ratta, N. Sakr, & J. Skovgaard-Petersen (Eds.), *Arab media moguls* (pp. 113–28). London, New York: I.B. Tauris.

Kraidy, M.M., & Khalil, J. (2009). *Arab Television Industries*. London: British Film Institute/Palgrave Macmillan.

Lebling, R. (2005, April 22). From Beirut to Jeddah: A desk editor reminisces. *Arab News*. https://www.arabnews.com/node/265757

Loqman, F. (1997). *Internationalizing the Arab press: Hisham and Muhammad 'Ali Hafez* [in Arabic]. Jeddah: Saudi Distribution Company.

Maxouris, C. (2019, September 30). Mohammed bin Salman denies personal involvement in Khashoggi killing in '60 Minutes' interview but says it was carried out by Saudi officials. *CNN*. https://www.cnn.com/2019/09/29/middleeast/crown-prince-mohammed-bin-salman-interview/index.html

Ministry of Communications and Information Technology (2019a, October 5). *MCIT releases framework to empower digital skills of Saudi youth*. https://www.mcit.gov.sa/en/media-center/news/183883

Ministry of Communications and Information Technology (2019b). https://www.mcit.gov.sa/en

Ministry of Media (2019). *About the Ministry.* https://www.media.gov.sa/en/about-ministry

Mubasher (2019, January 2). Mobile, Internet penetration nears 100% in 2018 in Saudi Arabia. *Zawya.* https://www.zawya.com/mena/en/business/story/Mobile_Internet_penetration_nears_100_in_2018_in_Saudi_Arabia-ZAWYA20190102050230/

Rasooldeen, M. D. (2013, March 18). Second STC CEO quits post in less than a year. *Arab News.* https://www.arabnews.com/news/445252

Rugh, W. A. (1980). Saudi mass media and society in the Faysal era. In W. A. Beling (Ed.), *King Faysal and the modernization of Saudi Arabia* (pp. 125–44). Boulder: Westview Press.

Sanjar, R., & Harissi, M. A. (2018, May 14). New Saudi TV station feeds into modernization drive. *The Jakarta Post.* https://www.thejakartapost.com/life/2018/05/14/new-saudi-tv-station-feeds-into-modernization-drive.html

Statista (2019). *Leading countries based on number of Twitter users as of April 2020.* https://www.statista.com/statistics/242606/number-of-active-twitter-users-in-selected-countries/

Trading Economics (2019). *Saudi Arabia.* https://tradingeconomics.com/saudi-arabia/population-density-people-per-sq-km-wb-data.html

7. United Arab Emirates: Media for Sustainable Development

Mohammad Ayish

Since the formation of the United Arab Emirates (UAE) in 1971, media have been key forces of socioeconomic development and nation building. During the almost 50 years of the UAE's post-independence history, the UAE media and communications sector has been entrusted by the state with supporting the nation's political orientations, promoting economic growth, fostering national identity, and strengthening international cooperation. But, while huge investments in this sector have indeed turned the UAE into a global media hub that boasts world-class infrastructure and human talent, an updated media regulation, the Emiratization of the communications sector, and a smooth transition into the digital mediascape remain major challenges to address.

Background

The UAE is a federation of seven emirates situated in Southwest Asia, bordered on the north and northwest by the Arabian Gulf and on the east by the Indian Ocean. The UAE Federation, comprising the Emirates of Abu Dhabi, Dubai, Sharjah, Ras Al-Khaimah, Umm Al-Quwwain, Fujairah, and Ajman, occupies an area of 83,000 square kilometers. Founded in 1971 by the late Sheikh Zayed bin Sultan Al-Nahyan and other Emirati leaders of the time, the UAE Federation replaced the old association of the Trucial States with Britain, which, for decades, had defined colonial geopolitics in that part of the world. By mid-2019, the

UAE population was estimated at 9.7 million inhabitants, and about 1.2 million of them were UAE nationals, while the remaining 7.5 million was composed of foreign expatriates from around 200 nationalities attracted to the country initially by the discovery of oil, and later by a booming diversified economy. While Arabic is the official language of the UAE, English is the number one international language spoken alongside other languages by the country's large expatriate communities. Islam is the official religion of the UAE, but members of other denominations, such as Christianity and Hinduism, are granted full freedom to practice their faiths. In 2016, the UAE established a Ministry of Tolerance, and 2019 was officially declared as the "Year of Tolerance" to emphasize the country's commitment to international and intercultural coexistence and diversity.

While the UAE hereditary monarchical system may be described as politically conservative, the country's socioeconomic and cultural policies, as defined by free market practices, the empowerment of women, world-class education, and inclusive international and intercultural engagements, have been hailed as highly progressive. The UAE political system, as defined by the country's constitution, guarantees all UAE citizens equal rights and opportunities, safety and security, and social justice. Article 45 of the constitution identifies five federal authorities: the Federal Supreme Council, the President and the Vice President of the UAE, the Cabinet, the Federal National Council, and the Federal Judiciary. The UAE Supreme Council, chaired by a UAE President and composed of rulers of six emirates, is the highest policymaking body while the Federal National Council (parliament) serves numerous oversight and legislative functions. In 2010, the UAE government launched UAE Vision 2021, which set the key themes for the country's social and economic development, calling for a shift to a diversified and knowledge-based economy. The UAE National Agenda, resulting from Vision 2021, incorporates a set of national indicators, including a cohesive society and preserved identity, competitive knowledge economy, world-class healthcare, first-rate education system, sustainable environment and infrastructure, a safe public, and fair judiciary (Vision 2021, 2019). At the local level, each emirate has its own functions and socioeconomic development agendas that are aligned with federal policies and strategies. Local policies and institutions cover areas such as socioeconomic development, media, culture, urban planning, industry, services, and education, while national defense and foreign relations are an exclusive concern of the federal government.

As the second largest economy in the Arab World (after Saudi Arabia), the UAE pursues a knowledge-based strategy that has won significant international recognition. In 2018, the International Monetary Fund (IMF) forecast the UAE's nominal gross domestic product (GDP) would grow 4.7% to AED 1.673 trillion (USD 455.8 billion) in 2019, which is close when compared with the actual GDP figure of AED 1.589 trillion (USD 429.45 billion) in that year (WAM, 2019). Though the UAE economy has traditionally been driven by oil and gas exports, the country's economic diversification strategy has effected significant shifts in the economy. The UAE per capita income was put at around USD 43,000 in 2018. In early 2017, 70% of the UAE's GDP was derived from non-oil sectors, such as extractive industries (29.50%), wholesale and retail trade (11.70%), financial and insurance activities (8.60%), and construction and building (8.40%) (UAE Government, 2018a).

Historical Developments

While some scholars trace the history of media in the UAE back to rudimentary publications in the late 1920s and mid-1930s, the real history of that sector began only in the post-Federation years (Tabour, 2000). The rise of the UAE in 1971 as a sovereign state marked a comprehensive process of socioeconomic development, driven by both the discovery of oil and the promise of a knowledge-based economy. The former Ministry of Information and Culture was established in 1971 to oversee information and communication activities in the country. In those formative years, the press, bolstered by expanding nationwide education and literacy strategies, was driven by a developmental approach to socioeconomic transitions. The launch of numerous Arabic-speaking publications across the country underscored the belief at the time in the power of the press to effectively communicate official views and positions on national development to growing local and expatriate populations. On 19 October 1970, *Al-Khaleej* newspaper was launched in Sharjah by brothers Taryam and Abdalla Omran. *Al-Khaleej*'s critical approach to British policies in the region at the time led to its closure in

1972, and it did not resume publication until 5 April 1980. On 22 April 1972, *Al-Ittihad* (formerly *Al-Ittihad Al-Dhibyanieh*) changed its format to a daily publication with the declared aim of promoting the principles and values of the emerging Federation (Nouwais, 1984). *Al-Bayan* daily newspaper was launched on 10 May 1980 as a Dubai government publication with a focus on economic and business news. English language newspapers that appeared in the UAE during the first three decades of the Federation included *Khaleej Times* (1978) and *Gulf News* (1979). The UAE national news agency, *WAM*, was launched in 1976 as the official voice for the UAE government, providing news services in several languages. Among other things, the first two decades of the UAE Federation also witnessed the institution of Federal Law (15) in 1980, commonly known as the Press and Publications Law, to regulate media functions across the country.

During the UAE's early years, broadcasting became an important facet of the emerging media landscape, with numerous radio and television stations carrying news and current affairs, entertainment, cultural and religious programs, and sports and talk shows on matters of interest to local communities in Arabic and in other languages. While some of those services were broadcasting to a pan-Arab audience on short-wave, most radio operations were using medium-wave and later FM transmissions to reach local audiences. Radio stations included specialized broadcasters, such as *Qur'an Radio*, *Folklore Radio*, and *Classical Music Radio*, in addition to Western-style radio stations drawing on live talk shows and music programs. The Abu Dhabi-based radio stations were operating as part of the former Ministry of Information and Culture, while other radio services were affiliated with local emirates' information departments. Television was first introduced to the UAE in August 1969 in black and white from Abu Dhabi. In 1972, Dubai had its first channel, followed some years later by the launch of *Channel 33*, a foreign program channel that, along with Abu Dhabi's *2nd Channel*, was transmitting to the large UAE expatriate community with English-language programming. In 1989, Sharjah launched its own channel with mostly cultural and religious programming (Boyd, 1999). In those years, some programs such as news, cultural shows, and entertainment, were locally produced, while the bulk of the content was imported from Arab countries such as Egypt and Jordan (Boyd, 1999).

The 1990s was a watershed decade for UAE media development, with the country's media landscape going through major transitions induced by the digital revolution and liberal-market policies. It was during the period of 1990–2020 that the UAE's media scene experienced major restructuring, new expansions, key regulatory changes, entrepreneurial media free zones, diverse players, and far more importantly, more advanced digital and networked technological infrastructures. In the early 1990s, the UAE joined other Arab states in embracing satellite television broadcasting, and by 2001, it had its first media free zones, in which different regulatory frameworks are enforced.

Political System and Legal Framework

When viewed through Rugh's (2004) Arab media typologies, the UAE media system seems to have features of the loyalist press model, in which communications operate in alignment with state orientations within broader national socioeconomic strategies. Indeed, media are meant to serve as a powerful voice of national identity and government orientation, but they are also seen as vehicles for education, entertainment, and cultural expression.

UAE-based media are subject to numerous legal and ethical regulatory frameworks, ranging from the 1980 Press and Publications Law to the 2018 Electronic Media Regulation, and from the Journalists Association's Code of Ethics to free zone policies and guidelines. Generally speaking, UAE media regulations seek to ensure media practices' alignment with the country's political, social, cultural, and economic strategies and agenda. Among other things, these regulations address potential abuses on a political level, such as disrespect for the state, national symbols, and the country's heritage and values, and incitement to sectarian violence and hatred, but also on an individual level, with regard to the invasion of privacy and intrusion on copyright. They also tackle potential violations entailing harm to the country's economy, children, women, and other social groups, especially those involving cyberbullying, extortion, and stalking. The common feature defining the regulations is a strong sense of social responsibility and a profound belief in media contributions to economic prosperity, social welfare, and cultural fulfillment by those making the rules. Generally speaking, UAE media regulations have been highly responsive to national, regional, and international political, social, economic, and cultural developments relating to society and the state. The 1980s Press and Publications Law (Federal Law No. 15) that applies to the conventional press and media forms has prompted calls for further updates and enhancement to reflect expansions and changing roles within the UAE communications scene. The law reflects the regulatory spirit of the second half of the twentieth century, when nations of the Global South were going through postcolonial phases of development that required cohesive media attitudes towards nation-building. It regulates printing and publishing activities in the UAE, applying only to traditional media, such as newspapers, magazines, book publishing, and film. It basically prescribes guidelines for materials prohibited from publication, and penalties imposed on individual and institutional violators. Federal Law No. 7 of 2002 on Copyrights and Related Rights protects all original works in the areas of literature, arts, or science, regardless of their description, form of expression, significance, or purpose. Federal Law No. 5 of 2012 on Combatting Cybercrimes, and its amendment by Federal Law No. 12 of 2016, address online communications issues relating to national security, privacy, public morality, financial communications, and others (Gibbs, 2019).

Secondary media regulations in the UAE cover a variety of functions related to advertising and electronic communications. In 2018, the UAE National Media Council began to implement a new regulation for all electronic and digital media activities on the mainland and in free zones. Electronic media activities addressed by the system include sites used to trade, present, and sell print, video, and audio materials, electronic publishing activities and on-call printing, and specialized websites such as the electronic advertisements, news sites, and any electronic activity that the council deems appropriate to be included in that category (National Media Council, 2018). One of the controversial aspects of the new rules relates to licensing social media influencers who make profit out of online branding and marketing activities. The National Media Council Chairman's Decision No. 20 of 2010 concerning media content standards is another secondary piece of regulation that emphasized content compliance with articles of the 1980 Press and Publications Law in both conventional and digital contexts. An updated regulation, in the form of an official advertising guide, was introduced by the National

Media Council in October 2018 to clarify standards for the advertising industry in the UAE and to protect the public from marketing promotions that do not conform to applicable standards. The document specifies the terms of licensing for advertising activities by individuals, companies, and institutions.

Media free zones across the UAE have been subject to special regulations. Dubai Technology and Free Zone Authority (DTFZA) does licensing and content regulation for hundreds of media and communications services based in Dubai Media City. Issued in 2001, DTFZA regulations cover a range of areas relating to registration, shares, management, and administration. The Abu Dhabi-based twofour54 Media Zone Authority Content Code sets out the editorial standards which must be maintained by entities established in the Abu Dhabi media free zone (twofour54) in the areas of publishing, broadcasting, and/or communication with the public. The Content Code requires compliance with generally accepted standards regarding the social, cultural, moral, and religious values that apply in the UAE. It prohibits the transmission of offensive content, including sexually explicit and violent content, unless it is generally appropriate due to its artistic or creative merit, beneficial to society, and factually accurate. The Dubai Internet & Media Free Zone (TECOM) Codes of Guidance require publishers and broadcasters to be mindful of and to take into account the prevailing social and religious customs of the UAE and the Middle East, and the Islamic religion generally. Examples of violations would include ridiculing religious practices and conventions, and promoting sectarian divisions in society.

Media in the UAE are also expected to comply with ethical standards established by the UAE Journalists Association (UAEJA), an independent professional body for UAE-based journalists and media practitioners whose members in April 2019 came to include digital media professionals with a minimum of one year of experience. The UAEJA is classified as a non-profit organization whose finances derive from membership fees, state subsidies, public donations, and other sources. UAEJA's code of ethics calls for respect of the truth and the right of the public to have access to true and accurate information. It also promotes values of journalistic freedom and professional integrity in news work. According to the UAEJA's code, a journalist is expected to serve as a voice of "fair and neutral comments and criticism" (UAE Journalists Association, 2018). It also emphasizes accuracy in news reporting and editing, while maintaining fairness and objectivity towards all sides involved. A key value stressed by the code is privacy, where Article (8) states that:

> "Respecting privacy is a main principle in the profession, and journalists should respect the privacy of individuals and not expose it by publishing anything without the consent of those individuals. If personal conduct clashes with public interest, such conduct may be covered without violating the personal rights of uninvolved individuals" (UAE Journalists Association, 2018).

While there are no cases of journalists being sanctioned by the UAEJA, the Association's General Assembly may look into complaints from members regarding possible ethical or professional violations.

UAE media development has been supported by key professional and institutional structures to sustain a steady professional and commercial growth of media industries. An example is Dubai Press Club, whose mission includes promoting dialogue and exchange between Arab and international media, recognizing excellence in journalism, developing the skills and capabilities of journalists, and providing in-depth analysis of trends and developments in Arab media. Dubai Press Club publishes the *Arab Media Outlook* report and organizes the Arab Media Forum which annually brings together leading Arab and international media leaders to discuss important issues of concern to media practitioners and institutions. Dubai Press Club also oversees the Arab Journalism Award, designed to motivate creativity in journalism in the region across different genres. The Sharjah Press Club, launched in 2016, seeks to enhance journalists' skills and promote national and international networking among media professionals. The Sharjah International Government Communication Center offers a government communication award and organizes the International Government Communication Forum. The UAE media ecosystem also includes a wide range of university media education programs that offer degrees in journalism, advertising, public relations, digital marketing communications, media studies, multimedia, and new media and broadcasting.

Economy and Ownership Patterns

In the UAE, media also serve as key pillars of the country's progress towards a sustainable knowledge economy through enhancing content creation in conventional and digital formats and supporting public engagement in the knowledge sector. While national state media function as government communication outlets, private media (both on-shore and off-shore) operate according to commercial standards. Hundreds of media companies, digital start-ups, advertising and PR agencies, digital marketing firms, and publishing companies employ thousands of people in the different areas of communications at five media free zones across the country.

The UAE adopts a free-market economy with credible state welfare components. This feature has been reflected in the country's national communications system, where state-sponsored/subsidized media operate alongside profit-making ones. At the local level, media organizations, such as the Abu Dhabi Media Company, Dubai Media Incorporated, and Sharjah Media Corporation, function as local government-subsidized operations that also receive revenue through commercial sources such as advertising, subscriptions and sponsorships. Unlike traditional state-supported media organizations that offer protocol-oriented content and rigid formats across the MENA region, UAE state-subsidized media harness the latest technologies and provide audiences with high-quality content in news, public affairs, and entertainment. Whether originating from local production or from Arab or international television imports, broadcast content in the UAE, such as documentaries, reality TV, drama, and talk shows, maintain high standards in production. Many of these television shows are broadcast with commercials for local and multinational companies catering to a regional MENA market. Some of the channels such as *Dubai TV* use artificial intelligence in their operations relating to augmented reality, news verification, and communication with audiences.

By mid-2019, the UAE's on-shore media outlets included 23 television channels, 30 radio stations, 15 newspapers, five magazines and nine website portals. On-shore media services, such as the *Al-Khaleej* newspaper, Al-Sayegh Media, Dubai Media Incorporated, Abu Dhabi Media Company, Sharjah Media Corporation, and *Ajman Radio Four*, reflect mixed patterns of ownership that include government-owned media, state-subsidized media, and private media. On the off-shore side of the media landscape, five media free zones host hundreds of international television channels, newspapers, radio stations, online news portals, PR agencies, advertising firms, film production houses, publishing houses, and digital communications companies with full private ownership zones: Dubai Media City, Dubai Studio City, Abu Dhabi twofour54, Sharjah Media City (SHAMS), and Fujairah Creative City. By June 2019, there were about 1,500 companies with over 25,000 workers of 142 nationalities operating from Dubai Media City, which was launched in January 2001. twofour54 aims to cultivate Abu Dhabi's media free zone and provide products and services to attract local, regional, and international media businesses to Abu Dhabi. SHAMS, Sharjah's media free zone, was launched in 2017 to attract small to medium enterprises (SMEs), entrepreneurs, and companies to start and grow their businesses in a creative Free Zone Hub in Sharjah. International media organizations such as *CNN International*, *Bloomberg*, *Reuters*, *Middle East Broadcasting Center Network*, *Sky News Arabia*, *Al-Arabiya TV*, and many others carry out their operations from UAE media free zones, attracted by its unique business opportunities. Dubai Media City, for example, offers media investors 100% foreign ownership, full repatriation of profits and capital, no personal, income, or corporate taxes (50-year exemption), exemption from customs duties for goods and services, world-class infrastructure to help support the growth of the cluster, and a 24-hour visa service.

Media convergence, which is defined as the blending of multiple media forms into one platform for the purpose of delivering a dynamic experience (Dwyer, 2010), is one common feature shared by UAE's on-shore and off-shore media. Ayish (2003) noted that the UAE was one of the earliest countries in the MENA region to apply convergence standards to its national media system. Operating with substantive state subsidies and advertising revenue, both Abu Dhabi Media and Dubai Media Incorporated stand out as examples of technological convergence, where media organizations serve as umbrellas for multiple communications functions and channels, generating wide-ranging content. Under Abu Dhabi Media there are four major publications: the *Al-Ittihad* newspaper, *Zahrat Al-Khaleej* magazine, *Majid* children's magazine, and *National Geographic Al-Arabiya* magazine. Television channels include *Al-Emarat TV, Abu Dhabi TV, Abu Dhabi Sports 1, Abu Dhabi Sports 2, Yas, Majid TV, National Geographic Abu Dhabi,* and *Abu Dhabi Drama*. Radio stations include *Qur'an Kareem, Emarat FM, Abu Dhabi FM, Star FM, Abu Dhabi Classic FM, Radio Mirchi, Radio 1,* and *Radio 2*. Digital media platforms include *Ana Zahra, Zayed Digital TV,* and *Mohtawa*. In addition, Dubai Media Incorporated is an umbrella organization housing a range of publications, radio stations, television channels, and digital services, which includes five television channels, two newspapers, five radio stations, two online outlets, and two printing and distribution services. In 2019, Dubai was declared the media capital of the Arab World in recognition of its role as a regional and global media center. The Sharjah Media Corporation also houses four television channels, four radio stations, and one online news service. UAE-based media free zones also apply convergence practices as they operate in highly advanced networked and digital communications infrastructures.

Though the global financial crisis seemed to have cast shadows on commercial profits in the private media sector, communications companies, beefed up by a notable rise in entrepreneurial start-ups, have continued to provide communication services to corporate and government clients. Data from 2016 show that television ad expenditure in the UAE was estimated at USD 14 million, but was expected to experience some decline in the following years. Television has the highest weekly reach in the UAE across all ages. Among millennials, the second most frequently-used medium is the Internet, and for consumers aged 35 or older, it is the radio (Statista, 2016). *Emirates 24/7* reported that the UAE topped Gulf Cooperation Council (GCC) countries in terms of advertising in the first quarter of 2017, with the equivalent of around USD 400,000, accounting for 44% of total GCC advertising spending. The UAE is followed in second place by Saudi Arabia with USD 220 million, then by Kuwait with 191 million, Qatar with 70 million, the Sultanate of Oman with 35 million, and Bahrain with 29 million, respectively (Emirates 24/7, 2017).

Technology and Infrastructure

Media and communications in the UAE have evolved within the country's vision of technology as a key agent of positive social change. The UAE is one of only a few countries in the region with declared sustainable technology adoption and development strategies pertaining to space, artificial intelligence, and the fourth industrial revolution (4IR). The UAE was globally ranked second in 2018 on the Telecommunications Infrastructure Index and eighth on the UN E-Government Development Index Report (Federal Competitiveness and Statistics Authority, 2019). In the country's duopolistic Internet and telephony market, the two telecom companies, *Etisalat* and *du*, provide a range of data, telephony, and cable television services to individuals and businesses. The International Telecommunication Union's (2018) statistics show that the UAE experienced exponential growth in mobile subscriptions, from 1.4 million in 2000 and 11 million in 2010 to 20 million in 2018. Internet subscription also experienced similar leaps, from 24% in 2000 and 68% in 2010 to 95% in 2017. In 2017, the UAE government launched the UAE Strategy for the Fourth Industrial Revolution to strengthen the nation's position as a global industrial hub, and to increase its contribution to the national economy by means of advancing innovation and future technologies. The UAE Strategy for the Fourth Industrial Revolution focuses on a number of key fields, embracing innovative education, adoption of intelligent and personal genomic medicine and robotic healthcare, and research in nanotechnology. The 4IR strategy also aims to achieve future security of water and food supplies by using bioengineering sciences and advanced renewable energy technologies, to enhance economic security by adopting digital economy and blockchain technologies in financial transactions and service, to optimize the utilization of satellite data in planning future cities, and to establish advanced defense industries by developing national capacities in the field of robotics and autonomous vehicle technologies (UAE Government, 2018b). In addition, the UAE has been the only country to establish a Ministry of State for Artificial Intelligence, which has evolved into the Artificial Intelligence Strategy 2031 "to enable the country to become a fast adopter of emerging AI technologies across government, as well as to attract top AI talent to experiment with new technologies and work in a sophisticated, secure ecosystem to solve complex problems" (UAE Government, 2019).

Although the UAE media's relationships with the public continue to be under-investigated, a survey commissioned by the National Media Council (Al Bayan, 2017) on public trust of media outlets showed that mobile phones accounted for 97% of respondents' information sources, while traditional television accounted for 83%, newspapers 14%, home Internet service 76%, car radio 63%, and subscription television 27%. The results also showed that 42% of respondents use social media and the Internet to obtain information. While respondents' trust in newspaper coverage of local, national, and international events ranged from 12% to 26%, the range for television was from 29% to 43%, and for social media, it ranged from 25% to 51%. *Facebook* and *Twitter* stood out as the main sources of information for respondents on local events and issues, according to the survey. The public trust index developed by the study generated a score of 63% for reliance on local media, 86.3% for confidence in the most recently followed type of media, 93.4% for professional and ethical evaluation of practitioners, 78.7% for opinion and news analyses, and 69.6% for specialized media coverage. The overall trust index was 80.4% for all categories. A MENA media use study by Northwestern University in Qatar (2018) noted heavy UAE user engagement with new media to access news, play video games, and listen to podcasts, especially via mobile devices.

Challenges

It is clear that the UAE media present a unique case of a technological ecosystem marked by a strong sense of social responsibility, amicable state relations, significant technological innovation, mixed state-subsidized and commercial sustenance, and profound intercultural engagement. As elsewhere, the UAE media have challenges to address and opportunities on which to capitalize. The UAE public trust in media study (Al Bayan, 2017) identified UAE media challenges as including, among other things, incompetent practitioners, insufficient focus on regional issues, news credibility and transparency, an absence of Emirati media personalities, and a lack of discussion about issues relating to Emirati youth. The representation of UAE nationals in the communications workforce has also been a controversial issue on the country's media development agenda. It is widely believed that, in order for UAE media to truly reflect UAE national identity and cultural heritage, a credible component of professional Emirati communicators is critically needed. Though there have been some National Media Council initiatives to integrate more Emiratis into the media market, more has yet to be done in this area. Factors impeding UAE nationals' integration into the media sector have ranged from lacking material incentives to competition from a burgeoning government communication sector that has lured a huge number of local talents with attractive employment packages. Over the years, the UAE has seen the rise of prominent media leaders and journalists, including Ibrahim Al-Abed (co-founder of the UAE News Agency), Abdul Hamid Ahmad (*Gulf News* Editor-in-Chief), Mohammed Al-Hammadi (Chair of the Journalists' Association), the late Habib El-Sayyegh, former Chair of the Arab Writers Union, and Aysha Sultan (columnist), who have all served as successful role models in their professional communities.

Another challenge faced by the UAE media sector is related to the outdated Federal Law (15) of 1980 that was enacted at a time when print media dominated the national communications landscape. The growing irrelevance of the law in respect to the emerging UAE digital and networked communications transitions has attracted much attention at official and media levels, with more voices calling for updates to the legislation to reflect the changing face of UAE media in the early part of the twenty-first century. At the Fifth Emirati Media Forum, held in May 2019, participants echoed the need to update the legislation by adding new provisions that reflect the huge transitions experienced by UAE media over the past four decades (El Emarat Al Yawm, 2019). The current law addresses media as print publications (newspapers and books), while visual media are addressed as film with a focus on ownership, imports, printing presses, distribution, and banned content. It is true that the UAE has initiated cybercrime laws (2012) and an electronic media regulation (2018) to address potential abuses online. But the emerging features of the country's journalism, as marked by mobile and online engagement, dictate the development of a new legislation that fully accounts for those transitions. It is widely believed that draft changes to Federal Law

(15) are awaiting the right political, national, and regional moments to be officially endorsed.

A third challenge facing UAE media is the declining finances of conventional media operations, as induced by global financial crises and regional conflicts. As the UAE online and networked communications experience greater expansions in technological sophistication, audience consumption, and global reach, conventional media stay on the losing end of the proposition. State subsidies are clearly keeping government print and broadcast media afloat, but the threat to the physical structures, distribution methods, and consumption patterns remains highly existential. To deal with this challenge, all UAE newspapers and broadcast outlets have launched their own online versions with a wide range of multimedia features that reflect the unique nature of virtual communications. Websites for television services post previously-broadcast shows online with full user access. Live audio and video streaming services have become standard features of the emerging online landscape. Newspaper websites show increasing levels of audience engagement as evident in social analytics relating to users' views, likes, sharing, and comments. All UAE media have also harnessed social media platforms to expand their reach and enhance engagement with Arab and global audiences. The online migration trend has been generally represented by the rise of fully dedicated online news services catering to local and regional audiences, such as *UAE-24*, *alain_4u*, *Sharjah-24*, *Mohtawa*, and *Dubai Post*.

Outlook

Media in the UAE have much to gain from the country's economic development, cultural diversity, and technological innovations. A robust economy would certainly provide sustainability for media industries, while demographic diversity would enhance cultural pluralism in the country's public sphere. In addition, further technological innovation would help media keep a strong competitive edge and foster engagement with local and international audiences, while quality media education would provide the media industry with young talent highly conscious of digital market dynamics. However, for UAE media to maintain their function as voices of national identity and tools for information, education, and marketing, much has to be done with respect to the regulatory environment. The clear duality in the country's political conservatism and its progressive social and cultural policies needs to be addressed through incremental media transitions into more open and participatory governance options. The UAE media have been at the forefront of advocating womens' empowerment, human tolerance, and cultural diversity, but have taken a backstage position on critical conversations in the public sphere. New legal frameworks that enable media to accommodate greater political diversity and genuine engagement are indispensable for creating and sustaining economic, cultural, and technological momentum. As the UAE announced its preparations for the next 50 years, the development of the media sector, as informed by increasing regional competition and domestic indigenous representation in the public sphere, has been placed high on the nation's agenda.

References

Al Bayan (2017). National Media Council Reveals Study on Media Credibility [in Arabic]. Dec. 10. https://www.albayan.ae/across-the-uae/news-and-reports/2017-12-10-1.3126797

Ayish, M. (2003). Media convergence in the United Arab Emirates: A survey of evolving patterns. *Convergence*, 9(3), 77–87. https://doi.org/10.1177/135485650300900306

Boyd, D. (1999). *Broadcasting in the Arab world: A survey of the electronic media in the Middle East*. Ames: Iowa State University Press.

Dwyer, T. (2010). *Media Convergence*. Berkshire: Open University Press.

El Emarat Al Yawm (2019, May 27). *Al Jaber: National media are genuine partners in sustainable development* [in Arabic]. https://www.emaratalyoum.com/local-section/other/2019-05-27-1.1217652

Emirates 24/7 (2017, April 14). *UAE tops advertising spending in Gulf region*. https://www.emirates247.com/business/uae-tops-advertising-spending-in-gulf-region-2017-04-14-1.651315

Gibbs, J. (2019). Business news in a Loyalist Press environment. *Journalism*, (October), https://doi.org/10.1177/1464884919878352

International Telecommunication Union (2018). *Global and regional ICT data*. https://www.itu.int/en/ITU-D/Statistics/Pages/stat/default.aspx

National Media Council (2018). *Electronic media regulation.* http://nmc.gov.ae/en-us/NMC/Documents/Electronic%20Media%20Regulation.pdf

Northwestern University-Qatar (2018). *Media use in the Middle East.* http://www.mideastmedia.org/survey/2018/

Nouwais, A. (1984). *Mass media in the United Arab Emirates* [in Arabic] Abu Dhabi: Sahwa Publishing and Distribution Company.

Rugh, W. A. (2004). *Arab mass media: Newspapers, radio, and television in Arab politics.* Westport: Praeger.

Statista (2016). *Advertising expenditure in the United Arab Emirates from 2004 to 2018, by medium.* https://www.statista.com/statistics/386530/advertising-expenditures-by-medium-uae/

Tabour, A. (2000). *The development of media organizations in the UAE and its effects on cultural development* [in Arabic]. Abu Dhabi: Cultural Foundation.

UAE Government. (2018a). *Economy.* https://u.ae/en/about-the-uae/economy

———. (2018b). *The UAE strategy for the fourth industrial revolution.* https://u.ae/en/about-the-uae/strategies-initiatives-and-awards/federal-governments-strategies-and-plans/the-uae-strategy-for-the-fourth-industrial-revolution

———. (2019). *UAE Artificial Intelligence strategy.* https://ai.gov.ae/about-us/

UAE Journalists Association (2018). *Code of Ethics* [in Arabic]. https://uaeja.org/ar/pages/30/ميثاق-الشرف-الصحفي

Vision 2021 (2019). *National agenda.* https://www.vision2021.ae/en/national-agenda-2021

WAM (2019, April 17). *IMF forecasts UAE's nominal GDP to grow 4.7 percent to AED1.673 trillion in 2019.* http://wam.ae/en/details/1395302756253

8. Qatar: A Small Country with a Global Outlook[1]

Ehab Galal

The State of Qatar is a new, small, and extremely rich country, ruled by the Al-Thani family and with a population of which a majority are non-Qatari nationals. It is also a country mostly known for the satellite channel *Al-Jazeera*. This cocktail of small size, royal rule, and money is crucial for understanding the media landscape in Qatar, which in basic terms must be divided between the national media and the global satellite consortium of *Al-Jazeera*. Despite their different audiences, both media types are used and managed to consolidate and strengthen the rule and influence of Qatar and the Al-Thani family.

Background

Qatar is a peninsula of 11,500 square kilometers, located on the east coast of the Arabian Peninsula. Surrounded by the Arabian Gulf to the north, east, and west, the coastline makes up most of the country's borders in addition to its southern border with Saudi Arabia. The country has been an independent state since 1971, when Great Britain renounced the protectorate of Qatar that had existed since the First World War. Previously, the country had been part of the Ottoman Empire for about 400 years. However, the local power has been in the hands of the

---

[1] The research for this article formed part of the research project *Mediatized Diaspora (MEDIASP)—Contentious Politics among Arab Media Users in Europe*, which is financed by the Independent Research Fund Denmark (funding ID: 8018–00038B).

Al-Thani family since the mid-1800s, and when Great Britain decided to withdraw, negotiating with several Gulf countries, Qatar—together with Bahrain—insisted on independence instead of becoming part of a union of smaller Gulf emirates. Thus, while the UAE became the union of seven emirates, Great Britain handed over the sovereign power to the Al-Thani family in 1971 to form the independent state of Qatar. Sheikh Tamim bin Hamad Al-Thani has been the Emir of Qatar since 2013 after he replaced his father, Sheikh Hamad bin Khalifa Al-Thani, who ruled from 1995 until his abdication.

As in other Gulf countries, the majority of inhabitants are non-nationals. Out of a population of 2.8 million people in Qatar, only about 12% are Qatari. While the total number of people fluctuates because of seasonal work, the fact that the number of men is almost three times the number of women further reflects the country's large foreign labor force, which is employed by the oil and gas, construction, and related industries. The majority of labor immigrants are from Southeast Asia with smaller numbers from Arab countries, mainly Palestine, Syria, Lebanon, and Egypt. The official language is Arabic, but due to its oil and gas industry, its huge non-Qatari and non-Arab population, and the country's attempt to play a role in the international scene, English is a widely used second language.

Islam is the official religion of Qatar, and the national law is based on secular principles as well as Shar'ia law. Because of the high number of immigrants, other religions also exist. Statistics from 2010 estimate that 67.7% of the population are Muslims, 13.8% are Christians, 13.8% are Hindus, and 3.1% are Buddhists, whereas the rest belong to other religions or are unaffiliated (Pew Research Center, 2012). Most Qataris are Sunni Muslims who follow the Wahhabism tradition, while from 5% to 15% are Shi'a Muslims. Qatar allows non-Muslims to worship in specially designated locations, but they are not allowed to proselytize. Public worship is restricted, and religious groups have to formally register.

Once a poor British protectorate with its main income coming from pearling, Qatar became an affluent state with oil and natural gas resources after gaining independence. Although the oil production took off in the 1950s, and the high oil prices in the 1970s changed Qatar's economy significantly, it was the natural gas that, according to the latest Human Development Index figures by UNDP, placed Qatar as the richest country in the world measured by gross national income per capita in 2018. Today, Qatar is the largest exporter of natural gas accounting for a third of the world trade. Due to its wealth, there is no income tax, and the state heavily supports Qatari nationals financially.

When leaving its protectorates in the Gulf, Great Britain also left border conflicts to be resolved by the countries themselves. For Qatar, there were two conflicts to solve: one with Saudi Arabia about the Khafo area and one with Bahrain about the Zabaarah area. While the latter was resolved in 2001, Saudi Arabia has repeatedly claimed its right to the Khafo area. This border conflict has recurred as soon as other conflicts in the area have broken out, and in 1992, the two countries also went through a short-term armed conflict. In this continuous conflict with Saudi Arabia, Qatar realized it was falling behind when it came to media coverage. The Saudis had strong media that were available outside Saudi Arabia, while media in Qatar were weak. It was on this premise that Sheikh Hamad bin Khalifa Al-Thani founded the satellite television channel *Al-Jazeera* in 1996. However, he also initiated and facilitated international involvement including more active participation in the Gulf Cooperation Council (**Al-**Hawik, 2013). Both *Al-Jazeera* and Qatar's international involvement would later cause new conflicts.

Historical Developments

The media development in Qatar can be divided into three periods. In the first period, which extended from 1961 to 1995, the media were a tool for nation-building, while the second period from 1995 to 2011 was characterized by liberalization. Starting in 2011, the third period expanded Qatar's use of and investments in media as part of its soft power policy, which referred to a country's reliance on "resources of culture, values, and policies" (Nye, 2008, p. 94).

Operating in a young nation, the media in the first period came to serve as a channel for communicating national and political imaginaries. To ensure that these imaginaries were in accordance with the ideas of the ruling family, the media were either owned or subsidized by the state. The first radio was *Mosque Radio*, which started broadcasting in the beginning of the 1960s. Also, in 1961, the print media were established, and the state launched an official gazette announcing new laws and decrees. The development of both radio and press sped up as the country moved closer to independence. On 25 June 1968, the state-run *Qatar Broadcasting Service* started transmission, and *Mosque Radio* continued transmitting for only a few months after that point. In 1969, *Qatar Radio* joined the Arab States Broadcasting Union (ASBU) under the Arab League. Starting with five hours daily transmission in 1968, *Qatar Radio* gradually increased the hours of transmission, reaching 13 hours in 1969, 19 hours in 1982, and 24 hours on 27 June 2003 (Al-Mua'ssasah Al-Qatariya lili'laam, 2018). In 1971, transmission in English followed, Urdu in 1980, and French in 1983 (Al-Jaber, 2012, p. 56). In 1992, *Qur'an Radio* was established with programs on the Qur'an and Hadith, Islamic science, and debate of modern issues. From its inception until today, the role of radio has been to communicate the identity and heritage of Qatar. Consequently, around 85% of the programs are locally produced. The rest are imported programs that include documentaries, religious programs, songs, and plays (Al-Mua'ssasah Al-Qatariya lili'laam, 2018).

Compared with other Arab countries, the print media emerged in Qatar rather late. The reasons were the lack of printing presses and high illiteracy, among others (Mellor, Ayish, Dajani, & Rinnawi, 2011, p. 53). Starting in the late 1960s and into the 1970s, the state launched a number of magazines covering different issues. In the 1970s, the transfer of professional foreign workers, among them journalists, to the new, rich Qatar, established a basis for setting up professional media. In 1969, *Al-Mash'al* magazine, which focused on oil and energy, was released together with *Al-Doha* magazine, which focused on culture and arts and was issued by the newly established Department of Information. In 1970, *Education* magazine was published by the Ministry of Education. In 1977, the sports magazine *Al-Saqr* was issued by the Ministry of Defense, and in 1980, the monthly *Al-Umma* began publication, which focused on Islamic matters and was issued by the Presidency of Shar'ia Courts and Religious Affairs in the State of Qatar. In 1986, the state decided to close down all the Qatari state's magazines as a result of declining oil prices.

In addition to the state press, the private press also appeared in the 1970s. Though media outlets were entitled to be private, the state ensured their loyalty by providing financial support to local newspapers until the early 1990s, when the funding was suspended. The first private magazines were *Al-Urooba* and *Gulf News*, launched in 1970. The latter was an English-language magazine that was published twice a month. In 1972, the *Al-Arab* newspaper started publishing as the first political daily, and in 1974, *Al-'Ahd* became the first political weekly. The first women's magazine, *Mijalit Al-Johara*, and the first sports newspaper, *Al-Dawri*, both appeared in 1977. *Al-Arab* was closed in 1996 after the death of its founder Abdullah Hussein Nema when the heirs sold the license of the newspaper, which did not reappear until 2007.

As for television broadcasting, *Qatar TV* began broadcasting in black and white in 1970 and color in 1974. Starting with a few hours in Arabic, it extended its transmission to nine daily hours when introducing color television. Similar to other Arab countries, a foreign language channel was soon introduced. *Channel 2* in English started broadcasting in 1982 with programs on culture, sports, and entertainment, including those of foreign production (Al-Jaber, 2012, p. 58).

The second period of media development was initiated in 1995 when the new Emir, Sheikh Hamad bin Khalifa Al-Thani, introduced his reform program. Due to new freedom from interference by the government, international newspapers such as *The New York Times*, *Time Magazine*, *The Financial Times* and *Al-Quds Al-Arabi* became available in Qatar (Al-Jaber, 2012, pp. 49–50). Also, Qatari media appeared nationally, for example, with *Al-Watan* newspaper which offered more critical coverage of national issues in Qatar, and transnationally with the launch of *Al-Jazeera*.

Qatar opened up to the world and this was the beginning of a third period starting in 2011, when Qatar expanded the *Al-Jazeera* network by launching several new international channels, allowed private television in Qatar, and increasingly backed and/or financed media based in or outside Qatar. Strongly induced by the Arab uprisings, *Al-Jazeera* now openly supported Arab oppositions such as the Muslim Brotherhood in Egypt and the Islamist opposition in Tunisia, Syria, Yemen, and Libya. Thus, during the Libyan Civil War in 2011, *Libya Al-Ahrar TV*, a Libyan television channel, started broadcasting by satellite from Doha. Its focus was Libya's revolution and its political future. In 2012, the first private television channel *Al-Rayyan TV* was launched to specifically target the Qatari community. Its support for the Qatar National Vision 2030 and emphasis on Qatari history and tradition illustrates its loyalty towards the regime. In 2016, it launched its second channel. Another example is the Qatari online and print newspaper *Al-Araby Al-Jadeed* and the *Al-Araby* television network, both based in London (Roberts, 2014). This multidirectional media strategy reflects Qatar's soft power policy, which includes the support of not only Islamist oppositions but also liberal voices, such as the Egyptians Alaa Al-Aswany, Iman Nour, and others, who continuously have been allowed speaking time at *Al-Jazeera*.

A study of media use from 2010 to 2012 showed that Qataris still preferred daily newspapers as a source of local news in contrast to expatriates that increasingly preferred online media (Meeds, 2015). As of 2019, Qatar had four daily newspapers in Arabic: *Al-Arab*, established in 1972, *Al-Raya* (1979), *Al-Sharq* (1987), and *Al-Watan* (1995), and three in English: *Gulf Times* (1978), *Peninsula* (1996), and *Qatar Tribune* (2006). All papers are pro-government with regular headlines about and links to the ruling family and offer little criticism of domestic or foreign policy. With regard to television, the population in Qatar prefer different types of programming. Whereas Qatari nationals and Arab expats primarily watch television programming on free television (72% and 64%, respectively), Asian and Western expats prefer to watch subscription television (44% and 57%). The reason is probably that subscription television offers another kind of programming that is more attractive to non-Arabs (Meeds, 2015).

Political System and Legal Framework

The political system in Qatar is based on the acknowledgement of the Emir's sovereign authority. The Emir is not only the head of state, but also the commander-in-chief of the armed forces. The power is based on the separation of the legislative powers held by the Al-Shura Council, the executive powers headed by the Emir, and the juridical powers in the hands of the courts. Political parties are not permitted, and the only elections for direct representation are for the Central Municipal Council that has 29 elected members and an advisory role (Freedom House, 2019). The council was founded in the 1950s, but free elections took place for the first time in 1999. In that election, women were able to participate for the first time, both as voters and candidates. On the Ministry of Foreign Affairs' English website, the election is highlighted as "a historic event" that "represented the first steps of the country towards democracy in its civil sense," also highlighting the new role of women (Ministry of Foreign Affairs in Qatar, 2019). As such, the elections are still used as a showcase for the democratic intentions of the country. In 2003, a referendum took place giving the Qataris the right to vote for the country's first constitution. This happened, however, without mobilizing the citizens or fostering any wider public discussion (Al-Hawik, 2013, pp. 236–37).

When Sheikh Hamad bin Khalifa Al-Thani came to power through a coup removing his father from the throne in June 1995, he inherited an autocratic country built on tribal structure. His ambition was to build a civil society by introducing a number of legal reforms, including more freedom for national media. Looking closely, however, it appears that he, and later his son, had endorsed a policy that carefully navigated a balance between transformation and status quo or, in other words, between liberalization and control.

Qatar's first official censorship law was issued in 1979 with the aim to regulate and control the press, publishing houses, bookstores, artistic production, and advertising agencies. Based on the law, many non-Qatari newspapers and books were forbidden to be imported because they were not in accordance with the government's political, economic, or religious perspectives adopted as the basis for nation-building. The responsibility of regulating media, particularly radio and television, has been ceded to different institutions. Starting with the Media Department that was established in 1969, the Ministry of Information followed in 1974, which later became the Ministry of Information and Culture in 1990 (Al-Mua'ssasah Al-Qatariya lili'laam, 2018). In 1998, the new Emir abolished the Ministry as the controlling body of all media activities, including media censorship, thereby sending a strong signal of his wish to create freer media. As an alternative, the National Council for Culture, Arts and Heritage and the Qatar General Broadcasting and Television Corporation were founded as independent bodies to promote free public debate. In 2009, the Qatar Media Corporation was established as the official broadcasting authority for the state of Qatar. It carries on its dual role of pursuing the newest updates of media and technology while "maintaining and enforcing broadcast standards and content guidelines and developing programming that promotes Qatar's interests" (Government of Qatar, 2020).

In the new constitution from 2003, Article 48 states: "Freedom of the press, printing and publication shall be guaranteed *in accordance to the law.*" According to Anas (2012–2013), the old press law from 1979 continued to be in force, even after Sheikh Hamad bin Khalifa Al-Thani announced his visions for a new Qatar, as no other law was drafted before 2011. By referring to the 1979 law, it was possible to practice censorship of both domestic and foreign publications, as well as broadcast media, "for religious, political, and sexual content prior to distribution" (Anas, 2012–2013, p. 37). Furthermore, according to Anas, similar to cases in other Arab countries, one could be prosecuted for criticizing the government, the ruling family, or Islam. Although the Advisory Council had drafted a new press law in 2011, it had still not been approved by the Emir in 2016. The law was particularly intended to protect journalists against prosecution, while regulating the online media (Freedom House, 2019). Finally, in September 2018, a new draft law was approved by the government to regulate and organize the circulation of publications, publishing, media activities, and arts. In the Qatari daily *Gulf Times*, this law was presented as an answer to the technological development and protection of freedom of opinion, freedom of expression, and human rights. It abolishes prison sentences for publishing with reference to freedom of expression, but it also incorporates the publications and Publishing Law of 1979 and the Decree Law of 1993 on regulating the practice of advertising, public relations, artistic production, and artistic works. The freedom of journalists is assured, but the law also emphasizes the general obligation to abide by the code of ethics of the press (*Gulf Times*, 2019). Importantly, other laws such as the anti-terrorism legislation and the cybercrime law also restrict media and freedom of expression. The cybercrime law criminalizes the distribution of "false news" the violation of "social values or principles" online behavior that threatens state security, and online defamation. Violation may lead to either imprisonment or huge fines (Freedom House, 2019).

This development of press and media freedom is two-sided. On one hand, a number of reforms have been introduced to strengthen the presence of free media in Qatar. On the other hand, restrictions by the state are still more the rule than the exception, although they might have become more subtle. The many changes of laws and bodies involved in managing media reflect the ambivalent policies that the Qatari regime adopts when simultaneously promoting freedom and restricting access to power. The overall result of this media climate is that most outlets adopt a government-friendly approach and perform considerable self-censorship (Freedom House, 2019).

The most famous result of the attempts of liberalization was Sheikh Hamad bin Khalifa Al-Thani's establishment of *Al-Jazeera TV* in 1996. In contrast to the national media that work to strengthen the Qatari regime within the national framework, *Al-Jazeera* was directed towards a transnational audience and enhancing the position of Qatar transnationally. The channel quickly became a tool to amplify the influence and visibility of a small country, becoming an instrument for Qatar's soft power strategy.

Excursus: *Al-Jazeera*

Al-Jazeera TV, later known as *Al-Jazeera Arabic*, has become the most influential Arab television station internationally. The local presence of its correspondents during the US-led invasions in Afghanistan and Iraq, and later the Arab uprisings, has especially made the coverage of the station into a reference for international media. The network is viewed as an exception, both in Qatar and the Arab world, due to its critical outlook and global reach. From the beginning, it was organized as a private satellite television station, regardless of being established and financed by Sheikh Hamad bin Khalifa Al-Thani. *Al-Jazeera* became an element in his strategy of reaching out globally to constitute a new and stronger position of the country, while at the same time promoting new ideas of Arab democracy and critical thinking. Internationally, the Emir tried to create better relations with a number of countries such as Israel and Iran, and Qatar came to act as a mediator in Iraq, Saudi Arabia, UAE, Sudan, Eritrea, and Pakistan (Miles, 2010).

Since its establishment, *Al-Jazeera* has grown gradually from a small studio in a small Arab capital to a large transnational network of various thematic television channels that offers a multi-channel, multi-platform, and multilingual package addressing a global audience. It has offices around the world as well as online platforms. *Al-Jazeera Mubasher/ Live* was launched in 2005 and transmits live events and debates on current issues 24/7. *Al-Jazeera English* was launched as a news channel on 15 November 2006. In 2011, *Al-Jazeera Balkan* started transmitting international news from its headquarters in Sarajevo in Bosnia and Herzegovina. *Al-Jazeera Mubasher Misr* covered the Egyptian uprisings in the period from 2011 to 2013, when the President Morsi, aligned with the Muslim Brotherhood, was removed from power. In the period from 2013 to 2016, *Al-Jazeera America* was offering the Americans a perspective on the Middle East while prioritizing American news with the ambition to create a mix between *CNN America* and *CNN International*. Also in 2013, *Al-Jazeera Sport* was rebranded under the name *beIN Sports*. In addition to its many news channels, the network added *Al-Jazeera Children's Channel* (2005) and *Al-Jazeera Documentary* (2007). In 2014, the *Al-Jazeera* media network launched the online news site *Al-Jazeera Turk* in Turkish. The aim was later to establish a television channel, *Al-Jazeera Turk*, in Turkey. This never became a reality, because the online version did not succeed and was shut down in 2017.

Al-Jazeera has its own training center and a media research institute. The staff is international, comprising journalists educated in Western countries, and has a broad network of correspondents worldwide. Similar to *CNN* and *BBC*, *Al-Jazeera Arabic* transmits around the clock, but the programs are more varied, combining news coverage with political and cultural programming. From the very start, the network adopted a confrontational style, addressing issues considered taboo in the Arab world, thereby indirectly challenging Arab national media's ability to control the coverage of a story. However, it has been criticized for its uncritical coverage of Qatar's ruling family.

In the aftermath of 11 September 2001, *Al-Jazeera Arabic* started to become an important player in the coverage of conflicts inside and outside of the Arab world, where its strength—and vulnerability—have been its physical presence in conflict areas. The channel's critical coverage of global conflict has since then stirred up controversy and conflict inside and outside of the Arab world. Its unpopularity among Arab regimes has triggered several attempts to restrict the channel by closing down *Al-Jazeera*'s local or regional offices periodically or permanently. In particular, *Al-Jazeera*'s coverage of and presence in the epicenter of global conflicts, including the American invasion of Afghanistan in the wake of 9/11, the Gulf Wars, and the Arab uprisings, have triggered such responses. In any conflict it has covered, the network has been accused of being biased and has therefore been given numerous and often contradictory labels such as pro-Iraqi, pro-Israeli, pro-American, pro-Taliban, etc. (Sakr, 2006). During the Arab uprisings of 2010–2011, the channel played a significant role by providing the Arab and global audiences with live coverage of street protests, while clearly siding with the protesters against dictatorships. This univocal positioning once again made Qatar unpopular among Arab regimes.

Economy and Ownership Patterns

In Qatar, there is a tendency for the media to be either state-owned, owned by prominent members of the ruling family and/or government, or by businessmen with close connections to the ruling elite. Thus, all radio stations in Qatar are government-owned, whereas the *Al-Raya* and *Gulf Times* newspapers are owned by a private company led by a board that includes the oil minister, a former senior official, and several prominent businessmen. The *Al-Watan* newspaper, launched after the Emir's abolishment of censorship in 1995, introduced a more critical approach to local issues, but was owned by the foreign minister in association with a leading businessperson (Rugh, 2004). The paper adopted a relatively critical policy, which got it into trouble vis-à-vis with a number of ministries and institutions, and a court case was initiated against its editor Ahmad Ali (KUNA, 2001). Also, both existing *Al-Sharq* and *Peninsula* newspapers were owned or co-owned by the Qatari foreign minister (Rugh, 2004).

A characteristic of the third period, starting in 2011, has been the investment in media in all forms as part of Qatar's soft power policy and a strategic direction in its relationships with regional and international allies and enemies. Most of Qatar's new media ventures are, however, based outside Qatar, perhaps to avoid any escalation of conflict with its neighboring countries or to be relieved from the pressure they exert in the region. Whereas *Qatar TV* is state-owned, *Al-Rayyan TV* was launched in 2012 by Al-Rayyan Media and Marketing Company that also had produced programs for *Qatar TV*. The *Libya Al-Ahrar TV* is mostly funded by Libyan expatriate businessmen, while Qatar provides facilities and technical staff through *Al-Rayyan TV*. A

Qatari-owned private holding company, *Fadaat Media*, owns *Al-Araby TV* and the *Al-Araby Al-Jadeed* newspaper, but both were initiated by Azmi Bishara. Bishara is a prominent Christian Israeli Palestinian, who is a secularist and pan-Arabist. He is the chairman of *Fadaat Media* and *Al-Araby Al-Jadeed* network, also functions as advisor to the Emir, and is the director of the Doha Institute (Roberts, 2014). *Fadaat Media* also owns *Syria TV*, a satellite channel that has been broadcasting from Istanbul. Over concern that the diversity of digital media outlets has been limited, there are allegations that they are being financed by Qatari media companies, but it is difficult to get a confirmation of exact ownership. Furthermore, in 2017, a media city was established in Doha in order to make Qatar attractive to international and regional media outlets. To further this effort, the city advertises that it offers the newest technologies and provides no editorial limits except for a code of ethics.

Regarding *Al-Jazeera*'s funding, the intention from the outset was transferring it to pure private financing after five years of operation. While part of its financing comes from advertising, it is rather unclear how it is financed today, with no doubt that Qatar still supports the channel and its offspring financially. In 2014, *beIN Sports* was separated from *Al-Jazeera* and now operates 60 channels across 34 countries. In 2016, it also bought Turkey's largest pay-television operator, *Digitürk*, profiting from the rapid growth of pay-television in the Middle East (Oxford Business Group, 2018).

Regionally, Qatar is one of the biggest spenders on advertising. Newspapers are the most important platform, with online channels being a new platform. Advertisers have changed over time, not the least due to lower oil and gas revenues, but the state remains the dominant advertiser and spends "on advertising for major projects, such as infrastructure improvements and initiatives under the framework of Qatar Vision 2030" (Oxford Business Group, 2018).

Technology and Infrastructure

With the access to satellite technology, Qatar followed the trend practiced by other Arab countries and transformed its ground television station to satellite television in 1998, transmitting via the satellites

ArabSat, *NileSat*, and *Hot Bird*. In 1993, Qataris already had access to 31 satellite channels via the Qatari cable system network known as *Qatar Cablevision* (*QCV*), challenging the monopoly of *Qatar TV* by offering channels such *CNN*, *BBC*, *Fox Sports*, and Arab satellite channels (Miles, 2013, p. 43). With the rapidly increasing number of Arab satellite channels, *Qatar TV* in 2000 changed the format of the channel in response to the growing competition. It changed its logo, style of programs, intervals, and announcements, and new young faces appeared on the screen. Despite the competition from outside, *Qatar TV* is still popular among viewers in Qatar, whereas many Qataris feel alienated by *Al-Jazeera*, according to Miles (2013, pp. 44–45). The Qatari satellite company *Es'hailSat* launched the country's first satellite in 2013 to support *beIN Sports* and the *Al-Jazeera* network. In 2018, it launched its second satellite and began offering commercial services in the region. In the telecommunications realm, the only provider of Internet in Qatar is the government-owned *Qatar Public Telecommunications Corporation* (*Q-Tel*). Owning the entire IT infrastructure, it provides a list of banned websites and blocks material that is deemed as being against Qatari values. An example is *Doha News*, which was blocked in November 2016. As a private initiative, it had developed from a *Twitter* account, then a *Tumblr* blog, to a popular English-language website that was not afraid of criticizing Qatari politics. In the end, the owners sold *Doha News* to a foreign company due to problems with getting licensed (Napieralski, 2018). When raising a case, the authorities typically warn the local journalists, while non-Qataris employed by Qatari media outlets risk being deported or imprisoned.

With regard to Internet use, a six-country (Jordan, Lebanon, Tunisia, Qatar, Saudi Arabia, and United Arab Emirates) study by Northwestern University in Qatar found that Qataris are "among the most digitally connected citizens in the Arab Region" (Dennis, Martin & Wood, 2017). According to this study, 95% of the population has access to the Internet, and they spend 60% more time online than the populations from the other five Arab countries of the survey. They also found that, while the most popular social networks are *Facebook*, *WhatsApp*, *YouTube*, and *Instagram*, the users in Qatar spend less time playing video games or using *Facebook* in comparison with the other five countries. Instead, they use the Internet to watch news, comedy, sport, and religious/spiritual programs online. The study also showed that watching television online, either by streaming or download, is practiced by a third of Internet users in Qatar. Arab expats seem to especially prefer this option. The Internet appears to have become the most preferred form of media for users who are interested in political news (Meeds, 2015).

Challenges

Qatar's transnational media expansion has created a major source of conflict in recent years. In 2014, Bahrain, Saudi Arabia, UAE, and Egypt, the only non-member of the Gulf Cooperation Council (GCC), accused Qatar of supporting or financing terrorist groups in Egypt and Yemen. As a result, Qatar entered into a deal with the Gulf states not to support hostile media that function as a platform for opposition groups in other countries in the region. Later, another deal followed where Bahrain, UAE, and Qatar agreed to support the stability in Egypt and to prevent *Al-Jazeera* from working as a platform for opposition groups. These agreements seemed to have postponed the conflict from escalating after it broke out in 2017 when Saudi Arabia, the UAE, and Bahrain demanded that Qatar close down *Al-Jazeera*. The new Emir, Tamim bin Hamad Al-Thani, refused. This led Egypt, Bahrain, Saudi Arabia, and UAE to break off all diplomatic relations with Qatar in June 2017. Shortly after, Yemen, the Maldives, Mauritania, and Senegal also severed their relations with Qatar. Jointly, the countries would later present 13 demands that had to be met before contact could be resumed. Among these demands were to minimize contact with Iran and associated groups (a not very subtle reference to Hezbollah in Lebanon and Hamas in Gaza), to shut down the Turkish military base in Qatar, to stop financing terrorism, to stop all relations with terrorist organizations and individuals, and to shut down *Al-Jazeera*. Qatar rejected all accusations, demanded proof of the allegations, and refused to close down *Al-Jazeera* with reference to the need for freedom of the press (Naheem, 2017). This incident clearly illustrates how media are used to legitimize a political conflict, which in this case, according to Naheem (2017), has been a media war between UAE and Qatar. The conflict also underlines how *Al-Jazeera* plays a particular role as a transnational tool of Qatar's foreign policy. Where local national media in Qatar risk repercussions should they forget their loyalty towards the Qatari rulers, the same rulers use *Al-Jazeera* to position themselves within a conflictive international political field with no intention of restricting their activities.

Outlook

In the young nation of Qatar, with its history of around 50 years of national media, media play a key role in the construction of a modern Qatari state. Whereas the national media are restricted by regulations that assure their loyalty to the Qatari nation and its conservative values, the investments in and/or support of transnational media, including *Al-Jazeera*, play the role of strengthening the sovereignty—and more liberal values—of Qatar in an Arab region haunted by conflict. By concentrating media ownership among the ruling family and loyal businesspeople and setting up restrictions for obtaining media licenses, the Qatari rulers manage to control the national narrative and their own power. To control the international responses to *Al-Jazeera* appears more of a challenge, but until now, the Qatari rulers have not given in to threats and demands from outside. Two key issues will be crucial to the future media landscape of Qatar. One is how the continuous struggle with other Arab countries concerning *Al-Jazeera* evolves. As a small country, Qatar is dependent on international collaboration, and therefore, one likely scenario is that the countries will find a compromise where *Al-Jazeera* moderates the critique of other Arab regimes or turns its attention to other countries. However, if political changes in neighboring countries, such as Saudi Arabia, do in fact occur, Qatar may need to find new allies, which potentially could strengthen the role of *Al-Jazeera*. Another key issue concerns the advancement of new technologies wherein Qatar has invested heavily. This applies to technology itself but also to investments in Arab and English online news media globally, which have particularly provided Qatar with new platforms for influencing Arab perceptions of national and regional politics and identities. Although it is difficult to predict the future, Qatar will still be a small country with a majority of non-Qatari inhabitants, which makes it essential for the rulers to protect and control the symbolic (and physical) borders internally as well as externally.

References

Al-Hawik, H. (2013). *The Arab News satellites between two globalizations* [in Arabic]. Beirut: Al-Maaref Forum.

Al-Jaber, K. (2012). *Audiences' perceptions of news media services in three Arab countries* (doctoral thesis). University of Leicester.

Al-Mu'assasah al-Qatariya lili'laam [Qatar Media Corporation] (2018). *Qatar Radio: Golden Jubilee 1968–2018* [in Arabic]. http://www.qmc.qa/

Anas, O. (2012–2013). The changing profile of media in the Arab State. *Global Media Journal–Arabian Edition*, 2(1–2), 28–46.

Dennis, E. E., Martin, J. D., & Wood, R. (2017). *Media use in the Middle East, 2017: A six-nation survey.* http://www.mideastmedia.org/survey/2017/

Freedom House (2019). *Country report: Qatar.* https://freedomhouse.org/country/qatar/freedom-world/2019

Government of Qatar (2020). *Media.* https://portal.www.gov.qa/wps/portal/topics/Culture+Arts+and+Media/Media

Gulf Times (2019, February 6). *Qatar consolidates freedom of media with draft law.* https://www.gulf-times.com/story/621369/Qatar-consolidates-freedom-of-media-with-draft-law

KUNA (2001). *Qatari newspapers request police protection since the al-Watan newspaper incident last June* [in Arabic]. https://www.kuna.net.kw/ArticlePrintPage.aspx?id=1186747&language=ar

Meeds, R. (2015). Changing roles of traditional and online media as trusted news sources in Qatar and their relationships with perceived important issues and interest in politics. *Journal of Middle East Media*, 11, 34–61. https://doi.org/10.12816/0023481

Mellor, N., Ayish, M., Dajani, N., & Rinnawi, K. (2011). *Arab media: Globalization and emerging media industries.* Cambridge: Polity Press.

Miles, H. (2010). *Al-Jazeera: How Arab TV news challenged the world.* London: Abacus.

——. (2013). The other face of Qatari TV broadcasting. In T. Guaaybess (Ed.), *National broadcasting and state policy in Arab countries* (pp. 42–48). Basingstoke: Palgrave Macmillan. https://doi.org/10.1057/9781137301932_4

Ministry of Foreign Affairs in Qatar (2019). *Political system.* https://www.mofa.gov.qa/en/qatar/political-system/general-information

Naheem, M. A. (2017). The dramatic rift and crisis between Qatar and the Gulf Cooperation Council (GCC) of June 2017. *International Journal of Disclosure and Governance*, 14(4), 265–77.

Napieralski, M. (2018). The rise and fall of Doha News. *Qatarexpats.* https://medium.com/qatarexpats/the-rise-and-fall-of-doha-news-d191130f417c

Nye, J. S. (2008). Public Diplomacy and Soft Power. *The Annals of the American Academy of Political and Social Science, 616*(1), 94–109. https://doi.org/10.1177/0002716207311699

Oxford Business Group (2018). *Qatar maintains strong standing in regional and international media markets.* https://oxfordbusinessgroup.com/overview/tuned-country-maintains-strong-standing-both-regional-and-international-markets

Pew Research Center (2012). *Table: Religious composition by country.* https://assets.pewresearch.org/wp-content/uploads/sites/11/2012/12/globalReligion-tables.pdf

Roberts, D. (2014). Qatar and the Muslim Brotherhood: Pragmatism or preference? *Middle East Policy, 21*(3), 84–94. https://doi.org/10.1111/mepo.12084

Rugh, W. A. (2004). *Arab mass media: Newspapers, radio, and television in Arab politics.* Westport: Praeger.

Sakr, N. (2006). Challenger or lackey? The politics of news on Al-Jazeera. In D. K. Thussu (Ed.), *Media on the move: Global flow and contra-flow* (pp. 104–18). London, New York: Routledge.

9. Bahrain: Media-Assisted Authoritarianism

Marc Owen Jones

> The media ecosystem in Bahrain has primarily been shaped by the security interests of the ruling family and its formal and informal protectors, initially the British, and following Independence in 1971, Saudi Arabia and the United States. From its inception just before the Second World War, to the Uprising of 2011, television, radio, and the local press have been leveraged as a means of distributing state propaganda and public relations. Technological change has been embraced, but only to the extent to which it facilitates Bahrain's neoliberal development as a commercial ICT hub. The rise of citizen journalism, social media, and de-spatialized technologies has prompted some resistance to this top-down media-assisted authoritarianism, but the regime has adapted to instrumentalize these new technologies as tools of surveillance.

Background

Bahrain is a small archipelago of 33 islands in the Persian Gulf. Within this archipelago, Bahrain Island is the most populous and the largest, forming around 83% of Bahrain's total landmass of around 780 square kilometers. Bahrain is situated off the Eastern Province of Saudi Arabia and connected by the King Fahd Sea Causeway, which terminates in the Saudi city of Khobar. Its other immediate nearby neighbors include Qatar, to the east of Bahrain, and Iran to the north.

Arabic is the official language, but English and Persian are widely spoken by Bahraini citizens. Although Bahrain is small, it is densely populated with about 1.6 million people, of whom around 800,000 are non-Bahrainis (Information and eGovernment Authority, 2020). Like most Gulf states, large segments of the non-native population are workers from South Asia and the Philippines. As such, many other languages are commonly spoken, including Malayalam, Tagalog, Urdu, and Hindi. The majority of the native population are Muslims, broadly divided into Sunni Muslims and Shi'a Muslims. However, this sectarian simplification belies the fact that Bahrain's Muslim communities are characterized by diversity, both in terms of schools of thought and political opinions.

Bahrain is a nominal partial democracy, with an elected lower house and an appointed upper house. Bahrain has a constitution, although any amendments must be ratified by two-thirds of the lower house and appointed upper house, rendering change highly improbable. However, the ruler, King Hamad bin Salman Al-Khalifa, has the ability to rule by decree.

Like most Gulf states, Bahrain's political system has been defined in a number of ways, from a liberal autocracy, to a low-quality democracy, to an authoritarian regime (Jones, 2016). While the country is often characterized as a Sunni minority ruling over a Shi'a majority, this places too much emphasis on religious ideology. To clearly understand the current media system in Bahrain, one must consider that the media function in what has been called by some a kleptocratic autocracy. In this system, the ruling Al-Khalifa family monopolizes the country's material resources so that the institutions of state, including the media, function to prevent the occurrence of regime change which would otherwise alter the disbursement of this wealth to a broader segment of the population, most of whom have historically been Shi'a.

Tribal rule has profoundly influenced the media system in Bahrain. The Al-Khalifa family conquered Bahrain in the late 1700s and has since dominated positions of government. Initially, it subjugated the indigenous *baḥārna* population of mostly Shi'a Arabs to a form of feudal rule. This population was often subject to brutal oppression by the Al-Khalifas and their tribal allies. However, Bahrain's small size has meant that the Al-Khalifa regime has always derived much of its power and legitimacy from external sources. In the 1800s, the British signed a series of peace treaties with the Al-Khalifas and other ruling tribes across the Gulf. The overarching consequence of these treaties was that the British would thereafter protect the ruling tribes of the Arabian littoral as long as the tribes prevented piracy on British shipping.

Issues of domestic politics were generally overlooked by the British, although this began to change in the 1920s. Reforms imposed by the British designed to mitigate oppression of the *baḥārna* also resulted in consolidating the power of the ruling family. As far as the British were concerned, the Al-Khalifas supported British interests in the region, and were useful allies, despite the political costs.

Indeed, one of the most salient characteristics of Bahrain is its dependence on outside actors for legitimacy and support (Khalaf, 1998), which has had a profound role on the securitization of the media. During the 1950s and 1960s, two significant uprisings demanded increased citizens' participation in the political system. This further enforced the protectiveness of the Al-Khalifa-dominated institutions of the state, particularly those that were seen as a mobilizing force, such as the media.

Following independence from Britain in 1971, Bahrain increasingly turned to Saudi Arabia and the US for the support once offered by the British. Growing hostility from Saudi and the US administration towards Iran, especially after the 1979 revolution, brought a reversion to past practices of oppressing the local Shi'a population. This was not just the *baḥārna*, but also the *Ajam*, the Persian-speaking Bahraini citizens who originally came from Iran and settled in Bahrain. Growing Saudi influence and paranoia about Shi'a/Iranian expansionism resulted in the securitization of Bahrain's Shi'a community. Within this system, Shi'ites became second-class citizens, often prevented from entering positions of high office, whether in the government, media, or the military. This repression was one of the triggers for the 1990s intifada (uprising), where thousands of Bahrainis mobilized to demand political reform.

In 2002, Bahrain's King Hamad pushed forward the National Action Charter, a series of political reforms that created nominal democratic institutions. While this saw some media liberalization, it was short-lived. In 2011, thousands of Bahrainis took to the streets, demanding further political reform. They were, however, brutally repressed. Since then, the ruling family has not simply sought to contain the opposition, but to instrumentalize the media—both state-owned and privately-owned—in order to execute their divide and rule strategies that serve to keep Bahraini society segmented and stratified in order to better control it.

Historical Developments

The growth of media in Bahrain in its modern form can be traced back to the 1930s when newspapers arrived in Bahrain under much suspicion. The British adviser Charles Belgrave, who was in Bahrain from 1926 and 1956, was responsible for formative media policy. His dislike of Arabic newspapers criticizing British imperialism in Bahrain and the Gulf resulted in a rather hostile environment for fledgling press outlets. As such, visas were required for all journalists in Bahrain. Belgrave became the *de facto* embedded foreign correspondent in Bahrain, writing English-language articles for *The Times*, and ensuring international news about the country was generally positive.

The first local newspaper, *Jaridat Al-Bahrain*, opened in 1939 and was designed primarily as a vehicle for British war propaganda. The *Bahrain Broadcasting Station* was also launched in 1940 and broadcast as far as East Asia. Like *Jaridat Al-Bahrain*, its primary purpose was to broadcast war propaganda and counter Germany's anti-British propaganda being disseminated across the Middle East from *Radio Berlin*. Given their limited purpose and scope, both *Jaridat Al-Bahrain* and the *Bahrain Broadcasting Station* closed down by the end of the Second World War in 1945 (Al-Rumaihi, 2002).

In 1950, the weekly paper, *Voice of Bahrain*, began publication. The years 1953–1956 also saw a blossoming of more critical media, defining the first true epoch of printed media in Bahrain. Newspapers such as *Al-Qafila*, *Al-Watan*, *Al-Shula*, and *Al-Mizan* were widely circulated in Bahrain. It was a time of growing Arab nationalism and anti-imperialism. Due to their nationalist leanings, which provoked the Al-Khalifa regime and their British protectors, all of these newspapers were closed by 1956, leading to years of press stagnation. One editor, Abdulrahman Al-Bakir, was even deported to the British territory of St. Helena for his alleged role in plotting to overthrow the regime. Following anti-imperialist and prodemocratic unrest in the 1950s, the government reacted by introducing draconian press policies (Jones, 2020). Fear of another media renaissance that might offer support to other social movements led to stringent controls on publishing and broadcasting.

After 1956, the British kept tabs on any left-leaning publications, until they eventually decided that the lack of media was actually a problem. From the British perspective, it was held that the media should exist to promote the achievements and reforms initiated by the Bahraini government. Once again, the media in Bahrain were reimagined primarily for public relations and propaganda purposes. For this reason, the Bahrain PR Office was initially headed by a British officer, who ensured that all published material met with British approval. The mentality was that a response was needed to counter the propaganda pouring out of Egypt, Syria, Iraq, and later in the 1970s and 1980s, Iran. The British felt they could stave off unrest by reassuring the people about the modernization of Bahrain (Jones, 2020). Primarily, they believed they could convince Bahrainis that modernization under the Al-Khalifa regime was better than the alternatives in any other Arab republics.

Tentative steps by the government to liberalize the political system post-independence drove a number of media reforms. From 1976 to 1989, a total of 12 weekly, quarterly, daily, and monthly newspapers and magazines were created. Some of these were trade magazines for the Bahrain Petroleum Company (BAPCO) or the Bahrain Medical Association. However, the most prominent of these perhaps were Bahrain's daily newspapers, *Al-Ayam*, *Akhbar Al-Khaleej*, and the English-language the *Gulf Daily News*, the circulations of which reached 21,565, 22,000, and 9812 respectively in 2002 (Al-Rumaihi, 2002).

While *Bahrain Radio* reopened in 1955, it did so under tight restrictions, broadcasting mostly entertainment. This again reflected regime paranoia about propaganda. It was only in the 1960s that the quality of programming started to improve. An English service, *Radio Bahrain*, was introduced in 1977 to cater to Bahrain's blossoming non-Arabic speaking community. By 1991, *Bahrain Radio* had extended its broadcasting to 24 hours. As with many stations, it is now possible to listen to *Bahrain Radio* online, theoretically giving its audience unlimited reach.

Television broadcasting in Bahrain began in 1973 to coincide with the creation of Bahrain's National Assembly. This fledgling move towards representative democracy was one of many instances that showed that autocracy was loosening politically and, consequently, in the media sphere. Indeed, Bahrain was one of the few Gulf countries to license the creation of news broadcasting to the American company *RTV International*. This was short-lived, however, reflecting the rising ascendency of the conservative prime minister Khalifa bin Salman Al-Khalifa. Along with the dissolution of the short-lived National Assembly in 1975, *Bahrain TV (BTV)* was brought under the Ministry of Information, ostensibly due to *RTV*'s financial difficulties and rumored connection with the CIA (Al-Rumaihi, 2002).

As one of the first countries in the Gulf to undergo modernization, Bahrain was often technically ahead of the curve. It was the first country in the Gulf to broadcast in full color in 1977 when it started broadcasting news from Europe. By 1986, *Bahrain TV* had both an Arabic channel (*Channel 4*) and an English-language channel (*Channel 55*). By 1994, *BTV* was broadcasting about 540 hours per week across five channels (Al-Rumaihi, 2002). Yet, the content was often considered too parochial and unappealing to Bahrain's mixed demographic. While the media environment had tried to exclude foreign news over which there was little editorial control, efforts at internationalization sped up in the 1990s. This was partly driven by the 1991 Gulf War and public demand for information (Al-Rumaihi, 2002). Bahrain was also the earliest adopter of *ArabSat* in the Gulf. In the 1990s, Bahrainis were receiving via satellite content from *CNN*, Egypt, and the pan-Arab *MBC*, among others.

In the 1990s, Bahraini politics were defined by the intifada, where people once again took to the streets to demand reforms from the government. The media environment mirrored this, with its tight government hold on newspapers and television. Human rights organizations also reported multiple instances of trial by media, where political prisoners were paraded in front of national papers before trial, prejudicing their right to a fair hearing. Indeed, the role of state media in underscoring repressive policy, especially during times of crisis, was clear. Upon the death of Bahrain's ruler Shaykh Isa bin Salman Al-Khalifa in 1999, his son Hamad bin Salman Al-Khalifa came to power. After making himself king, Hamad introduced steps towards political liberalization, including the superficial relaxing of rules around media outlets.

Political System and Legal Framework

As with most authoritarian states, and despite Bahrain's nominal democratic institutions, political control over state media is largely centralized under the Al-Khalifa-appointed government. This is increasingly evident in a stifling legal framework that seeks to strictly govern the behavior of publishers and journalists, imposing heavy fines for those who contravene the Press Law. The formalization of media laws began in the middle of the twentieth century. The democratic movement of the 1950s and the strikes of 1965 prompted the authorities to abandon any notion of progressive media reform. The shutting down of Bahrain's budding press in 1956 was crystallized firmly in 1965 with the introduction of the Press Law, which set the tone for all future media restrictions in Bahrain. Criticism of the ruler or his family was, and remains, outlawed, as was any news that criticized allied countries or harmed Bahrain's economy. Any form of published material, from newspapers to pamphlets, was subject to the Press Law. The law expanded an existing law prohibiting the performance of plays, public concerts, or recitals without permission. Both the media and any avenues of cultural production were, and remain, closely monitored. Books and videos imported into Bahrain were often checked to see if they contained information critical of Bahrain.

Successive rulers of Bahrain have demonstrated hostility towards and suspicion of any media (Jones, 2020). Examples abound. During the election of newly formed labor committees in the 1970s and 1980s, the government instructed the media to keep coverage of the elections to a minimum. By 1985, the Ministry of Information's control of the media had exceeded that which was stipulated in the Press Laws, and a culture of self-censorship had emerged. The existence of this media culture of self-censorship was backed up by tough fines and potential prison sentences which were firmly embedded in law. This culture of censorship remains in place today. Following King Hamad's National Action Charter in 2001, a new era of relative press freedom was heralded in. As with independence in 1971, King Hamad sought to create a clear break from the past and ostensibly bring in a new era of political and social reform. The newly launched Bahraini constitution of 2002 guaranteed, albeit in a heavily caveated fashion, freedom of the press under Article 23. However, prior to the formation of the parliament, the government exploited this opportunity to pass a series of statutory decrees limiting certain freedoms, including the new Press Law of 2002. Like its predecessor, this Press Law prevents criticism of the king, the regime, Islam, and other Arab and Muslim countries, among other things (ARTICLE 19 & Bahrain Institute for Rights and Democracy, 2016).

Despite this restrictive environment, the reforms saw the launch of *Al-Wasat* newspaper in September 2002, one of Bahrain's only opposition-leaning legal daily newspapers. Founded by Mansour Al-Jamri, *Al-Wasat* published op-eds by members of the Bahraini political opposition and was one of the only non-loyalist papers in Bahrain, along with the short-lived *Al-Waqt*, a leftist-nationalist-leaning paper published from 2006 to 2010. Founded by Khawla Mattar, *Al-Waqt* was the first newspaper in Bahrain to have a woman as editor-in-chief (Mattar & Seikaly, 2012). It included articles by political exiles, such as Abdulhadi Khalaf, who was briefly a Bahraini MP in 1973 but was then expelled for political activism. However, *Al-Waqt* closed following reported financial difficulties. In 2009, both *Al-Waqt* and *Al-Wasat* had estimated circulations of around 20,000 and 30,000, respectively (Fanack, 2016). While their criticism was at times quieted, they often called out government repression, investigating, for example, political gerrymandering that discriminated against the Shi'a population.

However, the relative media pluralization that followed the reforms of 2001 was short-lived. Saudi-led fear about Shi'a empowerment after the fall of Iraq's Saddam Hussein in 2003 once again prompted a sectarian and security-orientated contingent of hardline members of the ruling family to influence media policy. Former US Ambassador to Bahrain, William Monroe, noted that "royal court elements" had a "direct hand in a scathing press campaign launched by Arabic daily *Al-Watan* against NDI, the National Democratic Institute, other NGOs, and even the US Embassy" (Monroe, 2006). *Al-Watan* itself was known for its close ties to the royal court. At times, this level of personalistic influence by the likes of the Prime Minister and other elements of the royal court indicated the extent of the Al-Khalifas' overreach in media affairs.

In 2006, Shaykh Ahmed Atayatalla Al-Khalifa, a conservative and influential member of the ruling family, reportedly established two media watch committees under the auspices of his office to intimidate journalists and editors into not writing articles that were deemed anti-regime. Shaykh Atayatalla's interference signified the influence of elements of a ruling Al-Khalifa core in controlling press freedom despite superficial institutional and constitutional safeguards. Like most political crises, the 2011 uprising that began on 14 February generated further securitization and coordination of media in Bahrain. The general harassment and intimidation of local journalists escalated sharply during the 2011 uprising. Bahrain was listed by Reporters Without Borders as one of the ten most dangerous places for journalists in the world after two journalists were killed and a number were detained and tortured (Bassiouni, Rodley, Al-Awadhi, Kirsch, & Arsanjani, 2011). In early 2011, *Al-Wasat* was targeted by pro-government thugs who attacked the company's printing press. The newspaper was eventually suspended on 2 April 2011, after the government used a raft of legal arguments to quash it. It was permanently shut down on 4 June 2017, signaling the end of any critical newspapers in Bahrain.

After the reforms of 2001, the government attempted to create the illusion of political distance from the media, turning the Ministry of Information into the Information Affairs Authority (IAA). Initially, this was headed by ruling family member Fawaz bin Mohammed bin Khalifa Al-Khalifa, and later Sameera Rajab. After the 2011 uprising, however, the IAA was subsumed under the Ministry of Information Affairs (MIA), which was created in 2014. The Ministry's role is to set policy and legislation and to oversee the media sector and its activities as well as to represent the "media sector before the Cabinet and the legislative authority" (Ministry of Information Affairs, 2020). The IAA remains the executive body for the media sector in Bahrain. It is tasked with operating official state media outlets, namely *Bahrain Radio, Bahrain TV*, and the official state news agency. The IAA also implements the policies issued by the MIA.

The Bahraini Independent Commission of Inquiry Report of 2011 stated that the media in Bahrain had been highly partisan during the

2011 uprising and that journalists, medical staff, and others in the state-controlled media had been defamed for their support of political reform (Bassiouni et al., 2011). As a result, the government set up the High Authority for Media and Communication (HAMC). The MIA describes the HAMC as an entity that proposes rules and regulations necessary to "upgrade the professions of media and communication" (Ministry of Information Affairs, 2020). It is also tasked with setting standards for "monitoring media and advertising content in different media and communication outlets." While the MIA claims that the HAMC is independent, its management is appointed by the government (Universal Periodic Review, 2017a). The ombudsman has not abated the authoritarian trajectory of media regulation in Bahrain. For example, in July 2016, the MIA issued Edict 68/2016, which requires newspaper outlets to obtain an annual license for disseminating printed or electronic content. It also forbids newspapers to livestream or produce videos longer than two minutes (Universal Periodic Review, 2017b). In general, the online media environment in Bahrain is so oppressive that people have been jailed for simply retweeting criticism of the king (Amnesty International, 2017). More insidiously, the Ministry of the Interior announced that anyone who even followed on *Twitter* the critics of government would be held legally accountable (Ministry of Interior, 2019). Thus, the aim again has been to dismantle the independent non-state social media news and information networks that formed after 2011.

The uprising prompted Saudi Arabia to ask Bahrain for cooperation among its media agencies to adopt strategies to counter what it stated were efforts by foreign agencies (most likely Iran and Lebanon's Hezbollah Party) to attack the reputation and stability of Bahrain. Saudi and the Al-Khalifas' fear of Shi'a empowerment in Bahrain, as well as historically rooted sectarianism, has compounded the obstacles to the development of media plurality in Bahrain. Even prior to 2011, the government had refused to issue newspaper and television licenses to predominantly Shi'a opposition groups such as *Al-Wefaq*. Consequently, in 2015, the Bahraini authorities quickly pulled the plug on Saudi Prince Al-Waleed bin Talal Al-Sa'ud's television channel *Al-Arab* within 24 hours of its first broadcast, reportedly because it aired an interview with a senior member of the Shi'a opposition group *Al-Wefaq*. This reflected the government's desire to not give the Shi'a any type of political platform. Indeed, the country's Shi'a have long complained of marginalization not only in participatory politics but also in the country's media and cultural production in general. As one Bahraini merchant once told *The Washington Post*, "if you switch on the T.V., there is not a single program that refers to us, our history, our folklore, our geography. We are nothing" (Lawson, 2004).

Economy and Ownership Patterns

In addition to the lack of sovereignty and the growth of Saudi overrule, the privileges afforded to the ruling family by oil revenues have incentivized continued control over positions of authority. A devolved media structure and relaxation of ownership would fly in the face of long-held beliefs that a pluralistic media may generate criticism of government that could lead to revolution. At the same time, the need for direct foreign investment has driven the government to put emphasis on projecting an image of "business-friendly Bahrain" (Khalaf, 2013). In order to successfully project this image, the government has seized control of the ability to dominate messaging about Bahrain. As such, ownership is tightly controlled by the state, even if it is permitted privately. The strictures of the Bahraini Press Law ensure that only those of a sound reputation can own a media outlet. This is a means of ensuring government control of their patrons in the media both in theory and in practice.

Historically, there has been nominal private ownership of newspapers. For the period of 1962 to 1976, Bahrain's publications can be grouped into three categories: those owned privately by Bahrainis, those owned by the government, and non-Bahraini publications regularly read in Bahrain (Nakhleh, 2011). These included *Al-Adwa*, *Sada Al-Usbu*, the *Gulf Weekly Mirror* (English), *Al-Mujtama' Al-Jadid*, and *Al-Haya Tijariyya*. Given Bahrain's small size, the average circulation of these publications ranged from 2,500 to 3,500. Nakhleh's (2011) analysis of these publications concluded that none were critical of the government. Ideologically speaking, *Al-Adwa* and *Sada Al-Usbu* were considered by Nakhleh to be "moderate."

The two dominant Arabic language papers in Bahrain from 1976 to 1989 were *Al-Ayam* and *Akhbar Al-Khaleej*, both of which are still operating today. While *Al-Ayam* is owned by the eponymous Al-Ayam Press, Akhbar Al-Khaleej Press owns both *Akhbar Al-Khaleej* and its sister English-language paper the *Gulf Daily News*. As well as extensive government oversight, the circulation of Bahrain's press during the 1960s and 1970s was also stymied to some degree by illiteracy levels.

By 2011, six of Bahrain's seven daily newspapers were owned by pro-government Bahrainis or those affiliated with the royal family (Project on a Middle East Democracy, 2012). This, of course, has resulted in a lack of editorial diversity. Indeed, one archaic regulation of Bahrain's Press Law is that those who run a newspaper should be of "good character." Such subjective terminology essentially means that only those approved by the Al-Khalifa dominated ministry will be granted such a position. With the closing down of *Al-Wasat* in Bahrain, a significant number of Bahrain's most circulated English and Arabic language papers, including the *Gulf Daily News*, *Al-Ayam*, and *Akhbar Al-Khaleej*, are owned by only two companies. While these are privately-owned, they are still subject to the state's tight control.

Al-Watan is more vociferously pro-government and nationalist. Set up in 2005, it has a mostly Salafist board and is heavily influenced by Saudi Arabia. By 2009, *Al-Watan* had an estimated circulation of around 30,000 copies (Fanack, 2016). Its columns have generally reflected Sunni political opinion in Bahrain, especially after 2011 where it took an anti-opposition, rather than entirely loyalist, stance. When Saudi forces entered Bahrain in 2011 to put down the uprising, the Salafi Islamist political party, *Al-Asala*, took out an advertisement on the front page welcoming the Saudi forces (Monroe, 2012). The Minister of Information, Sameera Rajab, often writes a column in *Al-Watan*. Thus, ownership in Bahrain is largely irrelevant in the domestic press sector as it is so tightly controlled by the government.

Bahrain's television market is relatively small. The five main terrestrial channels are operated by the Bahrain Radio and Television Corporation (BRTC). In 2007, Bahrain's first privately-owned television channel, *Atlas Travel & Culture*, was launched. It was owned by businessman Jamil Wafa (Toumi, 2007). Pay-television and direct-to-consumer (DTH) are more popular than free-to-air (FTA) channels, with *Orbit Showtime Network*

(*OSN*) being one of the major players. While most radio stations are also state-owned, private channels such as the *South Asian Hindi* station and *Your FM* also operate (Dubai Press Club, 2018).

Technology and Infrastructure

While Bahrain's media are politically regressive, Bahrain has been an early adopter of technological change. It was one of the first Middle Eastern countries to launch the Internet in 1995, the first country in the Middle East to install a mainframe computer (1962), and the first to install a satellite station (1969). It was also one of the first countries to have commercially available 5G networks in 2019. Bahrain's small size and limited oil supplies have encouraged it to diversify into other sectors extremely quickly. It has had limited success with this, briefly becoming a regional banking hub following the civil war in Lebanon. While the 2011 uprising damaged this status, Bahrain is turning towards information and communication technologies (ICTs) to attract foreign direct investments through a partially deregulated economy, at least by Gulf standards.

Today, the Bahraini government, through the Telecommunications Regulatory Authority, is pushing forward the Fourth National Telecommunications Plans (NTP4), which seeks to improve Bahrain's communication and technology infrastructure for the country's 2030 Vision—a comprehensive economic plan for Bahrain. Bahrain's Economic Development Board has been keen to promote the fact that Bahrain offers 100% foreign ownership, unrestricted VoIP calls (e.g., Skype), and a free trade agreement with the US that offers "highly credible" intellectual property legislation. Above all, Bahrain asserts that it offers the most liberal ICT market in the Middle East, with the most robust infrastructure. As with many other Gulf countries, Bahrain is keen to project itself as open for business with regards to its media and digital infrastructure, as long as these will not deployed to criticize Bahrain's government policies.

Bahrain's relatively substantial wealth and small size have facilitated the rollout of a comprehensive Internet infrastructure. Internet penetration is extremely high, with 96% of households and 100% of businesses able to access broadband. By 2018, broadband subscriptions had reached 2.16 million, representing a penetration rate of around 144%. A significant proportion of these were mobile subscriptions. In the same year, there were approximately 81 licensed operators in the telecommunications sector. Mobile phone penetration rates are currently around 133%. However, the majority of telecom sector revenue is held by three companies: *Batelco*, which is Bahrain's state-owned operator, *Viva Bahrain*, and *Zain Bahrain* (Telecommunications Regulatory Authority, 2018). As part of NTP4, Bahrain is rolling out a national fiber-based network to support ultrafast broadband.

The high penetration of mobile technology has resulted in Bahrain having a high take up of social media. From 2010 to 2014, Bahrain had from 500,000 to 600,000 *Facebook* users, of whom the majority (around 68%) were male. By March 2014, Bahrain had about 62,200 *Twitter* users. There was, however, more gender parity with *Twitter*, with 44% of users estimated to be women (Salem, 2017). Despite the affordances of these new platforms, which allow for citizen journalism and emerging forms of media expression, the authorities have cracked down heavily on those choosing to criticize the government or institutions of state. Social media are highly monitored and have been weaponized as a tool of state surveillance (Jones, 2013, 2020). Web censorship has been centralized, with Internet service providers instructed to install specific web filtering software to block specific websites. The encrypted messaging app *Telegram* has also been blocked.

Despite the blocking of websites, citizens are still able to use mainstream social media platforms to produce critical content. The years from 2011 to 2013 saw the proliferation of citizen journalism and revolutionary cultural production—all disseminated via *YouTube*, *Twitter*, *Facebook*, and *Instagram*. This marked a shift from traditional online criticism of politics, which mainly centered around messaging boards such as *Online Bahrain* (Jones, 2017). However, those caught engaging in such activities were and continue to be harshly punished.

The Telecommunications Regulatory Authority oversees much of the communication infrastructure in Bahrain. It is also highly responsive to the state security apparatus. The chairman of the board of directors is a member of the ruling family, while the board also includes a major general from the Ministry of the Interior. The government has the ability to localize Internet curfews during times of political unrest and did so for the village of Duraz for over 100 days starting in June 2016, switching off certain 3G and 4G cell towers between 7 p.m. and 1 a.m. every evening. This allows the government to strictly enforce repressive measures, making the need for wide-scale, nation-wide information control less necessary.

Challenges

Bahrain's media system is very much reflective of its authoritarian ecosystem. With most ministries dominated by members of the ruling family and no substantive democratic representation, it is unlikely that Bahrain's media system will ever be considered free, pluralistic, or critical, so long as the current political system remains in place. Tentative attempts at media pluralization have generally been short-lived, tempered by political crises that provoke reactionary measures by the government. Given Bahrain's regular political crises that tend to flare up every two decades, it is unlikely any liberalization will be sustained. Nonetheless, Bahrain's media environment is considerably more pluralistic than it was. Socially liberal ideas are generally tolerated, yet platforms for political demands are controlled. As such, availability and demand for on-demand streaming services such as *Netflix* have skyrocketed.

Politically, Bahrain's' dependency on Saudi Arabia is also a large contributing factor to the lack of media dynamism in the country. It was Saudi displeasure that was the likely reason for the cancelling of the television channel *Al-Arab*. Despite the political reforms going on in Saudi Arabia under Mohammed bin Salman (MBS), a free media is a long way off. As such, any media reforms that emerge in Bahrain are always going to be hampered by MBS's desire to maintain control of the media's portrayal of the region. Indeed, it was the rise of MBS that was credited with the fact that Qatar's *Al-Jazeera*, one of the Arab world's most popular broadcasters, was blocked in Bahrain, the UAE, Saudi, and Egypt after the aforementioned countries severed political ties with Qatar in 2017.

Outlook

It is expected that Khalifa bin Salman, the country's prime minister and driver of some of Bahrain's most conservative policies, will eventually step down or become unable to continue to exert influence. If significant political influence shifts to his technical successor, Crown Prince Salman bin Hamad, who is widely seen as more progressive, it is possible that there may be a step change in the constitutional makeup of Bahrain, and the inclusivity of the media. However, this will be defined ultimately by external (Saudi) influence.

Most state-funded and private media companies have made efforts to migrate or have a heavy digital presence across social media and through websites. It is unlikely that state media will ever be fully subsumed or replaced by external media content, digital or otherwise. While Bahrainis consume lots of content from abroad, such as through *Netflix*, the government will likely retain its official news outlets for the purpose of propaganda, PR, and crisis communication. The suspension of *Al-Jazeera* highlights the regime's willingness and ability to block content it deems to be threatening or not in line with its political outlook.

Social media sites, while monitored, are likely to remain popular. However, Bahrain's economic need to project an image of neoliberal modernity necessitates the embrace of modern communication technology. Failure to do this would be harmful to the economy. As long as the government maintains the ability to guide, control, and monitor people's consumption of media, the actual availability of platforms, websites, and news content will likely continue to flourish.

References

Al-Rumaihi, E. M. H. (2002). *The development of mass media in the Kingdom of Bahrain* (doctoral thesis). University Exeter.

Amnesty International (2017). *Bahraini Activist Risks 7 years in Jail for Retweets*: *Yaser Mawali.* https://www.amnesty.org/en/documents/mde11/6825/2017/en/

ARTICLE 19 & Bahrain Institute for Rights and Democracy (2016, October 4). Joint Submission for the UPR of Bahrain: For consideration at the 27th session of the UN working group in April–May 2017. *Universal Periodic*

Review. https://www.upr-info.org/sites/default/files/document/bahrain/session_27_-_may_2017/js2_upr27_bhr_e_main.pdf

Bassiouni, M. C., Rodley, N., Al-Awadhi, B., Kirsch, P., & Arsanjani, M. H. (2011, November 23). Report of the Bahrain Independent Commission of Inquiry. *BICI*. www.bici.org.bh/BICIreportEN.pdf

Dubai Press Club (2018). *Arab media outlook 2016–2018: Youth, content, digital media.* https://dpc.org.ae/-/media/1adce79686d148a1a98a6e1044156b2e.ashx

Fanack (2016, November 7). *Bahrain's media landscape: An overview.* https://fanack.com/bahrain/society-media-culture/media/

Information and eGovernment Authority (2020). *Bahrain open data portal.* https://www.data.gov.bh/

Jones, M. O. (2013). Social media, surveillance and social control in the Bahrain Uprising. *Westminster Papers of Communication and Culture, 9*(2), 71–91. https://doi.org/10.16997/wpcc.167

———. (2016). Saudi intervention, sectarianism, and de-democratization in Bahrain's uprising. In T. Davies, H. E. Ryan, & A. Milcíades Peña (Eds.), *Protest, social movements and global democracy since 2011: New perspectives* (Vol. 39) (pp. 251–79). Bingley: Emerald Group Publishing Limited. https://doi.org/10.1108/s0163-786x20160000039011

———. (2020). *Political repression in Bahrain.* Cambridge: Cambridge University Press.

———. (2017). Satire, social media and revolutionary cultural production in the Bahrain uprising: From utopian fiction to political satire. *Communication and the Public, 2*(2), 136–53. https://doi.org/10.1177/2057047317706372

Khalaf, A. (1998, August 12–16). *Contentious politics in Bahrain: From ethnic to national and vice versa.* Paper presented at the Fourth Nordic Conference on Middle Eastern Studies: The Middle East in a Globalising World, Oslo, Norway. www.smi.uib.no/pao/khalaf.html

———. (2013, February 28). The Many Afterlives of Lulu. The Story of Bahrain's Pearl Roundabout. *Ibraaz.* https://www.ibraaz.org/essays/56

Lawson, F. H. (2004). Repertoires of contention in contemporary Bahrain. In Q. Wiktorowicz (Ed.), *Islamic activism: A social movement theory approach* (pp. 89–111). Bloomington: Indiana University Press.

Mattar, K. M., & Seikaly, M. (2012). *The Arab Spring: Impacts and consequences on the GCC.* http://grm.grc.net/index.php?pgid=Njk=&wid=MjQ=

Ministry of Information Affairs (2020). FAQ. https://www.mia.gov.bh/the-ministry/faq-ar/?lang=en

Ministry of Interior (2019, May 30). Anti-cybercrime: Those who follow inciting accounts that promote sedition and circulate their posts will be held legally accountable [Tweet]. https://twitter.com/moi_bahrain/status/1134148380312178689

Monroe, S. L. (2012). Salafis in Parliament: Democratic attitudes and party politics in the Gulf. *Middle East Journal*, 66(3), 409–24. https://doi.org/10.3751/66.3.11

Monroe, W. T. (2006, May 24). Bahraini political scene part II: Royal family conservatives tighten reins on politics. *WikiLeaks*. https://wikileaks.org/plusd/cables/06MANAMA907_a.html

Nakhleh, E. (2011). *Bahrain: Political Development in a Modernizing Society*. New York: Lexington Books.

Project on a Middle East Democracy (2012, November 12). *One year later: Assessing Bahrain's implementations of the BICI report*. http://pomed.org/wp-content/uploads/2013/12/One-Year-Later-Assessing-Bahrains-Implementation-of-the-BICI-Report.pdf

Salem, F. (2017). *The Arab social media report 2017: Social media and the Internet of Things: Towards data-driven policymaking in the Arab World* (Vol. 7). Dubai: MBR School of Government. https://www.mbrsg.ae/getattachment/1383b88a-6eb9-476a-bae4-61903688099b/Arab-Social-Media-Report-2017

Telecommunications Regulatory Authority (2018). *TRA annual report*. https://www.tra.org.bh/Media/Interactive_Annual_Reports/2018/en/index.html#page29

Toumi, H. (2007, April 8). Bahrain to air first private TV channel. *Gulf News*. https://gulfnews.com/world/gulf/bahrain/bahrain-to-air-first-private-tv-channel-1.171527

Universal Periodic Review (2017a). *27th session, April-May 2017, contribution of UNESCO to compilation of U.N. information (to Part I. A. and to Part III – F, J, K, and P): Bahrain*. https://www.upr-info.org/sites/default/files/document/bahrain/session_27_-_may_2017/unesco_upr27_bhr_e_main.pdf

Universal Periodic Review (2017b). *UPR submission of the UNCT in Bahrain*. https://www.upr-info.org/sites/default/files/document/bahrain/session_27_-_may_2017/js0_upr27_bhr_e_main.pdf

10. Kuwait: From "Hollywood of the Gulf" to Social Media Diwaniyas

Fatima Alsalem

> The media in Kuwait is relatively free and includes a wide variety of platforms expressing disparate views in a unique, competitive culture. The press in Kuwait has always been privately-owned by influential elites, allowing for wide range of opinion expression, but it has been limited to some degree by censorship and media laws. Nevertheless, the press exerts a strong influence on public opinion. Private broadcast media emerged in 2004 when the state ban was removed. Although private television and radio stations enjoy a fair amount of freedom in Kuwait, especially when compared with other Gulf states, they are subject to government laws and regulations.

Background

Kuwait is one of the smallest countries in the Middle East, located adjacent to the northwest corner of the Arabian Gulf, with an area of 17,818 square kilometers. The country shares borders with Iraq and Saudi Arabia and enjoys a significant and important commercial status in the region due to its strategic location, natural passage to the northeast corner of the Arabian Peninsula, and, of course, its vast oil resources. The country has a desert-like climate, and a population of 4.1 million, including approximately 30% Kuwaiti citizens and 70% non-Kuwaiti nationals (World Population Review, 2019). Although

English is widely spoken, the official language of Kuwait is Arabic. The population is 85% Muslim, with Protestant and Catholic Christians, Hindu and other religions combined to account for the remaining 15%. At 96%, the literacy rate in Kuwait is one of the highest in the world due to the government's expenditure on education and the country's free educational system. Kuwait can be viewed as the most democratic country in the Gulf region. Compared with other Gulf countries, it has a thriving democratic society with a democratic government. It is a constitutional hereditary monarchy ruled by descendants of the Al-Sabah family. Nonetheless, the legislative branch is democratically elected by Kuwaiti males and females over 21 years of age. Women gained the right to participate in elections and vote in 2006. Since women received the right to vote, almost all Kuwaitis vote; only military personnel are excluded.

Kuwait had been, for many centuries, an independent sheikhdom living on trade, fishing, and pearl harvesting. In the early eighteenth century, tribes such as Al-Utub and Al-Sabah fled to Kuwait from the Arabian Peninsula, away from danger and dispute with other tribes. After they had settled in the town of Kuwait, the small town developed into a commercial hub and began to thrive because of its location overlooking the head of the Arabian Gulf. This led Kuwait to become one of the most prosperous countries in the region. The Al-Utub and Al-Sabah tribes voted for Sabah bin Jaber Al-Sabah as their leader, or "governor," in 1762. Although Kuwait has been ruled by 15 different rulers since its establishment by the Al-Sabah family, Sheikh Mubarak Al-Sabah (1896–1915) is seen as the founder of the modern Kuwaiti state. After being threatened with occupation by the Ottoman Empire, Mubarak Al-Sabah signed an agreement with the British, and Kuwait became a British protectorate from 1899 to 1961.

After the discovery of oil and the beginning of its export in the middle of the twentieth century, Kuwait City and its villages witnessed a great urban renaissance. In addition, the country experienced a period of stability and prosperity driven by the oil resources and its liberal atmosphere. This was a turning point in the history of Kuwait. By 1952, the country had become the largest oil exporter in the Gulf, and this attracted many foreign workers to the state.

In 1961, Kuwait declared its independence from Britain and called for elections for a constituent assembly, tasking it with drafting a new constitution (Salem, 2007). The assembly, however, was not the first of its kind in Kuwait. The democratic experience before Kuwait's independence had major influences on the significant changes in its social and political life. The first elected legislative council was established in June 1938—with 150 voting members from elite families—for the purpose of advising the ruler on such matters as the creation of the economic and educational systems and the taxation system as well as the drafting of the first constitution. Kuwait is specific in the Arab region because of the participatory style of governing between the ruling family and the people, and it was among the first to draft a constitution and form an elected parliament, which it did in 1962. Although the constitution limited some legislative powers, it guaranteed civil liberties, such as equality, freedom of expression, and freedom of the press.

After independence, the government supported a democratic constitution that granted significant power to the legislative branch (Kuwait National Assembly, 2019). Its constitution and the elected parliament set Kuwait apart as a political model and has inspired many countries in the Gulf and beyond to take similar measures (Asiri, 2007). The participatory political system in Kuwait strengthened people's political orientation and their interest in politics. This is reflected in the growing number of registered voters, a relatively high voter turnout, and the advanced nature of Kuwaiti elections' advertising campaigns.

There are several sociocultural, political, and economic factors that have influenced Kuwaiti citizens to become more politically active compared with those in many Arab nations. First, there are the sociocultural factors related to the country's original organization, which was based on tribal and Bedouin families. The tribal system enhanced political participation early in the country's establishment when the three main power factors in the country (politics, business trading, sea trading) were divided among the leaders of the three main tribes. This suggests that the idea of participatory governance was embedded early in Kuwait's history.

Historical Developments

Kuwait enjoys a more outspoken and critical media environment than most other nations in the Arab world. There is unrestricted news accessibility in Kuwait, with a large amount of media freedom that ranks the country as a "partly free" press system and the only Gulf country represented in this category (Freedom House, 2019). Thus, Kuwait's media may be described as one of the most open media systems in the Middle East due to its diversity and early emergence. In particular, from the 1960s through the 1980s, Kuwaiti media became one of the most developed and influential media systems in the Middle East.

Yet, the Kuwaiti press was established rather late compared with the emergence of the first Arab newspaper in Egypt in the early nineteenth century. The Kuwaiti press began not as a government tool but as private endeavors (Al-Rasheed & Chenoufi, 2008). In February 1928, Abdulaziz Al-Rasheed published the first Kuwaiti magazine, *Majalat Al-Kuwait*. Although it did not last long and closed down after two years of publication, a new newspaper was published in 1947 by the House of Kuwait (student union) in Cairo, under the name of *Al-Bitha*. *Al-Bitha* played a prominent cultural role for the Kuwaiti students in Cairo as it covered news from the country and gave students the opportunity to express their viewpoints on political and social affairs. *Al-Arabi* magazine, one of the leading cultural magazines in the region, was established in December 1958 when the Kuwaiti government decided to publish a magazine concerned with Arab cultural affairs. Since its initial publication, *Al-Arabi* magazine has been keen to discuss Arab and international developments and cultural issues. The magazine has been a pioneer publication for leading Arab writers, poets, intellectual elites, and scholars, including Taha Hussain, Abbas Al-Akkad, Najib Mahfouz, Nizar Al-Qabbani, Abdel Hadi Tazi, Ihsan Abbas, Youssef Idris, Salah Abdel Sabour, Jaber Asfour, Farouk Shousha, and others. Since the publication of the first issue more than 50 years ago, *Al-Arabi* has become a cultural Arab symbol and has succeeded in introducing a new form of cultural magazine.

During World War II, only a few people in Kuwait owned radio devices, yet Kuwaitis used to gather in *diwaniyas* (cultural halls) to tune in to radio stations such as the *BBC*, *Radio Cairo*, and *Radio Baghdad*.

Inspired by this experience, Mubarak Al-Mayal, who served in the military, suggested using an old radio transmission device owned by the Ministry of Interior and the Kuwaiti military to set up a new radio station with the help of a Pakistani technician, Mohammed Khan (Al-Enezi, 2015).

"This is Kuwait" were the first words broadcast on-air, spoken by Mubarak Al-Mayal to announce the establishment of Kuwaiti radio on 12 May 1951. Since then, Kuwait has taken serious steps to develop the station and introduce more diversified programs, while also extending the transmission time. In the 1960s, radio played a vital role in Kuwaiti lives during the period of independence. Radio has also played a leading role in guiding Kuwaiti public opinion, spreading the spirit of patriotism and national pride, for example, during Iraq's threats to Kuwait's independence in the 1960s.

Television emerged in 1951 and was privately-owned by a local Radio Corporation of America (RCA) television dealer who wanted to promote television set sales. Later, the Emir of Kuwait, Sheikh Abdullah Al-Salem Al-Sabah, bought the television transmission from RCA to bring it under government control. Official broadcasting started on 15 November 1961, and *Kuwait TV* became one of the earliest television stations broadcasting in the Arab world after the emergence of television in Lebanon, Iraq, and Egypt and was the first and only broadcast operator in the Gulf region.

The Ministry of Information continued to develop *Kuwait TV* and bought the first outdoor shooting cameras and equipment in the region. The cameras attracted many Arab artists to Kuwait to shoot their music videos. This made the archive of *Kuwait TV* one of the most substantial visual libraries in the region.

Initially, *Kuwait TV* broadcast its programs in black and white for four hours a day until mid-March of 1974. In 1974, color broadcasting began, followed by the grand opening of the new television building in the Ministry of Information complex in February 1979.

At that time, television sets were costly, and citizens who were able to afford them shared their viewing with family and neighbors. Kuwaiti families who owned television sets used to have home cinema style gatherings where neighbors and friends gathered to watch shows and television series.

Kuwait TV soon became the leading broadcaster in the Gulf and many of its programs and soap operas were broadcast abroad. Since its emergence, *Kuwait TV* has been considered one of the best and has competed with Egyptian television, which was considered the leader at that time. During the 1970s and 1980s *Kuwait TV* produced the top dramas and shows in the region. At that time, most of the Gulf states did not have the infrastructure necessary for television broadcasting; thus, the Kuwaiti government opened a branch of *Kuwait TV* in the United Arab Emirates (UAE), sending content and programs daily by air for UAE viewers. The leadership role of Kuwait television was not limited to helping other GCC countries establish their television. It also produced television dramas (soap operas) that aired in all Arab countries. The 1980s marked Kuwaiti drama's golden age, and Kuwait was named "Hollywood of the Gulf" due to the international popularity of its soap operas and theatre. This led many Gulf and Arab actors and performers to settle in Kuwait to establish their professional careers.

The state took serious steps to improve the media technically and financially. However, the Iran-Iraq war during the 1980s and, in particular, the Iraqi invasion of Kuwait and the subsequent war in 1990–1991, resulted in an economic crisis which affected media development in Kuwait. Iraq bombed the Ministry of Information building as soon as it occupied Kuwait in an attempt to control the media and obscure the reality of what was happening. The attack on the Ministry's building broke down the radio transmitters. However, shortly after the breakdown of the official radio transmission in the country, Kuwaitis rushed to transmit radio broadcasts from a military camp before moving to a new studio in the Dasma residential area and transmitting their broadcasts from Failaka Island. The transmission lasted only two days before the Iraqi army found out about the transmission in Failaka and closed it down. However, Kuwaiti media did not stop at that point but decided to continue to broadcast from Khafji in Saudi Arabia and Cairo, Egypt. During the invasion, Kuwaitis also launched the international radio station *Sawt Al-Kuwait* to address Kuwaitis at home and in the world. *Sawt Al-Kuwait* station, which aired from a secret site, helped Kuwaitis stay connected, voice their opinions, and support the legitimacy of the government.

However, after Kuwait was liberated in 1991, a rebuilding process took place based on a new and modern foundation. This process required a lot of effort because the invading troops had taken or damaged all the production equipment, including cameras, studios, tape recorders, and the archives, resulting in damage estimated to be USD 150 million.

Political System and Legal Framework

During the second half of the twentieth century, Kuwait faced many political challenges that led to an ambivalent stance towards media and the freedom of expression. Since its establishment in 1963, the National Assembly has been dissolved eight times and early elections have been called for due to the impasse between the legislature and the government (Shayji, 2009).

The continued conflict between the executive and the legislative branches has led to an increase in politically active movements in the country. For example, activist youth groups, opposition members of the government, and some members of parliament joined in a broad-based movement named "nabeha khams" ("We Want It Five") in 2006, which aimed to shrink the number of electoral districts from 25 to 5, in order to minimize corruption in the voting system. This campaign involved street demonstrations, rallies, blog posts, and text messages, leading the government to call for new elections within a few weeks. In 2011, the opposition coalition also campaigned against the prime minister and his cabinet to end corruption in the National Assembly. The campaign, known as "irhal" ("Leave"), utilized many digital media tools, including *YouTube* videos, social media tools, and text messages.

More recently, Emir Sabah Al-Ahmed Al-Jaber Al-Sabah issued a decree that amended the basic electoral law and decreased the number of votes allowed per person from four to one in elections for the National Assembly. The old voting system was perceived to enforce the tribal system, because people were used to electing a slate rather than dividing their votes among a larger group of candidates. Therefore, the new voting system of "one person, one vote" was thought to favor the less well-organized and more liberal Kuwaiti families. In a reaction to the Emir's voting amendment, a coalition of young people, Sunni Islamists, tribal activists, and some liberals staged demonstrations, rallies, political speeches, and sit-ins to campaign against the new voting system (Central Intelligence Agency, 2019). Campaigns, such as "karamat watan" ("The Nation's Dignity") or "kate'a" ("Boycott"), used *Twitter*, *Instagram*, and *YouTube* as mobilization platforms for their election boycott campaigns. However, the supporters of the voting amendment also ran a political campaign on social media to raise the public's awareness of the importance of voting as a civic duty. The "s'osharek" ("I'm Going to Participate") campaign, for example, was organized by pro-government activists, former members of parliament, political candidates, and activists. The main objective of this campaign was to call for participation in support of the government and the sovereignty of the constitution.

This active political sphere in Kuwait and the challenging relationship between Kuwaitis and their government have influenced the status of the media in the country. On the one hand, parts of the elite and the public have demanded a greater role in the democratic process by newspaper ownership and media influence. On the other hand, the Kuwaiti government continuously tries to impose control over the media. For example, the Kuwaiti government had imposed a total ban on issuing licenses for new newspaper publications since the mid-1970s, leaving only five daily newspapers (owned and managed by elite business families) to operate until a change of the law in 2006. The total ban of newspaper licenses was imposed by the government to help them control, deal with, and censor their content. This ban, however, has resulted in Kuwaiti newspaper journalists facing pressure not from direct government control but from newspaper owners' personal relationships with government officials. The close relationship that elite families and newspaper owners have with the government makes it difficult to freely criticize the government due to shared interests and fear of losing economic benefits from the government. In a television interview that was aired on *Kuwait TV 1* in 2016, *Al-Qabas* newspaper's editor-in-chief, Waleed Al-Nusif, admitted that owning a newspaper in Kuwait brings significant power and influence to the families that own them. In the same interview, he said that newspapers do not represent the whole society, although they "claim" they do, but their owners' goals and interests do limit them. Nevertheless, Kuwaiti newspapers criticize the government organizations. In fact, newspapers are free for the most part to publish what they want, but only in accordance with the Press and Publications

Law (Dashti & Fadhli, 2011). However, newspapers tend to respect and follow the country's political strategies and principles and, therefore, support the country's policy, especially in its international affairs and relations.

In 2006, the Kuwaiti government passed a revision of the Press and Publication Law of 1961. It provided several reforms, including the government's agreement to allow the publication of new daily newspapers, which ended the publication ban that had lasted three decades. Still, newspaper publishers are required to obtain an operating license from the Ministry of Information. The new law no longer classifies press offenses as crimes to be sanctioned with imprisonment, yet offenders can be charged with fines. The Press and Publication Law has also set limits to certain types of criticism, such as criticizing the Emir, scrutinizing Islam, or publishing information related to the national security. Violating these limits can result in criminal charges against the author and the editor-in-chief of the newspaper.

The Internet is considered to be a relatively free medium in Kuwait and is protected by freedom of expression in Articles 36 and 37 of the Kuwaiti Constitution. Although the Internet is a means of communication and information, it is not regulated by the Ministry of Information but rather by the Communication and Information Technology Regulatory Authority (CITRA) under the supervision of the Ministry of Communication. Internet Despite the protection of freedom of expression by the Kuwaiti constitution, CITRA routinely blocks websites suspected of terrorism or inciting political instability and monitors Internet communication for defamation and security threats (Freedom House, 2019). Regardless of some government control on social media users, most Kuwaitis have unfiltered access to the Internet. Unrestricted social media use makes sense in a country that allows for a greater degree of freedom of expression than other countries in the GCC.

Economy and Ownership Patterns

Ownership in Kuwait can be characterized by a mix of limited privatization and governmental control. As for the press, since its emergence in the 1920s and expansion in the 1960s, Kuwait's newspapers have been entirely individually owned. This means that newspapers are owned by influential individuals of elite families in the Kuwaiti society, family partnerships, or joint stock organizations (Abu Shanab, 1987). Although profits are the main objective for the establishment of a newspaper in Kuwait, it has proven to provide other benefits to its owners, such as political and social influence (Abu Shanab, 1987).

Today, there are a total of 13 Arabic daily newspapers and three English dailies in Kuwait (Ministry of Information, 2019). The five newspapers that operated before the new press law in 2006 are still considered to be the most influential and include *Al-Rai* that started publication 1961, *Al-Seyasah* founded in 1965, *Al-Qabas* founded in 1972, *Al-Watan* which started publication in 1974, and *Al-Anbaa* founded in 1976.

When it comes to radio, Kuwaiti radio offers nine specialized English and Arabic stations that are owned and managed by the Ministry of Information, including *Al-Qur'an Al-Kareem*, *Super-station*, *Kuwait Radio One*, *OFM*, *Traditional Station*, *The Old Arabic Singing*, *Easy*, and *Kuwait Radio Two* (Ministry of Information, 2019). Private radio emerged in 2005 after the state domination of broadcast radio and television was eased by a ministerial order. Radio stations, such *Marina FM* and *Nabth Al-Kuwait* which are owned by the private sector, have changed the game. The government permission of private radio stations initiated competition which enriched the quality of the programs and professionalism of their presenters. Also, the emergence of private radio has increased advertising spending on this platform. Before private radio stations, advertisers had no great interest in radio because it was considered a government entity whose purpose was not to generate revenue. The establishment of private radio stations led the government to issue an Audio and Visual Media Law in 2007 to control and manage the private stations.

Similar to radio, the Kuwaiti government removed the state ban on private television in 2004 and granted the first television license to *Al-Rai TV*, followed by *Al-Watan TV* and *Funoon TV*, all owned by Kuwaiti business families, allowing for greater freedom and diversity of choice. The television licenses allowed the private sector to begin commercial broadcasting. The first private television, *Al-Rai TV*, followed by *Al-Watan*, offered daily news, documentaries, popular movies, talk shows, and late-night shows that gained huge popularity in the Kuwaiti society. Although the government permitted the establishment of private television, new private operators needed to obtain media licenses from the Ministry of Information and sign a consent form agreeing to obey the law and abstain from shows that would "undermine public modesty." Yet, state-owned television remains dominant, and the Ministry of Information broadcasts eight diversified satellite television channels, which also stream live on its website as well as through an Internet application that enables live television streaming on mobile phones (Ministry of Information, 2019). The eight channels are *KTV1*, *KTV2*, *KTV Sports*, *KTV Ethra*, *KTV Arabe*, *Al-Qurain*, *KTV Sports Plus*, and *KTV Al-Majlis*.

Technology and Infrastructure

Kuwait ranks first in terms of Internet penetration in the Middle East (followed by United Arab Emirates) with 100% of the population having access to the Internet. There are various economic and political reasons for such a high level of Internet penetration in Kuwait. In addition to bilingual education, which allows Kuwaitis to easily navigate the Internet, Kuwait's gross domestic product per capita is very high, and as a result, most Kuwaitis can easily afford to buy the latest Internet-enabled communication technologies and maintain Internet subscriptions.

The Kuwaiti government has taken serious steps towards the development of its e-government services and social media presence. The government has implemented laws and strategies to manage and control Internet service providers' prices and the quality of their service. In 2012, for example, the Ministry of Communication issued a regulation that limited the maximum cost of an Internet subscription, reducing the fees of some providers by at least 40%. The main objective of the law was to maintain high quality and efficient services.

Another factor for the high Internet penetration in Kuwait is the high degree of mobile phone penetration in the country. Kuwaitis' ability to purchase smartphones enhances their Internet accessibility and use of social media. A study of university students in Kuwait concluded that nearly 100% of participants already had Internet access at home in 2010, while more than 75% had Internet access on their mobile phones (Wheeler & Mintz, 2010). Statistics also show that Kuwait's mobile phone penetration had reached 179% as of 2018, indicating that nearly every Kuwaiti has two mobile phones. A report also determined that 100% of land area and population is covered by mobile networks, while the 4G LTE network has a 97% coverage according to the Consolidated Kuwait national ICT indicators report of 2016. Thus, the high mobile phone penetration in Kuwait fosters Internet usage as many Kuwaitis access the Internet and social media sites through their smartphones.

Statistics show that local Kuwaiti social media users prefer *Twitter* (73% of Internet users) over *Facebook* (41%). As for the expat community, figures differ with 88% of the Asian expats and 97% of the Arab expats using *Facebook*. *Twitter* is only used by 52% of the Arab expats and 35% of Asian expats living in Kuwait based on figures from the Consolidated Kuwait national ICT indicators report of 2016. *Twitter* gained great popularity in Kuwait and became an integral platform for political discussions and debate. Although Kuwait led the world in terms of *Twitter* penetration rate in 2014 (Saleh, 2016), it has been affected by government restrictions and electronic criminal laws which made users more aware of and practice self-censorship when engaging in political debate and criticism. Still, *Twitter* has been an important outlet for public opinion in Kuwait and political campaigning, and many government officials use *Twitter* for their press releases and as a tool for crisis management.

Instagram had 1.7 million users as of September 2018, and statistics show that nearly 93% of Kuwaitis were using the platform, while approximately 70% of Arab expats used it (CAIT, 2016). *Instagram* has gained great popularity in Kuwait and changed the way people shop for and advertise their products. People use it as an electronic storefront where they advertise their businesses, selling anything and everything (Greenfield, 2013). Also, *Instagram*'s boom in Kuwait is linked to social media influencers who use this site for their daily life by blogging and having live chats with their followers.

Social media created a new media reality in Kuwait, one that offers a greater space for public debate and discussions of political events. Few can deny that social media have become an essential political tool in Kuwait and that Kuwaitis' use of social networking sites has been described as the most "intriguing" in the Gulf region (Al-Qassemi, 2011). This is because of the effective use of social networking sites for participating in political discussions, grilling parliament members, and holding heated political debates. Scholars such as Wheeler and Mintz (2010) have argued that the citizens in Kuwait see a potential for political change through the Internet, and some recent usage trends indicate that social media are contributing effectively to the latest political movements in the country by enabling political mobilization and discussion.

Interestingly, a tradition that materialized in the so-called *diwaniyas*, and stimulated high levels of interpersonal communication among citizens, offers one explanation for the political implications of social media. Traditionally, *diwaniyas* have been male social clubs, which also provided their members with an opportunity for political organization and mobilization. *Diwaniyas* were usually held in either halls attached to Kuwaiti houses or a separate building with a hall to receive guests, neighbors, and friends to discuss current events and exchange views. Even today, *diwaniyas* have preserved their importance and remain an essential part of the social, political, and economic life in Kuwait.

However, contemporary *diwaniyas* have become more like political salons and cultural clubs; they are more organized and often feature planned events, specific topics of discussions, and guest speakers. However, it is still not widely accepted for women to join *diwaniyas*. A member of the ruling family, Rasha Al-Sabah, has held mixed *diwaniyas* where men and women sit together to discuss politics and several other issues. Similarly, Rula Dashti, a former minister and a former member of parliament in the Kuwaiti government, held female-only *diwaniyas* before her official appointment and, as a consequence, normalized the *diwaniya* culture for women (Tétreault, 2012). Najla Al-Naqi (lawyer) and Ghadeer Asiri (professor and social activist) also frequently hold mixed cultural gatherings, which are similar to the *diwaniya* concept, to discuss political and social issues and to invite guest speakers and the press.

At the same time, the emergence of social media is supplementing the traditional role of the *diwaniyas*. Studies have shown that the introduction of the Internet has affected *diwaniya* attendance negatively and that many young people would rather use the Internet than visit *diwaniyas* (Wheeler, 2003). However, it could be argued that the use of social media in Kuwait has become an extension of the *diwaniyas*, where people can interact with politicians and opinion leaders online, discuss politics among themselves, or simply express their opinions.

Thus, Kuwaitis' high level of engagement on social media might be described as "virtual" *diwaniyas*, where public opinion is formed, news and political information are exchanged, and political opinions are expressed.

Although the social media sphere is active in Kuwait and is seen as a hub for political participation and expression in the Gulf, it faces many challenges and hurdles. In 2016, the government issued Cyber Crimes Law No. 63 which was approved by the National Assembly and contains 21 articles that aim to regulate online activities in Kuwait. Articles 4, 6, and 7 of the Cyber Crimes Law have concerned many activists and human rights advocates around the world. These articles could be used to limit freedom of expression on social media and could as well target online activists and online journalists. The law imposes severe restrictions on freedom of speech and allows the government to police online activities due to its vague and unclear terms. Therefore, this law can be described as a black point in Kuwait's history of freedom of speech.

Challenges

Since Kuwait's independence in 1961 and the subsequent establishment of the constitution, Kuwaiti media have enjoyed a great amount of freedom unlike the media in many other Arab countries. The press, for example, has never been owned by the government, but is instead censored and regulated by laws. Therefore, the government has to go to court if it wants to take an action or revoke a license. However, critics have argued that going to court causes a lot of trouble for the government and provides extra publicity for the publication. Thus, Kuwaiti media, to some extent, criticize the government, and most newspapers publish opinion articles and editorials that encourage public dialogue and provide topics for discussion in the *diwaniyas*. There is no doubt that tight censorship and government control of the media would lead to resistance and political unrest, and as control is less tight than in other countries, Kuwait remained relatively calm during the Arab uprisings in 2011 because opposition views were absorbed rather than silenced. The Kuwaiti media created an open political arena for the exchange of opinions and allowed criticism. However, with the exception of a few cases, the Kuwaiti press has always practiced a degree of self-discipline and self-censorship to avoid clashing with the government. Nevertheless, this self-censorship has its price and has affected the quality of journalism.

Today, as in many other countries, newspaper readership is declining in Kuwait and many newspapers are budget cutting in their operations by shrinking the number of pages or by laying off their journalists and employees. The decline in newspaper readership cannot go unnoticed or be denied. Many newspapers have started to disseminate their printed editions for free in governmental institutions, banks, and supermarkets in order to gain higher numbers in their circulation and readership. Also, newspapers have discontinued publishing on Saturdays in order to lower their expenses. Furthermore, the Internet and free news accessibility via social media have affected advertising revenue of newspapers. Many advertisers (the main source of revenue for Kuwaiti newspapers) have redirected their newspaper spending to social media advertising and other outlets such as influencers' endorsements. In addition, social media and online sources have provided uncensored news and publish more freely, which has affected journalism in Kuwait to a great degree.

Other challenges the Kuwaiti media face are those related to the press law and the Ministry of Information's direct control and management of broadcasting. The 2006 Press and Publication Law is seen as an improvement on the old law because of new press licensing and the ban on journalists' imprisonment without final court orders. However, the new law still limits what Kuwait's 1962 constitution guarantees, freedom of expression and freedom of the press. Moreover, the government proposed some amendments to the 2006 Press and Publication Law in 2010, an action that was described by legal experts as making a law that was somewhat strict into a very restrictive one. Some people have argued that the law will not necessarily stop people from writing but will make them lose their motivation to do so. Moreover, it is important to note that censorship is tolerated in Kuwait and expected as a form of civic responsibility. This civic responsibility makes journalists feel that they are protectors of the state, resulting in a culture of self-censorship to protect national security. On the other hand, broadcast media face tighter control mechanisms than print journalism in Kuwait because of their mass audience features, and the state has mostly continued its dominance in this sector.

In August 2020, the National Assembly approved several amendments to the Press and Publication Law that lifted the Ministry of Information's control over and censorship of publications, mainly books, imported into the country. These amendments have been seen as an important step towards more media freedom after years of fierce battle and the banning of 5,000 books over the last seven years. However, many people argue that this end to the Ministry of Information's control over publications has simply shifted the power of censorship and control from the executive branch to the judicial branch.

Outlook

The further development of Kuwaiti media will require major media policy reforms. Kuwaiti media need a structural independence from the government and the parliament so that their television professionals, journalists, and program producers can act more freely and express their creativity without government control and censorship. Although newspaper ownership is privately organized, papers are still bound by hidden government rules and regulations. Therefore, unconditional freedom of the press in Kuwait is necessary in order to further develop journalism and its practices.

The media industry in Kuwait has been highly influenced by the rapid technological developments. Digital media is taking over traditional media, and many daily newspapers have closed down, while others have introduced augmented and virtual reality news stories in addition to their digital newspapers. Nevertheless, the media are facing huge challenges in terms of revenue due to the social media advertising boom and the dominance of influencer marketing. Moreover, media platforms are trying very hard to catch up with the people's changing habits of media consumption and the emerging new trends in mobile media. In the end, technology alone cannot make a successful media unless it is creative and content rich. Despite the fact that Kuwaiti media are adopting the latest technologies, freedom of expression remains an essential factor for their development. Kuwait needs an independent regulator that can manage and regulate Kuwaiti media. In addition, Kuwaiti media must increase their transparency and reduce the Ministry of Information's control and management of theircontent.

References

Abu Shanab, H. (1987). *Communications' strategy in the State of Kuwait.* Kuwait: Al-Resala Publications.

Al-Enezi, M. (2015). This is Kuwait, a term that signals Kuwait radio's history of success. *KUNA.* https://www.kuna.net.kw/ArticlePrintPage.aspx?id=2424349&language=en

Al-Qassemi, S. (2011, May 31). Gulf governments take to social media. *Middle East Online.* http://middle-east-online.com/english/?id=46414

Al-Rasheed, A., & Chenoufi, M. (2008). *Pioneer of Kuwaiti journalism: Sheikh Abdul Aziz Al Rasheed (1887–1938 AD) and Majallat Al Kuwait (1928–1930 AD).* Kuwait: Kuwait University.

Asiri, A. (2007). *The political system in Kuwait: Principles and practices.* Kuwait: Alwatan.

CAIT (2016). *Consolidated Kuwait national ICT indicators report 2016.* The Council Agency for Information Technology of the Kuwait government. https://www.e.gov.kw/sites/kgoArabic/Forms/Final_Consolidated_English_Report_single_Pages.pdf

Central Intelligence Agency (2019). *The world factbook.* Washington: Central Intelligence Agency.

Dashti, A., & Al-Fadhli, S. (2011). The Impact of Online Journalism on the Freedom of the Press: A Case Study of Kuwait. *International Journal of Instructional Media, 38*(1), 47–59.

Freedom House (2019). *Country report: Kuwait.* https://freedomhouse.org/country/kuwait/freedom-world/2019

Greenfield, R. (2013, July 12). In Kuwait, Instagram accounts are big business. *The Atlantic Wire.* https://www.theatlantic.com/technology/archive/2013/07/kuwait-instagram-accounts-are-big-business/313382/

Kuwait National Assembly (2019). *The process of democratic live* [in Arabic]. http://www.kna.kw/clt-html5/index.asp

Ministry of Information (2019). https://www.media.gov.kw/

Saleh, S. (2016, January 28). Kuwait tops the world in terms of Twitter use. *Al-Nahar.* http://www.annaharkw.com/annahar/ArticlePrint.aspx?id=627923&mode=print

Salem, P. (2007). Kuwait: Politics in a participatory emirate. *Carnegie Endowment for International Peace.* https://www.files.ethz.ch/isn/157954/CMEC_3_salem_kuwait_final1.pdf

Shayji, A. (2009, February 3). Kuwait: A democratic model in trouble. *Carnegie Endowment for International Peace.* https://carnegieendowment.org/sada/22700

Tétreault, M. (2012, November 1). Looking for revolution in Kuwait. *Middle East Research and Information Project.* http://www.merip.org/mero/mero110112

Wheeler, D. (2003). The Internet and youth subcultures in Kuwait. *Journal of Computer-Mediated Communication, 8*(2).

Wheeler, D., & Mintz, L. (2010, April 15). The Internet and political change in Kuwait. *Foreign Policy.* http://mideast.foreignpolicy.com/posts/2010/04/15/the_Internet_and_political_change_in_kuwait

World Population Review (2019). *Kuwait population.* http://worldpopulationreview.com/search/?query=kuwait

11. Oman: Time for Fundamental Changes

Abdullah K. Al-Kindi

This chapter examines the most prominent milestones in the development of mass media in the Sultanate of Oman, and the relationship between media and the political system as well as the legislative frameworks regulating media work in the Sultanate. At the end of this chapter, the author also discusses a number of challenges facing the Omani media, which are structural, legislative, and professional in nature. The author argues that the conditions and developments in the media industry globally and regionally seem to be conducive to bringing about fundamental changes in the media system in Oman, but those changes are totally linked to the political system's desire and decision to make these changes.

Background

On 23 July 1970, the Sultanate of Oman witnessed the beginning of a new political era led by Sultan Qaboos bin Said, succeeding his father, Sultan Said bin Taimur (1910–1972), who had ruled Oman for nearly 38 years from 1932–1970 (Marefa, 2019). At the beginning of his reign, Sultan Qaboos faced a communist movement in the southern part of the country, which had been launched in 1965. The new political system was able to suppress that movement in 1975 with international support led by the United Kingdom and the participation of some regional powers, mainly Iran and Jordan. This new political era, called "contemporary Oman," was characterized by comprehensive development, especially in education, health, and social development, and a return to the culture and heritage that has always been a staple of Oman. The contemporary Oman is also characterized by the consolidation of the idea of a civil state through the implementation of laws and legislation in various fields, and the organization of a civil service sector, which has witnessed several developments in the period from 1970 until today.

Oman is located in the southeast of the Arabian Peninsula and has land borders with three Arab countries: the United Arab Emirates to the northwest, Saudi Arabia to the west, and Yemen to the southwest. It also has maritime borders with Iran and Pakistan. The coastline of the Sultanate of Oman stretches over 1,700 kilometers, and the total area of the Sultanate is estimated at 310 square kilometers.

This geopolitical location led the Sultanate to establish a continuous interactive relationship with different countries in its neighborhood. One of the most important achievements of contemporary Oman was the signing of border agreements with the neighboring countries of Saudi Arabia (1991), Yemen (1992), and the UAE (1999), and maritime border agreements with Pakistan (2000) and Iran (2015).

The Sultanate places great emphasis on the establishment of friendly and equal relations with countries worldwide, noninterference in the internal affairs of others, and respect for international laws, covenants, and customs (Ministry of Foreign Affairs, 2013). Today, Oman has extensive diplomatic relations with many countries worldwide. It was a founding member of the Gulf Cooperation Council (GCC) and has maintained its membership since 1981, and it has been a member of the Arab League and the United Nations since 1970, as well as being a member of various other regional and international organizations (Ministry of Foreign Affairs, n.d.).

Oman has also avoided engaging in wars or conflicts with any of its neighboring countries or getting involved in conflicts have taken place between them in the period from 1970 to the present. Perhaps the only exception to this was its participation in the war to liberate Kuwait after the Iraqi invasion on 2 August 1990, as part of the joint military forces of the GCC. The Sultanate takes the role of a political and diplomatic mediator among its neighbors rather than taking sides between them and other countries of the world. It solidified this role by hosting the signing of the nuclear agreement between Iran and the P5+1 countries (USA, Russia, China, UK, France, and Germany) in 2015 (Gupta, 2015).

Arabic is the official language of the Sultanate, used throughout governmental and educational institutions, and it is the language of social, cultural, and media discourse. English is the second most widely-used language, especially in the private sector and university education and, particularly, in the fields of science and technology. In addition to Arabic, the population speaks certain ethnic languages that reflect the sociocultural diversity of the Sultanate. In northern Oman, some residents speak Swahili, which they acquired and inherited from their ancestors during the Omani presence in East Africa, in general, and Zanzibar, in particular. Some people in the north also speak Baluchi, which was the result of the extension of Omani empire in the seventeenth and eighteenth centuries in Asia and around the Indian Ocean, particularly Gwadar and Mekran, as well as other languages such as Zadjali and Sindhi (Al-Balushi, 2015, p. 9). Some speak Shihi, particularly in Musandam, located in the far north of Oman. In the south of the country, the population speaks Arabic as well as the languages or dialects of ancient South Arabic, such as Shahriyah, Jabaliya, Harsusia, and Btahriya. This multilingualism reflects the human and cultural diversity in the Sultanate (Al-Mashani, 2003).

The latest statistics by the National Center for Statistics and Information show that, as of September 2019, the population of the Sultanate of Oman is now 4.8 million, of whom 57% are Omani nationals and 43% are expatriates. Notably, approximately 74% of the expatriates in Oman are from India and Bangladesh (36.9% from India and 36.8% from Bangladesh) (National Center for Statistics & Information, 2019).

Oman consists of 11 governorates or geographic regions with 61 local states. The features of modernity in contemporary Oman include attention to education, health, parliament, arts and literature, and other areas where the state has achieved advanced results as a modern nation.

Historical Developments

Oman could be considered a latecomer in terms of its introduction of mass media in comparison with other Arab countries. The first radio station was established in Oman in Muscat on 30 July 1970. This radio station was only one kilowatt and was transmitted to limited areas of the capital city (Al-Mashiaki, 2015, p. 32).

However, several recent studies have indicated the possibility that Oman had established several radio stations before that time, pointing to the likely beginning of *Radio Muscat* in the 1960s. Another radio station was established in the southern city of Salalah in 1961, *Radio Al-Hisen*, however the transmission of this radio station and its activity was limited and therefore did not reach the general public (Ministry of Heritage and Culture, 2013, pp. 66–67).

Printed periodicals initially appeared in Oman with the establishment and publication of *Al-Watan* for the first time on 28 January 1971, as a private newspaper founded by Nasr bin Mohammed Al-Taie. *Al-Watan* is still published today.

It should be noted here that Omanis knew and practiced journalism as a profession before 1970, but this was done outside the borders of contemporary Oman. Some Omani pioneer journalists established newspapers on the island of Zanzibar in the early twentieth century. Omani presence in East Africa, specifically on the island of Zanzibar, dates back to the seventh century, when the first Omani families and individuals migrated to Zanzibar and East Africa as well. The official Arab Omani ruling of Zanzibar lasted for more than a century; from 1832–1964 (Al-Kindi, 2004, p. 48). Omanis were responsible for many cultural and civilizational influences, journalism and newspapers being one example. The first of these was *Al-Najah*, founded by Nasser bin Salim bin Odeiam Al-Rawahi in 1911. *Al-Falaq* was founded by the Arab Society in Zanzibar in 1929, *Al-Murshid* by Ahmad bin Saif Al-Kharousi in 1942, and *Al-Nahda* by Sayyed Saif bin Hamoud Al-Said in 1951 (Al-Kindi, 2004, pp. 71–72).

While it is important that the founders of these newspapers were all Omani and most of their coverage was devoted to local Zanzibar events, it is also worth noting that these newspapers were interested in covering the news of Oman and described it as the "motherland" or "great homeland" (Al-Kindi, 2004, pp. 86–87).

These newspapers ceased publication in 1964 or even earlier, as the AfroShirazi Party led a revolt against the regime and against the Arab presence in Zanzibar on 12 January 1964, a date that marked the end of the Arab presence and the rule of the Omani Al-Said family on the island of Zanzibar (Al-Riyami, 2009, pp. 367–77).

Television began broadcasting as a state-funded project across Oman on 18 November 1974 and has since witnessed several developments in its programs, broadcasting hours, and program quality. *Oman News Agency (ONA)* was established in 1986 as an official source of news and information, especially from the government. In 1997, the Internet was extended for public use, and in 2004, journalists and media personalities established their professional society, the Omani Journalists Association.

Political System and Legal Framework

Since 1970, the mass media in Oman have witnessed remarkable developments, especially in terms of increasing the number of media outlets, content, and policies governing media environment. Today, there are 12 radio and six television channels broadcasting in Oman.

Ownership of radio and television channels in Oman is divided equally between the government and the private sector in an attempt to balance ownership and to avoid monopolization by a single sector. The number of radio channels outnumbers television channels by a 12 to 6 ratio, which is related to the higher costs of investment in television channels. Therefore, the financially more potent government is the investor and operator of four television channels through the Public Authority for Radio and Television versus two private television channels. As for the ownership of radio channels, the private sector is ahead of the government sector. In terms of the interests of these radio and television channels, most of them tend to be of general interest (13 general radio and television channels versus five specialized channels). This reflects a lack of interest in specialized fields and the desire of these channels to reach out to different audiences and, thus, achieve adequate financial and advertising revenues to ensure their survival and continuity. As for the language used on these channels, Arabic dominates in 13 radio and television channels out of 18, compared with four in English, and one in Arabic and English.

The dominance of the Arabic language is expected, although it overlooks large groups of residents in Oman who do not speak Arabic or English, especially those coming to work in the Sultanate from the Indian subcontinent. There is no media to address them in their language.

Printed periodicals have witnessed many developments in Oman. According to the Ministry of Information (2018), there are about 84 periodicals published in Oman, including seven dailies, the most important of which are *Al-Watan*, *Oman*, *Al-Shabiba*, and *Times of Oman*. The private sector owns more daily newspapers and is also ahead of the government sector in its establishment of these newspapers. The private sector established the first daily newspaper in Arabic in 1971, and this sector also founded the first daily newspaper in English in 1975.

More than half of all Omani periodicals are owned and published by governmental and semi-governmental entities. These kinds of periodicals, however, could be described as public relations publications representing the concerned entities (Ministry of Information, 2018).

Unfortunately, there are no known or reliable circulation figures for the printed periodicals in the Sultanate, and there is no system for publishing and disclosing these figures to the public. However, these numbers are made available to advertisers in a very limited way.

The mass media in Oman have been an essential part of the Omani regime's project to build a modern state. Therefore, the establishment and emergence of mass media in contemporary Oman has been linked to the desire of the new political system, led by Sultan Qaboos bin Said since 1970, to employ these means in his comprehensive development project. The media is therefore meant to document the achievements of the Omani regime in various fields, comment on them, and provide the audience with appropriate explanations to support these achievements.

The political system in Oman is a hereditary monarchy, and the sultan is the head of goverment, the prime minister, and the final arbiter in all state affairs. The media system reflects the orientations of the authoritarian political system in which the mass media cannot violate the orientations of that regime or act contrary to its views (Abu Zaid, 1986). News stories sometimes note a departure from the general political orientation in one country or another, but such stories are rare, and are not representative of a mass media that is subject to an authoritarian political regime.

In Oman, the mass media are subject to direct and indirect regime control through specific institutions. The Public Authority for Radio and Television, as a governmental entity, supervises and operates five public radio and television channels, four of which are *Oman TV*, *Oman Cultural Channel*, *Oman Radio*, and *Oman Youth Radio*. The Ministry of Information also directly supervises and operates two daily newspapers in Arabic and English in addition to a quarterly cultural magazine and the *Oman News Agency*. Private broadcasting outlets are under the supervision of the Ministry of Information, which also regulates the work of these channels and gives them permission to broadcast. A special committee in the Ministry of Information is in charge of monitoring these channels. The Ministry of Information, through its publication's unit, also supervises all government and private print publications issued in the Sultanate. According to the Press and Publications Law of 1984, the Ministry of Information is the authority responsible for issuing licenses for the government and private publications.

Online media are subject to the technical supervision of the Information Regulatory Authority through the Telecommunications Regulatory Law of 2002. However, there is no specific government body responsible for licensing or permitting electronic online publications or radio and television channels. When any individual or company opts to produce any media using the Internet, they need to get a special domain assigned from within the Sultanate through the Information Technology Authority or register outside internationally. Thus, regime entities control the content published by both government and private mass media through a set of laws and legislation, as well as general policies and practices.

The public receives free radio and television broadcasts and buys daily newspapers and publications at nominal prices. A daily newspaper costs Bz 200 (USD 0.52), and the value of other periodicals offered for sale is not more than OMR 1 (USD 2.60). Many institutional publications are provided to ministries and companies free of charge.

Litigation procedures in case of any violation of the applicable laws include administrative procedures carried out by the Ministry of Information, as stated in the Press and Publications Law of 1984, and judicial procedures if the concerned people decide to take it further.

Economy and Ownership Patterns

Ownership of the mass media in Oman is divided between the government and the private sector. Private sector investments are more interested in radio stations, while investments in television channels remain limited. One potential reason for this is the relatively high financial cost required to invest in the establishment of a television channel compared with the fewer technical requirements for founding a radio station. Another reason is that the advertising market in the Sultanate remains limited compared with that in other countries in the region, such as the United Arab Emirates and Saudi Arabia.

Most of the private mass media companies in Oman can be described as family-owned businesses. *Al-Watan*, the first Omani Arabic daily newspaper, is owned by the Al-Taie family. Similarly, the *Times of Oman* (founded in 1975) and *Al-Shabiba* (founded in 1993) are owned by the Al-Zidjali family. The *Al-Roya* newspaper (founded in 2009) is owned by another member of the Al-Taie family, which is the case for quite a few of these newspapers and periodicals. These families invest mainly in media, but also hold certain other businesses, since they either belong to the business elite or maintain a strong relationship with them and organize their media activities through publishing houses.

Ownership laws in the Sultanate allow a single company to own more than one media outlet and to exist as "multi-activity" companies. This has allowed some companies to publish different newspapers using both Arabic and English languages since the 1990s. For example, the Omani Institution for Press, Printing, Publishing and Distribution, which has published *Al-Watan* since 1971, started publishing the *Oman Tribune*, a free weekly newspaper, in 2004, *Futon* in 2005, and a free weekly sports newspaper, *Al-Malaeb*, in 2007.

Recently, some media companies have been diversifying their media activities. Muscat House for Press, Publishing and Distribution—which has owned the *Times of Oman* (in English since 1975), *Al-Shabiba* (in Arabic since 1993), and a free weekly newspaper, *Al-Youm Al-Sabi'*, since 2007—established a radio station, *Shabiba Radio*, in 2018. The same is true for Al-Roya Press and Publishing, which has published the Arabic daily newspaper *Al-Roya* since 2009, and launched *Al-Roya Radio Voice* in 2017.

Allowing media companies to engage in multiple enterprises and outlets and, thus, encouraging a certain diversity of the means owned by them is a positive and healthy phenomenon that reflects the potential of these companies, their desire to expand within the market, and to get a greater share of advertising. This trend also reflects the state's confidence in these companies, their media line, and their relationships with the political system. But this trust may also evolve into a kind of monopoly or centralization of the mass media in the hands of a limited and narrow group of families and individuals who own these companies.

The economic system in the Sultanate allows private companies to own mass media in accordance with limited rules and conditions, the most important of which is the existence of financial efficiency, and the stipulation that over 50% of the company's capital and shares are owned by Omani nationals. The Sultanate has not attracted international investment in the media sector, perhaps due to economic laws that do not provide enough incentives in this regard, or because the media environment in the Sultanate is not encouraging enough to attract international media companies to operate from there in free media cities, as is the case in the United Arab Emirates, Egypt, Qatar, and Jordan.

Oman is not expected to open its doors to international investment in the field of media, as Dubai has already done for nearly 20 years or as Qatar has recently begun to do. From a political point of view, opening up to international investments might contradict the policy of neutrality and noninterference in foreign affairs, and there is also a concern that the state would lose its control over the media sector in such a scenario. International investors might require greater freedom of expression to say what they want in their media, which could cause embarrassment to the Oman on the world-stage.

Oman is classified as one of the Gulf Arab oil countries, which rely on oil as a main source of national income. According to the latest statistics and reports for 2019, the state's revenues from oil and gas reached OMR 7.4 billion (USD 19.7 billion), which comprises about 74% of its total revenue (PWC Middle East, 2019).

However, Oman's oil and gas revenues remain modest compared with those of other countries in the Gulf region, outperforming only Bahrain in oil revenues in the region. Since the beginning of the development movement in contemporary Oman, the state economic situation has positively impacted the media. The oil revenues that have flowed since the 1970s have helped to establish and develop many mass media outlets.

These revenues have also helped the government to support mass media institutions, especially in the form of donations and direct financial support, or advertisements, subscriptions, and tax exemptions. It was only in the mid-1990s that the state ended direct financial support of private newspapers and magazines in Oman. As the world witnessed a decline in oil prices beginning in 2015, the Omani regime reduced spending on advertising in the media and subscriptions, which affected many private mass media outlets, particularly newspapers, some of which reduced their publication frequency, number of pages, or stopped publishing altogether.

Technology and Infrastructure

Oman has a well-developed technical infrastructure and is categorized by some international reports on the Middle East and North Africa (MENA) region as one of the countries that invests most heavily in infrastructures that enable people to continuously use and spread technology. One report stated that "since 2007 Oman has completed fifty-four infrastructure projects, which is the highest number of any MENA country" (Göll & Zwiers, 2018, p. 3).

However, the problem of slow network speed should also be noted, especially in some remote areas or those affected by mountainous terrain. Calls to improve network services and reach all regions without exception continue to be made, as well as demands to reduce service pricing to enable the widest use. Regarding mobile telephony, the number of mobile and smart phone subscriptions is widespread. According to the latest statistics, there are about 6.7 million device subscriptions which amounts to 133% of the total population (Kemp, 2019).

Telecommunications services were once limited to a single company, *OmanTel*. Today there are six telecommunications service providers; only one of them is semi-governmental (*OmanTel*), while the rest are private and owned by Omani companies. These companies are under the supervision of a government authority, the Telecommunications

Regulatory Authority (TRA), which is responsible for issuing, classifying, and regulating work permits. In general, the contents of telecommunications and the Internet are subject to unspoken censorship. Advanced techniques are used for sorting, categorizing, and blocking certain content classified by government entities as "unaccepted contents," specifically those regarding political, social, or cultural issues, or any others considered sensitive.

Regarding Internet reach and saturation in Oman, the latest statistics as of mid-2019 indicate that the number of Internet users in the Sultanate reached 3.7 million users, a figure representing 80% of the total population. The number of social network accounts in the Sultanate has reached about 2.5 million of Internet users, and *Facebook* is ahead of other social platforms in terms of the number of users in Oman, attracting about 1.8 million users (Kemp, 2019).

Despite the many and varied options offered by state-of-the-art technology in all fields, including the media, traditional media companies are still in a slow transitional phase of integrating electronic publishing into their activities. Some of these publishing houses still place more emphasis on the hard copy and have not yet improved their electronic versions or linked them appropriately to social networks. Some traditional newspapers have not yet started using electronic applications in smartphones. In general, traditional newspapers and periodicals in Oman remain reluctant to undergo digital transformation.

This reluctance may be related to the lack of financial resources to bring about digital transformation appropriately. Beyond the traditional media, there are evolving initiatives to employ technology in media work. Almost eight full private electronic newspapers are published in Oman, along with a number of news sites and applications, most notably *Atheer*, *Al-Falaq*, *Wahag Al-Khaleej*, and *Wejhatt*. Recently, some digital podcasts have emerged as private projects. The creative digital content industry is also evolving in Oman and is being led by small businesses and individual initiatives that need more support for greater success in the future.

The technology resources available today in Oman are capable of developing both the traditional and new media sectors, and employing digitization for the ultimate benefit of the media content consumer. Nonetheless, there remains a strong need for further encouragement and support of this transition.

Challenges

The main challenges facing the current media system in Oman can be divided into three types: structural, regulatory, and professional challenges.

The political system in Oman deals with the media outlets—both governmental and private—as non-independent, subordinate forces. Accordingly, the regime controls the media, their orientations, and their content through certain laws, or even through direct and indirect instructions for media outlets to take certain positions or avoid covering certain stories or events. This trend imposes a pattern of "government media" in which there is little room for disagreement or criticism, especially regarding policies of the regime. A more public service-oriented media could ensure more space for a freer and more independent media.

One of the structural challenges facing the media system in Oman is the absence of a clear strategy directing media work in the country. To the best of the author's knowledge, there is no written or published strategy for media in the Sultanate, despite the importance of strategic planning in this field.

In addition to these challenges, there are several official institutions supervising and directing media work in Oman. This multiplicity is confusing, hampers media development, and leads to overlaps in tasks and responsibilities. For example, the Ministry of Information supervises all publications and private radio and television channels, as well as the *Oman News Agency*. At the same time, the Public Authority for Radio and Television operates and manages five radio stations and four television channels. Both the Ministry and the Authority work independently from one another and do not officially cooperate. The new media and its various applications are technically under the supervision and operation of the Ministry of Transport and Communications through the TRA and the Information Technology Authority (ITA). As for the new media, there is no specific body to supervise or even license these types of media outlet. In 2017, the Communications Center for Government Services was established. This institution is a central public relations agency whose main objective is to provide positive images about the regime's performance.

It is affiliated with the General Secretariat of the Council of Ministers and operates independently of the abovementioned media institutions, even if it cooperates with them to accomplish its various tasks. In order to overcome this supervisory chaos, the author proposes that these separate institutions be put under the supervision of a single umbrella institution in the form of a national media council to oversee these bodies and set broader policies for media work in the Sultanate.

Furthermore, the media legislative and regulatory frameworks in the Sultanate are outdated and not in line with the technical and objective changes witnessed in the media environment inside and outside the Sultanate. The Press and Publications Law, which is considered the most important legal document for regulating media work in the Sultanate, was first issued in 1984 and does not cover many of the changes in the media sector, especially in the area of new media and its various applications.

Because of the multiplicity of institutions operating and supervising media institutions, there are also numerous laws relating to media institutions. When assessing the organization of media work in the Sultanate, it is not only the Press and Publications Law (1984), Telecommunications Regulations Law (2002), and Radio and Television Private Establishments Law (2004) that must be considered, but also some other laws which have separate legal articles related to media work, such as the Penal Code (1974), the Commercial Companies Law (1974), the Trade Law (1990), and the Law of Declaring a State of Emergency (2008).

The Omani media also face professional challenges. Perhaps, first and foremost is the human and financial inability to incorporate the elements of media convergence, especially in the private sector outlets. There are limited possibilities for the current institutions to achieve this, and initiatives for media convergence on the level of media institutions and the messages they provide are lacking, along with the multimedia skills of journalists and media professionals.

Another professional challenge facing the Omani media is the absence of accurate indicators of public attitudes and their requirements from media in terms of programs and messages. There are, to the best of the author's knowledge, no monitoring centers for public opinion that can help the media in formulating their messages in more useful and influential ways. The National Center for Statistics and Information, established in 2012, may help to provide some information about the public's preferences, but it cannot serve as a professional center for measuring public opinion.

On the other hand, there is no accurate information on the Omani media's competitiveness, level of access and influence, circulation, distribution, readership, listenership, viewership, or other important information that might help in judging the performance of these media, and measuring their public presence and influence.

Outlook

Looking to the future, two fundamental changes are required. The first is related to the traditional media and requires a major political decision. The second is being led by the new media, and could be described as a gradual shift that began a while ago thanks to the efforts of individual citizens. On the level of traditional media, the future Omani media scene will require major restructuring. First and foremost, a shift away from the government media model is necessary in order to reduce the regime's control over media work and media outlets. In spite of difficulty of accepting this model, the Sultanate has important capabilities and experiences that can help in this gradual transition, which would require a political decision to start the process.

On the level of new media, social networks in particular have given individuals the opportunity to express themselves more freely, present their different views and readings to governmental and non-governmental institutions, and critique these institutions in an unprecedented manner. It can be argued that new media have provided a more dynamic, free, and diverse public space than traditional media. However, the content, attitude and level of criticism of state institutions of traditional media could greatly benefit from the advantages brought by new media.

References

Abu Zaid, F. (1986). *Journalism systems in the Arab World* [in Arabic]. Cairo: Book World.

Al-Balushi, K. (2015). *Multiculturalism in Oman: Its foundations and problems* [in Arabic]. Muscat: Oman Institute for Press, Publishing and Advertisement.

Al-Kindi, A. (2004). The beginnings of the Omani press in Zanzibar. *The Arab Journal of Human Sciences, 88*, 47–110.

Al-Mashani, M. (2003). *Dhofar hemiari contemporary tongue: Survey comparison study* [in Arabic]. Muscat: Oman Studies Center, Sultan Qaboos University.

Al-Mashiaki, M. (2015). *Media in the Gulf: Current and future* [in Arabic]. Al-Ain: Al-Falah Books for Publishing and Circulation.

Al-Riyami, N. (2009). *Zanzibar personalities and events (1828–1972)* [in Arabic]. Muscat: Beirut Bookshop.

Göll, E., & Zwiers, J. (2018). Technology trends in the MENA region: The cases of digitalization and information and communications technology (ICT). *MENARA Working Papers No. 23*. https://www.iai.it/sites/default/files/menara_wp_23.pdf

Gupta, S. (2015, July 23). Oman: The unsung hero of the Iranian nuclear deal. *Foreign Policy Journal*. https://www.foreignpolicyjournal.com/2015/07/23/

Kemp, S. (2019). Digital 2019: Oman. *Data Reportal*. https://datareportal.com/reports/digital-2019-oman

Marefa (2019). *Said bin Taimur*. https://www.marefa.org

Ministry of Foreign Affairs (n.d.). *Multilateral relations*. https://www.mofa.gov.om/?page_id=9327&lang=en

———. (2013). *Foreign policy*. https://www.mofa.gov.om/?p=796&lang=en

Ministry of Heritage and Culture (2013). Radio Al-Hisen [in Arabic]. In Ministry of Heritage and Culture (Eds.), *The Omani encyclopaedia: Volume I* (pp. 66–67). Muscat: Ministry of Heritage and Culture.

Ministry of Information (2018). *List of periodicals in the Sultanate of Oman* [in Arabic]. Unpublished report.

National Center for Statistics & Information (2019). *Population clock*. https://www.ncsi.gov.om/Pages/NCSI.aspx

PWC Middle East (2019). *Oman state budget*. https://www.pwc.com/m1/en/services/tax/me-tax-legal-news/2019/2019-oman-state-budget.html

12. Yemen: Unsettled Media for an Unsettled Country

Abdulrahman M. Al-Shami

> Throughout history, successive governments in Yemen have realized the importance of the media. Consequently, they have tightened the grip on the media by imposing a monopoly on ownership and by selecting editors-in-chief and other leading positions to ensure complete media control. Thus, media have functioned as a voice for the government rather than a voice for the public. A slight change has occurred since the Yemeni unification in 1990 in terms of allowing limited ownership and freedom of expression. However, as a result of the long monopoly and mismanagement, media in Yemen are facing huge challenges at the levels of infrastructure, technology, regulation, freedom of expression, training, and professionalism.

Background

Located in the southernmost portion of the Arabian Peninsula, the Republic of Yemen is bordered by Saudi Arabia to the north, the Arabian Sea and Gulf of Aden to the south, the Sultanate of Oman to the east, and the Red Sea to the west. In 2019, the population exceeded 29 million, with a growth rate estimated at more than 3% per year.

Yemen was for a long time divided in two parts. Before 1962, northern Yemen was under the rule of the Zaydi Imamate from 898 to 1962 until a revolution erupted in September 1962. Southern Yemen was under British colonial administration from 1839 to 1967 until another revolution began on 14 October 1967 (Varisco, 2017). In 1990, the two

Yemens—the People's Democratic Republic of Yemen or South Yemen and the Arab Republic of Yemen or North Yemen—unified and became one country under the name of the Republic of Yemen.

Yemen is a traditional society that has entered the era of modernization only recently, where tribes and clans stand out as active in and determinant of social structure (Al-Salahi, 2012, p. 14). The tribes have had a significant impact on Yemen and its social structure since ancient times. Under the modern state structure, the tribes still play a pivotal role in Yemen's political life (Rabe'e, 2012, p. 28). Tribal leaders and clans are the basis of state authority in rural areas (Al-Mawla, 2011, p. 121).

Most of Yemen remains religiously divided, with the Shi'a Zaydi school dominant in the north, and the Sunni Shafi'i School most common in the south and along the Red Sea Coast (Varisco, 2017). Sunnis represent about 70% of the population and Zaydis about 30%. There are also two minorities, one of which is an Ismaili sect that is classified as part of the Shi'ites, and the other is Jews, most of whom emigrated to Israel in the late 1940s as part of an organized plan to evacuate them from Yemen (Al-Salahi, 2012, p. 15). Some of the remaining Jews have migrated to Israel recently due to conflict and threats, mainly from the Houthis. The current state constitution defines Yemen as an Arab, Islamic state, and Islamic Shar'ia law is the basis for all legislation. The Arabic language is the official and dominant language in society and all aspects of life, as well as in the educational system.

According to the Yemeni Constitution, the political system of Yemen is based on political and party pluralism. The authorities are divided into three independent entities: the executive authority, represented by the President of the Republic and the Council of Ministers, the legislative authority, and the judiciary. However, actual practice reflects that full control of the executive lies in the hands of the president, as opposed to the other ministers (Al-Salahi, 2012, p. 16).

The Yemeni economy in the two Yemens, both before and after unification, is a rent-based economy. This type of economy has led to the fragility of the state, a lack of power and legitimacy, encouragement of non-official groups to rebel against the state, and a lack of stability on the economic, political, and social levels (Al-Fakih, 2012, p. 31).

Many factors have led to enduring political conflict, which has been ongoing over the last three decades: corruption, marginalized democracy, and a lack of political reform, as well as a failure to embrace the collective stance needed to build a modern state. This includes, but is not limited to, the secessionist movement in the south and the Houthi movement in the north, which culminated after the Arab uprisings in 2011. One year into the uprising, then-president Ali Abdallah Saleh stepped down after more than three decades in power and left a political vacuum in the country. Yemen's political elite acceded to the Gulf initiative in November 2011, which established a caretaker transitional government. The agreement, which was signed in Riyadh on 23 November 2011, stipulated a two-year transitional period and created a National Dialogue Conference (NDC) as a forum to solve the country's political problems (Schmitz, 2014). The Conference, which lasted for almost one year, concluded with agreement on most of the controversial and critical issues as well as a future road map. Thus, Yemen was referred to as one of the success stories of the Arab uprisings. Yet, within months, a rebel group, the Houthis, took over the Amran governorate and other important military camps and facilities. Motivated by popular frustrations over deteriorating living circumstances and lack of political reforms (Clausen, 2015), the Houthi forces and forces loyal to former president Saleh took control of Yemen's capital, Sana'a and much of the country on 21 September 2014. Consequently, the Yemeni state nearly collapsed (Human Rights Watch, 2019).

In March 2015, after Saleh's successor, President Abed Rabbo Mansur Hadi, who had fled to Saudi Arabia, appealed for international intervention, Saudi Arabia hastily assembled an international coalition and launched a military offensive aimed at restoring Hadi's rule and evicting the Houthi fighters from the capital and other major cities. Since then, the war has caused the deaths of thousands of Yemenis, including civilians as well as combatants, and has significantly damaged the country's infrastructure as well as its social fabric (Sharp, 2019).

Historical Developments

The media in Yemen have been through different historical developments. These can be classified into four major phases: 1) the British and Ottoman occupation, 2) revolutionary times and independence, 3) separation until 1990, and 4) the period after unification in 1990.

During the first phase, in 1872, the Ottomans introduced the first print media to Northern Yemen for official use, the *Yemen* newsletter, which was the first publication in Yemen in the Turkish language. In 1879, *Sana'a*, a weekly newspaper, was published as the first newspaper in the Arabian Peninsula in the Turkish language and later on in Arabic and Turkish languages (Al-Zain, 1995, pp. 17–32). The *Al-Iman* newspaper was published in 1926 and the *Al-Hekma Al-Yamaniya* magazine in 1938 (Al-Zain, 1995, pp. 60–69).

In Southern Yemen, *Aden* weekly newspaper was the first official newspaper, which was published from 1929. *Sawt Al-Jazeera Aden* was published in 1939, followed by other newspapers. The purpose of these publications was to clarify Britain's position on World War II and to highlight the victories of the Allied Forces against Germany. These publications also aimed to publish news of the colonial administration in Aden and its decisions. By 1960, the number of daily and weekly newspapers and magazines in Aden had increased to 34 publications issued by the government, parties, and syndicates (Mutahar, 2004, p. 68). These journalistic activities indicate that all competing parties in North and South Yemen, including the Imamate, the opposition, and the British colonizers, had recognized the importance of print journalism in the conflict.

South Yemen was first introduced to radio broadcasting in 1940 when the British occupation authority established a small radio station, *Voice of the Island*, in Aden. This station broadcast on short wave, targeting Yemenis and residents of Aden and announcing military victories of Britain and the Allied countries against Germany and its Axis allies. It also broadcast instructions to citizens on how to protect themselves against air strikes during World War II (Basaleem, 2003, p. 65). *Radio Aden* was established in 1954 as the first radio station to provide regular services in the region in the morning and evening periods. It broadcast programs for six hours per day and 10 hours on weekends (Mutahar, 2004, pp. 81–82).

In North Yemen, an American delegation came to Sana'a in 1946 to discuss with Imam Yahya the oil extraction in Yemen. They brought a 13-watt wireless device with them, which they gave to the Imam.

This device was then used for radio broadcasting. The radio station broadcast its programs every Thursday and Friday for one hour and 15 minutes only, with content limited to readings from the Holy Qur'an, Imam news, religious speeches, and military marches played by copper machines (Al-Soswa, 1998, p. 17).

The real birth of the Yemeni radio news came after the revolution of 26 September 1962, where radio played an important role in defending the revolution and the Republican system. After that point, broadcast transmission increased to cover the entire day and devoted two hours for broadcasting in the English language.

In the South, *Aden TV* began broadcasting on 11 September 1964, during the British occupation of Southern Yemen. The broadcast duration ranged from two to four hours daily and covered the city of Aden (Al-Fakih, 2000, p. 3). The second phase, during the 1960s, directly involved the popular struggle of the Yemeni people. Press publications reached a total of 19 newspapers and magazines. Their positions ranged from those who supported the armed revolt against the colonizer, to those who were pro-occupation, and to others who were in between. However, most of these newspapers were pro-revolutionary and supported the armed struggle against British colonialism (Mutahar, 2004, p. 70).

During the third phase, the separation of South Yemen, and after the end of British colonialism in 1967 and the establishment of the Socialist Party of Yemen, almost all newspapers in the south were suspended. During the period from 1970 to 1985, only two newspapers were published, *Defa'a Al-Sha'ab* and *Al-Rayah*, which was issued by the military in 1980.

In North Yemen after the 1962 revolution, three official newspapers appeared: *Al-Thawra*, *Al-Gomhoriah*, and *Al-Akhbar*. *Al-Thawra* was the first newspaper for the newborn republic. Despite the different names of those newspapers during that period, their content was almost identical in terms of addressing various issues related to the revolution and the fledgling republic, as well as questioning the past period in all its forms and manifestations. They were operated based on an informally unified framework to help in nation-building (Mutahar, 2004, p. 67).

According to the Ministry of Information, the total publications in North Yemen reached 46 (daily, weekly, and monthly) during the period from 1962 to 1978. This is considered the phase in which modern journalism was established in Yemen.

Aden News Agency was established in 1970 in South Yemen to collect and disseminate news, while in North Yemen, *Saba'a Yemeni News* was set up. They later merged into one news agency, the *Yemeni News Agency (Saba'a)*, after 1990, which is the main source of news for Yemeni official media inside the country, as well as for media institutions abroad. Also, *Sana'a TV* began broadcasting on 24 September 1975, transmitting from a studio of 100 square meters with little equipment.

Yemen General Corporation for Radio & Television was reorganized in May 1990 after the reunification through a merger of one corporation that was established in Sana'a in 1976 with another that was established in Aden in 1986. The headquarters are located in Sana'a. It comprises *Yemen Satellite Channel* and *First Channel* in Sana'a, *Second Channel* in Aden, *Public Radio Program* in Sana'a, and *Second Radio Program* in Aden as well as local radio stations in several governorates.

After 1990, Yemeni media have witnessed remarkable developments in terms of quantity, quality, and the level of form and content as well as the legislative aspect. The number of newspapers and magazines were doubled as more licenses were granted. However, only 191 of the 497 licensed newspapers have continued to be published on regular and semi-regular bases (Abdulwase'e, 2009). In addition, television transmission via the *ArabSat* satellite started in 1996.

The widening margin of freedom granted to the media has enabled partisan and non-partisan newspapers to appear, allowing all political, partisan, and civil society organizations to express themselves through print media, including nongovernment newspapers (42), party newspapers (22), governmental newspapers (19), nongovernment magazines (22), party magazines (3), and 42 governmental and official magazines (Basaleem, 2003, pp. 175–81).

This new free atmosphere and the evolution of satellite television broadcasting technology have allowed private television channels to appear as well. By the end of 2012, there were 13 television satellite channels: four of them are state-run channels and the rest are private. Two of the government channels are for general programming, *Al-Yemen* and *Aden*, and the others are specialized channels, such as *Sheba*, a youth and sports channel, and *Al-Iman*, a religious channel, both launched in

2008. *Al-Saeeda TV* was the first Yemeni private channel launched from Cairo in 2007, and it then moved its operation to Sana'a. In 2009, three channels were launched: *Suhail*, an opposition channel from inside the country; *Al-Aqeek* (Onex), which shut down after one year for financial reasons; and *Aden Live*, an opposition channel from abroad. Three more non-governmental channels were launched in 2011. These included *Yemen Today* (partisan channel), *A'azal* (belonging to one tribe leader), and *Yemen Shabab*, a youth and revolutionary channel as well as the *Belqees* channel, another youth and revolutionary channel owned by female Nobel Prize winner Tawakkol Karman. The channel used to broadcast from Yemen until 2015, when it was moved to Istanbul after being attacked by the Houthis. In 2012, two new channels were launched: *Al-Maseerah* (belonging to the Houthi Movement) and *Al-Sahat* (launched from Beirut in July) (Al-Shami, 2013, pp. 443–51).

Moreover, two new channels affiliated with Houthis have launched and are operating from Sana'a. They are *Al-Hawia TV*, which officially launched on 15 April 2018, and *Al-Lahda TV*, which launched in July 2018. In early 2020, *Al-Mahriah TV* was launched from Istanbul as the most recent channel broadcasting from outside the country.

Political System and Legal Framework

The Yemeni Constitution guarantees freedom of opinion and expression to all citizens. According to Article 42, every citizen has the right to participate in the political, economic, social, and cultural life of the country. The state shall guarantee freedom of thought and expression of opinion in speech, writing, and photography within the limits of the law. It also guarantees citizens the right to organize themselves in different manners. The state shall also guarantee freedom for the political, trade, cultural, scientific, and social organizations.

Law No. 25 on the Press and Publication, which was issued in 1990, has governed the Yemeni press up to this date. According to Article 33 of this law, the right to own and publish newspapers and magazines is guaranteed by the Constitution to all citizens, licensed political parties, individuals, public companies, popular organizations, ministries and government, as well as corporations. In the chapter on the rights and duties of journalists, Article 13 confirms that a "journalist may not be interrogated on opinions which he has expressed or published, and which may not be used to inflict harm on him/her provided what he/ she published is not contrary to the law."

Despite the abovementioned constitutional guarantees, Law No. 25 imposes several restrictions on the freedom of information and allows the imprisonment of journalists. Article 103 contains a list of restrictions that journalists must take into consideration. This list includes prohibits the following:

> a) Criticism of the head of state, or attribution to him of declarations or pictures unless the declarations were made or the pictures taken during a public speech.
>
> b) Anything which leads to the spread of ideas contrary to the principles of the Yemeni Revolution, is prejudicial to national unity or distorts the image of Yemeni, Arab or Islamic heritage.
>
> c) Anything that undermines public morals or prejudices the dignity of individuals or the freedom of the individual by smears and defamation.

Article 104 of the law emphasizes that anyone who violates this "shall be subject to a fine not exceeding ten thousand riyals or a period of imprisonment not exceeding one year." Moreover, they shall be tried before the Public Prosecutor's Office for Press and Publications, which was founded in 1993. The law also includes other punishments, such as the closure of newspapers or suspension of their work, confiscation of copies, and the prevention of journalistic practice (Article 19, 2008, p. 6).

Under this law, several violations against journalists were committed. These included, but were not limited to, the imprisonment of journalists, seizure of licenses, creation of copies of websites, threats to journalists, break-ins at media organizations' premises, murders and assaults of journalists, and confiscation of their equipment. Therefore, this law has been subject to much criticism throughout the last years from different actors, including individual journalists, the Journalists' Syndicate, civil society organizations, lawyers, and lawmakers. They have called for changes or at least amendments to it. In an attempt to regulate online journalism, which had started to play a role in influencing public opinion, as well as to respond to demands to allow forces other than the government to own broadcast channels, in 2010 the Ministry of Information proposed a new law for organizing broadcast and online media. This law was however very controversial due to its extreme restrictions and conditions for owning and launching media outlets. For instance, the proposed new law would require those who wished to obtain a license to establish a television channel to pay YER 30 million (around USD 135,000 at the time) and YER 20 million (USD 90,000) to establish a radio station or online websites. In addition, the same amount would have to be paid every two years for a renewal of the license. The fees for owning a multimedia service via mobile phone was to be set at 10 million riyals. However, the political conflicts in the years after the law was proposed hindered the process of finalizing and endorsing it by parliament. Consequently, Press Law No. 25 from 1990 still governs media in Yemen.

The government's constant attempts to legislate mass media reflect the importance it attributes to the media and its desire to control it. This has led it to adopt legal articles that reflect the interests of the ruling authority, not those of the press or journalists, and guarantee the authority complete control of the media. Consequently, this has led to a long conflict between the government, on one hand, and individual journalists, the Journalists' Syndicate, and civil society, including NGOs, on the other. It is worth mentioning that in October 2017, the Minister of Information under the *de facto* authority issued a bylaw for the regulation of online journalism.

It is noteworthy that the youth uprising in 2011 had pushed for more media freedom, including on the state-run television channels, in terms of providing space for different voices, particularly for opposition and anti-government voices. Following the uprising, talk show programs on the *Al-Yemen*, *Sheba*, and *Al-Iman* channels were dedicated to debating about protests, including the reasons that triggered them and their consequences. For several weeks, those channels hosted young people from the pro- and anti-government groups to openly debate on those issues. However, this approach lasted for only a short period of time, and those channels eventually returned to presenting a one-sided discourse.

After the Houthis took over Sana'a in September 2014, the media landscape in Yemen dramatically changed. They took control of all the state-run media, including television channels, radio stations, and print and online newspapers as well as *Yemeni News Agency* (*Saba'a*) and its website: *Saba'a Net*. They also closed down non-governmental media, including television channels, print and online websites, and community radio stations. Moreover, they attacked media premises belonging to opposition media organizations, confiscated their property, and imprisoned many journalists. According to Human Rights Watch, a group of local journalists has been detained in Sana'a for more than three years (Human Rights Watch, 2019). Thirty-five journalists have died in Yemen since 2011, and eight of them were killed in 2018. In addition, 53 kidnapping or arrest cases of journalists have been recorded since 2011, mostly perpetrated by the Houthis and the related government. The International Federation of Journalists (IFJ) and the Yemeni Journalists' Syndicate (YJS) reported that 135 cases of press freedom violations were registered from January to the end of September 2018. Moreover, the Yemeni media have become polarized along political and sectarian lines and have been viewed by the warring factions as the enemy (IFJ, 2018).

The Houthis also shut down offices of pan-Arab television channels such as *Al-Jazeera* and *Al-Arabiya* as well as other Arab channels, and they placed the Internet and mobile phones under censorship and surveillance.

The division of the country between the Houthi-controlled areas and the Saudi-UAE coalition-controlled areas has created two parallel media landscapes in Yemen that reflect the political situation. There are two versions of each medium, including *Yemen TV*, *Saba'a Net*, and the *Al-Thawra* website. One operates from Riyadh and the other from Sana'a, and each of them reflects the position of the individual controller. Moreover, some non-governmental television channels have migrated abroad. *Suhail TV* operates from Riyadh, and *Yemen Shabab* from Amman and Istanbul. *Belqees TV* operates from Istanbul, *Al-Sahat TV* from Beirut, and *Yemen Today TV* from Cairo.

The main media victims after the Houthis took control over Sana'a were community radio stations. According to Al-Moushaki, director of *Yemen Times* radio station and chair of the Yemeni Network for Community Radio, the situation for community radio stations deteriorated after 2015 due to economic problems resulting from the war. In addition, the premises of many stations were raided, and their property was looted. Some others had been suspended, and some turned to commercial entertainment models (Al-Reifi, 2019). Around mid-2016, community radio stations began to gradually reappear in the Sana'a, Hadramout, and Aden governorates, but with a new focus, concentrating on entertainment, social, and religious programs, and avoiding political issues. Currently, a few of them deal with political issues, but their coverage must be in line with the position of the *de facto* authority in Sana'a. This has enabled them to gain more advertisement revenue, especially with the disappearance of most print and online newspapers. On the one hand, these stations have represented a new venue for advertisers, and a source of profit for owners, on the other (Al-Reifi, 2019).

Economy and Ownership Patterns

Despite the many changes in the media landscape in Yemen over the last decades, the business models of the media remain almost the same. Since the Houthis took over Sana'a in 2014—and as the *de facto* authority—they have directly controlled governmental broadcast, print, and online media and financed them from the public treasury as a means of propagating their revolutionary discourse and political, social, religious, and economic interests. They also monitor all other types of media and means of communication. Houthis have blocked several websites, especially those belonging to their opponents. Blocked websites also include external websites like *Aljazeera.net*. According to a recent report, Yemen has the most significant share of Internet shutdowns in the Middle East (KeepetON, 2019).

An increase in the deployment of network control devices on YemenNet, the ISP controlled by Houthi forces, has also been observed (Insikt Group, 2019). On the other hand, the internationally recognized government has continued to finance copies of the same media operating from Riyadh. Moreover, the partisan and non-governmental media have continued to operate from abroad, mainly from Istanbul, Amman, Riyadh, and Beirut.

While the main political entities still seem to invest in television, printed newspapers have a very limited reach, and are therefore not invested in heavily. The print media landscape in Yemen can be classified into three basic types of funding. The first is the official one, which lacks many conditions of vitality, freedom, and the ability to keep abreast of global changes in professionalism and technology. The second is the partisan one, depends on the financial situation of parties in the public landscape, and yet their press reflects their miserable situation. The third is the nongovernmental press, that is, the press owned by private individuals (Abdulwarith, 2009). Al-Akbari (2005) concluded in her study that the Yemeni press, whether governmental, partisan, or privately-owned, is of minor interest to the public, and its impact is weak. The highest number of copies comes from the governmental newspaper *Al-Thawrah*, and this ranged from 5,000—12,000 copies during the period from 2013— to 2017.

Community and private radio stations may be the only exception to these long-standing media economic models. They have doubled in number since 2011, from less than a handful of radio stations to more than 30 stations. Before 2011, the government monopolized FM radio signals and granted them only to governmental radio stations. After the youth uprising in 2011, this monopoly was broken, and accordingly, community radio stations started to appear. *Yemen FM* radio, which belongs to the General People's Congress (GPC), was the first of these stations to be launched (in 2011).

As a result of the political vacuum that Yemen was experiencing at that time, other new FM radio stations were also launched. The *Yemen Times* newspaper, which was the first Yemeni English-language newspaper, used this opportunity to launch *Radio Yemen Times*, which was the second station after *Yemen FM*, followed by *Sawt Al-Yemen*. The period from 2011 to 2014 was significant for community radio stations in Yemen. Their discourse was varied and critical. They tackled issues ranging from the political to the social. The financial sources of these stations were not particularly clear as, similarly to other Yemeni media, their financial budgets were not declared. However, advertisements may have represented the main source of income. Others, such as *Nas FM*, received support from businesspersons.

As a result, there are now around eight community radio stations in Sana'a, and three in Hadramout. Some of them are general, and others are specialized. However, in Aden, there is only one community radio station, *Lana FM* radio (Studies & Economic Media Center, 2018, p. 11).

There are, moreover, 21 private radio stations. Fifteen of them are in Sana'a. They are either privately-owned by individuals or supported by political parties or religious groups. They include *Yemen FM*, *Iram*

FM, Yemen Music, Grand FM, Radio Yemen Times, Yemen Voice, and others. In Hadramout, there are five private FM radio stations, while in Aden, there is only one.

Technological developments—which have reduced the cost of radio broadcasting devices, such as transmitters and other equipment—have enabled the launch of small FM radio stations covering small, local areas. This fact, along with the granting of licenses by the *de facto* authority in Sana'a, has allowed these radio stations to flourish. However, a recent study on Yemeni radio stations concluded that the role of these stations in Yemen remains weak when it comes to essential issues. It revealed that social issues and basic services, such as electricity, water, road networks, and security problems, are represented in only a small percentage of radio coverage, accounting for just 20%, whereas entertainment, music, sports, and politics account for 80% of radio programming (Studies & Economic Media Center, 2018, p. 15).

Technology and Infrastructure

Over the past decades, the Yemeni government has exerted significant effort to keep up with technological developments, but often lagged behind other Arab states. This included shifting to a color television system in 1980 and expanding transmission to cover almost 70% of the total area of the country, and the whole country by 1996 via the *ArabSat* satellite. In 2001, Internet broadcasting was started through *ArabSat* (Mutahar, 2004, p. 80). However, the technological infrastructure is still modest. According to a recent report, the percentage of Internet users in Yemen is the lowest in the region, while prices are the most expensive in the world (Studies & Economic Media Center, 2018, p. 8). Internet users in Yemen were estimated to be more than 7 million in 2018, which amounted to around 27% of the population. However, while television transmission via Internet is very common in the neighboring countries, this is not so in Yemen due to its limited Internet speed and high prices. This kind of transmission seems still to be far off in the future.

In the era of media convergence, the country is still lagging behind. Many print newspapers have an online version as well as accounts on social media. However, videos and podcasts are notably still absent from these platforms. Some websites rely on uploaded videos from other Arab and international media outlets, like *Al-Jazeera*, *BBC*, and *YouTube*. This is due to the slow Internet speed and lack of resources and trained persons for producing such materials. This type of convergence has deeply affected print media circulation. However, official newspapers are still surviving. This is due to indirect financial support from the government through subsidy and advertisements. All ministries and other governmental institutions are obliged to subscribe to these newspapers, as well as to post advertisments in them.

Mobile users in Yemen amount to around 55% of the total population. Four main companies provide mobile services. One is a government company, which is *Yemen Mobile*, and the three others are private companies: *Sabafon*, *MTN*, and *Y Telecom*. At this point, 3G is the most common network used. Internet users in Yemen have significantly increased over the last decades, from 15,000 in 2000 to more than 7.9 million in 2019. Internet penetration in Yemen is now around 27%.

The number of social media network users in Yemen is growing rapidly. They increased by 19% from April 2019 to January 2020. The total number of users was 2.5 million in January 2020. Social media penetration in Yemen stood at 8.5% in January 2020 (Kemp, 2020). Smartphones play a significant role in the growth of social media as the majority of users have mobile phones, especially in rural and remote areas, and can thus access these platforms.

Facebook ranks as the top social network in Yemen. More than 8% of the population are using this network (NapoleonCat, 2020). According to Statcounter GlobalStats (2020), *Facebook* represents 85% of social media users in Yemen, followed by *YouTube* with 11% and *Twitter* with 3%. Other social media networks, such as *Instagram* and *Telegram*, are used by 1% or less of social media users.

Challenges

Yemeni media face several challenges, mainly with regard to legal, technological, economic and social aspects. In an attempt to keep the media under control, the Yemeni government has resisted legislation proposals to partially relinquish its control of the media. However, the law governing the media was implemented in 1990 and has become seriously outdated. In 2010, the Ministry of Information proposed a new law for audiovisual media that raised a lot of controversy. In respect to the technological factors, the fast-paced development in communications technology and multimedia communication represents a main challenge that Yemen in its current state of war cannot possibly meet.

Social media play an important role in all aspects of the daily life of Yemeni people, particularly young people. This role goes beyond facilitating social interaction between people in a very traditional and conservative society, such as Yemen, to a full-fledged medium of communication by all means. Social media have gained special importance since the Houthis' coup in 2014 that has led to blocking many online journalism websites and shutting down several newspapers, radio stations, and television channels. In such circumstances, these media have become the alternative media for the public to share information, publish news, and discuss and express opinions about several issues. Activists and journalists in particular heavily utilize social media for launching humanitarian relief and political campaigns as well as publishing breaking news. Thus, social media have become important players for influencing public opinion and enhancing awareness on political, social, and cultural levels.

Outlook

The future of Yemeni media will be determined by the future of the country itself after the current war ends. This war has produced many changes including a polarized media landscape. New players have forced themselves on to the political scene in the north (mainly the Houthis), as well as in the south (the Southern Transitional Council). Even the long-ruling party, the GPC, which controlled the country for more than three decades, has split into two divisions, one inside the country and the other abroad. However, the role of the media will remain essential for all actors and political players as a driving force for social and political changes as well as mobilization. The best media model for Yemeni media is to be independent from the ruling authority's control and to become a real public media that serves the interest of the people, not the ruling power. From a legislative perspective, in a country like Yemen, the best approach to regulate media is to have partnership among all stakeholders, journalists represented by Yemeni Journalists' Syndicate and other syndicates, academia, and experts. Joint efforts like this might lead to media laws that would achieve a minimum degree of consent on how media should operate in such a complex society. From a technology perspective, media in Yemen need to create a conducive environment for private investments that encourage the private sector to invest in the media industry and work in a competitive manner. Finally, freedom is the main pillar of the media: without freedom, the country will go nowhere, not only in the field of media but also in all aspects of life.

References

Abdulwarith, H. (2009). *Has the local press succeeded in shaping public opinion?* [in Arabic]. Paper presented at the symposium organized by the Ministry of Information, Sana'a, Yemen.

Abdulwase'e, N. (2009). *The Press and Publications Law and its application to reality and the possibility of its development in light of current developments* [in Arabic]. Paper presented at the symposium organized by the Ministry of Information, Sana'a, Yemen.

Al-Akbari, S. (2005). *Effects of attitudes of economic discourse in the Yemeni press on the public during the period of 1995/2005* (doctoral thesis) [in Arabic]. Cairo University.

Al-Fakih, A. (2012). Political economy and its role in forming active groups [in Arabic]. In C. Choucair (Ed.), *Informal actors in Yemen–causes of formation and ways of treatment* [in Arabic]. Beirut: Araba Scientific Publishers.

Al-Fakih, M. (2000). *The political role of television in Yemen* [in Arabic]. Cairo: Madboli.

Al-Mawla, S. (2011). *The Happy Yemen and the conflicts of religion and tribe* [in Arabic]. Beirut: Madarek.

Al-Reifi, A. (2019, June 9). *Community radio in Yemen: A distinctive experience amid the war* [in Arabic]. https://bit.ly/2Z7Gxjs

Al-Salahi, F. (2012). Society and the political system in Yemen [in Arabic]. In C. Choucair (Ed.), *Informal actors in Yemen–causes of formation and ways of treatment* [in Arabic]. Doha: Araba Scientific Publishers.

Al-Shami, A. (2013). Questioning the media: The role of Yemeni media in the youth revolution. *Journalism and Mass Communication*, 3(7), 443–51.

Al-Soswa, A. (1998). *Yemeni media constructing and modernization* [in Arabic]. Aden: 14 October Corporation for Press, Printing and Publishing.

Al-Zain, A. (1995). *Yemen and its media 1974–1982* (2nd ed.) [in Arabic]. Beirut: Dar Elfikr Almoasir.

Article 19. (2008). *Yemen freedom of expression in peril.* https://www.article19.org/data/files/pdfs/publications/yemen-foe-report.pdf

Basaleem, H. (2003). *Yemeni media handbook* [in Arabic]. Location: Yemen News Agency Printing Press.

Clausen, M. (2015). Understanding the crisis in Yemen: Evaluating competing narratives. *The International Spectator, 50*(3), 16–29. https://doi.org/10.1080/03932729.2015.1053707

Human Rights Watch (2019). *World Report 2019.* https://www.hrw.org/world-report/2019/country-chapters/yemen

Insikt Group. (2019). *Cyber threat analysis* (Recorded Future). https://go.recordedfuture.com/hubfs/reports/cta-2019-0312.pdf

International Federation of Journalists (2018). *End impunity campaign 2018: Yemen country report.* https://bit.ly/31wOXma

KeepItOn. (2019). *Targeted, cut off, and left in the dark.* (Report on Internet shutdowns). https://www.accessnow.org/cms/assets/uploads/2020/02/KeepItOn-2019-report-1.pdf

Kemp, S. (2020, February 18). *Digital 2020: Yemen.* https://datareportal.com/reports/digital-2020-yemen

Ministry of Information (2002). *Yemeni media: Evidences and achievements* [in Arabic]. Yemeni News Agency Printing Press.

Mutahar, B. (2004). *Introduction to the Yemeni media* [in Arabic]. Beirut: Dar Al-Kotob Al-Ilmiyah.

NapoleonCat (2020). *Facebook users in Yemen: January 2020.* https://napoleoncat.com/stats/facebook-users-in-yemen/2020/01

Rabe'e, H. (2012). *Yemen challenges of change and modernization* [in Arabic]. Beirut: Dar Al-Tawfik.

Schmitz, C. (2014). *Yemen's national dialogue.* https://www.mei.edu/publications/yemens-national-dialogue

Sharp, J. (2019). *Yemen: Civil war and regional intervention.* Congressional Research Service. https://fas.org/sgp/crs/mideast/R43960.pdf

Statcounter GlobalStats (2020). *Social media stats Yemen.* https://gs.statcounter.com/social-media-stats/all/yemen

Studies & Economic Media Center (2018). Journalists and citizens' access to the Internet: suffering, monopoly and blocking [in Arabic]. http://economicmedia.net/wp-content/uploads/2018/04/access-to-internet-yemen2018.pdf

Varisco, D. (2017). Islam in Yemen. *Oxford Bibliographies*. https://www.oxfordbibliographies.com/view/document/obo-9780195390155/obo-9780195390155-0093.xml

13. Egypt: A Divided and Restricted Media Landscape after the Transformation

Hanan Badr

Egypt's media landscape is marked by long years of struggle. This is a paradox: it is one of the pioneers of media industries in the Arab region, yet today, it has a massively restrained media system. The Egyptian media is marked by an unresolved identity struggle between its traditional roots in Arab and Islamic culture and an ambivalence towards modernized, Westernized lifestyles. It is also contending with a highly polarized media-politics parallelism in an environment which does not grant the media system space to develop fully and freely. Despite the great potential of the media system, the recent crackdown on freedom of expression has suspended the potential for the professionalization of an autonomous form of journalism.

Background

Located in Africa's northeastern corner, Egypt is the only country that extends into both the African and Asian continents through the Sinai Peninsula. Throughout its history, the deserts around the Nile Valley and Delta have functioned as natural geographic barriers, keeping the core Egyptian state intact for centuries. Egypt's location, overlooking two seas—the Mediterranean to the north and the Red Sea to the east—has historically made it a natural geopolitical hub for intercultural exchange and trade, as well as the site of colonization projects and the cradle of empires, as one of the world's most ancient civilizations.

Currently, all of Egypt's neighbors, from the Libyans and Sudanese to the Palestinians in the Gaza Strip, are witnessing either political upheavals or escalations of conflict. Regional conflicts in these neighboring countries cast their shadows on the military and security roles shaping Egypt's foreign relations. Recent major changes in geopolitics include the 2015 change of maritime borders with Saudi Arabia. That action caused a short-lived public stir, as Egypt refused to renounce its sovereignty over Tiran and Sanafir, the two islands, located near the touristic city of Sharm El-Sheikh.

Terrorism and armed struggle against ISIS-affiliated militias, especially in the Sinai Peninsula, have affected the levels of freedom of expression and public acceptance of security institutions and their rhetoric. These conflicts have advanced the validity of security concerns over terrorism on the political agenda, which has in turn strengthened the military's claim to power after Egypt's failed uprising in 2011.

Egypt's primary and official language is Arabic, whereas the English language is an informal language employed for business communication in international companies centered in the capital, Cairo, and Alexandria. French also has a notable presence due to the enduring Francophone cultural influence. Editions of Egyptian print media appear in both French and English languages to target the limited readership of high-income citizens, who are socioeconomically distinct from the majority of the public.

The population majority is Muslim, but there is a Coptic Christian minority estimated to account for between 5% and 10% of the population, although the exact figure is unclear, as there is no official census (Pew Research Center, 2011). Because Egypt is a socially conservative country, religious media have a considerable presence whether in the form of specialized media issued by the Islamic Al-Azhar institution, or by the Coptic Church in Cairo. While Egyptian society has many marginalized ethnic groups, such as Sinai Bedouins, Siwa Oasis Amazigh and Nubians, tensions frequently erupt over religious and ideological issues. The rise of political Islam from the 1970s onwards—in particular, the Muslim Brotherhood and its use of religious doctrine—constitutes an exclusionary ideology towards others. The Muslim Brothers offer fundamentally different answers to questions regarding Egypt's identity and international alliances. After a brief rise in power in the wake of 2011, the Muslim Brotherhood and other potentially contentious actors are now harshly excluded from society: since 2013, their members are tracked, exiled, or imprisoned under inhumane circumstances. Other ideological strands, such as remnants of the left wing, or progressive liberals, are weak and remain elitist in their constituency, outreach, and rhetoric.

With its 99 million inhabitants, Egypt has a massive youth cohort: those below 15 years of age constitute more than one third of the country's entire population. The state faces significant challenges in offering education and healthcare services, as well as employment opportunities. Although women have received more legal rights and gained limited representation—for example, the right to vote and the right to education—over the past century there are still disadvantages for women in this socially conservative country, within both Muslim and Coptic Christian communities. Egypt faces the long-standing challenge of illiteracy, as, according to the Central Agency for Public Mobilization and Statistics (CAPMAS), almost 25% of the overall population remain illiterate. Trends show higher illiteracy rates in women and in rural areas. Women still suffer—despite gradual progress—from social practices, such as domestic violence, and socioeconomic disadvantages, such as estate inheritance or access to education.

The aftermath of the Arab uprisings still shapes the current political sphere and rhetoric. Caught in between the public's fatigue and fear, the status quo is marked by demobilization, as those currently in power are clearly keen to intensify their mechanisms of authority. The polarizing events of 2013 are viewed by the opposition as a coup against the legally elected president, Mohammed Morsi of the Muslim Brotherhood, while they are viewed by the military and its supporters as a second, corrective revolution against an extremist leader. This has caused massive fragmentation with serious repercussions for Egypt. The events of 2013 resulted in moments of international isolation from 2013 to 2015, as Egypt was temporarily ejected from the African Union. In addition to intensive diplomacy, the state media aggressively sought to polish Egypt's image during this phase. Yet amid the rise of global right-wing authoritarianism, and Europe's fear of migration and instability, Egypt's current regime faces neither real pressure to democratize, nor political consequences for violations.

Historical Developments

Egypt is a pioneer of media industries as its media are among the oldest in the Arab region. Print media is more than 200 years old. It started in the late-eighteenth century when Egypt was still a province of the Ottoman Empire and France's Napoleon started an expedition to invade Egypt in 1798. The invaders brought the printing press to Egypt. The first newspaper was *Le Courrier de l'Egypte*, which was published from 1798 in French for Napoleon's soldiers to stay informed and in touch with their home country. After Mohammed Ali assumed power, he published the Arabic newspaper *Al-Khedive Journal* in 1821 to disseminate official news and connect the provinces to the centralized power in Cairo, the capital (Abdel Rahman, 2002, p. 102).

When Khedive Ismail relaxed the licensing policies for newspapers in 1875, Egypt's newspaper scene began to flourish rapidly: within only 15 years (by 1890), more than 200 newspapers were registered. Some of them are leading newspapers with a long tradition of journalism which still exist today, such as *Al-Ahram* (1875). Other newspapers importantly expressed the country's identity struggle and reflected the pluralism of Egypt's political culture. The wide range of new newspapers included the pro-British Westernized *Al-Mukattam* (1888), the traditional reformist *Al-Mo'ayed* (1889), the critical satirical *Al-Ustaz* (1892), and the Egyptian nationalist *Al-Liwa'a* (1900). The Egyptian print media initially benefitted from the influx of Levantine immigrants escaping harsh Ottoman rule, as well as from the gradual diffusion of the print press and growing literacy rates. Historically, this phase bears striking similarities to the era of mass press during the same time in Europe and the US.

1882 marked a political rupture in Egypt, as it brought the second bloody confrontation with Western powers after Napoleon's French expedition in 1798. Amid Britain's aspirations to expand its north-south nexus on the African continent and to connect to its vast colonies in India by means of the trade route running through the Suez Canal, Britain used Egypt's political instability and the supposed protection of the weak Khedive, the Ottoman governor, as a pretext to occupy Egypt. Egypt became an unofficial British protectorate before being formally designated as a protectorate with the onset of World War I, in 1913. These developments imported British, French, and Ottoman influences into Egypt, and these shaped the media landscape accordingly. The British rule, which began in 1882—in conjunction with the then still official rule of the Khedive Palace, which was loyal to the Ottoman Empire—tolerated the pluralized media scene, with occasional closures of overly critical newspapers, in the hopes of using the fragmentation of media voices against the other competing power. Egypt's media system was affected by conflict and political parallelism. The initial propagandistic mobilization and media-politics parallelism instituted during this era has never really ended. After drafting its first constitution in 1922, the so-called liberal experiment in Egypt, which lasted until 1936, proved how parties and print media could not only coexist, but also nourish each other. This turbulent time, which was marked by frequent protests in the urban centers, saw a rise in debates over Egypt's future and identity. Moreover, the expansion of education formed a new social class. This phase also witnessed the establishment of Egypt's legacy media houses such as *Al-Akhbar* and *Ruz Al-Youssef*, which are still operating today, but in a state-owned form.

In 1952, fueled by grievances against a system of unfair privileges within the army and society in general, the Free Officers Movement overthrew the monarchy and forced the British military forces to leave. President Gamal Abdel Nasser came to power in 1954 and established the Egyptian Republic. Abdel Nasser pushed for full control over the public sphere to ensure power over the young independent state. He established a new media house called Al-Tahrir, which published the *Al-Gomhouriya* newspaper. In 1960, Abdel Nasser nationalized all media under the pretext of protecting stability and serving the interests of the public.

Radio had an early start in Egypt during its vibrant, cosmopolitan era under British rule. In the 1920s, individual radio stations were founded, often by foreign nationals residing in Egypt in Cairo and Alexandria, primarily for entertainment purposes. This is called the age of "civic broadcasting stations" (El-Sherif, 2015). On 31 May 1934, an official radio program was established in cooperation with the British Marconi Company. As anti-colonial and national attitudes rose, in 1947, the prime minister decided to fully nationalize and arabize the radio stations and begin Egyptian production. To this day, Egypt is keen to invest in its elaborate radio program, which has 40 foreign-language radio stations as a part of its public diplomacy efforts, including English, French, and German, as well as less widely spoken languages, such as Hebrew and Swahili.

Like radio, Egypt's cinema has its roots in the cosmopolitan era of the late-nineteenth century. Egypt's film industry has a long tradition and popularity in the region: the first film was shown in Alexandria in 1896, only one year after the worldwide debut of cinema. The first production of a fictional film was in 1927 by the Isis Film Company. Dubbed "The Orient's Hollywood," the popularity of its productions is one of the reasons for the widespread use of the Egyptian dialect in Arab countries outside of Egypt. The cinema is a pillar of Egyptian soft power. The 1960s constituted a golden era for Egyptian cinema in terms of the number of films produced and the legacies of famous and popular stars, and despite its political socialist one-party system under Abdel Nasser, the state invested heavily in arts and cinema.

Television is by far the most popular media in Egypt as it is the number one source for news and entertainment. Historically, Egypt has monopolized terrestrial broadcasting in the famous radio and television building, Maspero, situated in downtown Cairo. Television broadcasting started in 1960 under President Abdel Nasser. Building on strong national sentiments, he used the television as proof of Egypt's new, modernized republic. His successor, Anwar El-Sadat, established the Egyptian Radio and Television Union (ERTU), as the body controlling the radio and television channels aired in Egypt. It slowly developed its program to add more controlled pluralism, by offering the news-oriented *Channel 1* and the lighter *Channel 2*. In the late 1980s, state television expanded its service to offer five additional regional channels, for the capital Cairo, Alexandria, the Suez Canal area, Upper Egypt, and the Nile Delta. In the 1990s, satellite channels were introduced into Egyptian households. They constituted a serious challenge, in that they bypassed the national regulative framework for broadcasting. The offer of competing channels to Egyptian households, as well as the massive brain drain from Maspero's ERTU media workers moving to better-funded Arab television networks, gradually led to a loss of the monopoly once held by the Egyptian Radio and Television Union in the country. Moreover, Egyptian journalists and media personnel who had left the country were instrumental in initially conceptualizing and managing many media that started in the Gulf countries.

The Internet was introduced in Egypt in 1993. Penetration grew steadily in society, with a rise from 1% of the population being Internet users in 2000 to 45% in 2017. The number of *Facebook* users alone amounts to 35 million in Egypt; hence, a third of the population is on *Facebook*.

Political System and Legal Framework

In his book *Sorrows of the Press Freedoms*, veteran Egyptian journalist and unionist Salah El-Din Hafez (1993) sketched the enduring and multiple constraints over print media. The title sums up the fact that Egyptian journalism's struggle for autonomy, is political, economic, and professional. Egyptian journalism has a long history of not being free, and an almost 200-year struggle for freedom (El-Gody, 2009, p. 732). Owing to strong centralization and executive control of media mobilization for national development purposes, as well as control of media regulations and ownership, Egyptian journalism has only had brief periods of liberalization (Richter, 2011). These brief intermissions have created some dynamism among journalists to push for freedoms and reflect on their profession. The latest window of opportunity was the transformation phase of 2011–2013 after the uprisings.

Egypt's political system has officially been a presidential republic since 1952. During the past seven years, two constitutions were issued: the (now annulled) Egyptian Constitution of 2012, and the Egyptian Constitution of 2014, in addition to constitutional amendments in 2019. This shows two mechanisms at work: first, that the political contest in Egypt has traditionally been settled through legislation; and second, that those in power wish to emphasize the rule of law, in order to protect their image abroad. However, since 2014, consistent regulatory and legal changes have demonstrated a strong re-autocratization and legislative authoritarianism (Hamzawy, 2017). The long-sought abolition of the Ministry of Information in 2014 also did not establish more freedoms, as had been anticipated.

A paradox exists between formally acknowledging press freedom on paper in the 2014 constitution and tightening control of it in practice. Free expression is formally guaranteed in the current constitution, in

Article 65 (freedom of speech) and Article 68 (access to information and official documents). Yet, the creation of three regulatory bodies and media councils in 2017 by presidential decrees narrowed the supposed freedoms given by the constitution. Three councils replaced the abolished Ministry of Information: the Supreme Media Regulatory Council, the National Press Authority (founded to oversee and manage state-owned print media organizations), and the National Media Authority (founded to oversee and manage state-owned audiovisual broadcasting services). Members of the three regulatory councils are appointed by the president, and include journalists, social scientists, and media managers (such as editors-in-chief, etc.).

These councils increasingly exhibit a tendency for greater censorship by using vague ethical rules as legal boundaries. One example of this is Article 215, where the National Media Council, which oversees print, audiovisual, and digital journalism, is responsible for a broad spectrum of media. According to this article, the National Media Council should guarantee media freedoms in their various forms, maintain media pluralism and avoid concentration, protect the public interest, shape the regulations and criteria that lead to the commitment of the media towards the professional traditions and ethics, preserve the Arabic language, and observe society's values and constructive traditions. Loose interpretations of this article can limit freedoms of expression, as demonstrated by legal prosecutions for threatening social values that have been brought against journalists who have published ideas and opinions on progressive issues such as women's rights.

In the wake of the uprisings, Egyptian journalism went through political turbulence, starting with a massive rupture of the system in 2011, and continuing until the gradual elimination of any margin for freedom today. The struggle for journalists' freedom in the post-2011 phase in Egypt was perceived as a window of opportunity to turn journalists' hopes and demands of urgent and overdue reforms in the profession into reality. Right after the "Tahrir Revolution", specific actions for media reform were needed in order to establish greater autonomy (Sakr, 2013, pp. ix–x). These included more independence from executive control, the abolition of the detention punishment, the establishment of strong local and regional journalism, the transformation of state-managed media into true public service media institutions, efforts to foster pluralism in journalists' associations, and finally, maintenance of good governance in media organizations.

The turbulent years of transformation from 2011 to 2019 can be categorized in four phases:

1. Phase I took place from 2011–2012, directly after Mubarak's resignation when the Supreme Council of Armed Forces (SCAF) took over power and led the initial stabilization maneuvers;

2. Phase II continued from May 2012 to June 2013 while President Mohammed Morsi headed a Muslim Brotherhood-dominated government. Both phases I and II represented the highest potential for a transformation of Egyptian journalism. The intensive euphoria and protests aimed at reforming the Egyptian media. Journalists shared critical self-reflections on the country's journalistic practices. A Freedom House report captured the euphoric 2012 moment when, for the first time in decades, it called the Egyptian media system "partly free." New, pluralistic media outlets mushroomed and catered to those with previously marginalized needs. The strongest newcomers were the Islamist media. Yet, even under these flourishing conditions of freedom, the situation for journalists was considered "precarious" (UNESCO, 2013, p. 76). Examples of this professional precarity include insecure work conditions or poor personal safety during clashes and political turmoil. During the Muslim Brotherhood rule, the press was the target of repeated trials to intimidate journalists.

3. In Phase III, from July 2013 to May 2014, after the SCAF expelled the late President Morsi from his office and introduced an interim president, the negotiation processes to develop the media scene were suddenly interrupted. No genuine processes addressed the core issues of journalism's professionalization, autonomy, and financial viability.

4. Finally, Phase IV started with the election of President Abdelfattah Sisi as president in 2014, and has continued

after his reelection in 2018. Recently, Egypt slid to position 166 (of 180) in the Reporters Without Borders 2020 ranking. The Cybercrime Law issued in August 2018 targets freedom of expression on blogs and social media. An example of direct intimidation occurred in November 2019, when security forces stormed *MadaMasr*, an independent online journalistic platform. This political climate has affected news media coverage and made it less diverse in moments of crisis or security-related concern. Increased control of foreign correspondents, as seen in the revoked accreditation of *BBC* correspondents in 2018 and 2019, aims at controlling non-Egyptian coverage.

One unprecedented moment of escalation between the state and the media occurred in May 2016, when police forces stormed the Egyptian Journalist's Syndicate building to arrest two journalists only one day before World Press Freedom Day.

While practicing journalism is open to all graduates from various disciplines, official protection is only given to members of the Journalists' Syndicate as the sole trade union representing print journalists. Other media professionals have a separate trade union, the Media Workers Syndicate, which is service-oriented and not politically active. The exclusionary and restrictive bylaws of this syndicate's membership discriminate against digital journalists who are prohibited from becoming members.

Economy and Ownership Patterns

The political economy of the media in Egypt demonstrates an unresolved conflict of interests, which predates the Arab uprisings. Indirect state capitalism controls the media economy and determines ownership structures. After the establishment of the Egyptian Republic in 1952, all private media were nationalized and transformed into state-run institutions. Party newspapers were gradually introduced in the early 1970s, and private media emerged in the mid-1990s. The tripartite ownership of Egyptian journalism (state-run, party, and private press) has created stark contrasts in the political economy, financial security, and journalistic practices. State-led print media receive full state subsidy, and follow the official government line more closely, with a very low margin of tolerance. Editors-in-chief have adapted their approaches and opt for mild criticism at most as a political survival strategy, since they are nominated and appointed by the state. At the same time, within the semi-liberalization strategies under former President Mubarak, the modernization of print technologies in the late 1990s led to huge investments in print technologies in the three largest publicly-funded, state-owned media organizations: *Al-Ahram*, *Al-Akhbar*, and *Al-Gomhouriya*.

State-run print media have low circulation, are overstaffed, and have accumulated significant debt, which amounted to USD 1.6 billion in 2015 (Miri, 2015). For example, the oldest daily newspaper, *Al-Ahram*, sells only 70,000 copies daily, compared with 2013 when the numbers were 10 times as many. Despite the financial losses, journalists in state media, who have the status of civil servants, are secure against layoffs due to the high political cost of such a decision. Corrupt and unethical practices, such as nepotism and an approach of mixing editorial content with advertising, are common (Ghali, 2015). New regulations since 2014 regard state media as a giant financial burden, without any real political benefit. In order to stop the financial drain, hiring ceased altogether. Media investment is not on the current political agenda; on the contrary, rulers view them as adversaries. Rather than make them more powerful, the current strategy is to weaken the media, as their loyalty and public influence are not guaranteed.

Private media institutions have a history of tolerating certain freedoms and are run as purely profit-oriented business models. Business tycoons purchase media to protect their stakes in other businesses (Roll, 2013). Although they incur losses, these are covered by the other non-media businesses. Compared with those who work for the state-run media, private media journalists earn more for high workloads. But major layoffs and shutdowns of enterprises have shaped the private media landscape since 2014. After a short-lived surge in sales from 2011–2012 where, for example, the private daily *Al-Masry Al-Youm* reached 650,000 copies per day, today it struggles to sell 60,000 copies per day. Moreover, party newspapers are well past their golden years of the 1990s and are struggling to survive.

The journalism crisis is severe: in terms of sales, print papers went from three million daily copies in 2000 and 1.5 million daily copies in 2010 to less than 200,000 daily sold copies nationwide in 2018 (personal communication with *Al-Ahram* distribution network officer, August 2019). In a country of 100 million people, this amounts to two sold copies per 1,000 inhabitants. Widespread poverty and illiteracy rates do not suffice to explain the decline in newspaper sales. In fact, young readers have increasingly drifted away from classic media. According to Baseera Think Tank polls, 65% of young Egyptians do not read newspapers, and only 7% "always" do (Egypt Independent, 2015).

Observation of recent media developments has shown nontransparent acquisitions and monopolistic practices in the media industry. At the same time, new private media companies have established strong ties with various state security and intelligence organizations through favored loyalist frontmen, who have acquired majority shares in all the private print media institutions (Reporters Without Borders, 2019b). Horizontal and vertical conglomerates in media enterprises are characterized by this kind of oligarchy. One example is the Egyptian Media Group (EMG), which is closely linked to President Sisi's supporters and intelligence agencies. It not only owns the three biggest private television networks (*Al-Hayah, On E, Extra News*) and holds major shares in private newspapers (*Al-Youm Al-Sabea*, and *Sout Al-Omma*), but also controls the cinema production landscape (50% of shares of Misr Cinema Company and 50% of Synergy Production) and has large shares of numerous advertising industry companies (Reporters Without Borders, 2019b).

60% of the television sector, which is regulated by the National Media Authority, is either owned by the state ERTU (*Channels 1* and *2*) or the Egyptian Media Group. Other players include former Mubarak loyalist cronies, who own *Dream TV* and *Sada El-Balad TV*, and businesspersons who closely cooperate in the advertising industry (*Al-Nahar TV*). In addition, there is the Saudi-financed media group MBC, which operates from Dubai and launched *MBC Misr* (Reporters Without Borders, 2019b). As a result, the television sector has become increasingly de-politicized after a vibrant era of intensive political talk-shows prior to mid-2013. At this point, entertainment content accounts for most of the airtime.

Digital journalism is still heavily regulated in Egypt: in October 2018, the Supreme Media Regulatory Council demanded that all native online newspapers legalize their status within two weeks. This was a manifestation of the highly controversial media regulatory laws passed in July 2018 by the Egyptian Parliament (Mamdouh, 2018). Regulation and surveillance of the digital space to curb online freedom of speech have increased, as the Egyptian government cooperates with numerous international tech giants like *Google* (Ryan, 2019).

Media usage in Egypt can be summarized as follows: almost the whole population—more than 97%—watch television, only 33% use the radio, and 16% of people read newspapers (Reporters Without Borders, 2019b). Social media is increasingly becoming a strong competitor of the established professional media. As in other countries, old media find this new competition with the free and not yet fact-checked social media, challenging.

Technology and Infrastructure

Egypt has been a pioneer in media and communication technologies in the Arab world. Having invested early in national television, it aimed at further securing its position as a regional leader in media. Under President Hosni Mubarak (1981–2011), Egypt worked to secure its technological leadership in the Arab region. Competing with the newly launched, Gulf-funded television networks and media cities, Egypt launched its first Arab satellite channel, the *Egyptian Satellite Channel* in 1990. It launched its first satellite, *NileSat* in 1998 to consolidate its position as a leader in news and entertainment in the Middle East. However, the project of launching more than 15 specialized channels did not hold up economically and caused extreme financial pressures on the publicly-funded ERTU. At the same time, the government invested in the Media City complex, located in the 6th October suburb of Cairo, to bolster Egypt's regional position and accommodate the ambitious film and drama productions. Media City hosts several studios for privately-owned satellite television stations, such as *DMC*, *Dream*, and *El-Mehwar*.

The relevance of new digital media in Egypt has increased over the past 15 years. In line with the modernization plans under former President Mubarak's rule, during the early 2000s, the state announced and invested in an ambitious Internet and communication technologies (ICTs) plan. It aimed to connect a PC in every Egyptian home to the Internet by 2008, a goal which was regulated by the Ministry of Communications and Information Technology (est. 1999) and the National Telecommunications Regulatory Authority (est. 2003). A partnership with Microsoft was set up to launch incentives to market PCs and 512 ADSL connections. These investments in the technology infrastructure made Egypt an attractive spot for foreign investments and industries. Despite Internet censorship and limited speed, these investments in ICTs paved the way for the evolving blogging and citizen journalism activities that contributed to the 2011 uprisings.

Many scholars and commentators have attributed the Arab uprisings directly to the rise of the Internet, as they are widely referred to as the "Facebook Revolution." However, this is a simplified view of the events and interactions between media and politics (Badr, 2019). Nonetheless, the prelude of the Egyptian uprisings was indeed marked by a rise in citizen journalism and efforts from the blogger scene to push counter-issues of dissent into the mainstream media and thereby create a "trickle-down effect" (Badr & Richter, 2018).

Rapid and massive progress in ICTs before the Arab uprisings shifted political communication towards less deterministic patterns, so a complete state monopoly on media was no longer possible. For example, political blogging expanded the prospects of dialogue, offering vibrant networks for individuals with similar perspectives (Pole, 2010, p. 1).

However, while this describes the state of affairs just before the uprisings, recently there have increasingly been signs of expanded control over the public spheres. Since 2013, and after the presidential elections of 2014 and 2018, zero-tolerance policies towards dissent and criticism have been applied through increased police control and imprisonment of journalists, takeovers of all semi-independent media outlets, and the use of surveillance technologies. In addition to blocking more than 500 websites and media, the authorities issued a law against cyberterrorism in 2018, which tightened restrictions on the overlooked Internet public sphere, for example by incriminating *Facebook* group administrators (Reporters Without Borders, 2019a).

In the telecommunications sector, Egypt has four mobile phone companies: three private companies with shares from the governmental

Egypt Telecom, and a fourth, the government owned *We*. Due to strict antiterrorism laws and state scrutiny of mobile service owners, the mobile phone penetration rate dropped from an oversaturated 112% in 2012–2013 to 95% in 2018, according to ITU data. Ownership follows the state doctrine of licensing telecommunications companies to trusted business tycoons, and has headed towards increased state regulation in recent years. *Orange Telecom* (formerly *Mobinil*) is 99% in the hands of *Orange S.A.*, and *Vodafone Egypt* (formerly *Click GSM*) is divided as follows: *Vodafone Group* (54.93%), *Egypt Telecom* (44.94%), and free float (0.13%). *Etisalat Telecom* is owned by the Emirati company *Etisalat* (76%), *Egypt Post* (20%), and other investors (4%). Finally, there is the most recent addition, the state-owned *We* by *Egypt Telecom*, where the Egyptian government owns 80%, and 20% of the shares are free float.

Challenges

Put simply, the current media system is not sustainable. Amid persistent power asymmetries and a highly repressive environment, the media system reflects an extremely constrained political system, from which any prior pluralism has been removed. Even the tolerated, semi-liberalized pockets of free expression under former President Mubarak seem luxurious when compared with the situation today. However, the massive restrictions have led to a flourishing of free expression outside the country. Exiled Egyptian journalism is rapidly expanding, as many independent journalists are prevented from working inside the country. Yet, the political economy of these exiled journalism initiatives is often dependent on competing regional powers, such as Qatar and Turkey (*Al-Sharq TV* in Istanbul or *Al-Araby Al-Jadeed TV* in London). In addition, other media with limited professional experience depend on media assistance programs, such as the critically acclaimed investigative *MadaMasr*, which is banned within Egypt.

Contextualizing the Egyptian media system within its political determinants is important, as it depends on possible freedoms. The latest rare and short-lived protests in September 2019 erupted after disclosures of corruption were aired on *YouTube* by a self-exiled whistleblower, and resulted in a massive crackdown in the fall of 2019. Those connections between critical voices in exile and those within the country are facilitated by new media and transnationalization. Situated within the context of the ongoing socioeconomic problems that caused the Arab uprisings, and encouraged by the current global rise of right-wing authoritarianism, the political system has attempted to achieve stability at any cost.

In addition, the professional media scene faces numerous crises, such as erosion of the economic viability of media, declining professionalism, reproduction of loyalist and propagandistic practices, and clientelist patronage within a restrictive environment. The fragmented professional community of journalists has moreover weakened efforts to unionize.

Outlook

Egyptian media are heading into the unknown: the "death of journalism," extreme de-politicization of the public sphere, and the restrictive media environment have all weakened the media system. Under the current circumstances, no political will is pushing for progress or open investments in the media sector. Although the Supreme Media Regulatory Council announced an ambitious digitization plan for the media, no clear agenda is visible, except tightening control and advancing loyalist media. Official governmental rhetoric is using modernization and innovation discourses to pass collaborations for digitizing randomly selected archives. Massive financial problems and a dependent political economy hinder any serious attempts to give the media a societal relevance when compared with social media. Egyptian media remains oblivious to this convergence. At the same time, the current, globally interconnected world still poses a serious challenge to those in power, as illustrated by the exiled, transnational media landscape. However, these reflect regional alliances that are volatile. The weakened and stifled Egyptian media system has immense potential if given the chance to grow autonomously: a strong legacy, unused economic assets, talented journalists, and a big market that constitutes one-third of the population of Arab countries. Yet, these unused resources still make it unlikely for Egypt's media system to witness better times anytime soon. Despite these recommendations, the situation is extremely unpredictable in the long term. Therefore, in case of a political opening, whether through reforms from above or the regime was forced to respond by a renewed public upheaval or international pressure, the potential for transformation of the media system is there.

References

Abdel Rahman, A. (2002). *Contemporary issues in Arab journalism* [in Arabic]. Cairo: Dar Al-Arabi.

Badr, H. (2019). Transformation, social media and hybrid media systems–Rethinking media visibility of counter-issues in North Africa before and after the Arab Uprisings. *IEMed Mediterranean Yearbook 2019*. https://www.iemed.org/observatori/arees-danalisi/arxius-adjunts/anuari/med.2019/Counter-Issues_Media_Visibility_North_Africa_Hanan_Badr_IEMed_MedYearbook2019.pdf

Badr, H., & Richter, C. (2018). Collective self-determination in autocracies? Agenda building in the interaction of (digital) media and activists during anti-torture protests in Egypt [in German]. *Medien & Kommunikation, 66*(4), 542–61.

Egypt Independent. (2015, April 30). Baseera: 32% of Egyptians believe media is free. *Egypt Independent*, https://ww.egyptindependent.com/baseera-32-egyptians-believe-media-free/

El-Din Hafez, S. (1993). *Sorrows of press freedom* [in Arabic] Cairo: Al-Ahram Center for Political and Strategic Studies.

El-Gody, A. (2009). The media system in Egypt [in German]. In Hans-Bredow-Institut (Ed.), *International handbook of media* [in German] (pp. 731–51). Baden-Baden: Nomos.

El-Sherif, S. (2015). *The special-interest media: TV and radio broadcasting* [in Arabic]. Cairo: Al-Nahda Publishers.

Freedom House. (n.d.). *Freedom House country reports on Egypt*. http://www.freedomhouse.org/country/egypt#.VDYl5hbYohY

Ghali, M. (2015). The journalists' vision on the financial and managerial corruption of official newspaper adminstrations. *Egyptian Journal of Journalism Research, 1*(1), 31–127.

Hackett, C. (2011, February 26). How many Christians are there in Egypt? *Pew Research Center*. https://www.pewresearch.org/2011/02/16/how-many-christians-are-there-in-egypt/

Hamzawy, A. (2017). Egypt after the 2013 military coup: Law-making in service of the new authoritarianism. *Philosophy & Social Criticism, 43*(4–5), 392–405. https://doi.org/10.1177/0191453717695367

Mamdouh, R. (2018). Egypt's new media laws: Rearranging legislative building blocks to maximize control. *MadaMasr*. https://madamasr.com/en/2018/07/17/feature/politics/egypts-new-media-laws-rearranging-legislative-building-blocks-to-maximize-control/

Miri, K. (2015). The National Journalism Authority. *Egyptian Currents, 13*(4), 77–80.

Pole, A. (2010). *Blogging the political: Politics and participation in a networked society*. London: Routledge.

Reporters Without Borders. (2019a). *Egypt country report*. https://rsf.org/en/taxonomy/term/156

——. (2019b). *Media ownership monitor: Egypt*. https://egypt.mom-rsf.org/en/owners/companies/

Richter, C. (2011). *Media strategies of Egyptian Islamists in the context of democratization* [in German]. Berlin: Frank & Timme.

Roll, S. (2013). Egypt's business elite after Mubarak: A powerful player between generals and Brotherhood. *SWP Research Paper*. https://www.swp-berlin.org/en/publication/egypts-business-elite-after-mubarak

Ryan, V. (2019) Google is Deepening its Involvement with Egypt's Repressive Government. *The Intercept*. https://theintercept.com/2019/08/18/google-egypt-office-sisi/

Sakr, N. (2013). *Transformations in Egyptian journalism*. London: I.B. Tauris.

UNESCO (2013). *Assessment of Media Development in Egypt. Based on UNESCO's Media Development Indicators*. Paris: United Nations Educational, Scientific and Cultural Organization.

14. Sudan: Media under the Military–Democratic Pendulum

Mahmoud M. Galander

> This chapter describes the impact of the incessant political changes that have taken place in Sudan and highlights the impact of the country's shifts from democratic to military governments since independence on the performance of the media. In particular, the chapter describes the role of newspapers in the development of nationalism in the early 1920s, and in the development of partisan politics after independence. The chapter explores how, as radio and television remained public in their early years, they served as government propaganda and education tools, but later with the advent of satellite transmission and reception, how private entertainment radio and television services prevailed. The chapter discusses the impact of the numerous political systems that have shaped the media-politics relationship and, in particular, the effect of the various media laws that were promulgated in the country by the different political regimes.

Background

Until the secession of South Sudan in 2011, Sudan was one of the largest African and Arab countries in terms of area. The country borders Chad and the Central African Republic to the west, Ethiopia and Eritrea to the east, Egypt and Libya to the north and, since 2011, the Republic of South Sudan to the south. Although Sudan's culture is predominantly Muslim Arab, its ethnic constitution is a mixture of African, Nilotic, and Arabic. The history of the land is closely tied to the Pharaohs, as several indigenous "Mereoitic" and "Kushite" kingdoms had links to them. Christianity dominated in northern Sudan for several centuries before Islam and Arabism "migrated" to the country, around the twelfth century, through two corridors: Egypt in the north and the Grand Maghreb in the west.

The traditional nature of Sudanese society has helped in maintaining its homogeneity. The Islamic impact on Sudanese journalism is noticeable in the writings of early (and even current) Sudanese journalists. Arabic poetry, Qur'anic verses, and Arabic proverbs are widely used to create the strongest impact on the audience. Examples of this effect are well-documented in Sudanese archives, sermons, and utterances of the Mahdi, the leader of the Mahdist revolution who was able to win the hearts and minds of the public (Abu Salim, 1979). Successful political and persuasive writings rely on a mixture of modern analytical approaches with appropriate quotations from Qur'anic verses, the Hadith, and famous utterances of Islamic figures (Galander, 2003). Although Arabic is the lingua franca, there are several vernacular languages that are confined to some parts of the country. For example, the Beja in the eastern Red Sea area speak their own "Tibdawi" language, whereas some tribes in the north speak the "Mahas" and "Dungulawi" vernaculars.

According to the latest census, the current population of the country is 43 million, with a median age of 19.7 (World Population Review, 2020). Ethnicity lines are clearly drawn and well-established; the famous North-South conflict, which lasted for decades until the secession of the South, reflects these lines of division. Major areas of social conflict include famous parts of the country, such as Darfur in the west, the Ingessana in the southeast, the Beja in the east, and the Nuba in the west. Most of the conflicts are related to underdevelopment, as many of the regions lack the basic healthcare, employment, and education, but they have escalated into political conflicts, thus leading to armed struggle. Although the majority of the population is Muslim, major cities in the country have several churches that reflect the multireligious nature of the society.

Historical Developments

By the early-sixteenth century, Sudan was overwhelmingly under the influence of Islam, as two Muslim Sultanates, the Sinnar (or Funj) and the Fur Sultanates, ruled most of the land. Under these sultanates, social modes of communication prevailed. Religious leaders and traditional educators transmitted knowledge and information orally among members of society, and social and political news was communicated through traditional media, such as town criers, who traveled from village to village to announce major social and political news (Galander, 2001).

In 1821, the Ottoman Empire brought Sudan under its control for the next 60 years before it was driven out in 1885 by Mohammed Ahmed Al-Mahdi, who besieged Khartoum and ended the Ottoman rule of the country by defeating the famous British officer, General Charles Gordon. The Mahdi established the first independent Islamic state, the *mahdiyya* State. During the *mahdiyya* period, the mosque served as the basic center for dissemination of political and social news. Written communication was used on a limited scale for political propagation during the early days of the Mahdist movement, but when the movement developed into a revolution, and later into a state, both written and oral forms of communication were used. However, written communication was confined to formal messages exchanged among state officials.

After the occupation of the Sudan in 1898, the British colonial power sought to modernize the country by educating an elite that would help in the administration of the country, but would also remain loyal to it (Galander, 2003). As such, the sons of loyal tribal leaders were sent to schools and brought up to populate the administration. This educated elite was, however, ultimately behind the rise of a local press that became the vanguard of the call for independence.

Print journalism dates back to 1903, when a non-Sudanese publisher began publishing the newspaper *Al-Sudan* with the permission, but also under the watchful eye, of the British administration (Salih, 1971). A few years later, several newspapers began to sprout up, and by the 1920s as a nationalist movement swept the country, several Sudanese published newspapers and used the press as a political platform for calls for independence. In response to these developments the colonial power introduced several restrictions to curb nationalistic enthusiasm by licensing the press, practicing censorship, and denying government employees the ability to write in the daily press (Babiker, 1985).

Born under a colonial administration, Sudan's broadcasting service was to serve as the main means of disseminating propaganda for the Allied Forces fighting in North and East Africa during the Second World War (Awad, 1994). The half-hour daily radio service, which started in 1940, primarily broadcast news of the war to the Sudanese public, who followed the conflict closely because of the involvement of several battalions from the Sudan Defense Force (SDF).

With independence in 1956, Sudan embarked on a multiparty form of democracy that copied the British bicameral parliamentary system. However, this first democratic experience did not last long; two years later, the democratically elected prime minister, citing sectarian bigotry and senseless political wrangling, collaborated with the army and handed over rule to a military junta. The following six years of military rule were brought to an end by a popular revolution in October 1964. A multiparty system was thereafter restored, but it too ended only four years later, when another military coup in 1969 dragged the country into 16 years of socialist and, later, Islamist rule. In its first two years, General Ja'afer Nimeiry's government adopted socialism and nationalized the banks, international companies, and private businesses. In its last two years, the socialist military government adopted Islamic Shar'ia law and dealt harshly with its violators. In 1985, another popular revolt brought the second military government to an end and ushered in the third democratic period, which lasted from 1985 to 1989. These four years of democracy were mired in political wrangling that was further exacerbated by a raging war in South Sudan. As a result, on 30 June 1989, Islamist elements in the Sudanese army conspired with the National Islamic Front (NIF) party and engineered a coup that brought the Islamists—under Omar Al-Bashir—to power for 30 years (1989–2019).

The 30 years of Islamist rule put the country under international scrutiny, as the government was accused of harboring international terrorists and rogue Islamist elements, such as Osama bin Laden, as well as committing crimes against humanity in the province of Darfur. Consequently, the country was severely sanctioned by the US government for almost all of the government's 30 years, while civil wars crippled the economy. Under continued external political and economic pressure and as a result of an incessant internal civil resistance, the Islamist-military government of Omar Al-Bashir was finally brought down by a popular revolt within the so-called second wave of the Arab uprisings that lasted for four months until April 2019.

Political System and Legal Framework

Few countries have experienced anything like Sudan's constant political oscillation between military and democratic forms of government. The country has also witnessed the replacement of three military dictatorships through civilian dissention, the latest of which were the December 2019 uprisings, which ended the longest authoritarian government in the history of the country. Such swings from democratic to military governments are important for understanding and explaining the dynamics of media operations in the country.

The media of the country have, no doubt, suffered from such an incessant oscillation between liberalism and authoritarianism. As the country stumbled from democratic to military rule, the media existed in an environment unconducive to the healthy growth of the profession.

During the first democratic government after independence in 1956, the private and partisan press mushroomed, and a truly free press system operated for a brief period until the coup of 1958 brought the first military rule, which clamped down on the free press. Although the military did not ban the private press, it printed its own newspaper as the official voice of the government. In 1964, a popular revolution restored liberal democracy, and reinstated the free press, but several newspapers were banned from publishing as a result of accusations of collaboration with the defunct military government (Galander, 2001). In 1969, another coup brought the second military government to power. As it subscribed to leftist ideologies, the government of General Ja'afer Nimeiry nationalized the press, and replaced 40 private newspapers with two government dailies and a weekly military paper. A press council was also established to guide media operations in the country, and the first indigenous press law replaced the colonial press act of the 1930s. The press law confined all mass media ownership to the ruling Sudan Socialist Union (SSU), and, consequently, the media were turned into mouthpieces of the government party, and forbidden to publish substantive criticism.

In 1985, the second popular revolution forced General Nimeiry to resign and brought back a democratic government that restored press freedom and lifted restrictions on private ownership of the press. This sudden return of the private press led to an unprecedented rise in the number of private media outlets, and created a situation that bordered on journalistic chaos, with increased violations of the basic ethics of journalism. Such conditions, according to some sources, helped the next military coup of General Omar Al-Bashir to rationalize the takeover, by citing unverified stories of corruption and crime that had appeared in the press (Galander, 2001).

The third military government began with a scheme of publishing two government-owned papers, but later allowed the private press to publish after shackling them with a series of restrictive press laws, enacted in 1994, 1996, 1999, and 2004 (Galander, 2016). These laws provided several strategies for curbing free expression of opinion, including censorship, jailing of journalists, closure of papers, and confiscation of printed issues.

As for radio, the first military government of General Abboud (1958–1964) began to expand radio services to the southern region of the country, where a civil war was flaring up and the need for a government voice was strong. By the time of the second military government of General Nimeiry, and as microwave and satellite technologies became available, regional radio stations were established all over the country. During the 30-year period of General Al-Bashir's rule, with the advanced technologies of radio transmission, private radio stations were allowed, and as a result, several FM radio stations, such as *Radio Al-Rabiaa* and *Khartoum University Radio,* appeared, but most of these stations were non-political and confined their discussion and progamming to sports and music.

Television was introduced in Sudan by the first military government. It was then expanded, and put to political use by the second military government, and was further expanded to broadcast regionally and internationally by the third. The government of General Abboud introduced television in 1962, but the service was a privilege only enjoyed by a small middle-class elite that lived around Greater Khartoum.

The government of General Nimeiry expanded television coverage to almost all regions of the country and utilized the service for political mobilization (Galander, 2003). The government of General Al-Bashir considered television a strategic resource for the propagation of its self-declared embodiment of the "civilized Islamic orientation" form of government.[1] Today, several television channels such as *Al-Shurooq*, *Blue Nile*, and *Sudaniya 24* are in operation.

With respect to the legal dimension, the first press law of the land was the 1930 Press Act passed by the British administration, which served at the time as an important restraining factor against the involvement of the local population in newspaper publishing by placing heavy financial burdens on any media venture. After independence, the first postcolonial government (1956–1958) did not abolish the press law of the colonialists, as there was little need to use the law against the press, especially as it was not adversarial or irresponsible (Sa'id, 1989). However, the first military government that succeeded the British in 1958 amended some articles of the colonial law and used it to deal with the press from a security perspective (Galander & Starosta, 1997, p. 216). Though no new press laws were initiated after the return of democracy in October 1964, the governments of the period had a record of violations of the basics of press freedom as they suspended newspapers, dragged some journalists to court, and planned to publish a government-owned newspaper (Galander & Starosta, 1997, p. 216). The second military government, led by General Nimeiry, introduced the 1973 Press and Publication Act, which established complete state control of the mass media, and introduced a press council that became, and has remained, the mainstay of Sudan's media ever since. The council served as the watchful eyes, and the iron fist, of the government with respect to journals and journalists: all publications were to be approved and licensed, and all journalists were to be vetted by the council (Galander & Starosta, 1997, p. 225). With the downfall of General Nimeiry's government and the return to democracy, a new press law was put into effect, which, "though couched in liberal terms suited to the prevailing democratic spirit, [...] retained some of the articles of the previous 1973 Press Act" (Galander & Starosta, 1997, p. 231).

---

1   The Arabic term used to describe the system was *Al-Tawajjuh Al-Hadari Al-Islami*.

The third military government of Omar Al-Bashir depended, at first, on "revolutionary" decrees to organize press activity. By 1993, the blowing winds of global change obliged the government to introduce amendments to the media; hence, it promulgated what became the first of many laws, the 1993 Press and Publication Act, which legalized the independent press under strict conditions. The law banned individual or family ownership of newspapers, and it outlined several punitive measures to be used against violators of the law. The law established a press council as the regulatory agency of the press and as a tool for curbing the enthusiasm of the economically unable and the politically undesirable investors. Three years later, the government abolished the 1993 Act and introduced a new 1996 Press Act that was no different from the previous one in its treatment of the press, except for a few "liberal" articles, such as one that allowed the press council members to elect the president of their council (Mahjoub, 2003).

With the political developments that signaled a probable return to liberal democracy, a new 1999 Press Law repealed the 1996 Press and Publication Act (Press Law, 1999). The law legalized the partisan press as it stipulated that any legally registered political organization could publish a newspaper. However, the increased pressure on the government in 2000, as a direct result of the liberal environment that prevailed, led them to introduce more punitive articles to the law; the most notorious of these sought the establishment of a "press court" by the chief justice "to deal with violations to this law" (Press Law, 1999). Other amendments included an assortment of punishments that the council and the press court could impose on journalists.

By 2004, a process of national reconciliation brought several political opposition groups back into the country, and a new political atmosphere conducive to democratic practices developed. Responding to the blowing winds of change, the government took the initiative of repealing the 1999 Press Law, and it introduced a new 2004 Press and Press Publications Law. The law gave more attention to the political role of the press council by including in its membership representatives of the political groups that signed the peace agreement. Despite the liberal atmosphere, the 2004 law did not only give the press council all the punitive measures of the previous laws but added a new one: the ability to cancel a journalist's license (Galander, 2017).

In 2009, a new press law replaced the 2004 law, with only minor changes to the extent of punishment or prerogatives of the press council. The new law came into effect during a critical political period in the country, as legal wrangling mired any progress and resulted in increased penalties against the press. A notable feature of the 2009 law was the inclusion of three sources of punishment, which an article on the issue labeled "the tripartite sources of press punishment" (Galander, 2017, p. 375). The article named these three sources as the Press Council, the National Security Bureau, and the Press Court. Each of these institutions had, from 2009 to the end of the third military government, imposed numerous penalties that created a crippling environment for the Sudanese press.

Currently, since the 2019 uprisings, the country is now engaged in the process of overhauling the public media. The interim government has, for example, closed down the media outlets that were owned or operated by the security apparatus. The administration of the state-owned Radio and Television Corporation has also been changed. As for the private media, the government has opted for this sector to be regulated by a press council. It must be mentioned that radio stations and television channels were operated and/or licensed during the last military government of Al-Bashir by the ministries of information in the capital and in individual states.

Economy and Ownership Patterns

As the country has swung between the two extremes of liberal and authoritarian rule, the ownership of media has been much affected by the existing political and economic system. Although the private press existed during the early years of independence (even under the first military government), the second military government of Nimeiry adopted socialist policies and, hence, nationalized or confiscated the press, including publishing houses and printing presses. Under the socialist government, the media were owned and operated by the single government party, which sought to mobilize the Sudanese masses towards the implementation of a socialist state.

The end of General Nimeiry's government signaled the return of the private press, but as the economic conditions were not conducive to this shift, newspapers did not perform well, and many were closed down. The situation had political consequences, as some outlets fell prey to foreign and local political exploitation (Galander, 2001). A leader from the NIF told this author that they were ready to give financial aid to newspapers that would support the party's cause, whereas an inquiry into feature articles in favor of Ethiopia and Libya in a private newspaper revealed that they were adverts in disguise (Galander, 2016).

The third military government of General Omar Al-Bashir demonstrated an extreme distrust of the media by denying private ownership at the beginning of its rule and, later, by controlling the media with restrictive laws. A clandestine scheme of media acquisition and control by the government was also adopted (Galander, 2017). The government's security apparatus established its own printing press and an advertising agency that distributed government adverts to favored newspapers, and developed a plan for the gradual takeover of financially troubled newspapers. In this way, the government crippled unfavorable newspapers and forced them either to stop publishing or to fall for the Security Bureau's scheme of forced acquisition under an arrangement that would leave the owners as ineffectual shadow owners (Galander, 2017). Before the demise of the last military government of Al-Bashir, historically famous newspapers such as *Al-Ayyam*, *Al-Sahafa*, and *Al-Khartoum* were unable to continue publishing, while only government-supported (or government-supporting) papers such as *Al-Sudani*, *Al-Watan*, *Al-Intibaha*, and *Al-Ahram* were abundantly available in kiosks. The number of newspapers published in Khartoum, during the last days of the government, was estimated at 41 political and sports papers.

For many years, radio and television control remained in the hands of the different governments, democratic or military, hence less emphasis was placed on the economic sustainability of radio and television operations. However, with the advent of FM facilities, several private radio stations sprang up in the country. Improved satellite equipment has also allowed television channels to expand out of the country, and as a result, few privately-owned television channels currently exist. Today, private ownership of television channels in Sudan is a reality and, with the advent of Internet services, several of Sudan's private and government television channels, and some radio stations, are available online. However, similarly to what is presently the case in some Arab countries, the new trend of private ownership of radio and television has also been clouded by government attempts at intrusion. For example, it is well-known that the *Al-Shurooq TV* channel is owned by the Islamist Party through a close confidant of the Al-Bashir government, while another television and radio station (*Taiba TV*) was mentioned during the trial of General Al-Bashir as having received millions of dollars from him.

Technology and Infrastructure

The role of Nimeiry's government in laying down the foundation of a strong communications-related infrastructure cannot be denied. His government is credited with the expansion of television broadcasting as it built the first satellite reception station in the country, and used both this and the microwave network to expand service to regions and areas far from Khartoum.

General Al-Bashir's government put even more emphasis on television as a medium for the propagation of political views, not only nationally, but also regionally and internationally. The government invested heavily in modern communication technology, such as satellite transmission, reception equipment, and modern television production facilities. The plans for extending the range of transmission materialized in the late 1990s as *Sudan TV*, according to several government sources (Center for Strategic Studies, 1999, p. 404), could be watched in several neighboring African and Middle Eastern countries. As satellite and Internet technologies expanded transmission globally, *Sudan TV*'s channels were then made available on several satellites. On the national level, the number of local or regional television channels increased dramatically due to the fact that 25 regional radio stations and television channels were established as the public property of the 25 states that comprised the individual regions of the country (Center for Strategic Studies, 1999).

Advances in Internet and mobile telephony in Sudan have become more rapid and robust. *MTN*, *Zain*, and *Kanar* are the current international service providers of the service in the country. The establishment of a government-based telecommunications authority in 1995, accompanied by the installation of new satellite equipment and the building of 36 reception stations, increased the capacity of reception and transmission more than tenfold (Galander, 2003). These new technological developments, as well as the shift to fiber optics in 1995, constituted the basis for the country's rapid advancement in communications, which was manifested in the spread, as in the 1990s, of Internet cafés and increased public use of mobile telephony, including smartphones. The latest data on Internet services in the Sudan indicate that Internet users total around 31% of the population.

With the expansion of the use of mobile phones in the new millennium, the use of social media in Sudan has risen to a remarkable level. Analyzing the situation, *The Guardian* wrote that as the press has been adversely affected by the clampdown on freedom of speech, the young generation has been left with only social media to exchange news and views (Albaih, 2015). According to 2017 data, mobile phone use had surged to include 72% of the population. Although *Facebook* is most popular among the population, *WhatsApp* use has recently risen to an extent that *The Guardian* prophesied it as "fueling a sharing revolution" (Albaih, 2015). The newspaper remarked that "the app has become a major source of news to Sudanese people, thanks to the ease of sharing that it offers and the wide reach of the group chat option, which has also helped connect the large diaspora to the latest wedding pictures and local gossip" (Albaih, 2015).

The recent December 2018–April 2019 uprisings confirmed *The Guardian*'s prophecy as they emphasized the role that *WhatsApp* (and, to a degree, *Facebook*) played in the dissemination of the opposition's public mobilization tactics. An article on the situation during the last years of Al-Bashir described the resort to social media in search of political information as so overwhelmingly unprecedented that the government's security bureau had to establish an "electronic Jihad brigade" to counter the barrage of anti-government sentiments that filled social media sites (Galander, 2017).

No better confirmation of the impact of social media on public opinion can be found than in the developments in the aftermath of the fall of General Al-Bashir's government. The opposition cleverly utilized social media and successfully mobilized the masses in the streets of cities to demand the handover of power to a civil government. Reluctant to hand over power to civilians, the ruling Military Council became frustrated by the political strength endowed to the opposition by social media and, eventually, took an unprecedented drastic decision of enforcing a country-wide Internet blackout. To emphasize the impact of social media on political developments in the country, a member of the Transitional Military Council (TMA) considered the Internet "a threat to national security." This move to deprive the public of access to social media was meant to disable the public revolt by denying the opposition communication with the masses and preventing the organization of the planned civil disobedience.

Challenges

The major challenges faced by the media are the result of the unstable nature of Sudanese politics. Throughout its history, the press has suffered from continued pressure, not only from the military governments, but also from rival elements in the different democratic governments.

During the last three decades, Sudan's mass media have been under all sorts of pressures, political, legal, and economic, while global technological advances keep challenging the industry and putting these media at an extreme disadvantage. Local economic conditions are unfavourable for both the printed press and broadcasting, despite the newly-gained liberal atmosphere that is promising for a free press system in the future. As such, a new approach to the country's "classic" mass media may be needed.

As this chapter is being written in 2019, an interim government is in power, and in three years' time (in 2022) a full democratic government is anticipated. Although the prospects of a full-fledged free press are on the rise, the most daunting issues are the current realities surrounding the future of the printed press, not only in Sudan, but worldwide, and the rising costs of newspaper production. At least for the time being, the economic realities in the country make it very difficult for the private press to prosper, unless the government lends a helping hand. As seen in some European countries, press subsidies may have to be put into effect. For instance, as in Sweden, there may be a need for platform-neutral media subsidy schemes that could provide a more stable press capable of rising to the responsibilities expected of it as a watchdog of a new democracy.

Despite these realities, the Sudanese media, particularly the printed press, have played an important role in national politics. Since Sudanese independence from the British, rulers have been aware that the press is a major tool of political education and can be used for enlightening the masses. This perhaps explains the continued harassment that the several military juntas which ruled the country exerted against the Sudanese press.

Outlook

As the country enters into a new era in which the power of the people has brought down military governments three times, the role and place of media in the new era should receive close attention from concerned scholars and authorities. As the country, whose economy was left in disarray by the previous government, is entering into a new era of liberal democracy, the large number of daily newspapers would need to be brought down through a scheme of mergers and/or acquisitions that would strengthen the financial conditions for many of these papers. The same may also apply to private broadcasting ventures, some of which have been closed down because of lack of funds. Such steps need to supersede the shift to a multiparty democracy that has been planned to occur within the next three years.

Internet-based media are in a better position than other media, as many of them rely on the advantages offered by the nature of the technology. The obvious popularity in the use of the net in the country must be followed by developing profit-making schemes to benefit the media that use the Internet for broadcasting their programs. The current overwhelming and obvious impact of social media demonstrates the future of modern communication technology as fundamental to the development of communication policies everywhere. As Sudan is approaching a new phase of democratic rule, policymakers must take the changing nature of communication into account when designing policies.

References

Abu Salim, M. I. (1979). *The mahdiyya directives* [in Arabic]. Beirut: Dar Al-Jil.

Albaih, K. (2015, October 15). How WhatsApp is fueling a 'sharing revolution' in Sudan. *The Guardian*. https://www.theguardian.com/world/2015/oct/15/sudan-whatsapp-sharing-revolution

Awad, I. A. (1994). *Half a century of Sudanese radio broadcasting* [in Arabic]. Khartoum: Azza Publishing House.

Babiker, M. (1985). *Press and politics in the Sudan*. Khartoum: Khartoum University Press.

Galander, M. (2001). *Mass media in Sudan: Toward a history of media-politics interplay*. Kuala Lumpur: IIUM Research Centre.

——. (2016). Necessary illusions: The role of press in politics in Sudan [in Arabic]. In H. Ibrahim (Ed.), *Sudan's independence: 60 years of trial and error* [in Arabic]. Cairo: Dar al-Hadara.

——. (2017). Watching over the watchdogs: Triangulation of press punishment in Sudan. *Journal of Applied Journalism and Media Studies*, 6(2), 395–75.

Galander, M., & Starosta, W. (1997). Press controls in the post-colonial Sudanese press. In F. Eribo & M. Jong-Ebot (Eds.), *Press freedom and communication in Africa* (pp. 211–42). Trenton, Asmara: Africa World Press.

Mahjoub, F. (2003). *The dilemma of the fourth estate: About the situations and laws of Sudanese press* [in Arabic]. Khartoum: Azza Publication.

Sa'id, B. M. (1989). *Opinions on the future of Sudanese press* [in Arabic]. Unpublished manuscript.

Salih, M. M. (1971). *Half a century of the Sudanese press* [in Arabic]. Khartoum: Khartoum University Press.

World Population Review. (2020). *Sudan Population 2020*. https://worldpopulationreview.com/countries/sudan-population/

15. Libya: From Jamahirization to Post-Revolutionary Chaos

Carola Richter

"From house to house, from apartment to apartment, from alley to alley", he would "cleanse Libya of dirt and filth." With this statement, Mu'ammar Al-Qadhafi threatened rebels during the Arab uprisings in a thunderous speech delivered on 22 February 2011 on Libyan state television. As he had so often done, he tried to use 'his' medium to explain, justify, and mobilize. The media—and television, in particular—were understood by the self-proclaimed "Brother Leader" to be a direct channel to the masses since he had come to power in 1969.

William Rugh (1987) classified the Libyan media system as a mobilization system. Mobilization media intend to shake people up, make them good citizens, and, at best, educate them. In practice, however, this approach involved disseminating regime propaganda through media, which, in a simple sender-receiver model, the regime assumed to have immediate effects on the audience. This conception of the media as instruments for disseminating ideology to a supposedly receptive audience is still prevalent in the Libyan media system today even after the fall of the Qadhafi regime.

Background

Libya is, in principle, a rich country with the largest oil reserves in Africa. In 2012, its 6.7 million inhabitants yielded a GDP of USD 15,597 per capita. However, this had dropped to below USD 8,000 by 2018.

Libya had already previously faced economic difficulties, particularly during the era of UN-imposed sanctions from 1992 to 2003 that caused a low GDP of USD 4,120 per capita to be recorded in 2002. Import bans on many technical products such as computers also slowed down consumption and modernization of infrastructure until the mid-2000s.

Prior to this period, in the 1970s and 1980s, Qadhafi's modernization policy, which was financed by oil rents, strongly developed the country and brought benefits to citizens such as free basic education for all. Whereas 90% of the population was illiterate at the time of independence in 1951, today, almost all inhabitants can read and write. The population of Libya is young despite significantly declining birth rates: 28% are under 15 years of age.

The country consists of three historically distinct regions, namely Tripolitania with Tripoli as the capital in the west, the Cyrenaica with the metropolis of Benghazi in the east, and the Fezzan, the desert region with the city of Sabha in the south. Most people live in Tripoli and Benghazi as well as in other coastal cities along the Mediterranean Sea. The vastness of the country has always created challenges for media infrastructure. Transporting newspapers to the desert regions has been a major problem—even in the 2000s, they arrived in the cities of the hinterland two to three days after publication. Even national radio and television did not reach many of the country's regions before the arrival of satellite technology.

In such a huge country, there are several factors that influence identity formation. Despite Qadhafi's attempt to impose a revolutionary transformation on society and his focus on "Arabness" (Smith, 2013, p. 176), traditional tribal identities remain strong. Ethnic affiliations, such as the Imazighen (or Berbers) in the west, and the Tuareg in the south, who make up about 10% of the population and maintain their own language, also constitute potential areas of conflict. Until 2011, the media were banned from using Amazigh, the Berber language, but now it is present on local radio stations and in newspapers. Being a native of western Tripolitania or eastern Cyrenaica around Benghazi also plays a major role in identity formation. Since Italian colonial rule, the East has been regarded as a stronghold of resistance against the authorities. In 2011, the fall of Qadhafi was also heralded there. Both traditional tribal loyalties as well as modern political affiliations are partly responsible for the country's current power struggles and formation of militias (Lacher, 2013).

However, there are no significant religious minorities; 97% of the population are Sunni Muslims. In general, Libyan society can be described as moderately conservative. The dissolution of state structures after 2011 and the resulting migration of Islamist fighters from Syria to Libya, Mali, and Nigeria has led to radicalization among some groups in Libya. For some time, the Islamic State (IS) had strongholds in some regions in Libya.

Under Qadhafi, women were legally equal to men. In everyday life they could pursue a variety of professions but did not have and still do not have the same public presence as men.

Historical Developments

Libya's modern media development can be divided into four major stages, all of which have been characterized by an authoritarian state approach. This style of approach provided a clear orientation of the media within the context of a regime policy: under the brutal colonial rule of the Italians from 1911–1943, the British Mandate from 1943–1951, the rule of conservative King Idris from 1951–1969, and that of Qadhafi from 1969–2011. Even after the fall of Qadhafi, the media have found it difficult to break away from this legacy.

Compared with its Arab neighbors, Libya was a laggard in terms of press development. It was not until 1866 that the first Turkish-Arabic weekly, *Tarabulus Al-Gharb*, appeared as an official organ of the Ottoman Sultan. From then until 1929, only 13 newspapers were published within Libya. With the Treaty of Lausanne, the Ottomans handed over Libya to the Italians in 1912, and before the end of that year, all newspapers were discontinued and replaced by government-owned propaganda papers such as *Barid Barqa*. Even the first developments in radio brought nothing but Italian propaganda for the Libyans. Italian shortwave stations from Rome were transmitted via loudspeakers to many Libyan cities from 1937 onwards (Al-Zilitni, 1981, p. 114). In contrast to other colonized states in the region, Libya underwent no modernization whatsoever during the occupation. On the contrary, Italian colonizers exterminated one-eighth of the Libyan population in concentration camps between 1922 and 1939.

After an interim period under the British Mandate, Libya gained formal independence through the UN on 24 December 1951. The anti-Italian resistance movement of the Sanussiya Brotherhood subsequently placed its leader Idris Al-Sanussi on the newly created throne of a federal Libyan kingdom. After the discovery of oil in 1959, a period of cautious modernization began which transformed the media sector. A Ministry of Information and National Leadership was established, which was responsible for all official press and broadcasting. The private and official press coexisted. The spirit of optimism that many Libyans returning from exile in neighboring countries brought with them to their homeland led to a rapid resurgence of the press (Mattes, 1986, p. 42). For Libyan writers, the press represented the only possibility of publication, since book production only began in the late 1950s. As a result, most newspapers were more concerned with literary, cultural, and social problems. For this reason, the press was seen as a "public university" (Al-Zilitni, 1981, p. 104) with a strong educational function. However, Press Law No. 11 of 1959 imposed severe restrictions on the media. The royal house felt pressure from the burgeoning Arab nationalist movement, which emanated from Egypt and grew with the struggles for independence within the still colonized neighboring states (Richter, 2004). Under Idris, the inhabitants of Tripoli were able to receive radio programs from the nearby Wheelus Air Base of the US forces. In 1956, the Americans and British handed over the newly developed radio program *Voice of Libya* to the Ministry of Information. The first national television station, set up in 1968, was also financed to a large extent by the US.

1 September 1969 marked a great turning point in Libya's history. Riding on the wave of anti-colonial sentiment, Mu'ammar Al-Qadhafi and a group of young military men carried out a bloodless coup against King Idris. Following the example of Egypt's president Nasser, who had turned radio into a revolutionary medium, "the very first act" (Al-Zilitni, 1981, p. 121) after taking over power was to put the radio facilities into the hands of Libyan revolutionaries. Qadhafi's speeches, which often lasted hours, were henceforth broadcast completely live on radio and television. The radio was directly subordinate to the Revolutionary Command Council (RCC), and private newspapers were

systematically forced out of the market from February 1970 onwards as state advertisements were withdrawn from their pages. In addition, all foreign language media closed down for lack of an audience after the American and British bases were evacuated and Italian settlers were expelled from the country.

From 1972 onwards, a complete restructuring of the press landscape took place. Competition was seen as a useless function of the media system. After the ban on all private newspapers in October 1973, all media became part of state institutions. The so-called Green Book, a 100-page manifesto written by Qadhafi himself in 1975, drew up a "Third Universal Theory" alongside capitalism and communism, and was henceforth regarded as a kind of state constitution. The media system played a key role in transforming Libya into the "people's mass state" (*jamahiriya*) that Qadhafi had envisaged. As a result of this "Jamahirization", a tripartite media system was installed. It consisted of a one-dimensional press of the respective syndicates, in which doctors, policemen, peasants, etc. had to organize themselves into syndicates, revolutionary corrective media with the *Al-Zahf Al-Akhdar* newspaper as the leading force, and centrally controlled national media. Over the course of this restructuring process, salary payments to writers were stopped as journalism was perceived only as an activity to make money.

However, the result was unsatisfactory for Qadhafi. Therefore, in a "cultural revolution" in 1980, the central press organization was completely abolished, and the revolutionary committees took over the radio and news agency *JANA*. The prisons were filled with intellectuals, including many journalists. This so-called cultural revolution was accompanied by a devastating economic and armament policy and a grueling war with Chad, and by the mid-1980s, these events had almost led Libya into bankruptcy. Therefore, Qadhafi initiated yet another radical change of policy related to domestic and economic liberalization. In March 1988, Qadhafi even announced that the borders would be completely opened and introduced a human rights charter and freedom of the press. The imposition of UN sanctions in 1992 because of Libyan involvement in the airplane attack over Lockerbie led, however, to new economic difficulties, including a newsprint crisis that lasted until the mid-2000s. It was not until 2003 that the sanctions were completely lifted.

Thereafter, and in the course of the attempted enthronement of Mu'ammar's second oldest son, Saif Al-Islam Al-Qadhafi, there was a brief period that saw a kind of pseudo-critical media flourish (Richter, 2013). Saif Al-Islam propagated a reform program called "Libya of Tomorrow" (*libya al-ghad*) in 2006. Although this program remained politically overoptimistic, Saif Al-Islam succeeded in launching two new newspapers (*Oea* in Tripoli and *Quryna* in Benghazi), a radio station, several news websites, a new news agency, and two satellite television channels (*Al-Libiya* and *Al-Shababiya*) and thereby significantly expanded the Libyan media system. These newspapers and programs appeared much more professional than the rest of the media. Foreign press was also suddenly accessible and international press agencies were allowed to open offices. A member of the exiled opposition called this phenomenon "Al-Ghad journalism", highlighting the fact that this was by no means an expression of general liberalization under Qadhafi, but merely a very limited freedom (Al-Mohair, 2009). Criticism of Qadhafi himself was absolutely inadmissible. As a result of increased resentment from the Revolutionary Committees, all of these media organs were reinstated in 2009, and *Al-Libiya* was taken over as the second state television channel. Although this put an end to the pseudo-liberalization, *libya al-ghad* remained a good school for Libyan journalists who went on to successfully establish their own media after the fall of the regime in 2011 (Wollenberg & Pack, 2013, p. 204).

Political System and Legal Framework

The uprising of Qadhafi's opponents, which began on 17 February 2011 in Benghazi and was supported by NATO, became a triumphal procession for rebels, and put an end to Mu'ammar Al-Qadhafi's 42-year rule in August 2011. The political and legal frameworks that had been in place until then were completely suspended.

The Libyan media had experienced 80 years of strong dependence on ruling elites and tight control of all media outlets. Thus, in 2011, during the early phase of the transition period and after rigid control mechanisms had vanished, one could observe a "media stampede" in Benghazi and later in Tripoli. In Benghazi alone—a city with a population of roughly 600,000 people—120 new newspapers, five radio stations, and five television stations were launched (Wollenberg & Recker, 2012, p. 6). The breakdown of state control over mass media and public communication allowed long-oppressed ethnic minorities, dissidents, and other formally marginalized groups in society to finally voice their opinions. To participate in public debate on the future of their country was an opportunity that many had been longing for and, in the sudden absence of restrictions, this unprecedented freedom allowed media outlets to blossom (Wollenberg & Pack, 2013). Although most of the newly emerging channels eventually failed due to a lack of funding in the years following their establishment, the importance of public articulation in a formerly repressed society became clear.

Still, the new era provided many challenges. The so-called National Transitional Council (NTC) ran all political operations until a regular government under Prime Minister Ali Zaidan was finally formed after the first elections in November 2012. However, the government remained weak in the face of the *de facto* power of the still existing militias, which had legitimized themselves as combat troops against Qadhafi. In the summer of 2014, a war between rival militias plunged Libya into an unresolved leadership crisis that threatened to gradually divide the country into regions under the rule of different groups (Watanabe, 2016).

Since that time, Libya has been both geographically divided and politically fragmented. In the east of Libya, including the city of Benghazi, one main political entity emerged: an alliance called the Libyan National Army (LNA), which included remnants of the old regime and was led by former general Khalifa Haftar. This alliance also comprised the 2014 elected and displaced House of Representatives (HoR) in Tobruk and the interim government in Al-Bayda. In 2014, the LNA launched a military campaign called "Operation Dignity," claiming its mission was to rid Libya of Islamist forces, and succeeded in conquering mainly the eastern cities of the country. In reaction to this campaign, several changing coalitions were set up in the western part of the country, including Islamist forces. The unifying umbrella was their opposition to the LNA, and they formed what came to be known as "Operation Dawn." In particular, the Dawn coalition consisted of dozens of rival networks built on tribal interests and local loyalties (Lacher, 2015). All of these actors were also competing for international support, for example, from the United Arab Emirates (UAE), Saudi Arabia, and Qatar, which considered Libya as a battleground within which they could enlarge their spheres of influence. Daraghi (2015) concluded that "Libya's conflict has become more than ideological; it is also about the interest and relative power of different groups—and a fear of losing that power" (p. 50). This fear is also reflected in more recent developments. After the 17 December 2015 Skhirat Agreement was negotiated by the UN, the Government of National Accord (GNA), headed by Fayaz Al-Sarraj, was established in Tripoli to follow up on the intermittent transition process. Observers have argued, however, that instead of unifying the country, the GNA has become the political arm of an alliance of militias that exploits state resources (Lacher, 2018). The *de facto* separation of the state remains in place, with two main players—the LNA in the east and the GNA in the west—but there are also many local militias that exist and function within and between these players.

The resulting political confusion has had a massive impact on the organization of the media sector, which is now completely unregulated and governed by arbitrariness instead of law. Although the NTC had immediately appointed a media commission in 2011 to consider media regulation, the latter was abolished by the end of the year, and a newly established Ministry of Culture was entrusted with this task (Wollenberg & Pack, 2013, p. 201). In May 2012, the NTC attempted to establish a High Media Council (HMC) appointed by the NTC to oversee the media and draw up media policy guidelines. Immediately after the formation of the government, the parliament rejected the idea of the council in November 2012 and installed a Ministry of Information, as in authoritarian times, because, as one member of parliament put it, "Freedom is not equal to chaos—and that is what we have at the moment" (Grant, 2012).

In December 2011, with decree 7/2011, the decision was made to continue to operate state media and to transfer pre-existing staff into new institutions. Starting in May 2012, the government operated three television stations through the state-owned Libyan Radio and Television Network (LRT): *Libya Al-Wataniya TV* (the former *Al-Jamahiriya TV*) with a 24-hour program, *Libya Al-Rasmiya TV* (the former *Al-Libiya TV* founded by Saif Al-Islam), and a sports channel. After the arrival of the GNA, all three channels were placed under its control.

Some local terrestrial stations, such as *Misrata TV* or the *Benghazi Broadcasting Network*, had also received state funding until 2014. In addition, the news agency *LANA* (formerly *JANA*) remained a governmental body after the replacement of its executive board. Moreover, a press support committee (CESP) was set up to publish the daily newspaper *Febrayer* and several weekly newspapers and to provide other support for publications (El Issawi, 2013, p. 24).

Several radio and television stations have been licensed since 2011, increasing the number of broadcasting outlets to more than 50 by 2012 alone. Press and online organs were able to publish without a license, and dozens were founded and often disappeared just as quickly (Wollenberg & Recker, 2012). With the outbreak of fighting in mid-2014, many media ceased publishing or changed their political orientation or formats. For example, the popular *Al-Assema TV* in Tripoli was stormed by militias and had to close down completely. After the militias took over power, new channels emerged. These were either instruments of or, at least, loyal to the new rulers, such as *February TV* or *Libya 24* (Fhelboom, 2014). Currently, there is no regulatory body that oversees and governs Libyan media in either the East or West of the country.

Today's situation has resulted in journalism once again becoming an instrument of particular interest groups. Thus far, there has been no move to establish a new press or media law to replace the one from the 1970s. Although the interim constitution of August 2011 guarantees freedom of opinion and the press in Article 14, influential warlords generally define what may be said and written.

In this climate, the media and journalists have become frequent targets of militant attacks. Human Rights Watch counted 91 attacks or threats against journalists from 2012 to November 2014, including 30 cases of kidnapping and eight murders. There were also 26 armed attacks on television and radio stations (Human Rights Watch, 2015, pp. 1–2). At the same time, ever since the factual partition of the country, the media have been forced to take sides or refrain from politics altogether. This has resulted in less violent attacks against journalists because many now practice self-censorship for the sake of protection against reprisals. In fact, even before the war of militias, journalists had begun to form their own professional associations in order to organize their interests and to agree on journalistic ethical standards. In June 2012, the representatives of the General Media Union (GMU) were elected in Jadu (Legatum Institute, 2012), but due to the fragmentation of the country these efforts fizzled out.

Economy and Ownership Patterns

Media ownership under Qadhafi was clearly regulated, and only public corporations were allowed to publish media outlets. The underlying credo that Libyan people would acquire control over the media remained an ideological construction. In reality, it was a nationalization of the media. Media production was largely financed by the country's oil rents. Libya also currently has the third-largest share (11.2%) in the USD 500 million *ArabSat* satellite system, which is jointly operated by the states of the Arab League, after Saudi Arabia and Kuwait.

Under Qadhafi, broadcasting was financed entirely by state funds without costs for the population. Until 2007, there was only one television station; nevertheless, Libyan national television and radio employed about 5,000 people, the press 1,200, and the national news agency about 240. Although many of these employees worked in administrative or technical departments, media institutions were overstaffed. Until 2011, the entire press operation of the country had an extremely low combined distribution total of only a couple of thousand copies. As a rule, the authorities and embassies ordered large amounts of quotas, even paid a surcharge on the normal price and then distributed the newspapers to their employees free of charge. In addition to direct state subsidies and advertisements by state companies, these indirect subsidies ensured the survival of print products (Richter, 2004, p. 55). However, as a result of the lack of professionalism and quality of the Libyan media, no real reading culture had yet developed. For this reason alone, it was extremely difficult for new press outlets established after 2011 to find a permanent sales market. Privately financed newspapers still struggle to develop strong business models given the problems associated with print media. Hardly any national daily newspapers exist today; most of the 200 newspapers that still existed in 2012 were local papers with only a small circulation of a few hundred or thousand copies (Wollenberg & Recker, 2012).

In contrast to the dying print media, broadcasting is thriving. A media mapping of 2018 revealed that there are now 14 Libyan television stations and 122 local radio stations throughout Libya in both urban and rural areas, as well as some transmitting from outside Libya (Wollenberg & Richter, 2020). These are significant numbers, given the small size of the population, which is estimated to be around only 6.7 million inhabitants. According to the media mapping, each of the three strong and adversarial camps that dominate Libya's political landscape has their own media wing. One camp is supported by the LNA and its allies in the east of the country. All broadcasters in this sector are fully or partly funded by the respective government authorities. An equally strong camp is supportive of the GNA in the area of Tripolitania, and six broadcasters within this territory are directly funded by the GNA. Finally, there is a variety of media outlets operated or supported by different Islamist movements in Libya, namely the rather moderate Muslim Brotherhood and Jihadist groups such as the Islamic Fighting Group and the Saudi-backed ultraconservative Salafi Madkhali movement (Luck, 2018). With 35 affiliated outlets, Islamist groups control a significant proportion of media outlets with diverse political interests and agendas. The Salafi Madkhali movement operates 17 radio stations throughout the country, which all broadcast Qur'an recitations, sermons, and seminars that are in line with their school of thought.

A substantial number of television channels (6 out of 14) are broadcast from abroad, eight of which receive funding from sources outside Libya. *Libya 24* has been operating from London since 2014, allegedly with funding from Libyans in the UAE. Likewise, the channels *TV218* and *Libya's Channel*, both with headquarters in Amman, purportedly receive funding from sources in the UAE. *Libya's Channel* was founded in Jordan in March 2015 by the brother of the Libyan ambassador to the UAE (Libya Herald, 2015). Libyan benefactors who live abroad provide funding for *Libya Al-Watan*, which has operated from Tunisia since 2017. Another example of this external media production and funding model is *Al-Nabaa*, an outlet affiliated with the Muslim Brotherhood, which relocated from Tripoli to Istanbul in 2017 and is known to receive funding from the state of Qatar. Moreover, *Libya Al-Ahrar*, which is also closely linked to the Muslim Brotherhood, similarly receives funding from Qatar, although its headquarters are in Istanbul. In fact, *Libya Al-Ahrar* was founded by long-term Libyan exile Mahmud Shammam on 30 March 2011 in Doha, Qatar before it moved to Istanbul. Many media outlets also switch sides, according to the respective situation. For example, the defunct *Libya Dawliya TV*, which was founded in Tripoli in 2012, had connections to the pro-government Alliance of National Forces until it was "turned around" by the Dawn Coalition in Tripoli and filled with new journalists (Fhelboom, 2014).

The ownership structure and available financial resources of private broadcasters are largely non-transparent, which means that any discussion surrounding the business models of these companies is often only speculative. However, content and ownership in the television sector is characterized by severe polarization.

The situation with the radio sector, on the other hand, is different and goes beyond polarized instrumentalization. There are 122 locally broadcasting radio stations in the country. What appears to be a surprisingly high number of radio stations is, indeed, unusually high compared to neighboring countries. The BBC Media Action of 2014 reported that 47% of the Libyan male and 25% of the female population listen to the radio every day (Dowson-Zeidan, Eaton, & Wespieser, 2014). The radio is therefore as important to Libyans as the Internet, which is used by 32% of the interviewees on a "regular" basis (weekly or daily). However, these numbers definitely lag behind television, which is used by 76% of the population every day (Dowson-Zeidan et al., 2014).

After the collapse of the Qadhafi regime in 2011, local radio stations continued operating, mostly with volunteer workers and activists who could use and maintain the equipment at much lower costs compared with that of centralized TV infrastructure. In terms of the ownership and funding of all local radio stations, 71 of these 122 are still connected to public bodies; 34 are directly related to government institutions, such as ministries, and 37 are related to municipalities and publicly funded local organizations, such as universities. Nevertheless, editorial autonomy of local media entities is fairly high, as most outlets experience minimal control from governmental institutions and tend to follow public opinion on the community level. The remaining stations are operated by private entrepreneurs; 34 are based particularly in the Tripoli area, and 17 are clearly affiliated with the Madkhali Salafists (Wollenberg & Richter, 2020).

Technology and Infrastructure

Qadhafi announced in 2001 that he was an avid Internet surfer and that every Libyan should own a PC and a mobile phone. However, the expansion of digital infrastructure was and continues to be a very slow process, and "the underdeveloped state of the telecommunications network, which suffered from a lack of expertise and competition, was especially significant" (St. John, 2013, p. 95). As sanctions were lifted in 2003, communications technology was slowly upgraded. It was only after the political problems with the US had been resolved that the Libyan authorities were able to obtain the country's own top-level domain of.ly (Internet Assigned Numbers Authority, 2004). Until 2011, technological infrastructure was operated centrally by Libya Telecom and Technology (LTT) and the mobile phone providers *Libya* and *Al-Madar*, which were under the control of Qadhafi' oldest son Mohammed. For a long time, Qadhafi saw no reason to block the Internet or even satellite television, although the Internet in particular promoted a hotbed of political opposition. The portals *akhbar-libya.com*, *almanara.org*, and *nfsl-libya.com* were operated by exiles in the US and UK, and these shaped international perspectives on Libya. However, as the increase in networking opportunities was perceived as a threat to the regime, sites owned by the Libyan opposition abroad and all social media sites were blocked from 2010 onwards (Reporters Without Borders, 2011). In March 2011, Qadhafi completely disconnected the Internet and mobile communications from international data traffic. Despite these official restrictions, rebels secured channels to the outside world via proxy servers and satellite telephones.

While only around 14% of Libyans had access to the Internet in 2010, this number jumped to 22% in 2017, which was still very low. However, the situation seems to have changed very rapidly since then. Recent social media statistics, for example, show that 60% of all Libyans use *Facebook* and stream television programs either through media websites such as *TV218* or through *Facebook* pages (Democracy Reporting, 2019).

In respect to communications technology, mobile phones are particularly well distributed, with 92% of the population being connected. They also serve as the main gateway to the Internet. Three state-owned operators, *Libiyana*, *LibyaPhone*, and *Al-Madar* provide services and mainly cover the country's two big cities and some of the coastal areas. However, due to Libya's ongoing military conflict, Internet connectivity is often disrupted, and outside Tripoli and Benghazi, technological infrastructure is still insufficient.

Challenges

The Qadhafi era has left behind a media structure and culture of journalistic production that is inadequate for today's requirements. After 2011, reforms were started only hesitantly and did not change the premises of the system. In the context of political fragmentation, the media system has fallen back into the old pattern of political instrumentalization. As expected, the legacy of the Qadhafi era and the country's inexperience with any other legal and organizational framework means that the process of redesigning state institutions, including the media, poses an enormous challenge. Questions of media ethics, as well as the institutionalization and regulation of media are still completely unresolved.

For the time being, a culture of mutual accusation prevails in the television sector, which strongly reflects the partition of the country into two opposing political camps. This instrumentalization not only presents a challenge from an ethical point of view, in terms of journalistic autonomy, but might also have significant effects on the population and hinder future efforts for reconciliation after the war ends. At the same time, the public seems to be aware of biased reporting. People are frustrated by the "lack of useful and relevant information on television about issues that matter to them" (Dowson-Zeidan et al., 2014, p. 16), and they mostly trust friends and family as their main sources of information (Dowson-Zeidan et al., 2014, p. 36). Indeed, the UN-led consultations with 7,000 Libyans indicated that the population seems to be tired of political polarization and reported that "[t]he Libyans consulted requested an end to the transition period. They highlighted the need to unify State institutions" (UN Security Council, 2018, p. 2). Therefore, the existing culture of media instrumentalization needs to be overcome.

Another challenge is to provide an independent regulation for the media. As of now, no adequate media laws exist, and the ruling bodies either do not regulate at all or do so arbitrarily. In most parts of the country, media production is allowed as long as content creators align with the ideological orientation of the ruling entity or stay completely away from politics. This situation has brought about two trends. On the one hand, media production has been largely deterritorialized, and major players and financial support come from abroad—which keeps any regulation of licenses and content out of the hands of a potential national regulator. On the other hand, a considerable number of local initiatives have started their own media production, mainly radio, to serve the local communities. However, they are forced to refrain from political reporting to avoid any trouble.

Outlook

Both institutionally and socially, a new media system has yet to develop. This seems very problematic at the moment as military conflict continues to contribute to the increasing disintegration of state structures. The fact that many local initiatives produce content to serve the community offers a ray of hope, as this could provide a breeding ground for more independent non-instrumentalized journalism in the future. However, at the moment, these initiatives are vulnerable to any changes in the political situation and have no legal protection. Before Libya's media system can be reformed, the country's current political situation needs to be consolidated and the wars between militias need to be brought to an end. Only then will the existing challenges to the media system be overcome.

References

Al-Mohair, K. (2009, March 6). Two Qadhafi-related websites generate controversy with unusual criticism [in Arabic]. *Al-Jazeera*. http://www.aljazeera.net/news/archive/archive?ArchiveId=1171188

Al-Zilitni, A. M. (1981). *Mass media for literacy in Libya: A feasibility study* (doctoral dissertation). Ohio State University.

Daraghi, B. (2015). Libya: From euphoria to breakdown. *Adelphi Series*, 452(55), 39–58. https://doi.org/10.1080/19445571.2015.1114755

Democracy Reporting. (2019). *Libya social media report.* https://www.democracy-reporting.org/libya-social-media-report/march/pdfs/DRI-LY-DE_SMM-Report_Annex%20I_2019-04-05.pdf

Dowson-Zeidan, N., Eaton, T., & Wespieser, K. (2014). After the revolution: Libyan and Tunisian media through the people's eyes. *BBC Media Action Research Dissemination Series.* http://downloads.bbc.co.uk/rmhttp/mediaaction/pdf/research/libya_tunisia_media.pdf

El Issawi, F. (2013). Libya media transition: Heading to the unknown. *London School of Economics.* http://www.lse.ac.uk/media@lse/Polis/documents/Libya%20Media%20Transition%20Heading%20to%20the%20Unknown%20.pdf

Fhelboom, R. (2014, November 25). Journalism under siege. *Correspondents.* https://correspondents.org/en/2014/11/25/journalism-under-siege/

Grant, G. (2012, November 26). Libyan media to be regulated by new Ministry of Information. *Libya Herald.* http://www.libyaherald.com/2012/11/26/national-congress-votes-to-create-new-ministry-of-information/#axzz2yCPKrZXM

Human Rights Watch. (2015). *War on the media: Journalists under attack in Libya.* http://www.hrw.org/sites/default/files/reports/libya0215_ForUpload.pdf

Internet Assigned Numbers Authority (2004). *IANA Report on the Redelegation of the.ly TopLevel Domain.* http://www.iana.org/reports/2005/ly-report-05aug2005.pdf

Lacher, W. (2013). Fault lines of the revolution: Political actors, camps and conflicts in the new Libya. *Stiftung Wissenschaft und Politik.* http://www.swp-berlin.org/fileadmin/contents/products/research_papers/2013_RP04_lac.pdf

——. (2018). Tripoli's militia cartel: How ill-conceived stabilisation blocks political progress, and risks renewed war. *Stiftung Wissenschaft und Politik.* https://www.swp-berlin.org/fileadmin/contents/products/comments/2018C20_lac.pdf

Legatum Institute. (2012). *Libya media wiki.* https://lif.blob.core.windows.net/lif/docs/default-source/default-library/libya-media-wiki---snapshot-of-a-country-in-transition.pdf?sfvrsn=0

Libya Herald. (2015, March 3). New privately-owned Libyan TV channel launched from Amman, Jordan. *Libya Herald.* http://www.libyaherald.com/2015/03/03/new-privately-owned-libyan-tv-channel-launched-from-amman-jordan/#axzz3TPbQ9pd7

Mattes, H. (1986). The development of the Libyan press 1969–86 [in German]. *Communications, 12*(3), 41–60.

Reporters Without Borders. (2011). *Libya: The birth of „free media" in Eastern Libya.* https://ifex.org/images/libya/2011/06/27/free_media_libya.pdf

Richter, C. (2004). *The media system in Libya: Actors and developments* [in German]. Hamburg: Deutsches Orient-Institut.

———. (2013). Libyan broadcasting under Al-Qadhafi: The politics of pseudo-liberalization. In T. Guaaybess (Ed.), *National broadcasting and state policy in Arab countries* (pp. 150–65). Houndmills: Palgrave Macmillan.

Rugh, W. A. (1987). *The Arab press: News media and political process in the Arab world* (2nd ed.). New York: Syracuse University Press.

Smith, H. (2013). The South. In J. Pack (Ed.), *The 2011 Libyan uprisings and the struggle for the post-Qadhafi future* (pp. 175–89). New York: Palgrave Macmillan. https://doi.org/10.1057/9781137308092_7

St. John, R. B. (2013). The post-Qadhafi economy. In J. Pack (Ed.), *The 2011 Libyan uprisings and the struggle for the post-Qadhafi future* (pp. 85–111). New York: Palgrave Macmillan. https://doi.org/10.1057/9781137308092_4

UN Security Council. (2018). *United Nations support mission in Libya: Report of the Secretary-General*. Report no. S/2018/780. https://undocs.org/en/S/2018/780

Watanabe, L. (2016). Libya: Small steps out of the chaos [in German]. *CSS Analysen zur Sicherheitspolitik*, 193. http://www.css.ethz.ch/content/dam/ethz/special-interest/gess/cis/center-for-securities-studies/pdfs/CSSAnalyse-193-DE.pdf

Wollenberg, A., & Pack, J. (2013). Rebels with a pen: Observations on the newly emerging media landscape in Libya. *The Journal of North African Studies*, *18*(2), 191–210. https://doi.org/10.1080/13629387.2013.767197

Wollenberg, A., & Recker, S. (Eds.) (2012). *Reinventing the public sphere in Libya: Observations, portraits and commentary on a newly emerging media landscape*. Berlin: MICT.

Wollenberg, A., & Richter, C. (2020). Political parallelism in transitional media systems: The case of Libya. *International Journal of Communication*, 14, 1173–93.

16. Tunisia: The Transformative Media Landscape after the Revolution

Noureddine Miladi

The media landscape in Tunisia has witnessed significant transformations since the revolution of 14 January 2011. After decades of being direct controlled and tightly monitored by the dictatorial regimes of Bourguiba and Ben Ali, the country has shifted to a new era of a diverse media market. Public service media have been consolidated and made independent from government interference. Newly established television and radio channels have been thriving and stand in competition with the public service broadcasters. This diversity in the media market has also been accompanied by regulatory frameworks which guarantee free speech and the independence of journalists. In spite of its slow development, the independent television and radio regulator Haute Autorité Indépendante de la Communication Audiovisuelle (High Independent Authority of the Audiovisual Commission, or HAICA), has been integral in transforming the nature of the audio-visual market to meet international standards.

However, despite these recent advances in media development, I argue in this chapter that, similar to any other transitional democracy, in the case of Tunisia, ideological forces, the power of business magnates, and overseas influences remain key factors which affect the operation of various media outlets.

Background

The Arab uprisings, which were triggered in Tunisia by ousting Zain El-Abidin Ben Ali from power on 14 January 2011, have set a landmark for change in all aspects of the locals' lives. The one-party ruling regimes of Ben Ali and his predecessor Habib Bourguiba came to an end and gave way to a new democratic era. As a result, Tunisia, after living through decades of dictatorships, has been undergoing significant transformations regarding democratic governance, freedom of speech, and empowerment of civil society organizations. This transformative scene has evidently reinvigorated and changed the shape of the media market in terms of ownership, governance, editorial policies, and regulations.

Situated in the north of Africa and overlooking the Mediterranean Sea, Tunisia is bordered by Algeria on the northwest and Libya on the south. The population reached 11.8 million in 2020, and its GDP dropped compared with that of 2014 from USD 47.6 billion to USD 39.9 billion in 2020. Although a sizeable portion of its southern region is located in the Sahara Desert, Tunisia has a rich farming landscape and self-sufficient agricultural production.

Tunisia's official religion is Islam. The Maliki school of thought represents a key source for jurisprudence. There exists a small minority of Jews in the north as well as in the southern part of the country on the island of Djerba. Arabic is the official language, and French is the second most spoken language and, to some extent, the language of the elites. Many business enterprises as well as educational institutions still use French as their main language for communication.

Tunisia's past reveals a rich antiquity that spans across three thousand years of successive civilizations. Although Islamic culture overwhelmingly constitutes the country's identity, Tunisia's long history has always included a multiethnic, cross-cultural character influenced by the Carthaginian, Roman, Arab, Islamic, Berber, European, and Ottoman civilizations. As the site of the Phoenician city of Carthage, and later, as the Africa Province, Tunisia was of strategic significance in connecting Africa and Europe during the Roman times and was known as the breadbasket of the Roman Empire.

Tunisia's economic divide can be readily seen in the marked differences between the North and coastal cities when compared with the rural and southern parts of the country. The regimes of Bourguiba and Ben Ali had heavily invested in infrastructure, education, health, and tourism in the main coastal cities of Tunis, Nabeul, Bizerte, Monastir, Sousse, and Sfax. By contrast, most of the southern regions of Elkaf, Gafsa, Jandouba, Kairouan, Sidi Bouzid, and Mednine, among others, still suffer from poor infrastructure, lack of investments, and high rates of unemployment. The resentment that arose from this regional divide constituted one of the key reasons for the outbreak of the Tunisian revolution in the marginalized city of Sidi Bouzid. This regional divide is also evident in the distribution of media organizations across the country, as both state and private television channels and radio stations, in addition to major newspapers, are still primarily based in the wealthy coastal cities.

Historical Developments

In the modern era, Tunisia was under colonial rule by France from 1881 until its independence in 1956. Soon after the French invasion, the Tunisian Bey (ruler) representing the Ottoman Sultan was deposed. As a consequence, the beylic system was replaced after the treaty of Bardo and the Convention of Al-Marsa in 1883 by a new French authority called the French Resident General. Immediately after assuming power, the new governor embarked on changing the political, economic, and social order of Tunisia. These measures affected all aspects of everyday life including changes in communication and culture, which were persistently resisted by the locals. Similar to its neighboring country Algeria, the Tunisian anti-colonization movement led a long and unremittent struggle for independence. The resistance movement gathered momentum especially after dramatic changes in the international geopolitical scene after World War II. That momentum had been partly aided by the circulation of newspapers and newsletters among the activists and emerging educated elite.

During the French colonization, print publishing thrived in both the Arabic and French languages. During the French occupation from 1881 to 1956, there were more than 100 newspapers and periodicals published in Arabic, in addition to tens of newspapers published in French. Newspapers served as significant platforms for the struggle against the French occupation (Instance Vérité & Dignité, 2018). Prominent newspapers at the time, such as *Sawt Attalib Al-Zaytouni*, *Al-Tunisi*, *Al-Hadirah*, *Azzahra*, *Al-Talia'*, *Sabilurashad*, *Al-Fajr*, *Assurour*, and *Al-Dustour*, were crucial in sustaining the anti-colonial movement and challenging the communication strategy of the occupation power. Immediately after taking control of the country, the French colonial power confiscated some newspapers, including the *Al-Raid Al-Tunisi* and *Al-Tunisi* newspapers, among others, and turned them into mouthpieces of the colonial administration. In 1911, the French colonial power censored every Arabic language newspaper except for one which was the official organ of the French colonials. Additionally, as a new measure to regulate and control the newspaper market, a Communication Control Council was set up after WWII and was headed by a general from the colonial council. Part of its mission was to issue new licenses and regulatory laws, and control content.

However, the post-independence era was not free of media repression. Up to the eve of the 14 January 2011 revolution, Tunisia had been ruled by only two presidents: Habib Bourguiba (1956–1987) and Zain El-Abidin Ben Ali (1987–2011). Both had led dictatorial regimes and held control of every branch of the Tunisian state including the media sector. Both eras witnessed dark times as well as instances in which restrictions on free speech were slightly loosened (Zran & Ben Messaoud, 2018). Soon after the country's independence, the self-appointed president Habib Bourguiba not only prevented pluralism in radio and television broadcasting and the press but also monopolized the management and decision-making process in key media outlets. On 31 May 1966, the first television network began broadcasting and later became the Tunisian Radio and Television Corporation. This Tunisian broadcaster emerged as an official government body, which did not have the sovereignty of public service broadcasting institutions. Senior and middle managers were directly appointed by the presidential palace. Leadership positions were also allocated on the basis of strict allegiance to the ruling party, the Rassemblement Constitutionnel Démocratique or Constitutional Democratic Assembly (RCD) (Zran & Ben Messaoud, 2018).

As for the printed press, Bourguiba allowed, in the early years of his rule, the publication of only four newspapers: *Al-Amal* (in Arabic) and *L'Action Tunisienne*, which both functioned as organs of his political party (Free and Constitutional Party), as well as *La Press*, which was the mouthpiece of the government, and its Arabic version *Al-Sabah*. Although the two latter publications were declared as independent, they followed strict editorial guidelines set by the Ministry of Interior. Tight legislations governing the press and broadcasting first appeared within Article 8 of the 1 June 1959 Constitution. The document stipulated that freedom of speech and freedom of the press were guaranteed, but the specific legislation governing the field of media and communication was repressive and arbitrary.

In 1961, the *Tunisian and African Press Agency (TAP)* was launched. For decades, it remained the main and official source of news, focusing mainly on the regime and serving its agenda. During this period, the propaganda machine employed every possible means of state media and communication in order to establish political legitimacy and hegemonic influence in the public sphere. Through the Office of State Media, established on 31 May 1956, Bourguiba directly monitored and controlled all media outlets. In the mid-1960s, Tunisia witnessed further setbacks on civil liberties and free speech, which included closing down several media outlets and often forcing their owners to leave the country. This period coincided with the incarceration of the leaders of the Yousfi movement (named after its leader Ahmed ben Yousuf) and banning the activity of the Tunisian Communist Party.

Journalism education was yet another component of Bourguiba's regime. With the aim of breeding new generations of journalists, on 30 December 1967, he inaugurated the first college of journalism in the country and the region, the Institut de Presse et des Sciences de l'Information (IPSI). The institute served as an incubator for future generations of qualified journalists who fed both press and broadcast journalism institutions over the years.

Bourguiba dominated the content of daily news bulletins on state television and national radio, as well as on official and pro-government newspapers. These platforms repeatedly reported on his daily presidential engagements such speeches, meetings, and visits to various places. Due to this controlled discourse, broadcasting outlets seriously lacked depth and diversity and were characterized by a top-down indoctrinatory style of communication that was well orchestrated by the head of state (Hajji, 2004).

During this period, Tunisia witnessed its darkest epoch in media censorship and the repression of free speech. Total control of the media and self-censorship were the norm. Human rights and political activists rarely dared to openly criticize the ruling regimes. Those who crossed the line even at small gatherings, seminars, or academic symposia were arrested and subsequently given prison sentences. Scores of journalists fell victim to Bourguiba and Ben Ali's media censorship. Bashir ben Ahmed, one of the early diplomats who headed the Ministry of Information, could not tolerate Bourguiba's dominant persona and founded *Jeune Afrique* magazine in 1961 after resigning from office. After he settled in Paris in 1962, *Jeune Afrique* continued to operate as a significant platform for news and current affairs analysis about Tunisia and the African region, attracting not only a large readership among the Tunisian diaspora but also among the Tunisian elites back home. It remains to this day an influential publication.

Th state's tight control over media outlets did not change during the mandate of Ben Ali (1987–2011). However, a key feature of this era was that Ben Ali's family members became influential in every sphere of public life including the media. His political party, RCD, was the tool through which the Ben Ali regime managed to infiltrate every media institution.

The Ministry of Information and the External Communication Agency (ATCE) were two official bodies employed by the Ben Ali regime as instruments to control the media (Ben Letaif, 2018). The ATCE was in charge of out-of-state propaganda campaigns for the regime. Mainly through bribing journalists and media companies, the ATCE generously paid writers and PR organizations in Europe and the US to report fake economic successes of the regime and falsified claims about stability, freedom, and respect for human rights at a time when Tunisia witnessed one of the darkest episodes of its modern history. The ATCE, argued Ben Letaif (2018), "paid mercenaries and foreign political figures to promote the image of Ben Ali in their respective countries" (p. 3).

A further measure employed by the Bourguiba regime and later maintained during Ben Ali's rule was the 1975 Press Code that aimed to censor information and exercise tight control over free speech. The "legal deposit" requirement compelled all publishers to submit a copy of their publications before distribution. This gatekeeping policy allowed regime regulators to censor every form of media content and punish every journalist critical of the regime, such as through heavy fines and sometimes prison sentences Under such a regime defamation was a politically manipulated legislative tool used to accuse and imprison political dissidents and independent journalists. Tailor-made court sentences for attempting to jeopardize state security and public order or causing offence to the head of the state and other government figures were always in place (Human Rights Watch, 2005).

Among the notorious cases documented by international human rights organizations were those related to the ordeals faced by various journalists, political as well as human rights activists. Um Ziyad, a Tunisian female journalist, was imprisoned and tortured for a month in 2003 after using her blog to highlight problems within the country's education system and calling for proper reform of this sector. Hamadi Jebali, former editor of the *Al-Fajr* newspaper in the 1980s, and later a prime minister in the coalition government (2012–2013), was imprisoned for over 15 years under Ben Ali's rule for spearheading a newspaper that heavily criticized the regime's corruption. Because Internet platforms posed another challenge for the Ben Ali regime from 2000 onwards, systematic blocking of activists' homepages, *Facebook*, and *YouTube* was common practice. For over 10 years, the websites of *Al-Nahdah Net*, *Al-Kalima*, *Tunis News*, and *Al-Bawwaba*, among other critical news sources, were censored in Tunisia. However, such news sites continued to function as thriving platforms for discussions and news reporting about Tunisian politics in the diaspora. This struggle for freedom of speech among oppositional media, in addition to ongoing political changes in the country, has meant that Tunisia has set a benchmark in terms of democratic governance and media freedoms for other Arab uprising countries

Political System and Legal Framework

On 23 October 2011, Tunisia witnessed its first free democratic general elections that brought Ennahda, an Islamist political party headed by

Rashid Ghannouchi, to power for the first time. Moncef Marzouki, a former exiled political activist and founder of the Congress for the Republic party was proposed as their preferred presidential candidate. As a result, the country announced its first democratically elected government after over 60 years of dictatorship. A three-party coalition was formed among Ennahda, the secular party Ettakatol, and the Congress for the Republic (CPR) which ruled in Tunisia after the 2011 Constituent Assembly election.

Social and political instability kept mounting due to increasing unemployment, economic uncertainties, and shrinking foreign investment in the country. Political tension between the troika-led government and opposition parties, specifically from the extreme left, continued to simmer and took a dangerous turn after the assassination of two political activists, Chokri Belaïd in February 2013 and Mohammed Brahmi in July 2013. The political deadlock worsened as a result of hundreds of strikes organized by the General Labour Union in various parts of the country, which led the Ennahda Party to withdraw from power and opened the way for a general election. The legislative election held on 26 October 2014 and the presidential elections of 23 November 2014 brought the newly formed Nidaa Tounis (headed by Beji Caid Essebsi, a career minister from the Bourguiba era) to power. This guaranteed the success of a democratic and peaceful political transition and saved the country from falling into the same scenario as Egypt, Libya, or Syria which led either to the return of dictatorship or civil war.

The abovementioned challenges have impacted the media scene in terms of its operation and development. For instance, tension among various political parties has found its way to the front pages of newspapers and heated discussion programs on television and radio stations. As Tunisia has lived through decades of government media control, it will take time for a culture of free speech and free media to mature and develop. Nonetheless, this process is gradually taking place in Tunisia through the development of public service broadcasting, which is empowering independent and community media and strengthening the role of independent regulatory bodies. In fact, the biggest achievements of the Ennahda-led troika government were arguably the writing of the Tunisian constitution and the establishment of the independent council for media, HAICA. The HAICA was set up in May 2013 as the new regulatory body for monitoring television and radio content, issuing new licenses for both the public and private sectors. The establishment of this new independent regulatory body was preceded by the dissolution of the Ministry of Information and the ATCE, which had been used as the strong arms of the Ben Ali regime in controlling information.

It can be argued that the Tunisian media market has been significantly transformed because of the historical shift in the political scene. Its unprecedented growth has encompassed not only satellite television, but also radio stations, newspapers, and Internet platforms. From a handful of media outlets mainly controlled by the former Ben Ali regime, dozens of radio stations, television channels, and online news platforms, in addition to a plethora of newspapers and magazines, have been launched since 2011. The Decree-Law No. 115 (on the Press, Printing and Publishing) passed in February 2011 concerns both print and electronic media. This new law repealed the 1975 Press Code and paved the way for freedom of the press and organization of the market, and regulated ownership and control of newspapers and magazines. However, unlike the audiovisual market, the printed press is not yet under the umbrella of an independent regulatory authority.

Compared with the Ben Ali era, the post-revolutionary period witnessed a dramatic expansion of the broadcasting market. Today, there are 12 television channels and over 21 radio stations transmitting from various parts of the country. These channels and stations are now licensed and regulated under Decree-Law No. 116 by the Broadcasting Authority, that is, the HAICA. The analogue television market is currently dominated by three television channels, *Al-Watania 1* (known as *Tunis7* before the revolution) and *Al-Watania 2* (known as *Tunis21* before the revolution), both of which cover almost all of the Tunisian territory, while *Hannibal TV* covers only 45% (Office National de la Télédiffusion, 2014). The digital market currently includes the abovementioned two channels (*Al-Watania 1+2*), in addition to nine private channels: *Hannibal, Nessma, Ezzitouna, Attounissia, El-Hiwar Ettounsi, Attessia TV, M Tunisia, Tunisna TV, Al-Insen, Telvsa TV, Al-Janoubia,* and *Carthage+* (Office National de la Télédiffusion, 2014). In September 2020, the Press Council was set up as a culmination of collaborative efforts between various civil society organizations. The council functions as an independent, not-for-profit body that works to establish self-regulation for the media in order to protect freedom of the press, and to defend Tunisian citizens' right to obtain quality information. Its key roles are to assist media institutions in establishing mechanisms that abide by the ethics of the profession, to mediate between the profession and the public, and to improve legislation related to the media sector, especially in the written and electronic press.

This new environment has significantly widened the scope of free speech to a level not experienced before. The global freedom index of Freedom House, for instance, rated Tunisia "very high" in terms of freedom of expression. Although blasphemy remains illegal, the new constitution stipulates that freedom of belief and conscience should be guaranteed for all citizens. It also "bans campaigns against apostasy and incitement to hatred and violence on religious grounds" (Freedom House, 2020). Article 31 states that "Freedom of opinion, thought, expression, media and publication shall be guaranteed. These freedoms shall not be subject to prior censorship." Also, Article 32 confirms that "The state shall guarantee the right to information and the right to access information. The state seeks to guarantee the right to access to information networks." As a reflection of the new free media environment, television and radio stations now host shows and discuss issues that would have been impossible to air before the revolution. Talk shows about political reform, corruption, education, the role of the police, civil society, human rights, culture, and sports have become the digest of scores of channels. This has provided a critical space for members of the public to express their views regarding the shape of the new democracy in the country. The public service network is rapidly adapting to the challenge of finding its role in light of the competition from private channels. However, the public television network is caught in the middle of ideological tensions. These tensions exist partly among a few influential key players from various political parties who have infiltrated these media institutions and, to some extent, the regulatory body, HAICA, and the National Journalism Syndicate.

Economy and Ownership Patterns

Ownership and control of Tunisia's media organizations has also been subject to transformations. After decades of total control under the Bourguiba and Ben Ali regimes, ownership of television channels, radio stations, newspapers, and magazines has taken a dramatic turn since January 2011. This boom has brought new players into the market, many of whom are state funded, while others are privately funded or receive support from external bodies. Although private media organizations claim independence, direct links between media proprietors and political affiliation are highly visible. Nabil El Karoui, founder of *Nessma TV*, for instance, was also one of the founders of the political party Nidaa Tounis, later a founder of Kalb Tounis, and eventually a presidential candidate in the elections of October 2019. Tahar ben Hassine, the founder of *Al-Hiwar Ettounsi*, was also one of the founders of Nidaa Tounis and an influential member of the previous regime of Ben Ali. Larbi Nasra, founder of *Hannibal TV*, is a key figure in the party Voice of Tunisia People. Oussama ben Salem, founder of *Zitouna TV*, is a member of Ennahda, and his father was also one of the founders of Ennahda. Mohammed Ayachi Ajroudi, owner of *Janoubia TV*, is a key figure in the Tunisian Movement for Liberty and Dignity. Although a few of the abovementioned media owners/founders sold their shares before entering politics (namely Oussama ben Salem and Tahar ben Hassine) to comply with the HAICA regulations, political influence over various channels during election campaigns openly continued. *Nessma TV* was accused by the regulatory body HAICA of blatantly promoting the presidential candidate Nabil Karoui and his party Kalb Tounis during the legislative elections of September 2019 and presidential elections of October 2019 (HAICA, 2019). According to the same report, *Nessma TV* dedicated 24 hours and half of its airtime during the legislative election campaign to promote Kalb Tounis and its leader: six hours were direct propaganda and about 18 hours were various other political promotions such as advertising the humanitarian campaign of Nabil Karoui and his relief organization Khalil Tounis.

Technology and Infrastructure

Compared with other African countries, Tunisia has one of the most "sophisticated telecommunications and broadband infrastructures in North Africa," according to Lancaster (2020). Mobile and Internet technologies were also rated among the highest in the region in terms of coverage and penetration. Governance of the Internet has been relaxed since 2011 following a liberal turn (de la Ferrière & Vallina-Rodriguez, 2014). The Telecommunications Act of 2013 put an end to Internet censorship and encouraged competition between online platforms. Also, the laws supporting e-commerce have boosted online marketing and digital business activities. ADSL service is primarily provided by *Tunis Telecom*, a state-owned telecommunications company. Other main players in the market include the Qatari-based *Ooredoo* and *Orange Tunisie*. Both are licensed as fixed-line operators and have launched DSL and fiber-to-the-premises (FTTP) services. The Digital Tunisia 2020 program launched by the government aims to boost Internet connectivity and improve service in underserved areas all over the country.

Tunisia is reasonably developed when it comes to mobile phone technology. In 2016, the state issued three licenses to major networks in order to provide 4G technology, which enabled faster services and telecommunications coverage in every part of the country. These licenses came with a commitment from each service provider to reach 98% of the country by 2031 (Instance Nationale des Télécommunication, 2016, p. 37). Looking ahead, the regulatory body has also confirmed that 5G licenses are expected to be released in 2021.

These developments in telecommunications technologies have also been reflected by Tunisians' increasing Internet and social media use even before the revolution of 2011. In early 2020, Internet users reached 7.55 million (64% of the population) and active social media users constituted 62% of the population (7.3 million). *Facebook* remains the most popular social media platform among Tunisians. The number of total users of *Facebook* reached 6.9 million, which constitutes 75% of the population over 13 years of age. Although *Twitter* is a very popular platform in other Arab countries such as those the Gulf region, those who prefer this social media platform in Tunisia do not exceed 272,500, whereas *Snapchat* attracts 765,000 users, *Instagram* 1.9 million (21%

of the population), and *LinkedIn* 1.2 million (14% of the population) (Hootsuite, 2020).

Much has been said about social media networks as platforms for promoting social activism and resistance. *Facebook* and *Twitter* were considered instrumental in the Tunisian uprisings, operating as tools with which protesters challenged the brutality and censorship of the Ben Ali regime. Although it is hard to measure such influence, it was evident that social networks became alternative platforms for news. As argued by various studies on the Tunisian uprisings (Castells, 2012; Chomiak, 2011; Karolak, 2018; Miladi, 2016; Zayani, 2015), thanks to these digital platforms, protesters managed to get their voices heard by and stories out to the world. Marginalized youth proved that they were not mere observers or followers of news but could become shapers of mainstream media's news agenda. Most noteworthy was that they gained influence in disrupting the Tunisian regime's information management and its political communication channels both locally and internationally. Ben Ali's External Communications Unit, for instance, faced challenges in controlling the barrage of information spreading via social media and reaching out to an international audience via satellite television. Constant monitoring and partial blocking of *Facebook* in December 2010 was the last resort of the failed regime's attempt at containment and control.

The post-revolutionary period in Tunisia has witnessed the growing influence of social media platforms. For instance, with reference to the Tunisian elections of 26 October 2014, social media, it can be argued, assumed an effective watchdog role. For example, the youth-led civil society organizations of I-Watch and ATID harnessed social media platforms during the presidential and legislative elections of 2019 to monitor the election campaigns as well as the voting process. Thus, they not only monitored occurrences of possible corruption among candidates, but also checked media coverage against any possible ideological influences. At the same time, an analysis of the candidates' online activism during that election period revealed that contenders learned from the lessons of previous years and understood that social media was equally as important as traditional media, especially for reaching out to young voters (Miladi, 2016). Activities in the online sphere indicated that *Facebook* and *Twitter* had become battlegrounds for ideological fights, which the contestants and their supporters had to navigate skillfully. Yet again, *Facebook* pages became critical platforms for a thriving citizen journalism (Zayani, 2015).

It is evident that social media networks have become indispensable tools for communication, news sharing, and political campaigning in Tunisia. Whether employed by activists and opposition groups or political leaders, such networks have increasingly advanced communication and information sharing in various situations, such as political or social campaigns.

Challenges

The media scene in Tunisia has dramatically changed since the 2011 revolution. A new era of media plurality has not only seen a plethora of television channels, radio stations, and newspapers emerge across the country, which reflects a diverse political and cultural spectrum, but has also freed public broadcasting from government control. However, these changes have not come without challenges in terms of media ownership and regulation. The road to democracy in Tunisia still seems rough given the various obstacles that continue to crop up (Richter, 2017). The current government of Hisham Al-Mishishi, which came to power in August 2020, still needs to radically improve three main areas: 1) sustainability of media's business model, 2) ideological manipulation, and 3) elitist orientation.

Regarding the issue of sustainability, the print market witnessed the closure of hundreds of newspapers and magazines soon after the boom in newspapers and the audiovisual media market from 2011 to 2015. By 2017, the number of printed papers had dropped to 50 after reaching 250 in the post-revolutionary period. For instance, *Akhbar Al-Jumhuriyah* was suspended on 11 October 2017 after 25 years of operation. The broadcasting market has also faced similar challenges. For instance, *First TV* closed down in October 2017 because it was not financially viable. Restructuring, however, has been taking place for a few channels such as *Al-Mutawasit TV* and others.

In respect to manipulation of the media, the growth of the media market has meant increased challenges for regulatory bodies and has caused genuine concerns regarding the influence of new online media outlets. As such, this post-revolutionary period has also witnessed unremitting tensions between influential media enterprises and Tunisia's first democratically elected government. This is partly due to the conflicting understanding of the media's role in a transitional democracy and attempts to manipulate the media by rich entrepreneurs and ideological lobbies. This raises the question of media independence under the liberal consensus of the market (Johnson & Jacobs, 2004). In this context, concerns about external influences in the Tunisian media market are becoming more prevalent. Many of the challenges faced by the media are directly related to external funding, which has been given to certain media outlets arguably to promote certain political interests.

In terms of the issue of elitist orientation, the class base for the broadcasting and newspaper markets has remained mostly the same even though the state media in Tunisia has dramatically shifted from being government-controlled to a public service media and the regime change has brought new political players to the forefront of politics in the country. The national television broadcaster *Al-Watania TV1* can be seen as part of a divisive process that was firmly established in the decades of dictatorship under Ben Ali and Bourguiba and has continued to shape and strengthen its influence after the revolution. In this post-revolutionary period, particularly during election campaigns, a large number of media outlets are split along ideological and elitist lines rather than adhering to professional norms of journalism practice which, at their core, intend to serve public interests (Miladi, 2019). Public service media are expected to raise awareness about corruption rather than attempt to eliminate it, and are required to bring the public's attention to social problems rather than endeavor to force change in society. The power struggle that has surfaced during the last few years has revealed how a few ideological and elitist groups have attempted to set the agenda for public opinion by using media platforms such as television and radio.

Outlook

Changes to the telecommunications market, although significant, do not "change how the elements which constitute the deep state govern on a daily basis. Nor does such a change reform the political culture of submissiveness and bullying that allows the repressive state apparatus to coerce cooperation on behalf of ISPs without any independent oversight" (de la Ferrière & Vallina-Rodriguez, 2014, p. 652). Applying this to the whole media system, one could argue that, during this transitional period that Tunisia has been witnessing, the media remain a sophisticated space of manipulation and power struggle among the emerging power structures in the country. This power struggle is taking place primarily in public spaces, although evidence of it can also be found on television screens and radio airwaves as well as social media networks.

Extensive debates have been taking place across platforms on how to consolidate freedom of speech and strong, diverse, and independent media. These debates have also discussed the best model for regulating the media in Tunisia, and have been supported by various initiatives such as the decree-laws and the establishment of HAICA. In spite of these achievements, more attention needs to be directed towards preventing political influences and overseas infiltration of certain media outlets in Tunisia, and setting up a regulatory body for the newspaper market.

Lastly, the future of the broadcasting market looks bright if the public service broadcaster *Al-Watania Network* steps up and adheres to its professional standards. The new editorial policy aims to reflect a politically, culturally, and economically diverse society. Yet, its news values, documented in the revamped editorial guidelines, are yet to materialize. Among Tunisians, public service media have been upheld as a cornerstone for consolidating a democratic climate in the country's emerging democracy. Tunisia's transition to democracy cannot happen without an ideologically neutral media that will constructively observe its role as a watchdog against the corrupt activities of certain politicians and influential power elites in society. Academics and media critics have stated that, although *Al-Watania* television network is an important public service broadcaster, it needs structural reform in its editorial policy, journalism practice, and professionalism standards before it can serve this crucial role of watchdog.

References

Ben Letaief, M. (2018). Freedom of speech in Tunisia: Texts and contexts. *MENA Media Law*. https://www.menamedialaw.org/sites/default/files/library/material/tunisia_chp_2018.pdf

Castells, M. (2012). *Networks of outrage and hope: Social movements in the Internet age*. Cambridge: Polity Press.

Chomiak, L. (2011). The making of a revolution in Tunisia. *Middle East Law and Governance*, 3(1), 68–83. https://doi.org/10.1163/187633711X591431

De la Ferrière, A. A., & Vallina-Rodriguez, N. (2014). The scissors and the magnifying glass: Internet governance in the transitional Tunisian context. *The Journal of North African Studies*, 19(5), 639–55. https://doi.org/10.1080/13629387.2014.975662

Freedom House. (2020). *Freedom in the world 2020*. https://freedomhouse.org/country/tunisia/freedom-world/2020

HAICA (2019, October 10). *Report on the major violations in the coverage of the legislative electoral campaign by non-licensed TV channels* [in Arabic]. http://haica.tn/media/%D8%AA%D9%82%D8%B1%D9%8A%D8%B1-%D8%B9%D8%A7%D9%85.pdf

Hajji, L. (2004). *Bourguiba and Islam: Headship and religious leadership* [in Arabic]. Tunis: Dar Al-Janoub for Publishing.

Hootsuite (2020). *Digital 2020: Tunisia*. www.hootsuite.com

Human Rights Watch. (2005). *False freedom: Online censorship in the Middle East and North Africa*. https://www.hrw.org/report/2005/11/14/false-freedom/online-censorship-middle-east-and-north-africa

Instance Nationale des Télécommunications. (2016). *Annual report 2016* [in Arabic]. http://www.intt.tn/upload/files/RAPPORT%20ANNUEL%20INT%202016%20AR.pdf

Instance Vérité & Dignité. (2018, December 19). *Publicity and disinformation apparatus* [in Arabic] [Video file]. *YouTube*. https://www.youtube.com/watch?v=0IIi2-MDb1Y

Johnson, K., & Jacobs, S. (2004). Democratization and the rhetoric of rights: Contradictions and debate in post-Apartheid South Africa. In F. Nyamnjoh & H. Englund (Eds.), *Rights and politics of recognition in Africa*. (pp. 84–102). London: Zed Books.

Karolak, M. (2018). Social media in democratic transitions and consolidations: What can we learn from the case of Tunisia? *The Journal of North African Studies*, 25(1), 8–33.

Lancaster, H. (2020). Tunisia–telecoms, mobile and broadband–statistics and analyses. *BuddeComm*. https://www.budde.com.au/Research/Tunisia-Telecoms-Mobile-and-Broadband-Statistics-and-Analyses

Miladi, N. (2016). Social media and social change. *Digest of the Middle East Studies, 25*(1), 36–51.

——. (2019). Public Service Broadcasting and the Democratic Transition in Tunisia [in Arabic]. In J. Zran & N. Miladi (Eds.), *Media & Democratic Transition in the Arab World*. (pp. 343–68). Tunis: AMCN and Sotumedias.

Office National de la Télédiffusion. (2014). *Broadcasting via terrestrial networks* [in French]. http://www.telediffusion.net.tn/index.php?yoca_caauaca

Reporters Without Borders. (2010). *World freedom index 2010*. https://rsf.org/en/world-press-freedom-index-2010

Richter, C. (2017). Media policy in times of transition: Tunisia's bumpy road to democracy. *Publizistik, 62*(3), 325–37. https://doi.org/10.1007/s11616-017-0340-x

Zayani, M. (2015). *Network publics and digital contention*. Oxford: Oxford University Press.

Zran, J., & Ben Messaoud, M. (2018). Broadcasting public service in the Arab World: Rupture and continuity. *International Journal of Social Sciences and Management, 5*(3), 98–112. https://doi.org/10.3126/ijssm.v5i3.20599

17. Algeria: The Costs of Clientelism

Nacer-Eddine Layadi

Translated by Abdelhak Bouifer

> This chapter highlights Algeria's media development, which is shaped by trajectories of French colonialism and a socialist-clientelist regime of governance since the 1960s. The rich history of its media is contrasted by major challenges on the political, economic, and professional levels.

Background

Algeria is located in the northwestern part of Africa. It shares borders with six countries: Morocco and Mauritania to the west, Mali and Niger to the south, and Libya and Tunisia to the east. With a 1,644-kilometer coastline along the Mediterranean Sea to the north and a land area of 2,400,000 square kilometers, Algeria is the largest country in Africa, the Arab world, and among the Mediterranean countries.

According to the latest calculations of January 2019, the Algerian population is 43,000,000, of which young people from 15 to 24 years of age make up 16%. The majority of Algerians are Muslims. Christians, on the other hand, represent a tiny percentage, which was estimated to be below 1% in 2009.

Algeria's history goes back thousands of years during which various tribal communities fought many wars on its territory. Despite these ongoing conflicts the country was put under Turkish protectorate rule in 1615, which was ended only by the French invasion of 1830. The

Algerians began to retaliate against French colonialism in multiple ways, starting with the popular revolts (1830–1871), expanding into political and cultural resistance (1900–1954), and finally culminating in a war for independence (November 1954–July 1962). The heavy colonial heritage had a huge impact on political and media system in Algeria's post-independence period.

Facing a high level of illiteracy among children following the colonial era, Algeria put an enormous effort into eradicating this phenomenon by increasing the number of learners over the age of 15 from 15% in 1962 to 75% between 2005 and 2016. The two official languages are Arabic, the language of the majority of Algerians, and Tamazight, spoken by the indigenous Imazighen (Berbers). The latter was declared an official language in 2016 after a long and fierce struggle, following the events of the Amazigh Spring in 1980 and the uprising in the Kabyle region in 2001. As a result, the Tamazight language has been taught at various levels of education since 1995. Similarly, the Arabic language in Algeria has faced difficulties in expanding into other sectors, as French is still used in the financial, economic, and education sectors as well as in the scientific fields.

The amendment of the Family Code in 2005 reflected the Algerian legislators' desire to build bridges between the principles of Islamic law and the requirements of contemporary life. Thus, Algerian women obtained additional rights after amendments to the nationality law, including the right to grant Algerian citizenship to their children if their husband is a foreigner. The most significant gain for Algerian women has been their increased presence in elected councils; for example, their representation in parliament jumped from 5% in 1962 to 31% in 2012. However, this statistic does not reflect the everyday reality of Algerian women. According to data provided by the National Centre for Statistics for 2015, women workers did not exceed 18% of all 11,000,000 Algerian workers. The rate of women with a university degree who are unemployed is estimated at about 9% compared with almost 52% of men with a university degree.

Historical Developments

After the conquest of Algeria, the French colonial army brought a printing press to print the first newspaper, *L'Estafette d'Alger*, to promote the expansion of the colonial army's control across Algerian territory. It was replaced in 1932 by another weekly newspaper, *Le Moniteur Algérien*, which was regarded as the official voice of colonialism in Algeria.

The French authorities encouraged settlers to launch their own newspapers in Algeria's largest cities to preserve their interests, and set up other newspapers that targeted the local population, for instance, *Le Messager* (1848–1928), which was published bi-monthly in two versions: French and Arabic. It was the third newspaper published in the Arab world at that time.

The French Press Law of 1881 abolished the system of prior authorization and financial guarantee. It established a system which repressed the crime of defamation without any possibility of prior censorship. This enabled French newspaper publishers to thrive. However, Algerian publishers were not entitled to benefit from this law because they did not enjoy their civil rights. The system imposed by this law partly explains why Algerians delayed launching their own newspapers until the end of the last decade of the nineteenth century. They were also subject to indigenous laws (1865) which stripped them of their identity and their civil rights.

Newspapers published by Algerians, notably in Arabic, were characterized by their short life due to a lack of funding, but more importantly, as a result of the 1895 law that prohibited the publication of any foreign language newspaper, since the 1838 law defined Arabic as a foreign language.

The historian Ali Merad (1964) argued that the Islamic press (or the indigenous press) in Algeria symbolized the formation of a civil society (p. 9). It partially replaced the absence of political parties, spreading reformist ideas within the local community. The emergence of this press can be seen to reflect the change in Algerian society's social and cultural structure under French colonial rule, which established a new elite consisting of two categories. First was that of the urban youth loyal to the French culture, who were employed as administrative agents or employees in sectors such as education, medicine, judiciary, and translation. The second category was the Arabized elite, who were teachers at religious schools, Imams, and judges who believed in the Arabic culture. They played a pivotal role in the rise of the indigenous press. In fact, the two categories were not actually separated, and both helped to launch the indigenous press, but the fear of its impact led the colonial authorities blocking its expansion and development.

The national movement parties, which were formed at the beginning of the twentieth century, used newspapers to promote their reformist ideas for equal rights between the Algerians and French and to revive the cultural, linguistic, and religious components of the Algerian nation as well as to claim national independence. The National Liberation Front (FLN) relied on the media in its liberation struggle, creating the *El-Moudjahid* newspaper on 22 June 1956 as the official voice of the FLN.

On the radio, the FLN launched the *Voice of Fighting Algeria* on 16 December 1956. This station changed Algerians' relationship with radio broadcasting. As Frantz Fanon (1972) noted, the radio in the colonial era was initially intended for Europeans and was perceived as a tool through which they imposed cultural pressure on people under colonial domination (p. 52). Therefore, its audience among the Algerians was very limited. Nevertheless, the armed revolution transformed the radio into a tool of liberation that helped to turn Algerian audiences into one nation.

After independence in 1962, Algeria established its Radio and Television Company by taking advantage of what was inherited from the French Radio and Television Company in Algeria. Radio and television were the best means to mobilize Algerians around the goals of the revolution due to the country's high percentage of illiteracy, which sat at 85% during this period. The public radio company launched 50 local stations, in addition to its three national Arabic, Tamazight, and French-language stations. It also established an international station (broadcasting in Arabic, French, English, and Spanish) and other stations dedicated to culture, religion, and youth.

Algeria had only one television channel prior to 1994 when the French-language channel *Canal Algérie* was established and began broadcasting to the Algerian community in Europe and North America. In 2001, *Algeria 3* channel launched programs for Algerian audiences living in Arab countries. On 18 March 2009, two other channels, a

Tamazight-language channel and the *Holy Qur'an* channel, were introduced to 'protect' Algerian viewers from religious extremist discourse promoted by some foreign satellite channels.

The rising number of public radio stations and television channels was encouraged by competition from foreign television channels and radio stations, and was financially supported by the increase in oil revenues that constituted the backbone of Algeria's national economy.

Fearing that the events of the Arab uprisings would spread to Algeria and promote Abdel-Aziz Bouteflika's election campaign for a fourth presidential term, a branch of the Algerian regime set up television channels in 2012 that only broadcasted from outside Algeria. Within three years, the number of these "hybrid legal" channels jumped to 45. Private television has been broadcasting in this informal manner since 2012. In 2013, the Algerian authorities granted only five of these channels (*Ennahar TV, Echourouk TV, Dzaïr TV, El Djazairia One,* and *Hogar TV*) licenses to operate for a yearly renewable term. Even today, these five channels continue to function as offices of foreign channels and not as Algerian channels, and are consequently referred to by the Algerian media as "Offshore Channels". Moreover, the government has turned a blind eye to the activity of other television channels broadcasting from abroad. However, if any channel opposes the political regime, its equipment will be confiscated and all activity will be banned under the pretext that the channel does not have a legal license, which is what happened to *Atlas TV* in 2014 and *Al Watan TV* in 2015.

After all colonial printed media became nationalized after independence, the Algerian authorities began to build their own press system. They initiated this process by launching the Arabic-language newspaper *El-Chaab*, on 11 December 1962, *Le Peuple* newspaper on 19 December, 1962, which was the country's first French-language newspaper, and *El-Moudjahid* newspaper on 5 July 1965.

In the west of the country, the French-speaking newspaper *La République* began publication on 29 March 1963, and the French-speaking newspaper *El-Nasr* was established on 28 September 1963 in eastern Algeria. The historical newspaper *El-Moudjahid*, the official voice of the FLN, was transformed from a daily newspaper to a weekly paper in July 1964, and only the Arabic version of this publication was retained. The *African Revolution* magazine was published in French in November 1962 to express Algeria's solidarity with other liberation movements around the world.

After independence in 1962, Algeria abolished regional and local media in favor of centralizing the media system. This was done because the idea of "regional", which in the official Algerian political dictionary refers to the division and dispersion of Algerian people, is assumed to hamper the national effort to build a strong central state that unites the aspirations of the people and underpins the construction of socialism. This is why Algeria's newspaper market maintained its national character and included only two newspapers outside the capital, Algiers.

The fusion of political and ideological streams in the FLN during the liberation war became a reference for political and media practices in the post-independence era. These practices were fed by populist ideologies that betrayed the political opposition and eventually led to the abolishment of political and media pluralism.

In 1990, a major change occurred following the deadly protests of 5 October 1988 (Rahal, 2017), and before the approval of the Information Law in 1990 which ended the state's media monopoly. On 19 March 1990, the government of Mouloud Hamrouche instructed all journalists working in public media to either join newspapers belonging to political parties or to create groups to publish their own newspapers and magazines. Pursuant to this order, 150 journalists left their media organizations to launch their own companies, most of which were printed media that enjoyed partial freedom of expression. The regime used these publications as a democratic interface with the political system, a cover for the transition to a market economy, and a forum for readers to express their anger over poor living conditions as well as the abuse of power.

The press in Algeria has remained an urban phenomenon, despite significant changes in its quantitative and linguistic dimensions. The number of daily newspapers jumped from six in 1989, with nearly 670,450 copies per day, to 140 in 2014, with 2,469,616 copies per day (Ministry of Communication, 2014). The numbers of newspapers in 2016 increased significantly to 150 editions, but only 21 of these ran 10,000 or more copies per day.

Political and Legal Framework

Since its independence in 1962, Algeria has chosen the socialist system for its development. It adopted a single-party political system that dominated the political and media landscapes. The proclaimed "unity of perception and socialist thought" framed the structure of media organizations and regulated journalistic activity. This was supported by the first Information Law in 1982, which entrenched state monopoly of the media. This law granted the authority to direct media companiesby means of the political leadership represented by the Ministry of Information and Culture and the ruling party information officer. It also made media managers merely an operational means. As an example, Article 35 states that a professional journalist is a combatant who "practices his profession responsibly and with commitment in order to fulfill the objectives of the revolution as defined by the official texts of the National Liberation Front."

Algeria's economy is dependent on oil revenues which constitute 97% of its total revenue. As oil prices declined in 1986 to less than USD 15 a barrel, the authorities adopted an austerity policy on importing consumer products. Protests increased across the country through a series of demonstrations, with the most notable on 5 October 1988, leading the regime to promulgate a new liberal constitution in 1989 that recognized the right to private property, and freedom of belief, expression, and the press. Furthermore, it recognized the freedom to establish political parties, which led Algeria to reach a total of almost 60 parties. At the same time, a new Information Law was passed in 1990 to divide up the media management methods that had prevailed over the previous 28 years. This law opened the door to media pluralism in the press and audiovisual sector; it also put an end to the state's monopoly of the media. To be more specific, its fourth article highlighted the right of political parties and natural persons, subject to Algerian law, to establish newspapers and magazines and to own a media company.

The years 1990–1992 were exceptional in the history of Algerian media. In addition to the publication of private newspapers, which openly discussed societal issues and political trends in the country, the public media, especially television, offered a platform for opposition parties to take part in political debates about Algeria's future. Nevertheless, the democratic transition in Algeria has not been achieved because the state has systematically rejected the idea of a rotation of power. Although the ruling authority sought to renew itself by establishing a "monitored" political pluralism and allowing the FLN to assume a dominant position over other political forces, it ultimately failed in its mission. The 1992 legislative elections resulted in the victory of another dominant party, the Islamic Salvation Front (FIS), which threatened Algeria's political system and its adherents and alarmed Western countries (Addi, 2006, pp. 139–62).

Ultimately, the electoral process was cancelled, and a High State Council (HSC) was created to assume presidential powers after the resignation of President Chadli Bendjedid. Parliament was dissolved and replaced by an "advisory council," followed by a transitional council made up of appointed members. A state of emergency was declared on 9 February 1992. The High Media Council, which had seized control of part of the Authority of the Ministry of Information, was abolished, even though its role had been more consultative than regulatory in terms of media practice. Public freedoms and freedom of the press declined following the establishment of special anti-terrorism courts and the circulation of a decree issued on 14 June 1994 to direct press managers on how to deal with security news. As a consequence, print media were pressured to reproduce the official discourse of the ruling authority, leading to the impoverishment of the media. The number of newspapers multiplied, but without producing real media pluralism. In addition, journalists who sought to oppose the official government line were prosecuted and their newspapers were suspended or even banned. In the aftermath of 1992, Algeria fell into a cycle of violence that claimed the lives of thousands of Algerians, including 103 journalists.

Following the events of the Arab uprisings in 2012, a new Information Law was passed to emphasize the general principles of freedom of expression and media pluralism. However, in reality, nothing changed. This new law intended to establish the Print Press Regulatory Authority, which was to have more of a censorship role than a regulating one for journalistic activity. Yet, after five years, this body still had not begun functioning.

The Audiovisual Law of 2014 tightened restrictions on the creation of private television channels permitting only thematic channels to be launched. The Audiovisual Regulatory Authority (ARAV) was stripped of its role to control audiovisual activity. Since then, this body has not carried out any activity beyond issuing occasional statements that remind certain television channels to respect the principles and ethics of journalistic work. The abovementioned Information Law did not allow journalists to be imprisoned for various misdemeanors, including libel, defamation, and insulting others. Nevertheless, a review of the Criminal Procedure Code in July 2015 made temporary detention an exceptional measure, and this did not exclude journalists from being subject to detention.

The impact of the Information Law on media practices in Algeria has been very limited, perhaps even nonexistent, because its implementation is subject to political and special interest considerations. Many of its articles have remained meaningless, while some are applied selectively. For example, the authority allowed Ali Haddad, president of the Business Leaders Forum (FCE), to publish the newspapers *Le Temps d'Algérie* in French and *Time of Algeria* in Arabic, although Article 25 of the Media Law of 2012 prohibits owning both a French and an Arabic newspaper. Under this same law the contract for purchasing the businessman Issad Rabrab's *El-Khabar* newspaper was dissolved in 2017 as Rabrab also owned the newspaper *Liberté*. In 2014, it allowed Ali Haddad[1] to own both *Dzaïr TV* and *Dzaïr News*, and permitted other oligarchs who financed the election campaign of the president, Bouteflika, to create private television channels. This practice promotes "neo-patrimonialism," which indicates the unusual marriage between the autocratic system and modern state institutions. It is manifested through a "customerism" character (Roudakova, 2008, p. 42) that is seen as a structural factor in societies where there are few or no borders between public and personal interests, or between public and private property. This type of clientelism can also be understood as a cultural feature of the idea that systemic and universal rules are less important than personal connections.

---

1   Ali Haddad's media empire began to collapse after President Bouteflika was removed from power on 2 April 2019, and since then, he has been in prison with other figures of the regime charged with unlawful accumulation of wealth.

Economy and Ownership Patterns

The state monopolized the ownership of newspapers from 1962 to 1990. Today, however, it owns only six newspapers, compared with 144 privately-owned newspapers in Algeria. These private newspapers consist predominantly of journalists who have left public media. As a first step, they launched their own newspapers with their previous salaries received over a three-year period. As a second step, the government provided them with a wide range of indirect subsidies, such as interest-free bank loans, tax exemptions, and share of advertising proceeds, and headquarters for their newspapers. Finally, the government eased the payment procedure for printing costs at state printing companies by either subsidizing the price of paper or erasing the debts of some newspapers. The 1991 Finance Act established a special fund of USD 22,000,000 as an additional form of support for private newspapers. This fund existed until 2015. However, it was distributed in an unfair and unequal method.

Transparency in the funding of private newspapers is a constant demand of publishers and readers. *L'Expression*, for example, a newspaper which publishes 20,000 copies per day, barely sells 50% of its copies on average, and has no influence on national political life, generated significant annual profits during the period of 2009–2016 through government advertising evaluated to be between USD 506,000 and USD 1,500,000. It became the most cost-effective newspaper in the press sector. This is one example that has led to the call for more transparency in the newspaper market.

The two largest private newspapers, *El-Watan* (a French-language newspaper) and *El-Khabar* (an Arabic-language newspaper), were exempt from the monopoly exercised by authorities on printing companies. Although they set up their own printing companies, which have reduced their expenses, the financial situation of these publications has not substantially improved. For example, *El-Khabar*'s sales contributed only 50% of its total income, while *El-Watan*'s sales only generated 30% of its overall revenue despite the fact that these two newspapers have consistently raised the price of their issues. Advertising remains the main income source for newspapers in Algeria, contributing anywhere between USD 25,000 and USD 50,000 to the proceeds of a single issue of a newspaper. However, the state controls almost 85% of the advertising market through the National Publishing and Advertising Company (ANEP). Private companies and public institutions have been banned from purchasing advertising pages directly from newspapers. Thus, the distribution of advertising to newspapers and the rest of the media is still not subject to market logic, and for that reason, media pluralism in Algeria has not been strengthened.

Powerful and dominant media groups have been forming in Algeria since 2012. One of these is led by Mohammed Moukaddam, who owns two newspapers, *Ennahar El-Djadid* and the sports newspaper *El-Chibak*, as well as other news websites, such as *Algérie 24* and *Algérie Confidentiel*, published in the French language. There is also the group owned by the businessman Ali Haddad, the owner of one of the largest construction companies (ETRHB) and publisher of the newspaper *Le Temps d'Algérie* in Arabic and French. Ali Fodil leads another group and is the owner of the *El-Chourouk Daily* and the weekly magazine *El-Chourouk El-Arabi*, in addition to other websites, including *El-Chourouk Sport*, *Jawaher El-Chourouk*, and *El-Chourouk Markets*. These three newspaper owners also own television channels. Moukaddam has one channel, Haddad has two channels, and Fodil has three channels: *El-Chourouk TV*, *El-Chourouk News*, and *El-Echourouk Bana* (a cooking channel). Other examples of oligarch media investors are Mahieddine Tahkout, owner of the Car Installation Company and the Student Bus Company, and Bachir Ould Zamirli, an "investor" in the field of real estate promotion. The owners of these channels dominate Algeria's television viewing market. However, the ownership of these channels is a debatable point; it is contrary to the Organic Audiovisual Law which affirms in Article 23 that "a natural person or a private person subject to Algerian law cannot be a contributor to more than one service of audiovisual communication."

Moreover, Article 45 states that the same shareholder of a television channel may not hold, directly or through the intermediary of other persons, including ascendants and descendants of the 4th degree, more than 40% of its share capital.

In addition to their legal status, the economy of private television channels in Algeria has attracted significant attention from researchers (Cherif, 2014; Djaballah, 2019; Mostefaoui, 2019; Dimitrakis, 2019; Djaballah, 2018).

Considering the practices of clientelism, which control the relationship of power and the media, can explain how channels belonging to Algerian oligarchs are funded. First and foremost, they took advantage of the state advertising windfall. Second, the price of one minute of advertising at peak time on private channels is estimated between USD 109 and USD 181 (Belfarag, 2016). This relatively low cost negatively affected the public media, for which the price of one minute of advertising at the same peak time is estimated between USD 2,000 and USD 4,500. Such practices have not only undermined the economic framework of public television channels, but have undermined all forms of media, such as one minute of prime time on radio is priced at USD 346, newspapers that sell the color pages to advertisers for USD 3,500, half colored page for USD 1,756, and a quarter page for USD 920.[2]

There are no laws that organize or regulate unfair competition among the media in Algeria's booming advertising market, which jumped from EUR 19,000,000 in 1999 to EUR 200,000,000 in 2016 due to high oil revenues. The budget of any one private television channel cannot be compared with that of the public television system with its five channels. In 2012, the public system's revenues came from the license fee imposed on citizens, which was estimated at USD 9,000,000, and advertising revenues and rebroadcast rights exceeding USD 18,000,000. However, these two amounts were not enough to cover its expenses, especially the salaries of 3,447 workers. This forced the state to award the company more than USD 90,000,000 to meet the public service requirements and pay for its satellite broadcasting (Ali, 2014).

Most of Algeria's online newspapers belong to the private sector. Their economic situation is more complex than that of the print media. Each online newspaper pays nearly USD 2,630 a month for hosting and maintaining its sites, which is in addition to Internet subscription and phone connectivity costs. Some online newspapers, such as *Maghreb Emergent*, have tried to get their users to contribute to their crowd funding, but to no avail. Alternatively, many online publications provide training course and other services for companies to gain revenues.

For its part, *Radio M* appealed to the French Agency for Media Cooperation for a subsidy to ensure its survival. From 2006 onwards,

---

2   According to the prices supplied by the daily newspaper *Liberté* on 13 July 2019.

the state's monopoly on radio broadcasting and the low cost of Internet broadcasting encouraged companies to create web broadcasts to provide different content from government radio stations This trend began with *Radio Algiers* and was then reinforced by radio stations with music content and associations' radio stations, such as *The Voice of Women*, a subsidiary of an association called Women in Communication. It is crucial to note that it is difficult to limit the number of web television programs in Algeria, which have a different legal status to radio. There is a variety of news, music, and sports television broadcasts online, including those of state-owned companies, such as the *Algeria Press Agency (APS)* and other private entities.

Technology and Infrastructure

Eight satellites, including *Alcomsat-1*, which was the latest satellite launched by Algeria in cooperation with China on 10 December 2017, broadcast the country's five public television channels and programs from 50 public radio stations, including local, national, and thematic ones. To modernize technological infrastructure, Algerian authorities have completed 7,000 km of digital microwave networks as well as 14 medium and large networks for television broadcasting, and have built 400 stations for rebroadcasting to cover the shadow regions and the Algerian Sahara, and four stations for powerful broadcasting on micro- and medium waves.

Algeria began building digital terrestrial television in 2010 and was able to cover 85% of the national territory by 2013. This figure rose to 95% by the end of 2019. Algeria was on the verge of completely abandoning analog technology in June 2020. During the mid-1980s, Algerians turned to French and Arabic satellite television programs to avoid watching the only public television channel that existed at the time. Today, 97% of Algerian homes own a satellite dish.

Although computers were first introduced in major companies in Algeria in 1980, the computer system has remained on the sidelines of industrial activity. One explanation for Algeria's delay in developing its digital economy can be attributed to the fact that the Ministry of Post and Telecommunications developed modern communication technologies instead of the Ministry of Industry (Khelfaoui, 2007, pp. 71–90. To be more specific, the development of the Internet in Algeria has been influenced by ongoing struggles for power between those advocating urgent socioeconomic claims and the political forces that fear losing control over the use of the Internet. This explains the slow development of the Internet and the continued monopoly of Algerian Telecom's fixed and mobile Internet for the last 17 years. Furthermore, the license to use 3G networks was delayed until 2013, and the mobile phone and Internet market is currently exclusively shared by three economic operators (*Algérie Télécom*, Algeria's public communications company *Djezzy*, which owns 51% of its shares, and Qatar's *Ooredoo*).

According to the Ministry of Post and Telecommunications, the number of mobile subscribers (GSM, 3G, 4G) of the three operators jumped from 33,000,000 in 2010 to 51,000,000 in 2018. The number of mobile Internet subscribers (3G, 4G) increased from 300,000 subscribers in 2013 to 40,000,000 subscribers in 2018. Despite this, Internet speed remains slow, with an average estimated at 9 Mbps. Algerians who actively use social media platforms constituted 54% of the total population (i.e., 23,000,000 people) as of January 2019. More than half of all Algerians (22,000,000) use the social platform *Facebook* (Kemp, 2019).

El-Watan was the first Algerian newspaper to have a website (1997). Today, all Algerian newspapers have their own websites; some of them are hosted abroad, in countries such as France and Switzerland to avoid possible censorship. Some newspapers have set up electronic editions, television channels and news websites, such as *El-Chourouk* and *El-Nahar*, however, they cannot live up to the expected level of convergence, in the sense of producing content suitable for presentation on a variety of platforms.

Challenges

The media system faces a number of major challenges, which can be summarized in terms of the following overlapping levels.

On the political level, the "neo-patrimonial" political system that is hampering Algeria's democratic transition represents the biggest challenge for the media system in Algeria. Although the state's monopoly on print and audiovisual media and the establishment of private media was extinguished, this did not guarantee freedom of expression and media pluralism because these institutions were not based upon transparent and fair media competition. This was potentially due to the fact that the state failed to apply many of the laws' provisions relating to the organization of media companies (some of which are mentioned above), as well as those relating to financial transparency, and thus allowed private television companies to operate in a hybrid legal situation. The failure to announce the criteria based upon which the government granted authorization to only four private television channels as foreign television channels in Algeria is also one of the factors that confirms the logic of clientelism that frames the Algerian media landscape.

On the economic level, the financial situation of media companies has become fragile and more difficult in the absence of a clear and transparent national policy, which has forced some broadcasters such as *KBC Television*, as well as dozens of newspapers, such as *La Tribune*, to declare bankruptcy. The newspaper crisis has been amplified by its turbulent relationship with printing companies, which is not based strictly on commercial interests but is also subject to political considerations. It is difficult to ascertain the size of the debts of private newspapers owed to state printing companies. The Ministry of Communication intentionally pays no attention to some oligarchs' newspapers that have set up television channels without paying their debts, such as *El-Adjwa*, *El-Nahar*, and *El-Chourouk*, whose debts alone amounted to about USD 5,000,000 (Djaafer, 2017).

The Algerian authorities use printing houses to exert pressure on refractory newspapers in several ways. For instance, they may reduce the number of copies printed temporarily or permanently suspend printing if a company fails to pay their debts, as was the case with *La Nation* in 1997 and *Algeria News* in 2014. In addition, the state still has a monopoly on the advertising market, and its revenues are distributed to newspapers outside market logic and not in keeping with the requirements of public service and freedom of expression.

For more than a decade, publicity has not been used to defend the directions of the ruling power as originally intended but has deviated from its economic and political role. Its proceeds have been turned into rents shared by those who have the power to distribute those without control or accountability. In this way, advertising—the key financier of the media—has become an obstacle to media pluralism.

On the professional level, the historical context in which the Algerian media were formed and developed has pushed the media to play a propaganda role. It has led them to violate their professional and ethical commitment by frequently publishing anonymous news without justification, resorting to slander and insulting others, and preventing the legally recognized right of reply. These practices have been reinforced by the predominance of the commercial character in the activities of many private media companies that have violated journalists' professional rights and taken advantage of their deteriorating social conditions and professional instability. They have also benefited from their failure to organize themselves in order to issue a code of ethics and to hold their activities accountable to the rules.

Outlook

As in many countries, the Algerian press is in a major state of decline. For example, the largest Arabic language newspaper *El-Khabar* dropped from 1,200,000 copies per day in 2000 to 200,000 copies in 2017. The French-language newspaper *El-Watan* also experienced a declinine from 160,000 copies per day in 2012 to 90,000 copies in 2017. The future of Algeria's press will be dominated by online newspapers whose increased demand has resulted from the development of basic technological infrastructure. This has required the state to develop a national policy that will assist the media in their necessary transition to the digital environment and help them to establish their economic strategy.

The increasing number of Algerians using the Internet and social networks, as well as the establishment of 15 web radio sites and ten web television sites, have prompted the state to monopolize radio and television broadcasting, exercise censorship over media content, shut down newspapers and television channels, prevent new radio stations and television channels from broadcasting from Algeria, and implement other practices that restrict freedom of expression. However, new developments might lie ahead; when Ammar Belhimer took office as Minister of Communication and spokesman of the government on 13

January 2020, he promised to hold workshops and engage in dialogue with journalists before launching a media reform.

References

Addi, L. (2006). Political parties in Algeria [in French]. *Revue des mondes musulmans et de la méditerrané*, 111–12, 139–62.

Ali, S. (2014). *Project for the collection of statistical data on film and audiovisual markets in 9 Mediterranean countries* [in French]. Council of Europe. https://rm.coe.int/1680788a6c

Belferag, A. (2016). Private television channels have shattered advertising prices [in French]. *Cap Algerie*. https://www.capalgerie.dz/les-teles-privees-ont-casse-les-prix-de-la-pub/

Cherif, D. (2014). The media in Algeria: A changing space [in French]. *Maghreb–Machrek*, 3, N° 221.

Dimitrakis, L. (2019). Economy of the information [in French]. http://www.almanach-dz.com/index.php?op=fiche&fiche=5579

Djaballah, B. H. (2018). Economy of the press in Algeria–Study day–Communication [in French]. http://www.almanach-dz.com/index.php?op=fiche&fiche=4938

———. (2019). Economy of the press and communication in Algeria [in French]. *Naqd*, automne-hiver, n°37.

Djaafer, S. (2017). Public printing houses reveal big debt figures for Echourouk newspaper [in French]. *Maghreb Emergent*. https://maghrebemergent.info/algerie-les-imprimeries-publiques-revelent-les-gros-chiffres-de-la-dette-du-journal-echourouk/

Fanon, F. (1972). *Sociology of a revolution* [in French]. Paris: Maspero.

Kemp, S. (2019) Digital 2019 Algeria. https://fr.slideshare.net/DataReportal/digital-2019-algeria-january-2019-v01

Khelfaoui, H. (2007). Individual and collective strategies for ICT integration in Algeria [in French]. In M. Mezouaghi (Ed.), *The Maghreb in the digital economy* [in French] (pp. 71–90). Tunis: Institut de recherche sur le Maghreb contemporain.

Merad, A. (1964). The formation of the Muslim press in Algeria 1919–1939 [in French]. *Revue de l'Institut des Belles lettres arabes à Tunis*, 27, 9–29.

Ministry of Communication. (2014). The communication notebooks [in French]. March.

Mostefaoui, B. (2019). Power games in media governance in Algeria through the prism of the popular movement of February 22, 2019 [in French]. *Naqd*, 37(1), 13–50.

Rahal, M. (2007). 1988–1992 Multipartism, and the descent into civil war. In P. Crowle (Ed.), *Algeria: Nation, culture and transnationalism. 1988–2015*. Liverpool University Press.

Roudakova, N. (2008). Media-political clientelism: Lessons from anthropology. *Media, Culture & Society*, 30(1), 41–59. https://doi.org/10.1177/0163443707084349

18. Morocco: Competitive Authoritarianism in Media Reforms

Bouziane Zaid and Mohammed Ibahrine

> The chapter provides an account of why the media structure in Morocco is an uneven playing field with the state having the advantage. It argues that observable configurations of power over media are mainly tied to a repressive media culture and heritage that can be fairly described as a competitive authoritarian regime. Argumentation is supported by an analysis of Morocco's history and the political economy of media.

Background

Located in northwest Africa, Morocco borders the Mediterranean Sea to the north, the Atlantic Ocean to the west, Algeria to the east, and Mauritania to the south. The Strait of Gibraltar spans 14 kilometers of water that separate Spain from Morocco, which makes the country a gateway for illegal immigration to Europe. As a result, Morocco became a key European ally in the effort to contain the flow of illegal immigration from sub-Saharan Africa. In terms of demographics, according to the 2017 government census bureau, the population was at 35.5 million, 27% of which were under the age of 15, 61% urban, 51% females, and 49% males. The unemployment rate was at 10.2%, and the illiteracy rate was high at 30%. Life expectancy at birth is currently 76. The official languages, as stated in the 2011 Constitution, are Arabic and Amazigh.

Amazigh is a branch of the Afroasiatic language family and is spoken by the Imazighen (Berbers), who are indigenous to North Africa.

The majority of Moroccans today are Muslims, but an influential minority of Moroccan Jews remains in the country. Christians and other religious groups make up 1% of the populace, consisting mainly of foreign residents.

Although the 2011 constitution guarantees equal gender rights, real equality is still a long way off. In 2004, Morocco adopted a family code known as the *mudawana*, which was hailed by women's rights groups in Morocco and abroad as a major step forward. Civil society groups, which are fighting for women's rights, are dynamic and have managed to introduce major changes in Morocco's laws. In addition to the *mudawana*, these groups mobilized the political elite in 2006 to change equal nationality rights, allowing Moroccan women to pass on their citizenship to their children the same way Moroccan men can. More recently, they led a national debate on Article 475 of the Moroccan Penal Code, which allows rapists to avoid prosecution if they agree to marry their victims. Street and online protests were sparked in March 2012 when 16-year-old Amina Filali took her own life after a seven-month ordeal in which she was forced to wed her alleged rapist. Women's rights activists successfully used street demonstrations and social media platforms to rally popular support for changes to the law. In January 2014, the parliament unanimously amended Article 475.

The Western Sahara represents an ongoing major conflict involving Morocco, the Polisario, and Algeria. It was annexed by Morocco after Spain left in 1975. The legal status of the southern territory and the question of its sovereignty remain unresolved. The threat of terrorism continues to be another important issue. On 16 May 2003 Morocco was subject to the deadliest terrorist attacks in the country's history. Five explosions killed 43 people and injured more than 100 people in suicide bomb attacks in Morocco's largest city, Casablanca. The 14 suicide bombers all originated from a poor suburban neighborhood in the outskirts of Casablanca. A public debate ensued in the print and broadcast media, questioning the relationship between poverty and extremism.

In the context of the Arab uprisings, a protest movement known as the February 20 Movement held rallies and marches throughout the country in 2011 to demand democratic reforms, a parliamentary monarchy, social justice, the end of absolutism, and the abolition of corruption. The movement triggered a series of reforms initiated by the monarchy. Two weeks after the first demonstration on 20 February, King Mohammed VI responded by introducing constitutional reforms. He promised to relinquish some of his administrative powers and to devolve some of his executive powers to the head of government and the parliament.

The promises made in the "9 March speech" did not materialize in the contents of the new constitution. A study (Madani, Maghraoui, & Zerhouni, 2012) of the new constitution found that the King remained "at the center of political and constitutional life" (p. 4). The study added that, in contradiction to the "9 March speech," in which the King insisted on the notion of accountability, the King had maintained executive powers without accountability to the Moroccan public (Madani et al., 2012, p. 50).

Despite these issues, Morocco's civil society is dynamic. Activists use their constitutional rights to protest and take advantage of various social media tools to educate, organize, and mobilize people on a wide range of issues. In April 2018, a group of activists launched a campaign to boycott products from three major companies to protest increases in the cost of living. The boycott targeted Centrale Danone (dairy products), Sidi Ali (mineral water), and Afriquia (gas stations). The economic impact of the boycott was evident ten days after it started when Afriquia and Centrale Danone recorded major drops in market value on the Casablanca Stock Exchange, with shares of each falling by nearly 6%.

In terms of media consumption, television remains the primary media of information and entertainment given Morocco's high rates of illiteracy, lack of local digital content creation, and shortage of digital literacy skills. In a recent survey, 68% of youths stated they watch television and 54.5% listen to the radio, spending on average two hours and 14 minutes watching television and two hours and 52 minutes listening to the radio (Morocco World News, 2019). Satellite broadcasting is the dominant form of transmitting television signals, and access to television and satellite dishes is almost universal. The most remarkable change in Internet use continues to be the growing interest in domestic portals (Zaid, 2017). In 2010, the country's top 10 most visited websites did not include any Moroccan news sites. By 2018, the list included six Moroccan websites—three news sites, two classified ad platforms (Avito and Jumia), and one sports site. In 2019, the country's top ten most visited websites included seven Moroccan websites, three news sites, one classified ad platforms (Avito), and two sports news websites. The remaining three are *Google*, *Facebook*, and *YouTube*. *Chouftv* surpassed *YouTube* to rank second, and *Hespress* and *2M* surpassed *Facebook* to rank third and fourth, respectively (Ibahrine, 2020).

For print newspapers, circulation is estimated at 350,000; less than one percent of the population reads a newspaper every day. These numbers are likely to decrease, given the easy access to online news (Ibahrine, 2020).

Historical Developments

Moroccan media roots can be traced back to the colonial period when Morocco was a protectorate of France and Spain from 1912 to 1956 (Ibahrine, 2009; Zaid, 2010). The colonial powers introduced the print press in its modern form, and Spain played an essential role in establishing several publications in the northern cities of Ceuta, Tangiers, and Tetouan. As early as 1820, the Spanish periodical *El Liberal Africano* was published in Ceuta (Ibahrine, 2009; Zaid, 2017). Unlike radio, which was controlled by foreign powers from 1928 until independence in 1956, print media represented a site of political struggle. Moroccan nationalists published their first Arabic papers, *Lisan Al-Maghreb* and *Sinan Al-Qalam*, in 1907 to promote nationalist ideas among educated Moroccan elites as tools of liberation. The French colonialists responded by introducing several Press Codes to administer and regulate the nationalist print press. The first legislation was the Dahir (Decree) of April 1912, followed by a series of decrees that demanded prior authorizations and allowed the colonial powers to shut down publications deemed too critical. After independence in 1956, the print press remained a tool that was used widely in the struggle between the state and the opposition parties.

The French were the first to start broadcasting in Morocco in February 1928, when radio signals were sent from the city of Rabat. The first television station, *Telma*, also in French, began airing its programs in 1952. After independence, the government launched the Radiodiffusion et Télévision Marocaine (RTM) in 1962, which consisted of four radio stations and one television station. In 1989, the first terrestrial pay-television channel in the Arab world, *2M International*, began transmission from Casablanca (Ibahrine, 2009; Zaid, 2010).

A brief look at the history of the Internet shows that it has been available to the public since November 1995. Research universities were the first to adopt and use it. Morocco's first Internet café opened in 1996 in Rabat. In 1996, there were about 50 websites, but in July 2019, there were 100,618 registered domain names, with 74,717 with the .ma extension.

Until the mid-1990s, the culture of media in Morocco was authoritarian, administrative, and partisan (Zaid & Ibahrine, 2011). It was authoritarian and administrative in that the state controlled the financing, regulation, production, and distribution of broadcast media, which was considered the most influential media. It was partisan in that print media were mainly controlled by political parties. Given the low literacy rates, print media was not seen as a great threat to the regime; instead, maintaining complete state control over broadcasting was seen as essential. Print media became, after independence, a site of political tension between the opposition political parties and the monarchy (Zaid, El Kaddoussi, & Ibahrine, 2020).

Opposition leaders used newspapers and magazines as their chief weapons of political contestation. The era from 1961 to 1997 under the rule of King Hassan II has been labeled the "Years of Lead" because of the rampant repression, injustice, corruption, and media censorship, and the widespread imprisonment, murder, and "disappearance" of journalists and political opponents of the regime (Zaid, El Kaddoussi, & Ibahrine, 2020).

Like many countries in the early postcolonial era, Morocco perceived the role of media as a nation-building instrument (Zaid, 2017). Morocco was a proponent of the modernization theory which conceived development in terms of industrialization, transfer of technology and innovation, and economic growth. According to a study by the Moroccan Ministry of Social Development (2006), development programs and policy in Morocco during the 1950s and 1960s were in line with the modernization paradigm and consisted of investments in economic infrastructure and technology. In this paradigm, the mass media, or what Lerner (1958) called the mobility multiplier, represents the main tool and transmitter of modern values and information, and could even function as a surrogate for travel. Morocco's state-controlled media system was therefore mandated at the outset with the role of modernizing the economy and serving as an instrument for education and social change (El Kadoussi, 2016). It was argued that privately-owned media would be motivated to seek profits, and this would deprive the Moroccan population of content that fulfilled educational and informational values. For instance, in the 1960s, King Hassan II (1961–1999) mobilized radio and television for political awareness and education, including preparations for the country's first general elections and a constitutional referendum in 1962 (Ibahrine, 2007). The primary purpose was to modernize; human rights were of secondary consideration.

The major improvements in the relationship between the political establishment and mass media occurred when the oppositional socialist government was elected in 1997, a process consolidated under the reign of King Mohammed VI. After he succeeded his father Hassan II in July 1999, Mohammed VI instantly became a symbol of hope for a more democratic and freer Morocco (El Kadoussi, 2016). The mission of the 1997 government was to enact political reforms aimed at promoting human rights, civil liberties, and an open, pluralist media, and to establish the rule of law. One of the first major pro-human rights measures under the young King Mohammed VI was the 2003 creation of the Equity and Reconciliation Commission (ERC), which investigated human rights violations from the "Years of Lead" to establish the truth. The Commission organized public forums in 2004 in which victims voiced their pain and suffering under the old regime. These forums were broadcast live on television—a very important moment in Moroccan television history. Another major initiative was the Family Status Law, or *mudawana*, decreed in 2004 to protect the rights of women. To safeguard and promote Amazigh language and culture, Mohammed VI created the Royal Institute of Amazigh Culture (L'Institut Royal de la Culture

Amazighe [IRCAM]). The Imazighen constituted a large ethnic group whose culture had been undermined for decades. These positive reforms earned the new king political capital and furthered his legitimacy.

The media benefited from this political opening. All sectors—print, broadcast, and digital—witnessed significant growth during the period. The High Authority for Audiovisual Communication (Haute Autorité de la Communication Audiovisuelle [HACA]) was established under the Dahir (Royal Decree) of 31 August 2002 as an independent administrative body in charge of regulating audiovisual communication. The partial liberalization and modernization of the audiovisual sector allowed new commercial radio and television stations to emerge. The new private radio stations, which grew from two in 2005 to 16 in 2009, reinvigorated the broadcast landscape, especially through their live debate shows and news programs. They introduced the impetus and space to create possibilities for national debates on a variety of social, educational, and health-related issues. Government restrictions on print media also eased.

During this period, a new generation of young journalists pushed the boundaries of the comfort zone of mainstream media and society at large. Many taboos were broken, from discussing the king's salary to reporting on the arrest of high officials close to the palace. Morocco was also spared the draconian measures used in other authoritarian countries against the Internet, such as the blocking of social media platforms or web content. Moroccan citizens can, to this day, create websites and write for blogs without any registration requirements imposed by the government (Zaid, El Kaddoussi, & Ibahrine, 2020).

However, while the ERC, the *mudawana*, and the IRCAM have been positive developments, they have not constituted serious opportunities for challenging the status quo in Morocco. The state continues to use legal and financial penalties to keep the most critical voices in line. A record number of libel and defamation suits were filed against print media in the years following these reforms. Broadcasts remained under close state supervision via HACA. Internet use was and remains closely monitored through state surveillance. These setbacks led to the 2011 protest movement during the Arab uprisings, leading to constitutional reforms.

Political System and Legal Framework

Morocco is a constitutional monarchy with an elected parliament, but the King maintains executive powers without accountability to the Moroccan public (Madani et al., 2012). Morocco's political regime can be best characterized as a competitive authoritarian regime.

Competitive authoritarian regimes use elements of democracy to ensure domination over the other opposition forces in the country. Levitsky and Way (2002) defined competitive authoritarianism as civilian regimes in which "formal democratic institutions are widely viewed as the primary means of gaining power, but in which fraud, civil liberties violations, and abuse of state and media resources so skew the playing field that the regime cannot be labeled democratic" (p. 4). These regimes are competitive in the sense that the democratic institutions are real and that "opposition forces can use legal channels to seriously contest for (and occasionally win) power; but they are authoritarian in that opposition forces are handicapped by a highly uneven—and even dangerous—playing field. Competition is thus real but unfair" (p. 4). Competitive authoritarian regimes are characterized by the presence of some democratic institutions and some democratic practices such as elections, a multiparty system, and, in this case, a self-proclaimed independent media regulator and a new press law. We argue that Morocco's media reforms are in line with this vision of governance, whereby the state creates democratic institutions to use as a site of struggle with opposition forces while steadfastly maintaining control by establishing an uneven playing field.

Morocco's media system offers a good illustration of the complex process of media reform during political transitions. As a competitive authoritarian regime, the state uses democratic institutions to reform its media system, while entrenching these institutions via authoritarian laws. Morocco has witnessed periods of tight authoritarian control and periods of reformist tendencies. This cyclical fluctuation has resulted in significant progress in media structure and performance and, at the same time, in the state maintaining its control over the media landscape through various mechanisms of repression.

A case in point is the public service sector. The legal framework and institutional structure provide the conditions for public service to materialize but do not guarantee its performance. The nondemocratic culture of the country is the main deterrent for public service media. A competitive authoritarian regime has stifled the attempt to transform broadcasting from a state-controlled institution into a public service entity. The 2005 Audiovisual Communication Law put an end to the state's monopoly over broadcasting management. The most positive development has been the establishment of a legal framework for private ownership. However, the law contains provisions that allow the state to interfere with program content and to put limits on private ownership.

In addition to HACA, Moroccan Radio and Television (Radiodiffusion et Télévision Marocaine), the institution that earlier managed state television and radio, was transformed from a subsidiary of the Ministry of Communication to a public entity, the National Company of Radio and Television (La Société Nationale de Radiodiffusion et de Télévision [SNRT]) in April 2005. Self-proclaimed as independent, the SNRT manages nine public television stations and six public radio stations and is not subject to administrative control and supervision by the Ministry.

However, HACA's High Council consists of nine members, five of whom are appointed by the king, including the president. The king also appoints the president of the SNRT. The state, therefore, assimilated the broadcast regulator into authoritarian strategies of governance, using them to upgrade their capacity to control broadcasting by entrenching them in a multilayered architecture of control, namely the unrepresentative appointment process of its decision-making bodies and the repressive media laws. State control over the appointment process of the regulatory bodies is not an uncommon practice in most democracies. But, in mature democracies, systems of checks and balances exist whereby political power is not concentrated in the hands of a few, and one governance entity cannot hold too much power (Zaid, 2018). This is not the case for Morocco, which failed to transform state broadcasting into public media and continues its history of state broadcasting as an instrument of propaganda and political control.

The 2011 constitution entails provisions that guarantee freedom of expression, as well as caveats limiting this freedom. Article 25 guarantees Moroccan citizens "freedoms of thought, opinion, and expression in all their forms," and Article 28 states that "freedom of the press is guaranteed and may not be limited by any form of prior censorship." (El Kadoussi, 2020).

However, Article 19 puts limits on Morocco's adherence to international conventions on human rights, which has direct implications for the media by introducing two constraining phrases "with respect for the provisions of the constitution's permanent characteristics and the laws of the kingdom." Although the 2011 constitution strengthened the judiciary as a separate branch of government, it is far from independent in Morocco, leaving the media without adequate protection by the law (El Kadoussi, 2018).

The 2016 Press Code brought about many positive advances, but a close look at the text shows that the oppressive nature of the legal environment in the country has not significantly changed. The positive adjustments include the elimination of jail sentences for journalists and the establishment of a self-regulatory body, the National Press Council. The law also carries specific provisions to regulate digital media. However, the three taboo topics—monarchy, Western Sahara, and Islam—were preserved in the new code, and jail sentences were replaced by steep fines. Failure to pay the fines can lead to jail terms, and at the same time, the Penal Law, which stipulates jail sentences for any offense against taboo topics, can be used to prosecute journalists. The Anti-Terrorism Law, passed in 2003 after the terrorist attacks in Casablanca on 16 May, gave the government sweeping legal powers to control any media content that is deemed to "disrupt public order by intimidation, force, violence, fear or terror." Ostensibly intended to combat terrorism, the authorities have wide latitude in defining vague terms such as "national security" and "public order," opening the door for abuse.

Moroccan authorities use nuanced means to limit online content and violate users' rights. For example, while websites are rarely blocked, problematic press and anti-terrorism laws place heavy burdens on intermediaries and result in the closure of news sites.

Reporters Without Borders (RSF) (2019) ranked Morocco 135th of 180 countries in its annual press freedom index primarily due to the prosecutions of journalists. Media watchdog organizations such as RSF and Freedom House include in their annual reports the number and names of jailed journalists each year. Moreover, many prominent publication directors and editors such as Aboubakr Jamai, Ahmed Benchemsi, and Ali Lemrabet have resigned from their positions and live in self-imposed exile in Western countries (Zaid, 2017).

Economy and Ownership Patterns

Morocco's media system consists of a mix of public and private ownership and allows the government's intervention to ensure public service. Moroccan media outlets use two main financing models. The first is advertising. The media firms expose audiences to advertising messages in exchange for free content. This is the dominant business model in Morocco's media which permeates both public service and non-public service media content providers. The second is subsidy. The government pays media firms in return for public service. This applies to public service television and radio, as well as political party newspapers. The aim, as stated by the government, is to help these media firms be more independent and distanced from all vested economic interests.

Whereas neither public service television nor political party newspapers are free of advertising, public service radio is advertising-free and offers a wide range of publicly relevant news and information programming. Against this backdrop, the advertising industry cannot support sustainable media business models. In addition to the deteriorating advertising market, an estimated 70% to 80% of Moroccan advertisers use global online platforms such as *Google* and *Facebook*, whose market share will continue to grow at the expense of local websites. According to the Group of Moroccan Advertisers, the total advertising market stood at USD 596 million in 2017, USD 18 million more than in 2016. In 2018, the big advertisers, the telecom operators, banks, and the food sector lowered their advertising budgets by 14.6%, 14.7%, and 10%, respectively (Hespress, 2019).

The advertising budget is distributed not based on professional, standardized, and transparent criteria, but on who is close to the center of power. Advertising revenue provided by the government or government-linked companies is not split equitably between independent and pro-government publications. In a recent example, the Office Chérifien des Phosphates (OCP) and Caisse de Dépôt et de Gestion (CDG), two state-owned companies that do not offer any particular products to Moroccan consumers, bought advertising time and space. This move was meant to secure advertising funding the state can use to reward obedience.

Current regulatory practices aim to reduce media ownership concentration, but they fail to encourage pluralism in media ownership. In Morocco, the absence of concentration does not necessarily imply an increase in pluralism. According to the Press and Publications Code, any media organization in the broadcast industry cannot hold an investment in the capital of more than one print media company. Any person owning 30% or more of a newspaper company has to declare it to the National Press Council. Any newspaper or magazine that owns 10% or more of the capital of another newspaper or magazine has to declare it to the National Press Council. Internet service providers (ISPs) cannot own part of the capital of another ISP (Le Desk & Reporters Without Borders, 2017). Article 21 of the Audiovisual Communication Law limits the concentration of ownership in broadcasting except for state-controlled television and radio. In the first and second waves of licensing in 2006 and 2009, HACA granted licenses only to state-owned television stations and to a mix of state and private radio stations (18 of the latter). Television stations such as *Arriadiya* for sports and *Al-Maghribia* for the Moroccan diaspora, and private radio stations such as *Hitradio* and *Aswat* were all licensed during this phase. Ownership of private radio reflects closeness to the regime power structure (Le Desk & Reporters Without Borders, 2017), hence, the lack of pluralism. The list includes owners of pro-government print media organizations, such as Abdelmounaim Dilami and Moulay Hafid El-Alami; members of the administrative (pro-government) political party, such as Abdelaziz Akhenouch and Mouncif Belkhayat; and former employees of the state-owned television and radio stations, such as Kamal Lahlou. In the second wave of licensing in 2009, HACA declined five private television license applications on the grounds of a "deteriorating situation in the advertising market," and the need to "maintain the stability and viability of existing public and private operators." It exclusively justified these decisions on a financial basis. Article 21 stipulates that any broadcasting company or shareholder can own shares in another broadcasting company up to a maximum of 30% of its holdings. This was intended to prevent any individual or company from controlling more than one media outlet. Aside from state control over broadcasting, only a handful of media companies owned by key pro-government political players, such as the Caractères Media Group, EcoMédias Group, and Maroc Soir Group, control a few media outlets in print, online, and broadcasting. No single company has control over a significant audience share.

Some of Morocco's billionaires, such as Moulay Hafid El-Alami, Aziz Akhannouch, Othman Benjelloun, and Meriem Bensaleh Chaqroun, have stakes in five of the nine French-language publications including *Aujourd'hui Le Maroc, La Vie Eco, Les Inspirations Eco, La Nouvelle Tribune*, and *L'Economiste*. Currently, two of them are also ministers (Le Desk & Reporters Without Borders, 2017). The publications are editorially pro-government, and they benefit from advertising despite their limited circulation. This close relationship between economic power and the French-language media has created an unhealthy media market because these newspapers receive an advertising budget regardless of their primary circulation and readership. This promotes a culture of clientelism, which is harmful to media transparency and professionalism. Ostensibly, media in Morocco have been strongly controlled by political and economic clientelism. These political leaders need these publications for reputation management and to play down corruption scandals and ensure electoral campaign success (Benchenna, Ksikes, & Marchetti, 2017). This clientelism is also a manifestation of the rentier state in Morocco. If the freedom of the press is to be respected, independence from government interference and big money are vital.

Technology and Infrastructure

In the context of the liberalization of the ICT sector in the 1990s, the 1996 Law 24–96 ended the monopoly of state-owned *Maroc Télécom*. Morocco set up a regulatory body to come up with the country's vision for ICT. Three companies provide telecom services in Morocco. Initially owned by the state, *Maroc Télécom* became private in 1998. The French firm *Vivendi* acquired 35% of its shares in the company in 2001. In 2013, *Etisalat*, an Emirati telecom operator, acquired 53% of *Vivendi*'s stake for USD 5.6 billion (Oxford Business Group, 2019). *Orange Morocco* became the first fully private operator to enter the Moroccan market in 2000 (known then as *Médi-Télécom*, a private consortium led by Spain's *Telefonica*). It is now the market's second largest telecom operator. In

2007, *Inwi* (formerly *Maroc Connect*) became the third largest telecom company in Morocco. *Inwi* is a subsidiary of the SNI group, the leading Moroccan industrial, financial, and services conglomerate owned by the monarch. Telecommunications is the most dynamic sector in the industry, with mobile data services leading the way.

In 2009, the government launched the national strategy "Digital Morocco 2013" to consolidate ICT industries, to support the automation of small- and medium-sized enterprises (SMEs), to boost e-government services, and to foster the dissemination of ICT usage among Moroccan households. Subsequent to Digital Morocco 2013, Morocco launched "Digital Morocco 2020," which relies on three main pillars: 1) adopting smart government services and facilitating the adoption of digital devices among Moroccan households; 2) positioning Morocco as a strategic digital hub in French-speaking Africa and enabling the development of business process outsourcing services with high added values; and 3) upskilling human capital to increase the competitiveness of the economy (Oxford Business Group, 2019). The government invested USD 750 million to reduce the digital divide by 50% through the digitization of administrative services, improved access to the Internet through free Wi-Fi in public spaces, and digital literacy programs (Ministry of Industry, Investment, Commerce, and Digital Economy, 2019).

One of the results of Digital Morocco 2020 is the expansion of e-commerce platforms. In 2015, Morocco managed to reach a total of 11.7 million credit cards (Oxford Business Group, 2019). The rise of e-commerce is supported by electronic payment. Out of a total of 18.3 million Internet users, 900,000 are considered regular e-consumers (Oxford Business Group, 2019). In 2019, e-commerce growth was mainly driven by increased smartphone penetration and the rollout of the 4G network.

The development of IT services has been supported by the many technology parks that host more than 100 IT companies, including Dell, IBM, Accenture, Atos, HP, and Logica and more than 1,000 start-ups. Over the last few years, Morocco has created four technoparks in the four largest Moroccan cities Casablanca, Rabat, Tangiers, and Agadir. The mission of these technoparks, which facilitate importing and exporting IT-related services, is to assist in the creation and development of companies in ICT and to promote innovation, training, and technological support.

Morocco is now among the top ten African nations in terms of digital development (Oxford Business Group, 2019). The government efforts have resulted in high proportions of households with Internet access. According to the Agence Nationale de Réglementation des Télécommunications (2019), 74.2% of Moroccan households are now equipped with Internet, 99.8% have mobile phones, and of these, 75.7% have smartphones. The leading motivation for the adoption of the Internet and mobile phones is to enjoy entertainment content, such as games and social media platforms (95.2%), and to access the news (86.1%). Despite significant efforts by the government to integrate ICTs properly into the country's development agenda, the ICT Development Index ranked Morocco 100 out of a total of 176 countries (International Telecommunication Union, 2017).

Challenges

Three main areas represent challenges to the current system: quality media content, economic sustainability, and disrupting technologies. The rise of sponsored content, misinformation, sensationalism, and poor-quality journalism, particularly in online media, have raised serious concerns about the quality of information Moroccan audiences receive. Entertainment and celebrity stories have increased at the expense of news on national affairs. This dismal picture is the result of several factors, including the fierce competition over audience attention, the logic of algorithm-driven platforms, and the integration of the editorial, marketing, and analytics functions in the digital news industry. The value of news stories is no longer based on the standard quality but on a range of metrics, including the number of visits, hits, and views.

Another factor that negatively affects the quality of content is the journalists' education and training. Journalism seems to have become the profession of those who have no profession. In November 2016 and on the occasion of the International Day for the Elimination of Violence against Women, the *2M TV* show *Sabahiyat* featured a tutorial to show women how to cover domestic violence facial bruises with makeup.

In January 2019, a journalist at *Al-Ayam* newspaper interviewed an orphaned seven-year-old girl about her experience of her mother's murder. Both events triggered a vast wave of criticism from social media users and activists who denounced the unethical practices of the journalists.

In terms of economic sustainability, clientelism and the unfair distribution of advertising money continue to represent a threat to media business models. In January 2018, the government placed an additional financial burden on the fragile media sector by imposing a 5% tax on digital advertising.

In terms of technology, disruptive technologies are aggravating the fragility of the business models of the print media, despite government subsidies. Moroccan websites depend on revenue streams built on the commercialization of media platforms such as *Google*, *Facebook*, *Twitter*, and other global tech companies. Reliance on social media platforms has created a major structural shift in news production, distribution, and monetization. The tech giants deprive local news websites of vital revenue streams and sources. A local business in Casablanca will achieve a higher yield return on investment when it advertises with *Google* and *Facebook* than with a local news organization. The former will deliver local customers to the local business in a more efficient way than a local news organization serving the local news needs of the same local customers. This situation has had severe consequences for the revenue streams of news websites. Digitalization has been making the profession of a journalist in Morocco more volatile and insecure.

In line with competitive authoritarianism, Morocco failed to liberalize the media and has continued its history of state-controlled media as instruments of political control. As a competitive authoritarian regime, the state created democratic institutions such as HACA and SNRT to reform its media system while entrenching these institutions via authoritarian laws. The locus of power over the media includes licensing and policy formulation, but it also reaches into editorial decisions. Without the sincere political will to reform the media ecosystem, positive change in the quality of content and revenue streams is likely to remain a long-term proposition.

Outlook

As elsewhere, news and content providers should improve their competitiveness and ensure that more readers browse their media platforms. However, to further enhance the level of attractiveness in a highly competitive media content market, these news content providers such as print media, broadcast media, and digital platforms are called to personalize their news content over multi-cross platforms and different devices. Rather than targeting readers as a whole, news and content providers (media organizations) will realize that real value is in the market of one reader/consumer. The emerging world of media has become more personal than ever before, where readers access their news and media content through their personal and mobile devices. The personalization of news and media content is likely to take another dimension when the superfast 5G enters the Moroccan telecom market. Huawei, a global provider of ICT infrastructure, has been closely working with the Moroccan government and the three Moroccan telecoms operators to launch 5G and will make Morocco the first country in Africa to do so.

Over the next five years, digital advertising will continue to thrive and become strong and mature due to factors such as the high levels of connectivity, social media usage, digital platforms penetration, and mobile device adoption. Moroccan policymakers are well-advised to design flexible regulatory frameworks to protect Moroccan readers and their data. At the center of any regulatory framework, the critical issues at hand should include business models, disruptive technologies, trust, and regulation.

References

Benchenna, A., Ksikes, D., & Marchetti, D. (2017). The media in Morocco: A highly political economy, the case of the paper and on-line press since the early 1990s. *The Journal of North African Studies*, 22(3), 386–410.

El Kadoussi, A. (2016). The Moroccan independent press: Issues of independence and political opposition. *International Journal of Social Science and Humanities Research*, 4(4), 299–306.

———. (2018). Four phases in the history of the Moroccan private press. *The Journal of North African Studies*, Online first. DOI: 10.1080/13629387.2018.1434510

———. (2020). The perception of self-censorship among Moroccan journalists. *The Journal of North African Studies.* Online first. DOI: 10.1080/13629387.2020.1771310.

Hespress. (2018, November 14). *Advertising budgets in Morocco decline* [in Arabic]. https://www.hespress.com/economie/412277.html

Ibahrine, M. (2007). *The Internet and politics in Morocco: The political use of the Internet by Islam oriented political movements.* Berlin: VDM Verlag.

———. (2009). Massenmedien in Marokko. In *Internationales Handbuch für Medien 2009* [in German]. Hans-Bredow-Institut. Baden-Baden: Nomos.

———. (2020). The emergence of a news website ecosystem: An exploratory study of

Hespress. *Journalism Practice.* 14(8), 971–90. https://doi.org/10.1080/17512786.2019.1679037

Le Desk & Reporters Without Borders. (2017). *Media ownership monitor: Morocco.* http://maroc.mom-rsf.org/en/

Lerner, D. (1958). *The passing of traditional society: Modernizing the Middle East.* New York: Free Press.

Levitsky, S., & Way, L. (2002). Elections without democracy: The rise of competitive authoritarianism. *Journal of Democracy, 13*(2), 51–65.

Madani, M., Maghraoui, D., & Zerhouni, S. (2012). *The 2011 Moroccan Constitution: A critical analysis.* https://www.idea.int/sites/default/files/publications/the-2011-moroccan-constitution-critical-analysis.pdf

Morocco World News. (2019). *Moroccans spend 2 hours watching TV, 2 minutes reading, exercising.* https://www.moroccoworldnews.com/2019/01/262899/moroccan-tv-reading-exercising-hcp/

Oxford Business Group. (2019). *New plan and updated legislation provide a boost for Morocco's IT sector.* https://oxfordbusinessgroup.com/overview/building-new-plan-and-updated-legislation-have-provided-boost-0

Reporters Without Borders. (2019). *Data of press freedom ranking 2019.* https://rsf.org/en/ranking_table

Zaid, B. (2010). *Public Service Television Policy and National Development in Morocco: Contents, Production, and Audiences.* Saarbrücken: VDM.

———. (2017). The authoritarian trap in state/media structures in Morocco's political transition. *The Journal of North African Studies, 22*(3), 340–60.

———. (2018). Comparative study of broadcast regulators in the Arab world. *International Journal of Communication, 12,* 4401–20.

Zaid, B., El Kaddoussi, A., & Ibahrine, M. (2020). The Uneasy Journey of the Moroccan Press. In N. Miladi & N. Mellor (Eds.) *Routledge Handbook of Arab Media.* London: Routledge.

Zaid, B., & Ibahrine, M. (2011). Mapping digital media: Morocco. *The Open Society Foundation*. https://www.opensocietyfoundations.org/publications/mapping-digital-media-morocco#publications_download

Conclusion

Carola Richter and Claudia Kozman

> What do we learn from comparing the individual media systems of Arab countries? We consciously refrained from building a typology for the eighteen Arab countries that are examined in this book. Instead, we have opted for highlighting major themes that we detected when carefully reviewing the seven dimensions that each author used in the analysis of the respective countries. These themes comprise 1) the state's approach to media, 2) media ownership, 3) fragmentation and polarization, 4) technological advancement and innovation, and 5) transnational mobility and connection. We explain how the media systems examined differ or concur with regard to these five themes.

Deconstructing Typologies, Reconstructing Themes

Comparing Arab media systems can lead to paradoxical results, given their ambivalent developments. A shared history has left its marks, albeit in different ways. Ongoing changes distinguish several dynamic fields, while at the same time a strong authoritarianism persists in other fields. What conclusions, then, can we draw for the present and future of Arab media?

Throughout its chapters, this book has confirmed that Siebert, Peterson, and Schramm's (1963) indication that the "press always takes on the form and coloration of the political and social structures within which it operates" still holds true today (p. 1). Nonetheless, these political and social structures change over time and, depending on other factors such as the economic power or the embeddedness of a country in transnational settings, may play out differently. Moreover, while this deterministic view seems to have allowed Siebert and his colleagues to assign the different political and social structures of all countries worldwide to only four distinct types, we have found it impossible to identify an appropriate typology for Arab media systems. Thus, we consciously refrained from building such a typology for the 18 Arab countries that are examined in this book.

Instead, we have opted to highlight the major themes we detected when carefully reviewing the seven dimensions that each author used in the analysis of their country. These themes will enable us to create new perspectives that could lead to more detailed discussions about the notion of state and business power, the role of transnational influences, and the impact of the particular social settings of Arab countries on the media. Which major themes, then, are characteristic of Arab media systems from a comparative perspective?

In the extant media system typologies, the nature of the state or the government is analyzed along with the kinds of intervention they apply to the media. In her chapter in this book, Sarah El-Richani, however, contends it is "important to take stock of the *de facto* situation... in addition to that which is *de jure*." This implies that the media in general might reflect the political and social structures of a given country, but there are still manifold ways in which these structures affect actual practices. While the legal written rules and regulations are often the focus of a media systems analysis, the chapters on the respective countries urge us to take a more general perspective that also reviews typical practices of control and influence beyond the written rules and regulations. Instead of considering only the legal framework, we consider the government or ***the state's general approach to media*** as an important theme. This includes the ways in which journalism and the performance of media workers are affected by red lines, unwritten rules, and the kinds of self-censorship resulting from the state's overarching approach to media being incorporated into its work practices.

Another major dimension in the extant global media system typologies is the ownership of media. While this has often been analyzed as a simple distinction between state-owned and private, or "public" and "independent" media, we instead consider the patterns that shape ***media ownership*** and their impact on content. Here, William Rugh's (2004) notion of "loyalist" media in the MENA region is important because it hints at the fact that media privatization does not necessarily result in pluralistic media landscapes or regime-challenging media. Additionally, Hallin and Mancini's (2004) idea of analyzing political parallelism in the media is to be taken into consideration when assessing ownership patterns because of the typical interwovenness of politics and business, and how this is mirrored in the media scene.

The notion of political parallelism reappears in audiences' preferences and journalists' performances. In all of the countries analyzed, we find strong patterns of both societal and political fragmentation and polarization. Arab media systems seem to be characterized by a division of audiences, journalists, and content owing to conflict driven by ethnic, religious, or political differences, which often come to light during times of crisis and war. We thus consider the nature and effects of *fragmentation and polarization* of the media system as another theme.

An aspect that is not reflected strongly—or at all—in existing typologies is *technological advancement and innovation*. Media systems are converging throughout the world; therefore, the traditional distinction between print, audio, and visual media is not very helpful in an era of pervasive Internet, since it fails to provide us with in-depth knowledge about the realities of media production, usage, and control. Thus, we need to take a critical look at a media system's achievements and performance in terms of technology and infrastructure. The country chapters indicate that this theme is of major importance, even when some states simply do not have the wherewithal to engage in technological advancement and innovation.

Finally, the MENA region has been characterized for centuries by a tradition of *transnational mobility and connection*, which is also evident in the realm of media and journalism. On the one hand, and due to a common language, the potential outreach of media to publics beyond national borders enables content and production to travel in a way that is not even imaginable in other regions of the world. On the other hand, transnational connectedness raises its own unique problems, such as the asymmetry between the civilian experiences on either side of wars or conflicts, as in those between Yemen and Saudi Arabia or Palestine and Israel. With regard to outreach, mobility, and ownership the theme of transnationalism has been highlighted in several country chapters and thus requires further attention.

In the following section, we examine these themes more closely by comparing and contrasting the findings of the 18 country chapters.

Arab Media Systems: A Comparative Perspective

1. The State's Approach to Media

Reflecting on the state's approach to media allows us to understand the ability and means of ruling elites to control the media, or influence its production and content to shape public opinion. Indeed, the most common feature of almost all Arab political regimes is their continuous effort to make the media suit their immediate policies. Ehab Galal, for example, argues in his chapter on Qatar that the state "carefully navigate[s] a balance... between liberalization and control" and Bouziane Zaid and Mohammed Ibahrine detect a "cyclical fluctuation" of liberalization and repression in Morocco.

In most of the Arab countries, constitutions or other guiding legal texts guarantee freedom of media and expression—but almost always within the limits of vague concepts such as "national security" and "public morals." It thus remains within the jurisdiction of the regimes to execute what is meant by freedom of expression or, more generally, what they want the media to be and do in society. We identified mobilization and modernization purposes as the two main goals regimes typically use to justify the instrumentalization of the media. In addition to this line of comparison, we found varying degrees of enforcement of laws and (unwritten) regulations, which prompted us to include a second dimension of comparison: the contrast between a *laissez-faire* approach and strong control of media (see Figure 1).

Mobilization, in this context, is often framed as an educational effort by self-proclaimed elites to enlighten the masses who seem to be "not there yet," that is, not yet in the state of mind the regime wants them to be. More often than not, mobilization has turned out to be propaganda used extensively by socialist—or those claiming to be socialist—republics, such as Algeria, Sudan, Yemen, Syria, Libya, and Iraq. Yet, mobilization in the sense outlined above is a vanishing characteristic of Arab media systems. As seen in their respective chapters, only Algeria and Sudan still appear to be aiming to mobilize the "uneducated masses," although

Sudan's approach is apt to change due to revolutionary transformation, and in Yemen, Syria, and Libya, a unified state approach is completely lacking, due to the de facto fragmentation of these countries. In the latter three cases, militias or opposing elites today instrumentalize the media using propagandistic means to mobilize it for their causes and to delegitimize opposition, therewith constructing a new kind of mobilization media that is not likely to vanish if the wars finally end.

In Iraq, the situation has changed since the US invasion in 2003, throwing out the idea of mobilization as a main feature to describe the state's approach to media. Similarly, in Lebanon and Palestine, state structures are weak and thus a kind of *laissez-faire* approach towards the media exists, with restrictive laws in place but rarely applied. In these cases, the state is not in a position to dictate a specific media policy, neither can it mobilize for its causes. In a way, this makes these media systems freer than others. The problem, however, lies in the inability of the state to provide legal security to media outlets and physical security to media workers, making them vulnerable to any kind of attacks. Tunisia is a special case here: it has created laws to guarantee a more autonomous media system, balancing protection and control and avoiding instrumentalization of the media. However, the actual practices resulting from this approach have yet to be observed more closely.

On the other side of the spectrum, Egypt and Bahrain exercise strict control over the media, often under the pretext of stabilizing national security and the modern state. Due to the political turmoil these countries have faced since 2011, their governments view the media as potential enemies that need to be controlled through restrictive laws, intimidation of media workers, and ownership.

In between these two extremes—the *laissez-faire* and the strong control approaches—many countries oscillate between control and liberalization under the pretext of modernization and development. With the exception of Bahrain, all of the Gulf states, as well as the kingdoms of Morocco and Jordan, legitimize control of the media as a means to foster national stability and unity, while at the same time somehow conceding to private (foreign) investors in order to bring to life their visions of media as revenue creators. These governments also invest strongly in building a high-end digital infrastructure in order to keep their promises of modernization with regard to digital media. In this context, media content often is not directly censored; instead, journalists commonly revert to self-censorship in order to avoid jeopardizing their own position in a media industry that these governments view as a must-have in creating a modern society.

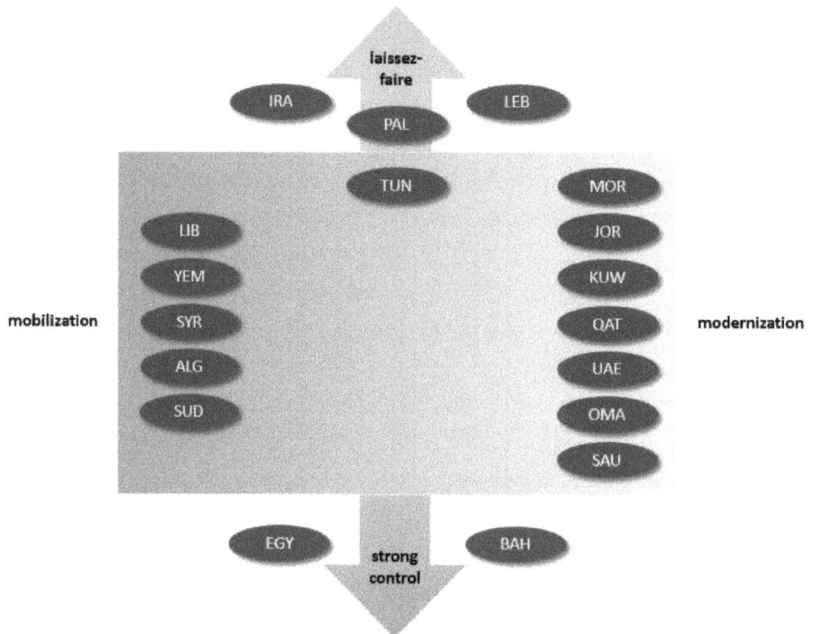

Fig. 1: The state's approach to media

2. Media Ownership

Media ownership reveals much about the distribution of power in the context of financial viability. It also raises questions about who is at the center or the margins of power, in addition to which role external donors play.

In the Arab world, state-owned and privately-owned media coexist, but to varying degrees. In some countries, such as Lebanon and Kuwait, print media have always been set up as entirely privately financed outlets without any state-ownership, while in most other countries, the print media market was at least liberalized in the 1990s or early 2000s, leading to the coexistence of state-owned, privately-owned, and party-owned press. The much wider reach of the broadcasting sector meant that regimes attributed much greater significance to it. Television, in particular, remained in the hands of governments and their ministries of information (or similar institutions) well into the mid-2000s. Lebanon is the only exception to this rule. One media type that is absent in the MENA is up-to-date public service broadcasting (PSB) that aims to represent all segments of society without governmental interference and commercial interests, although there have been some attempts to establish a PSB model similar to that of the *BBC* in Iraq. Currently, Tunisia faces the task of reorganizing state-owned broadcasting and turning it into a real PSB.

However, the simple facts of public or private ownership do not help us understand either the underlying patterns of media ownership or their effect on content. First, we must therefore glean patterns that shape ownership structures by taking into consideration the state's general approach to media as well as the availability of financial means by certain actors. Second, we have to consider Rugh's idea of "loyalist" media and pit it against its very opposite, which we term "confrontational" media (see Figure 2).

With regard to "loyalist" media, we find three distinct ownership patterns in our sample with one common characteristic: ownership of key media sectors, such as broadcasting and telecommunications, is almost exclusively in the hands of cronies or extended family members of the regimes. In countries such as Egypt, Sudan, and Algeria, the security apparatuses and the military play a huge role in the ownership of "privatized" media. In countries like Jordan, Kuwait, Morocco, Bahrain, or Oman, private ownership extends to influential businesspeople who have become successful due to their close links to the ruling family. These relationships allow them to make cross-sector investments in the media, for example to advertise their products. A third pattern is primarily linked to what we call "pan-Arab outsourcing" and applies mainly to Saudi Arabia, Qatar, and the UAE. While these countries still operate rather banal national state-owned television outlets, the main investments of the royal families and their allies go into pan-Arab consortia, such as *Rotana*, *Al-Jazeera*, and *MBC*, which provide professional journalism and high-end entertainment, but are entirely loyal to the political ideologies of their sponsors. None of these three ownership patterns is exclusive in any media system, rather they often greatly overlap within a single system. Here, we highlight the prevailing pattern for each country.

On the opposite side of the spectrum, "confrontational" media are prevalent in Libya, Syria, and Yemen, where media ownership is completely unregulated, at least from a national perspective. In these cases, media almost exclusively belong to actors involved in the conflict and consequently disagree with one another. At the same time, media loyalty is enforced in areas where one side dominates, such as in the Houthi-dominated north of Yemen or in east Libya, which is under the control of General Haftar. Here, media are typically owned by those who have the financial means to operate them and who are most often the conflicting parties themselves.

However, in the realms of both loyalist and confrontational media, a new development concerning small media has occurred. In some countries, small media, such as local radio stations or websites, are operated by local actors and provide a true alternative to the "big" national media, whereas in others, as in the cases of Libya and Iraq, they pop up unregulated, and often get support from external donors, such as European media development organizations. Still, in other countries, such as Tunisia, community media are part of the official new media scene. These examples indicate that small or alternative media could be a breeding ground for new media ownership models in the foreseeable future.

In addition to the patterns of enforced and unregulated media ownership, there exists another, more regulated kind of pattern on the "confrontationalist" side. In Lebanon, Tunisia, Iraq, and Palestine, media are owned by a variety of political and/or confessional actors, creating a rather pluralistic media landscape. While, in Iraq and Palestine, this can easily turn into the conflict model described above, in the cases of Lebanon and Tunisia, there seems to be a stable and healthy external pluralism.

Fig. 2: Media ownership

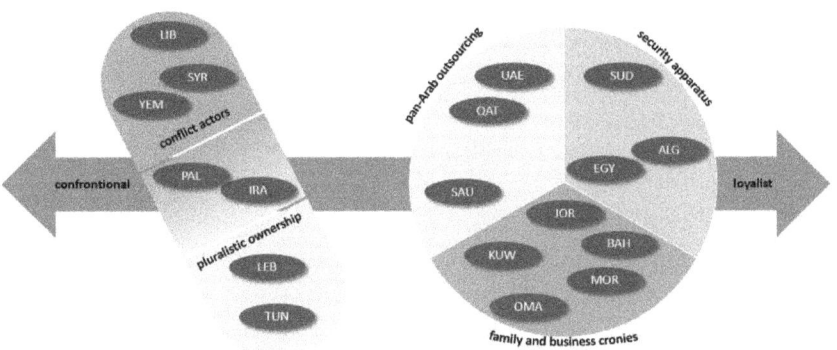

3. Fragmentation and Polarization

This theme identifies fragmentation and polarization as a result of lines of conflict driven by ethnic, religious, social, or political differences. It reflects the supremacy of power and control in dictating how social structures and divisions are represented. We identified two dimensions through which to compare the countries: how the political system deals with conflicts, and how the media represent conflicts. On the political level, the country cases indicate two opposing ways in which these phenomena are treated: either the lines of conflict materialize to such a degree that they are omnipresent in society and shape all societal discourse, or they are strongly suppressed so as to mimic political and social homogeneity for the sake of creating national stability. Different ways of representing these conflicts can be found on the media level, ranging from "conscious inclusion" to "conscious exclusion" of the voices of others (see Figure 3).

On one side of the political spectrum, in which strong political, religious, and/or ethnic divisions openly shape society, are post- and current-conflict countries that are mired in civil wars, including Libya, Syria, Yemen, Iraq, and Lebanon, or those that are shaken by major political rifts, such as that between Hamas and Fatah in Palestine. In all of these cases, media performance oscillates between providing an external pluralism of opinions and perspectives, on the one hand, and hate speech and denunciation of the opponent, on the other. With regard to each of Libya, Syria, and Yemen, where wars are still ongoing, a completely unregulated, polarized media is dominant, and there are only minor tangible efforts to overcome this polarization, such as small, local reconciliatory initiatives. This means a conscious exclusion of and fight against other actors' voices takes place in the respective media, thus reinforcing polarization through media discourse.

In the cases of Iraq, Lebanon, and Palestine, where the fragmentation of the media landscape along political and confessional lines has long been the case, more signs of professionalization, such as the use of less aggressive language or more objective reporting, can be observed. Thus, we can detect that some learning has taken place, perhaps due to the perceived necessity of including opposing voices of in different media in order to mimic openness and reduce polarization.

There is yet another way of dealing with conflict on the political level, as seen in Egypt, Tunisia, Morocco, and Jordan, each of which faces societal rifts in different spheres. Egypt has a large Coptic minority; Morocco comprises substantial Imazighen communities; Tunisia faces political rifts, severe problems with Islamists and an unresolved urban-rural divide; and Jordan's population is made up of many Palestinians and other refugee populations. These countries have found ways of responding to the demands of the various segments of society by providing better representation, either through special-language programs on radio and television, as in the case of Morocco, or by a quasi-natural inclusion, such as with the Palestinians in Jordanian society and its media landscape. In these cases—sometimes only after strong political pressures from the respective organized minorities—a gradual and closely monitored inclusion in the media system has taken place. Yet socioeconomic divisions, such as an urban-rural or class division, are not adequately addressed in most of the media systems that were observed here.

In other countries, societal conflict lines are strong, but their articulation remains suppressed, as in the case of tribal minorities in remote areas of Algeria and Sudan, such as Darfur, or in the cases of Saudi Arabia and Bahrain with religious minorities of other Islamic faiths. So far, no efforts have been made to provide a more inclusionary media landscape.

As for the small Gulf states of Kuwait, Qatar, Oman, and the UAE, indigenous citizens represent only a minority of the population, with the majority of the population comprising individuals originally from other Arab countries or South Asia, and typically dwelling only temporarily in these countries. It is worth noting that expatriates are oftentimes those behind media production both in the Arabic language (as in the case of *Al-Jazeera*), or the English-language newspapers, news agencies, and transnationally operating media. Although the foreign workers are not naturalized and therefore often lack political rights, the chapters on those countries paint a picture of harmonious coexistence, emphasizing the tolerance towards foreign religions, confessions, and ethnicities. Indeed, given the dependency on foreign staff, their inclusion in everyday life and the media scene is crucial for these regimes. It remains to be seen whether an adequate representation of the non-naturalized inhabitants' problems, needs, and demands—which revolve around human rights issues—is actually reflected in media production, or whether it is glossed over.

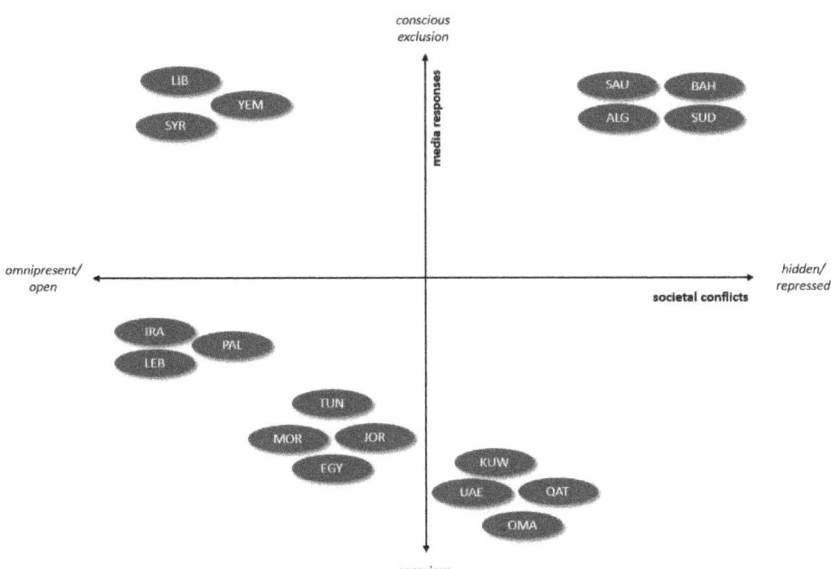

Fig. 3: Fragmentation and polarization

4. Technological Advancement and Innovation

Technological advancement reflects both the political ideology and economic power of a given state. We therefore approached this theme from two perspectives: first, the state of the infrastructure regarding Internet connectivity and telecommunications, and second, specific policies behind building a high-end infrastructure or the lack thereof—for example, whether a state makes it a priority to invest in the Internet, liberalizes the telecommunications market, or not. Taking these two aspects into consideration, we observe a spectrum with highly developed technological systems at one end, and poorly developed systems—due to a lack of prioritization—at the other (see Figure 4).

The rich Gulf countries, with their high-end infrastructure enabling literally everyone to be connected through the Internet and mobile phones, are positioned at one end of the spectrum. Statistics indicate an almost total connectivity amongst the populations in the small emirates of Kuwait, Bahrain, Qatar, and the UAE. For instance, mobile phone penetration sometimes hits the 200% mark, meaning that statistically every citizen has two mobile phone contracts. The geographically larger and more populated countries of Saudi Arabia and Oman follow a similar trend, although their penetration does not reach the same figure. In all of these countries, the regimes heavily invest in infrastructure and facilitate the establishment of international and leading technology companies in the region. The regimes regard these ventures as investments in their futures, actions that could diversify their economies and build a competitive infrastructure for businesses in general, as well as satisfying their citizens by providing state-of-the-art communications and a 'modern' lifestyle. At the same time, this state-of-the-art infrastructure comes with new forms of restriction. In order to keep their control of the online sphere, the incumbent elites have released a plethora of cybercrime laws and have invested, with the help of globally operating tech giants, in Internet security that not only aims to prevent financial fraud online, but in many cases is also used to limit freedom of speech on the Internet.

There are, of course, other countries in the region that have long realized how investing in Internet infrastructure in particular, and media infrastructure more broadly, can help to advance the countries' modernization and economic development. The governments that most strongly advocated for the distribution of computers and the development of an Internet infrastructure in the early 2000s were Tunisia, Egypt, and Morocco and, after some delay, Algeria. These countries started from a very low level of connectivity, and—due to their limited financial means, vast geographies, and still substantial illiteracy rates among the population—have reached only modest levels of Internet penetration (from 48% in Algeria to 64% in Tunisia). The early and controlled liberalization of the telecommunications market, however, has stimulated comparatively high levels of mobile phone penetration among citizens (which exceeds 100% in all countries but Egypt).

By contrast, in countries such as Lebanon and Jordan Internet penetration is comparatively better, but mobile phone use has for a long time been considered rather expensive and therefore has remained less common. In Lebanon, for example, regulation of the telecom market has favored cronies of the confessional regime, preventing a competitive environment that would push forward technological advancement.

Then, there are countries with an ambivalent record, such as Palestine, Syria, and Iraq, where a significant portion of the population is familiar with digital media due to advanced levels of education. While all three of these countries have witnessed major investments in Internet infrastructure and, in particular, in the telecommunications market, these investments continue to face major setbacks and destruction due to occupation, war, or violent conflict.

Yemen, Libya, and Sudan are situated at the opposite end of the spectrum of technological advancement, with the lowest rates of Internet connectivity. In these cases, the lag is the product of a mixture of general underdevelopment, war and conflict, and a severe lack of governmental determination to build an infrastructure until the 2010s.

Depending on the degree of state stability and investment security, technological advancement could develop rapidly in the two end groups. Regarding the two groups in the middle, policy directions and lack of financial means of investment seem to be the main problematic factors causing delays in development.

Fig. 4: Technological advancement and innovation

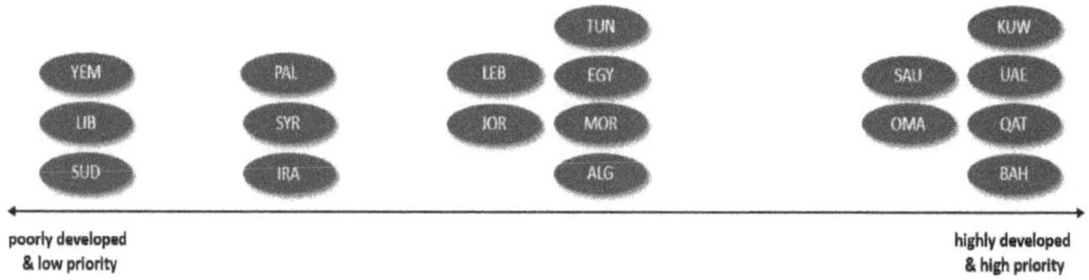

[Figure 4: A scatter plot showing countries arrayed from "poorly developed & low priority" (left) to "highly developed & high priority" (right). From left to right: YEM, LIB, SUD; PAL, SYR, IRA; TUN, LEB, JOR, EGY, MOR, ALG; SAU, OMA; KUW, UAE, QAT, BAH.]

5. Transnational Mobility and Connection

The fifth and last theme indicates how aspects of transnational connections mirror the multiple and changing relations between the different countries and their media systems. Aspects of transnationalism have featured strongly in most of the individual countries investigated here. They manifest in unique but overlapping ways. The main aspects to consider are: 1) the transnational circulation of media content, 2) the transnational circulation of media workers, 3) the role of the diaspora or those in exile in the media scene, and 4) the space that is provided to foreign or pan-Arab media in a given country (e.g. through hosting foreign channels). If we concentrate on the level of trans-Arab connections only, and exclude non-Arab mobility, we can identify five major groups of countries that can be distinguished in terms of these aspects (see Figure 5).

Oman represents the media system with the fewest transnational connections: it neither invests in pan-Arab content, nor hires large numbers of non-Omani Arab media workers. It also does not have a strong and active diaspora involved in media production, and does not host foreign media. But this is actually rather atypical for the region, as we can observe by examining the other countries.

A second group, comprising Bahrain, Sudan, Libya, and Yemen, boasts substantial and active diasporas that produce a sizeable volume of media content from abroad. Libyan and Yemeni political actors, for example, operate entire systems of television channels from abroad, while Sudan and Bahrain have active exile communities that are highly present online. The content these online spaces or channels produce is aimed at target audiences in the given home countries. Therefore, the transnational element in question here is the diasporic media production and transmission back to the country of origin, rather than the transnational circulation of content or media workers outside their home countries in general.

A third, very large group, including the Maghreb's Morocco, Algeria, and Tunisia, in addition to Iraq and Palestine, accounts for the countries of origin of many media workers who operate the pan-Arab television stations in the Gulf, such as *Al-Jazeera* or *MBC*. Moreover, these states also enjoy substantial diasporas spread over the MENA region and throughout Europe, in particular in France. These diasporas often consume the media of their home countries as well as adding to media production through a set of (mainly online) diaspora media outlets. Yet again, the content produced on these platforms is not directed beyond the respective national communities at home or abroad.

A fourth group consists of the Gulf countries Qatar, the UAE, and Saudi Arabia. These states dedicate their media investments to pan-Arab outlets, producing content that primarily targets transnational audiences. As the recipients of media workforces from other Arab countries, they have succeeded in building real pan-Arab working hubs. All three countries also provide platforms and financial support to other Arab political actors, enabling them to set up media abroad and directly target their own national audiences. All three have, for example, supported Libyan political actors and their media activities, and Saudi Arabia has provided media space for Yemeni political groups that have fled their country. Although Jordan does not fit seamlessly in this group, it does to a certain extent provide space for foreign media production, and hosts many international media producers in its Jordan Media City. Ultimately, however, it cannot compete with the Gulf states as a new pan-Arab media hub. Finally, until the 1980s Kuwait had been a major hub for pan-Arab content and workforce, but it has since lost this position to the Gulf states on the other side of the shore.

A fifth and final group includes the traditional hubs of pan-Arab transnationalism, Lebanon and Egypt, with their transnationally-oriented television, serial and cinema production, strong diasporas, and circulating workforce. Both countries have shaped the transnational flows of Arab media for decades. Before the current war, Syria had also played a strong role in pan-Arab serial production and the circulating workforce, but its transnationalism has since shifted towards the diaspora model, due to a significant decline in media production.

Fig. 5: Transnational mobility and connection

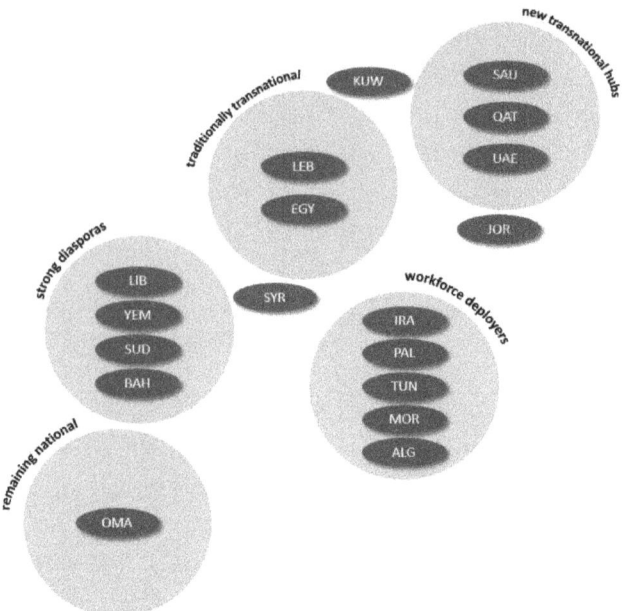

By identifying recurrent themes in the separate country chapters, and applying a comparative perspective when examining these themes, we tried to determine the similarities and differences among the 18 Arab media systems and thus provide an in-depth view of the current status quo regarding political, economic, societal, technological, and transnational dimensions. However, our analysis of different types of media systems should not be interpreted as suggesting that these types are set in stone. Developments in the region are so dynamic that the current situations displayed in our analysis and the figures included above should be understood as snapshots of a certain moment in time. The frequent lack of more accurate data in the MENA region still leaves us with uncertainty regarding many aspects. As a result, comparisons can only be tentative.

The Road Ahead: Challenges for Arab Media Systems

Finally, we will refer to some of the dynamic developments characteristic of the region, which also shape media landscapes globally, and whose directions and results cannot yet be predicted.

From the beginning, media in the MENA region have been tools for mobilization and modernization, and correspond to ownership patterns that reflect these approaches. Rarely in their history have they been considered as independent entities that exist to watch over the government and other ruling elites. Many of the Arab countries lack sustainable funding models for media beyond instrumental ownership by privileged actors. This has led to what the literature calls "media capture" (Schiffrin, 2018), that is, a state of affairs in which media outlets become a trading product of political or other actors who ensure an economic grip on it in order to remain in power. This kind of approach is no longer exclusively the domain of the state or its elites, but is also adopted by the business sector, security apparatuses, militias, and other political actors. The problem of media capture is certainly not limited to the MENA region, and has become a global phenomenon, as evident in European countries and the US. In some areas of the MENA region, community media, such as small radio stations or local online newspapers, which are in particular facilitated by the Internet, could evolve as alternatives to media capture on the national and transnational levels. Our authors highlight two main solutions to allow for a more autonomous and sustainable media environment: an accountable rule of law needs to be established for individuals inclined to invest time and money into media, and a real advertising market needs to be set up.

Another major challenge that will not be easily overcome is the fragmentation of societies that could ultimately result in the disintegration of entire countries, such as Syria, Yemen, and Libya, or in rising political and economic tensions, as in Iraq, Palestine, Lebanon, and Algeria. The fragmentation of societies and the concurrent instrumentalization of media by the various fragments are clear outcomes of these crises. Taking into consideration the historical developments and the colonial trajectories as well as the current (international) political interests in the Middle East and North Africa, we realize that crises are a common feature of the region, with only a few exceptions. The manifold transnational connections between the countries and the media systems, for example, investments in a joint *ArabSat* system or the pan-Arab workforce in many media channels, have not saved the region from infighting carried out via media. The recent outlawing of Qatar's *Al-Jazeera* by Saudi Arabia, the UAE, and Egypt is perhaps the most prominent example. Such infighting within or among states and the instrumentalization of media within them result in serious security risks for media workers, making journalism a dangerous occupation.

The digital transformation of the media is a major challenge globally, as well as regionally. Some Arab countries, in particular the wealthy Gulf states, seem to be well-placed to meet this challenge, thanks to their advanced infrastructure. They have the means to invest heavily in the latest technology and do so intentionally to respond to the pressing need to transform their economy from crude oil production to a more knowledge-based economy. Other MENA countries are lagging behind, which has created a digital divide in the region. Regardless of their progress, all these countries are faced with the question of Internet control and regulation, and what to permit and what to ban. In this context, several problems that are being discussed on a global level, such as data security, privacy, and prevention of disinformation and hate speech, present challenges that are crucial to authoritarian regimes in respect to their control of opinions and marginalizing the opposition. So far, it is not clear what the trend will be, considering that some regimes do not hesitate to slow or cut off Internet connections completely, as has been done in Iraq, or monitor content closely and impose cybercrime laws as in Egypt or Qatar and many other countries in the region.

The above challenges are critical and will affect all Arab media systems for the foreseeable future. Yet, the region has always shown strong dynamics and has even pioneered media-related developments. In Egypt, radio has long been exploited as a means of reaching out to the masses and creating stars, such as the singer Umm Kulthum and President Gamal Abdel Nasser in the 1960s. The immense role of satellite television in accessing not only national but transnational audiences has been largely driven by developments in the MENA region that had already started in the early 1990s. The Arab uprisings are ultimately connected to specific uses of social media that were unprecedented before 2010 or 2011 and that showed how savvy people could incorporate technologies into their political strategies. This inspired many movements all over the planet.

Arab media, the structures and systems behind the practices of their producers and users, and their impact and effects, will thus be of interest and relevance for many years to come.

References

Hallin, D. C., & Mancini, P. (2004). *Comparing media systems*. Cambridge: Cambridge University Press.

Rugh, W. A. (2004). *Arab mass media: Newspapers, radio, and television in Arab politics*. Westport: Praeger.

Schiffrin, A. (2018). Introduction to special issue on media capture. *Journalism*, *19*(8), 1033–42.

Siebert, F. S., Peterson, T., & Schramm, W. (1963). *Four theories of the press*. Urbana: University of Illinois Press.

Acknowledgements

The editors would like to thank Marilena Hohmann and Sabrina Schotten for their help in formatting and copyediting this book. We would also like to express our gratitude to the Jordan Media Institute (JMI), Amman, for hosting a motivating workshop to prepare this book. The Arab-German Young Academy of Science and Humanities (AGYA) has provided generous financial support for the preparation of this book. Finally, Freie Universität Berlin kindly supported the Open Access Publication with its funds.

Index

2M 306–307, 317
7amleh 49
7iber 67
9/11 136

Abbas, Ihsan 166
Abbas, Mahmoud 43, 47
Abboud, Ibrahim 238
Abdel Nasser, Gamal xxiv, 4, 58, 219–220, 252, 340
Abdul-Wahid, Shiswar 85
Abounaddara 31
Abu Dhabi 2nd Channel 112
Abu Dhabi Classic FM 119
Abu Dhabi Drama 119
Abu Dhabi FM 119
Abu Dhabi Media Company 117
Abu Dhabi Sports 1 119
Abu Dhabi Sports 2 119
Abu Dhabi TV 119
Abu Dhabi, UAE 109, 112, 115, 118
Addustour 58, 65
Aden 200, 202
Aden News Agency 202
Aden TV 201
Aden, Yemen 200–202, 207–209
Afaq 84
Afghanistan 135–136
Africa 215, 218, 233, 249, 268, 272, 278, 285, 303
Africa, East 183–184, 236
African Revolution 289
African Union 217
Africa, sub-Saharan xii, xiii, 303
Afriquia 305
AfroShirazi Party 184

Ahl Al-Bayt 85
Ahmad, Abdul Hamid 122
Ajam 147
AJL-TV 95
Ajman Radio Four 117
Ajman, UAE 109
Ajroudi, Mohammed Ayachi 277
Akamai Technologies 86
Akhannouch, Aziz 315
Akhbar Al-Jumhuriyah 280
Akhbar Al-Khaleej 149, 156
Akhbar Al-Khaleej Press 156
Akhenouch, Abdelaziz 314
Al-Abadi, Haydar 84
Al-Abed, Ibrahim 122
Al-Adwa 155
Al-'Ahd 131
Al-Ahd 84
Al-Ahram 3, 218, 225–226, 242
alain_4u 123
Al-Akhbar (Egypt) 219, 225
Al-Akhbar (Lebanon) 3, 5, 11
Al-Akhbar (Yemen) 201
Al-Akkad, Abbas 166
Al-Amal 271
Al-Anba' 11. *See also* Progressive Socialist Party
Al-Anbaa 172
Al-Aqeek 203
Al-Aqsa TV 43, 49, 98
Al-Arab 65, 74, 76, 131–132, 154, 159
Al-Arab Al-Yawm 65
Al-Arabi 166
Al-Arabiya xiii, 96, 104, 118, 206
Al-Araby 132

Al-Araby TV 138
Al-Araby Al-Jadeed 82, 132, 138, 229
Al-Armanazi, Najib 22
Al-Assad, Bashar 23–25, 29, 33
Al-Assad, Hafez 21, 23
Al-Assad, Maher 29
Al-Assema TV 257
Al-Aswany, Alaa 132
Al-Awqaf Al-Basriyya 76
Al-Ayam 149, 156, 318
Al-Ayam Press 156
Al-Ayyam 22, 242
Al-Azhar Institute 216
Al-Ba'ath 23. See also Ba'ath Party
Al-Babiliya 82
Al-Bakir, Abdulrahman 148
Al-Balad 12, 30
Al-Bashir, Omar 236–244
Al-Basra 76
Al-Bawwaba 273
Al-Bayan 112
Al-Bayda, Libya 255
Al-Bazzaz, Sa'ad 84
Al-Bina' 11. See also Syrian Socialist Nationalist Party
Al-Bitha 166
Alcomsat-1 297
Al-Dabbas, Fadhil 84
Al-Dawri 131
Al-Difa'a 59
Al-Din, Mayzar Nizam 24
Al-Diyar 11
Al-Doha 130
Al-Dustour 270
Al-Ekhbariyya 96–97, 103–104
Al-Emarat TV 119
Aleppo, Syria 20–21, 26, 31
Alexandria, Egypt 216, 219–220
Alfa 13
Al-Fajr 270, 273
Al-Falaq 184, 191
Al-Fallooja 85
Al-Furat 84, 87

Algeria xix, xxi, xxiii, xxiv, xxv, xxxi, xxxv, xxxvii, 41, 268–269, 285–300, 303–304, 326, 329, 332, 335, 337, 339
   1991 Finance Act 294
   Audiovisual Regulatory Authority (ARAV) 293
   Business Leaders Forum (FCE) 293
   Criminal Procedure Code 293
   French Press Law (1881) 287
   High Media Council 292
   High State Council (HSC) 292
   Information Law (1982) 291
   Information Law (1990) 290–291
   Ministry of Communication 299
   Ministry of Industry 297
   Ministry of Information 292
   Ministry of Information and Culture 291
   Ministry of Post and Telecommunications 297–298
   National Publishing and Advertising Company (ANEP) 295
   Organic Audiovisual Law 295
   Print Press Regulatory Authority 292
   Radio and Television Company 288
Algeria 3 288
Algeria News 299
Algeria Press Agency (APS) 297
Algérie 24 295
Algérie Confidentiel 295
Algérie Télécom 298
Al-Ghad 65–66, 254
Al-Ghadeer 84
Al-Gomhoriah 201
Al-Gomhouriya 219, 225
Al-Hadirah 270
Al-Hakeem, Ammar 87
Al-Hammadi, Mohammed 122
Al-Haqq Ya'alu 57
Al-Hayah 226
Al-Hayat 42, 100
Al-Hayat Al-Jadida 42
Al-Haya Tijariyya 155
Al-Hekma Al-Yamaniya 200

Al-Hikma 57
Al-Hiwar Ettounsi 277
Al-Hmayyim, Abdul-Lateef 85
Ali, Ahmad 137
Al-Iman 200, 202, 205
Ali, Mohammed 218
Al-Insen 275
Al-Intibaha 242
Al-Iqtissadiya 29
Al-Iraqiyya 81
Al-Ittihad 41, 112, 118
Al-Ittijah 84
Al-Jadeed 7, 9, 11, 13, 15
   New TV 11
Al-Jamahiriya TV 256
Al-Jamri, Mansour 152
Al-Janoubia 275
Al-Jazeera xxvii, xxxv, 43, 82, 95–96, 101, 104, 127, 129, 131–132, 135–136, 138–141, 159–160, 206, 210, 329, 333, 337, 340
   Al-Jazeera America 136
   Al-Jazeera Arabic 135–136
   Al-Jazeera Balkan 136
   Al-Jazeera Children's Channel 136
   Al-Jazeera Documentary 136
   Al-Jazeera English 136
   Al-Jazeera Mubasher 135–136
   Al-Jazeera Sport 136. See also beIN Sports
   Al-Jazeera Turk 136
Al-Jihad 59
Al-Jumhouriyya 11
Al-Kaaki, Awni 11
Al-Kalima 273
Al-Karbooli, Jamal 85
Al-Kateab, Waad 31
   For Sama 31
Al-Kawakibi, Abdul Rahman 21
Al-Khaleej 111, 117
Al-Khalifa, Ahmed Atayatalla 153
Al-Khalifa family 146–149, 153–154, 156
Al-Khalifa, Fawaz bin Mohammed bin Khalifa 153

Al-Khalifa, Hamad bin Salman 146–147, 150–151
Al-Khalifa, Isa bin Salman 150
Al-Khalifa, Khalifa bin Salman 150, 160
Al-Khalifa, Salman bin Hamad 160
Al-Khanjar, Khamees 85
Al-Kharousi, Ahmad bin Saif 184
Al-Khartoum 242
Al-Khazen, Jihad 100
Al-Khedive Journal 218
Al-Libiya TV 254, 256
Allied Forces 200, 236
Al-Liwa' 11–12
Al-Liwa'a 218
Al-Madar 261
Al-Maghribia 314
Al-Mahdi, Mohammed Ahmed 235
Al-Malaeb 188
Al-Maliki, Noori 84
Al-Mamlaka TV 63–64, 70
Al-Manar 9, 11, 58, 98
Al-Masar 84
Al-Maseerah 203
Al-Mash'al 130
Al-Mashriq 84
Al-Masry Al-Youm 225
Al-Mayal, Mubarak 167
Al-Mishishi, Hisham 280
Al-Mishraq 85
Al-Mithaq 57
Al-Mizan 148
Al-Mo'ayed 218
Al-Mosul 76
Al-Mudarrisi, Hadi 85
Al-Mudhik Al-Mubki 22
Al-Mujtama' Al-Jadid 155
Al-Mukattam 218
Al-Murr family 9, 11
Al-Murshid 184
Al-Mustakbal 11, 13. See also Future Movement
Al-Mutawasit TV 280
Al-Nabaa 259
Al-Na'eem 84

Al-Nahar TV 226
Al-Nahda 184
Al-Nahdah Net 273
Al-Nahyan, Zayed bin Sultan 109
Al-Najah 184
Al-Naqi, Najla 175
Al-Nujaba' 84
Al-Nusif, Waleed 170
Al-Qabas 22, 170, 172
Al-Qabbani, Nizar 166
Al-Qadhafi, Mu'ammar 249–255, 258, 260–262
Al-Qadhafi, Saif Al-Islam 254, 256
Al-Qafila 148
Al-Quds 39, 59, 131
Al-Quds Al-Sharif 39
Al-Quds Education TV (AETV) 42, 46
Al-Quds University 42
Al-Qur'an Al-Kareem 172
Al-Rafidayn 85
Al-Raid Al-Tunisi 270
Al-Rai (Jordan) 59, 61, 64–66
Al-Rai (Kuwait) 172
Al-Rai TV 172
Al-Rasheed 85
Al-Rasheed, Abdulaziz 166
Al-Rasid 84
Al-Rawahi, Nasser bin Salim bin Odeiam 184
Al-Raya 132, 137
Al-Rayah 201
Al-Rayyan TV 131, 137
Al-Rayyes, Najib 22
Al-Risalah 43
Al-Riyadh 95
Al-Roya 188
Al-Roya Press and Publishing 188
Al-Roya Radio Voice 188
Al-Sabah 81, 83, 86, 164, 167, 271
Al-Sabah family 164
Al-Sabah, Mubarak 164
Al-Sabah, Rasha 175
Al-Sabah, Sabah Al-Ahmed Al-Jaber 169
Al-Sabah, Sabah bin Jaber 164

Al-Saeeda TV 203
Al-Safir 5, 12
Al-Sahafa 242
Al-Sahat 203, 206
Al-Said, Qaboos bin Said 181, 186
Al-Said, Sayyed Saif bin Hamoud 184
Al-Salam 85
Al-Samarra'i, Ma'mool 84
Al-Saqr 130
Al-Sarraj, Fayaz 256
Al-Sa'ud, Al-Waleed bin Talal 154
Al-Sa'ud family 92, 101. *See also* Ibn Sa'ud; *See also* bin Salman, Mohammed
Al-Saudiyya 95
Al-Sayegh Media 117
Al-Seyasah 172
Al-Shababiya 254
Al-Shabaka 81, 86
Al-Shabiba 186, 188
Al-Shahba 21
Al-Sharq 57, 95, 132, 137, 229
Al-Sharq Al-Arabi 57. *See also The Official Gazette of the Hashemite Kingdom of Jordan*
Al-Sharqiya 84, 86
Al-Shaykh family 92
Al-Sherian, Daoud 96
Al-Shula 148
Al-Shurooq 239, 243
Al-Sudan 235
Al-Sudani 242
Al-Sumariyya 84
Al-Taie family 188
Al-Taie, Nasr bin Mohammed 184
Al-Talia' 270
Al-Tayr, Wissam 32
Al-Thani family 127–128
Al-Thani, Hamad bin Khalifa 128–129, 131, 133–135
Al-Thani, Tamim bin Hamad 128, 140
Al-Thawra 78, 201, 206
Al-Thawrah 208
Al-Tunisi 270
Al-Umma 130

Al-Urdun 57
Al-Urooba 130
Al-Ustaz 218
Al-Wafa'a 57
Al-Wahda 23. *See also* Ba'ath Party
Al-Wala' 85
Al-Waqt 152
Al-Wasat 152–153, 156
Al-Waseet 30
Al-Watan 29, 131–132, 137, 148, 152, 156, 172, 184, 186, 188, 242
Al-Watania TV1 275
Al-Watania TV2 275
Al-Watania Network 281–282
Al Watan TV 289
Al-Wefaq 154
Al-Yemen 202, 205
Al-Youm Al-Sabea 226
Al-Youm Al-Sabi' 188
Al-Zahf Al-Akhdar 253
Al-Zaman 86
Al-Zawra' 76
Al-Zidjali family 188
Amal Movement 11
Amazigh 216, 250, 286, 303, 304, 308. *See also* Imazighen (Berbers)
Amazigh Spring 286
Amman, Jordan 55, 58, 63–64, 66, 206–207, 259
AmmanNet 64
Ammon News 60, 67
Amouda, Syria 27
Ana Zahra 119
Anbar, Iraq 79
Ankawa, Iraq 75
An-Nahar 4, 10–12
Anti-Terrorism Law (2003) 312
Aoun, Michel 6, 9
Arabian American Oil Company (ARAMCO) 95
Arabian Gulf. *See* Persian Gulf (Arabian Gulf)
Arabian Peninsula xxxvii, 91, 93, 127, 163–164, 182, 197, 200
Arabian Sea 197

Arabic (language) xii, 3, 14, 27, 38–40, 43–44, 64–65, 75–76, 78, 91, 94–95, 110–112, 128, 131–132, 135–136, 141, 146, 148–150, 152, 156, 164, 172, 183, 185–188, 198, 200, 216, 218, 222, 233–234, 239, 251, 268–271, 286–289, 293–295, 297, 300, 303, 306, 333
Arab Journalism Award 116. *See also* Dubai Press Club
Arab League xiii, xxxv, 60, 103, 130, 182, 258
Arab Charter on Human Rights 60
Arab Media Corporation 66
Arab Media Forum 116. *See also* Dubai Press Club
Arab Media Outlook 116. *See also* Dubai Press Club
Arab News 95, 100
Arab Revolt 55
ArabSat xxxv, 103, 139, 150, 202, 209, 258, 340
Arab Satellite Organization 103
Arab Spring (uprisings) xix, xxiv, xxvi, 57, 131, 135–137, 176, 199, 217, 224, 228, 230, 237, 249, 268, 289, 292, 304, 309, 340
Arab States Broadcasting Union 66, 130
Arab Writers Union 122
Arafat, Yasser 43, 46
Armenian language 75
Arriadiya 314
ART xxxv, 99–100
Arta FM 27, 30
Asfour, Jaber 166
Asharq Al-Awsat 82, 100
Asia xii, 39, 74, 84, 91, 109, 128, 146, 148, 183, 333
Asia 132, 215
Asia Cell 86
Asiri, Ghadeer 175
As-Safir 4
Assembly of Catholic Patriarchs and Bishops 9
Assurour 270
Aswat 314

Atheer 191
Atlantic Ocean 303
Atlas Travel & Culture 156
Atlas TV 289
attacks 39, 43, 52, 82, 96–98, 104, 257, 304, 312, 327
Attessia TV 275
Attounissia 275
Aujourd'hui Le Maroc 315
Austria xxvii
Ayish, Mohammad xx, 109
Ayoub, Charles 11
Azzahra 270

Ba'ath Party 20–23, 25, 78
Baghdad, Iraq
    xiii, 74, 75, 76, 77, 78, 85, 86
Baghdadiya 82
Baghdad Radio 77
baḥārna 146–147
Bahrain xxiv, xxv, xxvii, xxx, xxxv, xxxvii, 91, 102, 119, 128–129, 140, 145–160, 189, 327, 329, 332, 334, 336
    Bahrain Island 145
    High Authority for Media and Communication (HAMC) 154
    Information Affairs Authority (IAA) 153
    Ministry of Information 150–151
    Ministry of Information Affairs (MIA) 153–154
    Ministry of the Interior 154, 158
    National Democratic Institute 152
    Press Law (2002) 151–152, 155–156
Bahrain Broadcasting Station 148
Bahrain Medical Association 149
Bahrain Petroleum Company (BAPCO) 149
Bahrain Radio 149, 153, 156
Bahrain TV (BTV) 150, 153
    Channel 4 150
Baladna 29
Balfour Declaration 37
Baluchi (language) 183
Bangladesh xxvi, 183

Barada 23. *See also* Ba'ath Party
Barazani, Masood 85
Barid Barqa 251
Basra, Iraq 75–76, 88
Batelco 158
BBC 40, 66, 80–81, 136, 139, 166, 210, 224, 260, 329
    Empire Service 40
Bedouin 165, 216
beIN Sports 136, 138, 139. *See also* Al-Jazeera: Al-Jazeera Sport
Beirut, Lebanon
    xiii, 3, 7, 100, 203, 206, 207
    Martyrs' Square 3
Beja people 234
Belaïd, Chokri 274
Belgium xxvii
Belgrave, Charles 148
Belhimer, Ammar 300
Belkhayat, Mouncif 314
Belqees 203, 206
ben Ahmed, Bashir 272
Ben Ali, Zain El-Abidin 267–270, 272–273, 275, 277, 279, 281
Benchemsi, Ahmed 313
Bendjedid, Chadli 292
Benghazi Broadcasting Network 257
Benghazi, Libya 250, 254–255, 262
ben Hassine, Tahar 277
Benjelloun, Othman 315
ben Salem, Oussama 277
Berbers. *See* Imazighen (Berbers)
Berri, Nabih 9, 11
Bidayyat 31
Biladi 84
bin Laden, Osama 236
bin Salman, Mohammed 91, 94, 96, 98, 99, 100, 102, 104, 105, 159. *See also* Al-Sa'ud family
Bishara, Azmi 138
Bizerte, Tunisia 269
Bloomberg 118
Blue Nile 239
Blum, Roger xviii, xx, xxv, xxxi, xxxii
Bonaparte, Napoleon 218

Bosnia and Herzegovina 136
Bourguiba, Habib 267–272, 274, 277, 281
Bouteflika, Abdel-Aziz 289, 293
Brahmi, Mohammed 274
Bravo 102
Bremer, Paul 79
British 199, 218
British colonial rule xxiii, 40, 45, 73, 77, 78, 111, 147, 148, 149, 164, 197, 200, 201, 219, 235, 239, 246. *See also* colonialism
British Mandate 37, 39–40, 45, 56, 251–252
British protectorates 127–128, 145, 148, 164, 218
broadcasting
    public service xxx, 270, 274, 329
Broadcasting Service of the Kingdom of Saudi Arabia (BSKSA) 99
Buddhism 128

Cairo, Egypt xiii, 98, 166, 168, 203, 206, 216, 218–220, 227
    Maspero television building 220
    Tahrir Square 222
Canal Algérie 288
Caractères Media Group 315
Carey, James xvi
Carthage+ 275
Casablanca, Morocco 304–305, 307, 312, 316, 318
censorship xxix, 22, 24–25, 32, 39, 45–47, 51, 97, 133–135, 137, 151, 158, 163, 174, 176–178, 191, 206, 222, 228, 236, 238, 257, 272, 276, 278–279, 283, 287, 292, 298, 300, 307, 312, 324, 328
Central African Republic 233
Centrale Danone 305
Ceuta, Morocco 306
Chad 233, 253
Chadwick, Andrew xiv, xxxiv
Chamoun, Camille 8
Channel 33 112
Chaqroun, Meriem Bensaleh 315
Chehab, Fu'ad 6
Chile 38

China 183, 297
Chouftv 306
Christianity xxv, 2, 4, 20, 38, 75–76, 110, 128, 138, 164, 234, 285, 304
    Catholicism 9, 11, 164
    Coptic Christianity xxv, 216–217, 332
    Maronite Christianity 6, 11
    Orthodox Christianity xxv
    Protestantism 164
civil war 2–6, 8, 55–56, 100, 131, 157, 236, 238, 274, 331
Classical Music Radio 112
clientelism 6–7, 293, 296, 299, 315, 318
CNN 96, 101, 104, 118, 136, 139, 150
Coalition Provisional Authority (CPA) 79–81
Cold War xv, xxiii, 20, 61
colonialism xii, xiii, xxiii, xxxvii, 1, 22, 39, 109, 197, 200, 201, 216, 219, 235, 236, 237, 239, 250, 251, 252, 269, 270, 285, 286, 287, 288, 289, 306, 339. *See also* French colonial rule; *See also* Italian colonial rule; *See also* British colonial rule
Committee to Protect Journalists (CPJ) 50
community radio 27, 202, 206, 208, 263. *See also* radio stations
Comoros, the xiii
Compagnie Libanaise de Télévision (CLT) 3
confessionalism xxv, 25, 83, 330, 332, 335. *See also* sectarianism
Congress for the Republic (CPR) 274
conservatism 26, 92, 105, 110, 124, 141, 150, 153, 160, 211, 216–217, 251
Coptic Church. *See* Christianity: Coptic Christianity
COVID-19 pandemic 7, 64, 66–67, 70
Curran, James xvi
cybercrime xxx, 14, 16, 32, 62, 102, 114, 122, 134, 176, 224, 334, 340

Daher, Pierre 11
Daily Star 12, 100
Damascus, Syria 20, 24, 28, 32
Daniel, Jamal 12

Daraj 12
Darayya, Syria 28
Darfur, Sudan 234, 236, 332
Darwish, Mazen 26
Dashti, Rula 175
Dasma, Kuwait 168
Defa'a Al-Sha'ab 201
Deir ez-Zor, Syria 26
Democratic Union Party (PYD) 25, 33
Denmark xxvii, 127
Derki, Talal 31
   Of Fathers and Sons 31
development xiii, xvi, xvii, xxii, xxiii, xxix, xxx, 19, 23–24, 27–28, 30, 32, 37, 39–40, 44, 49, 51, 55, 63, 66, 70, 77, 87, 94, 104, 109–111, 113–114, 116, 120, 122–124, 129–131, 134, 145, 154, 168, 173, 178, 181–182, 186, 189, 192, 211, 221, 233, 246, 251, 267, 274, 285, 288, 291, 298, 300, 307–308, 311, 316–317, 327, 330, 335
Dhammam, Saudi Arabia 93
diaspora xxxvi, 37, 43, 51–52, 244, 272–273, 314, 336–338
Digitürk 138
Dijla 85
Dilami, Abdelmounaim 314
Diwan 85
diwaniya 166, 175–176
Diyala, Iraq 75
Djerba, Tunisia 268
Djezzy 298
Djibouti xiii, xxxv
DMC 227
Doha Institute 138
Doha News 139
Doha, Qatar 130–131, 138–139, 260
Downing, John xv
Dream TV 226–227
du 120
Dubai Media Incorporated 117–119
Dubai Post 123
Dubai Press Club 116. *See also* Arab Journalism Award; *See also* Arab Media Outlook

Dubai Press Outlook. *See also* Arab Media Forum
Dubai Technology and Free Zone Authority (DTFZA) 115
Dubai TV 117
Dubai, UAE 28, 30, 34, 96, 109, 112, 115–119, 189, 226
Duhok, Iraq 74–75
Dungulawi (language) 234
Duraz, Bahrain 159
Dzaïr News 293
Dzaïr TV 289, 293

East Asia xii, 148
Eastern Europe xvi
Easy 172
Echourouk TV 289
EcoMédias Group 315
economic crisis xv, 6–7, 10, 15–16, 23, 65, 83, 119, 168, 253
Education 42, 130
Egypt xviii, xix, xxi, xxiii, xxiv, xxv, xxxi, xxxii, xxxiii, xxxv, xxxvi, xxxvii, 3–4, 13, 19, 30, 34, 38, 41–42, 58, 96, 98, 100, 112, 128, 131–132, 136, 140, 149–150, 159, 166–168, 189, 215–224, 226–230, 233–234, 252, 274, 327, 329, 332, 335, 337, 340
   Central Agency for Public Mobilization and Statistics (CAPMAS) 217
   Cybercrime Law (2018) 224
   Egyptian Constitution 219, 221–222
   Ministry of Communications and Information Technology 228
   Ministry of Information 221–222
   National Media Authority 222, 226
   National Media Council 222
   National Press Authority 222
   Supreme Council of the Armed Forces (SCAF) 223
   Supreme Media Regulatory Council 222, 227, 230
Egyptian Journalists' Syndicate 224
Egyptian Media Group (EMG) 226
Egyptian Radio and Television Union (ERTU) 220, 226–227

Channel 1 220, 226
Channel 2 220, 226
Egyptian Satellite Channel 227
Egypt Post 229
Egypt Telecom 229
El-Adjwa 299
El-Alami, Moulay Hafid 314–315
El-Attar, Hashem 21
El-Chaab 289
El-Chibak 295
El-Chourouk 295, 298–299
El-Chourouk El-Arabi 295
El-Chourouk Markets 295
El-Chourouk News 295
El-Chourouk Sport 295
El-Chourouk TV 295
El Djazairia One 289
El-Echourouk Bana 295
El-Hiwar Ettounsi 275
El Karoui, Nabil 277
El-Khabar 293–294, 300
El-Khuri, Bechara 3
El-Mehwar 227
El-Moudjahid 288, 289. *See also* National Liberation Front (FLN)
El-Nahar 298–299
El-Nasr 289
El-Richani, Sarah xxiv, 1, 324
El-Sadat, Anwar 220
El-Sayyegh, Habib 122
El-Sharq 11
El-Watan 294, 300
Emarat FM 119
Emirate of Transjordan 56
Emirates 24/7 119
Enab Baladi 28, 30
English (language) 27, 44, 64, 91, 94–96, 100, 110, 112, 128, 130–132, 139, 141, 146, 148–150, 155–156, 164, 172, 183, 185–187, 201, 208, 216, 220, 288, 333
English-language 12
Ennahar El-Djadid 295
Ennahar TV 289
Ennahda 273–274, 277

Erbil, Iraq 74–75
Eritrea 135, 233
Es'hailSat xxxv, 139
Essebsi, Beji Caid 274
Ethiopia 233, 242
Etisalat Telecom 120, 229
Ettakatol 274
Euro-Mediterranean Partnership (EuroMed) 61
Europe i, xii, xvi, xxi, xxiii, xxvii, xxix, 3, 12, 24, 27, 29–30, 34, 61, 74, 127, 150, 217–218, 245, 268, 272, 288, 303, 330, 337, 339
European Broadcasting Union 66
Extra News 226
Ezzitouna 275

Facebook 15, 32, 50–51, 65, 67, 84, 121, 139, 158, 174, 191, 210, 221, 228, 244, 261, 273, 278–280, 298, 306, 313, 318
Fadaat Media Group 28, 138
Failaka Island, Kuwait 168
Faisal, King of Saudi Arabia 94–95, 97
Falastin 39, 45
Fanon, Frantz 288
Fatah 43–44, 331
Fayyad, Feras 31
  Last Men in Aleppo 31
  The Cave 31
Febrayer 257
February TV 257
Federal Law (15)
  Federal Law 15 (1980) 112
Filali, Amina 304
First TV 280
Fodil, Ali 295
Folklore Radio 112
Fourth Industrial Revolution 120
Fox Sports 139
Foz, Samer 29–30
France xxiii, xxvii, 3, 19, 22, 30, 40, 55, 183, 218–219, 269, 288, 298, 306, 337
Freedom House xxviii, 223, 312
Free Patriotic Movement 9, 11

French Agency for Media Cooperation 296
French colonial rule xxiii, 19, 218, 269, 270, 285, 286, 287, 306. *See also* colonialism
French (language) 130, 216, 218, 220, 268–269, 286–289, 293–294, 300, 315
French Mandate 3, 22
Fujairah, UAE 109
Funoon TV 172
Furqan 81
Futon 188
Future Media 5, 13
Future Movement 11. *See also Al-Mustakbal*
Future TV 5, 9, 11, 13
 Future News 13

Galander, Mahmoud xx, xxi
Gaza Strip 38–41, 43–45, 47, 49–50, 140, 216
General People's Congress (GPC) party 208
German (language) 220
Germany xviii, xxvii, 148, 183, 200
Ghannouchi, Rashid 274
Ghrer, Hussein 26
Global South xvii, 114
Golan Heights 66
Google 50, 65, 227, 306, 313, 318
Gordon, Charles 235
GPC 211
Grand FM 209
Great Britain xxiii, 40, 55, 109, 127, 128, 129, 147, 165, 200, 218, 219, 236, 253. *See also* British colonial rule; *See also* British Mandate; *See also* British protectorates
Greece xvi, 9, 11, 73
Gulf Cooperation Council (GCC) 119, 129, 140, 142, 168, 171, 182
Gulf Daily News 149, 156
Gulf News 112, 122, 130
Gulf of Aden 197
Gulf states xiii, xxi, xxvi, xxxi, xxxii, xxxv, 66, 68, 128–129, 140, 146, 148, 150, 157, 163–168, 174, 189, 221, 327, 332, 334, 337, 340
Gulf Times 132, 134, 137
Gulf War 96, 101, 104, 136, 150
Gulf Weekly Mirror 155
Gwadar, Pakistan 183

HACA 309, 311, 314, 318
Hachten, William xvi
Haddad, Ali 293, 295
Hadi, Abed Rabbo Mansur 199
Hadikat Al-Akhbar 3
Hadith 130, 234
Hadramout, Yemen 207–209
Hafez, Hisham 100
Hafez, Mohammed Ali 100
Hafez, Salah El-Din 221
 Sorrows of the Press Freedoms 221
Haftar, Khalifa 255
hajj 92, 103
Hallin, Daniel xvi, xvii, xviii, xxii, xxiv, xxv, xxviii, xxxii, xxxiii, 325
Hamas 43–45, 50–51, 98, 140, 331
Hama, Syria 24
Hamsho, Mohammad 29
Hannibal TV 275, 277
Hariri, Rafik 4–5, 9, 11–13
Hariri, Saad 13
Hasakah, Syria 26
Hashemite Broadcasting System (HBS) 40
Hassan II of Morocco 307–308
Haute Autorité de la Communication Audiovisuelle (HACA) 309
Haute Autorité Indépendante de la Communication Audiovisuelle (HAICA) 267, 275–277, 282
Hebrew (language) 220
Hespress 306, 313
Hezbollah 5, 9, 11–12, 98, 140, 154
Hijaz, Saudi Arabia 94
Hikma Movement 84, 87
Hindi (language) 146
Hinduism 110, 128, 164
Hirak Protests 57, 62, 63, 68. *See also* protest

Hitradio 314
Hogar TV 289
Holy Qur'an 201, 289
Homs, Syria 20, 24
Hot Bird 139
Houthi movement 198–199, 203, 205–207, 211, 330
Human Rights Watch 199, 206, 257, 273
Huna Baghdad 84
Hussain, Taha 166
Hussein, Saddam 78, 80, 96, 152
Hutchins Commission (Commission on Freedom of the Press) xv

Ibn Sa'ud 91, 93, 94, 95, 101. *See also* Al-Sa'ud family
ICT Development Index 317
Idris, King of Libya 251–252
Idris, Youssef 166
Imam Yahya 200
Imazighen (Berbers) xxv, 250, 268, 286, 304, 309, 332. *See also* Amazigh
independence xii, xxiii, xxix, 3, 6, 19–20, 22, 32, 37, 56, 58, 61, 63, 69, 109, 128, 130, 145, 147, 149, 151, 165, 167, 176, 178, 200, 222, 233, 235–237, 239, 241, 246, 250, 252, 267, 269–270, 277, 281, 286, 288–291, 306–307, 315
   of media xxix, 27, 68, 77, 192, 228, 282, 310
India xxvi, 183, 218
Indian Ocean 109, 183
Indian subcontinent 186
Indonesia 102
Ingessana people 234
Instagram 15, 84, 139, 158, 170, 174, 210, 278
Institute of Modern Media (IMM) 42
International Federation of Journalists (IFJ) 29, 206
International Middle East Media Center 44, 52
International Monetary Fund (IMF) 111
International Telecommunication Union (ITU) 14, 31, 120, 229

Internet xiii, xxiv, xxvi, xxvii, xxxiii, xxxiv, xxxv, xxxvi, 8, 14–15, 24–25, 31–33, 38, 44–45, 49–50, 52, 62, 66–69, 78, 83–84, 86, 102, 115, 119–121, 139–140, 157–158, 171, 173–175, 177, 185, 187, 191, 206–207, 209–210, 221, 228, 242–246, 260–262, 273, 275, 278, 296–298, 300, 305, 307, 309, 314, 316–317, 325, 334–335, 339–340
intifada 39, 147, 150
   First Intifada 41–42, 45
   Second Intifada 42–43, 49
invasion xix, 74, 78, 113, 135–136, 168, 182, 269, 285, 327
Inwi 316
Iram FM 208
Iran xii, xviii, xxiii, 8, 12, 19–20, 74–75, 83, 88, 92, 100–101, 135, 140, 145, 147, 149, 154, 168, 181–183
Iraq xix, xxi, xxiii, xxiv, xxv, xxvi, xxx, xxxi, xxxiii, xxxv, xxxvii, 31, 41, 55–56, 73–88, 135, 137, 149, 152, 163, 167–168, 182, 326–327, 329–332, 335, 337, 339–340
   Ministry of Communication 78
   Ministry of Information 80
   National Communications and Media Commission 80–81
   Penal Law No. 11 (1969) 81
      Defamation Articles 82
   Publications Law No. 206 (1968) 81
   Radio Tax Law (1938) 77
   Rights of Journalists Law (2011) 82
   State Company for Internet Services (SCIS) 78
   Transitional Iraqi State Administration Law (2004) 79
Iraqi Commission for Broadcasting and Transmitting Services 80
Iraqi Media Network (IMN) 80–81, 83–84, 86, 88
Iraqiyya Radio 81
Isis Film Company 220
Islam xii, xxv, 2, 20, 43, 55, 73, 75, 79, 85, 92–94, 97, 110, 115, 128, 130, 134, 152, 164, 171, 198, 204, 215–216, 234–236,

239, 251, 268, 285–287, 292, 304, 312, 332
Islamic Dawa Party 84
Islamic Salvation Front (FIS) 292
Islamic State (IS/ISIS) 30, 33, 75–76, 79, 88, 216, 251
Islamism 28, 104–105, 131–132, 156, 169, 223, 236–237, 243, 251, 255, 259, 273, 332
Israel xxiii, 1–2, 4–5, 19–20, 22, 37–46, 48–52, 55–56, 58, 70, 88, 98, 135, 137–138, 198, 325
   Ministry of the Interior 45
Istanbul, Turkey 28, 98, 138, 203, 206–207, 229, 259–260
   Khedive Palace 219
Italian colonial rule 250–252
Italy xviii, xxiii
I-Watch 279

Jadu, Libya 258
Jamai, Aboubakr 313
JANA 253, 257
Janoubia TV 277
Jaridat Al-Bahrain 148
Jawaher El-Chourouk 295
Jebali, Hamadi 273
Jeddah, Saudi Arabia 94–95, 100
Jerusalem, Israel 38–40, 45, 56, 58
Jeune Afrique 272
Jihadism 259
Jordan xix, xxi, xxiii, xxvii, xxix, xxxiii, xxxv, xxxvii, 21, 29, 37–38, 40–42, 55–70, 74, 112, 139, 181, 189, 259, 327, 329, 332, 335, 337
   Access to Information Law (2007) 62
   Audiovisual Media Law (2002) 60
   Competition Law 65
   Court of Cassation 62
   Independent Public Service Broadcasting Channel Bylaw (2016) 63
   Law for Political Parties (1993) 61
   Media Commission 62
   Merger Law (1967) 58
   Ministry of Information 40, 61
   Penal Code 62
   Press and Publication Law (1993) 59
   Press Association Law 69
   Publication Law (1993) 61
   Radio and Television Corporation Law 63
   Jordan Press Association 63
   Jordan Press Foundation 59
   Jordan Radio and Television (JRTV) 64–66, 70
Jordan TV (JTV) 59, 63–64
Jo TV 64
journalism i, xxxii, xxxiii, 22, 40–41, 57–58, 67, 69, 76–77, 87, 116, 122, 145, 158, 177–178, 184, 200, 202–206, 211, 215, 218, 220–224, 226–230, 234–235, 238, 253–254, 257, 263, 271, 273, 280–282, 301, 317, 324–325, 329, 340
Judaism xxv, 37, 198, 268, 304

Kahaleh, Habib 22
Kalb Tounis 277
Kanar 243
Karbala 85
Karman, Tawakkol 203
KBC Television 299
Khafji, Saudi Arabia 168
Khalaf, Abdulhadi 152
Khaleej Times 112
Khalil Tounis 277
Khan, Mohammed 167
Kharabeesh 67
Khartoum, Sudan 235, 238, 242
Khartoum University Radio 238
Khashoggi, Jamal 91, 98, 104
King Fahd Sea Causeway 145
King Faisal. *See* Faisal, King of Saudi Arabia
King Hassan II. *See* Hassan II of Morocco
King Idris. *See* Idris, King of Libya
King Mohammed VI. *See* Mohammed VI of Morocco
Kirkuk, Iraq 75, 77
Korek Telecom 86

Kraidy, Marwan xxiii, xxxiii
Kurdish Democratic Party 85
Kurdish National Council 27
Kurdistan 31, 74, 76, 85
Kurds xiii, xxv, 19–20, 25–27, 30–31, 33–34, 75–78, 85, 87
Kuwait xiii, xix, xxi, xxiii, xxxv, xxxvii, 12–13, 56, 74–75, 78, 100–102, 119, 163–178, 182, 258, 328–329, 332, 334, 337
  Audio and Visual Media Law (2007) 172
  Communication and Information Technology Regulatory Authority (CITRA) 171
  Cyber Crimes Law (2016) 176
  Kuwaiti Constitution 171
  Ministry of Communication 171, 173
  Ministry of Information 167–168, 171–173, 177–178
  Ministry of Interior 167
  National Assembly 169, 176, 178
  Press and Publication Law (1961) 171
  Press and Publication Law (2010) 171, 177
Kuwait Radio One 172
Kuwait Radio Two 172
Kuwait TV 167–168
  Al-Qurain 173
  KTV1 170, 173
  KTV2 173
  KTV Al-Majlis 173
  KTV Arabe 173
  KTV Ethra 173
  KTV Sports 173
  KTV Sports Plus 173

L'Action Tunisienne 271
Lahlou, Kamal 314
LANA 257
Lana FM 208
La Nation 299
Lana TV 29
La Nouvelle Tribune 315
La Press 271

La République 289
Latakia, Syria 24
Latin America xii
La Tribune 299
La Vie Eco 315
League of Nations, the 19, 37, 76
Lebanese Broadcasting Corporation (LBC) 4, 9, 13, 15
  Lebanese Broadcasting Corporation International (LBCI) 7, 11, 13
Lebanon xviii, xix, xxi, xxiii, xxiv, xxv, xxvi, xxvii, xxx, xxxi, xxxiii, xxxv, xxxvii, 1–10, 12–16, 21–22, 24, 30, 34, 38, 41, 56, 84, 94, 96, 100, 128, 139–140, 154, 157, 167, 327–332, 335, 337, 339
  Cybercrimes Bureau 14
  Ministry of Information 8
  Ministry of Telecommunications 14
  National Audio-Visual Council (NAVC) 8–9
  National Pact 6
L'Economiste 315
Le Courrier de l'Egypte 218
legislation 10, 25, 32, 62, 88, 122, 134, 153, 157, 182, 187, 198, 210, 221, 271, 276, 306
Le Messager 287
Le Moniteur Algérien 287
Lemrabet, Ali 313
Le Peuple 289
Les Inspirations Eco 315
L'Estafette d'Alger 287
Le Temps d'Algérie 293, 295
Levant, the xxxvii, 3, 22
L'Expression 294
liberalism xvi, xviii, xx, xxi, xxxi, 4, 7, 12, 22, 25, 63, 94, 97, 105, 113, 132, 141, 146, 157, 159, 164, 169, 217, 219, 237, 239–241, 245–246, 278, 281, 291
Liberté 293, 296
Libiyana 261
Libya 261
Libya xiii, xix, xxi, xxiii, xxiv, xxv, xxvi, xxx, xxxi, xxxiii, xxxv, xxxvii, 131,

137, 216, 233, 242, 249–263, 268, 274, 285, 326–327, 330–331, 335–337, 339
General Media Union (GMU) 258
Government of National Accord (GNA) 256, 259
High Media Council (HMC) 256
House of Representatives (HoR) 255
Ministry of Culture 256
Ministry of Information 252, 256
Ministry of Information and National Leadership 252
National Transitional Council (NTC) 255–256
Revolutionary Command Council (RCC) 252
Libya 24 257, 259
Libya Al-Ahrar TV 131, 137, 259–260
Libya Al-Rasmiya TV 256
Libya Al-Watan 259
Libya Al-Wataniya TV 256
Libya Dawliya TV 260
Libyan Islamic Fighting Group 259
Libyan National Army (LNA) 255–256, 259
  Operation Dawn 255
  Operation Dignity 255
Libyan National Forces Alliance (NFA) 260
Libyan Radio and Television Network (LRT) 256
LibyaPhone 261
Libya's Channel 259
Libya Telecom and Technology (LTT) 261
LinkedIn 279
Lisan Al-Maghreb 306
Lockerbie bombing 253
London, Great Britain xiii, 96, 100, 104, 132, 229, 259
L'Orient le Jour 12
  L'Orient Today 12

Ma'an, Jordan 57
MadaMasr 224, 229
Maghreb Emergent 296

Maghreb, the xxxvii, 234, 337
Mahas (language) 234
Mahdi, the 234–235
  Mahdist movement 234–235
mahdiyya 235
Mahfouz, Najib 166
Majalat Al-Kuwait 166
Majid 118
Majid TV 119
Makhlouf, Rami 24, 29, 31, 33
Malayalam (language) 146
Maldives, the 140
Mali 251, 285
Maliki school 268
Mancini, Paolo xvi, xvii, xviii, xxii, xxiv, xxv, xxviii, xxxii, xxxiii, 325
Mandean language 75
March 14 Alliance 5–6, 11–12
Marconi Company 219
Marina FM 172
Maroc Soir Group 315
Maroc Télécom 315
Maronite Church. *See* Christianity: Maronite Christianity
Marzouki, Moncef 274
Mashriq, the xxiii, xxxvii
Mattar, Khawla 152
Mauritania xiii, 140, 285, 303
MBC xxxv, 96, 99–100, 104, 150, 226, 329, 337
McQuail, Dennis xiv, xvi
Mecca, Saudi Arabia 92–95, 104
  Grand Mosque 95, 97, 104
media. *See also* press, the
  alternative xxxiii, 211, 330
  control of xix, xxix, 28, 33, 65, 101, 151, 154, 159, 176, 197, 205, 210, 272, 274, 308, 318, 327
  digital xii, xxvi, 69–70, 91, 104, 114–115, 119, 138, 169, 178, 191, 227, 312, 327, 335, 340
  local xxxiii, 103, 121, 260, 290
  public service xxix, 222, 281, 282, 311, 313. *See also* broadcasting: public service

Media City 66, 115, 118, 138, 227, 337
media convergence xxxiv, xxxvi, 118–119, 193, 209–210, 230, 298
media policy 42, 97, 103, 148, 152, 178, 256, 327
media reform 68, 151, 222, 301, 310
Medina, Saudi Arabia 92–94
Médi-Télécom 315
Mediterranean Sea 215, 250, 268, 285, 303
Megaphone 12, 15
Mekran, Pakistan/Iran 183
Mellor, Noha xx
MENA region (Middle East and North Africa) xii, xx, xxi, xxii, xxiii, xxvi, xxvii, xxviii, xxx, xxxi, xxxiv, xxxvii, 117–118, 121, 190, 324–325, 337–340
Merad, Ali 287
Mesopotamia 73
  Akkadian Empire 73
  Chaldea 73
Middle East Broadcasting Center Network 118
migrants x, xi, xxxi, 75, 123, 128, 217, 218, 251. *See also* refugees
Mijalit Al-Johara 131
military xix, 20–22, 26, 28, 31–34, 38–41, 43–46, 49–50, 74, 76, 78, 100, 140, 147, 164, 167–168, 182, 199–201, 216–217, 219, 233, 236–242, 245–246, 252, 255, 262–263, 329
Misrata TV 257
Misr Cinema Company 226
mobile phones xxvi, xxxv, 14, 67, 86, 102, 121, 158, 173–174, 190–191, 205–206, 210, 228–229, 243–244, 261, 278, 298, 316–317, 319, 334–335
mobilization xix, 23, 170, 175, 211, 217, 219, 221, 239, 244, 249, 326–327, 339
Mobily 102
modernization xix, xxx, xxxiv, 10, 49, 59, 93–96, 103, 149–150, 198, 225, 227, 230, 235, 250–252, 297, 307–309, 326–327, 335, 339
Mohammed VI of Morocco 305, 308
  "9 March speech" 305

Mohtawa 119, 123
monarchy 56, 58, 60, 92, 99, 110, 164, 186, 219, 305, 307, 310, 312
Monastir, Tunisia 269
monopoly 8, 13, 23, 47, 60, 64, 74, 139, 189, 197, 208, 220, 228, 290–291, 294, 297–299, 311, 315
Monroe, William 152
Moroccan Dahir 306, 309
Morocco xix, xxi, xxiii, xxv, xxvi, xxxi, xxxii, xxxv, xxxvii, 285, 303–319, 326–327, 329, 332, 335, 337
  Agence Nationale de Réglementation des Télécommunications 317
  Anti-Terrorism Law (2003) 312
  Audiovisual Communication Law (2005) 311, 314
  Caisse de Dépôt et de Gestion (CDG) 313
  Casablanca Stock Exchange 305
  Digital Morocco 2013 316
  Digital Morocco 2020 316
  Equity and Reconciliation Commission (ERC) 308–309
  Family Status Law (2004) 308
  La Société Nationale de Radiodiffusion et de Télévision (SNRT) 311, 318
  Law 24–96 (1996) 315
  Ministry of Communication 311
  Ministry of Social Development 308
  Moroccan Penal Code 304
  National Press Council 312, 314
  Office Chérifien des Phosphates (OCP) 313
  Penal Law 312
  Press and Publications Code 312, 314
  Royal Institute of Amazigh Culture (IRCAM) 308–309
Morsi, Mohammed 136, 217, 223
Mosque Radio 129–130
Mosul, Iraq 75–76, 79
Moukaddam, Mohammed 295
Mroueh, Kamel 12
MTC Touch 13
MTN 210, 243

MTN Group Ltd. 31
 MTN Syria 31
M Tunisia 275
Mubarak, Hosni 223, 225–227, 229
mudawana 304, 308–309
Murr, Elias 11
Murr Televsion (MTV) 5, 9, 15
Musandam, Oman 183
Muscat House for Press, Publishing and Distribution 188
Muscat, Oman 183
Muslim Brotherhood xxv, 98, 131, 136, 216–217, 223, 259
Muslim Scholars Commission 85

Nabeul, Tunisia 269
Nabth Al-Kuwait 172
Nas FM 208
Nasra, Larbi 277
Nasserism 58
National Broadcasting Network Lebanon (NBN) 9
National Democratic Institute (NDI) 152
National Geographic Abu Dhabi 119
National Geographic Al-Arabiya 119
National Islamic Front (NIF) 236, 242
nationalism xxiii, 20, 22, 58, 93, 148, 152, 156, 218, 233, 235, 252, 306
National Liberation Front (FLN) 288, 289, 290, 291, 292. *See also El-Moudjahid*
nation-building 95, 114, 129, 133, 201, 307
NATO xix, 254
Nema, Abdullah Hussein 131
Nerone, John xvi
Nessma TV 275, 277
Netflix 104, 159–160
news agencies 25, 28, 64, 82, 112, 153, 202, 253–254, 257–258, 333
newspapers xiii, xvii, xxii, xxxii, xxxiv, 3–5, 8, 11–13, 22–24, 27, 29, 39–45, 57–67, 74, 76–78, 81–86, 94–95, 99–100, 111–112, 114, 117–119, 121–123, 130–133, 137–138, 148–156, 166, 170–172, 176–178, 184, 186–188, 190–191, 200–205, 207–211, 218–219, 224–227, 233, 235, 237, 239–240, 242, 244–246, 250–254, 257–258, 269–271, 273–275, 277, 280–282, 287–296, 298–300, 306–307, 313–315, 318, 333, 339
Nida' Al-Watan 12
Nidaa Tounis 274, 277
Niger 285
Nigeria 251
Nile River 215
 Nile Delta 215, 220
NileSat xxxv, 139, 227
Nimeiry, Ja'afer 236–239, 241, 243
Ninar FM 29
Nineveh, Iraq 75
Nobel Prize 203
North America i, xvi, 288
North Korea xviii
Northwestern University in Qatar 121, 139
Nour, Iman 132
Nuba people 234
Nubians 216

occupation 2, 19, 37–42, 44–45, 48–52, 55–56, 73–80, 164, 200–201, 235, 251, 269–270, 335, 340
Oea 254
OFM 172
Okaz 95
Olayan, Mohammad 65
Oman xxiii, xxx, xxxv, xxxvii, 91, 119, 181–194, 197, 329, 332, 334, 336
 Commercial Companies Law (1974) 193
 General Secretariat of the Council of Ministers 193
 Law of Declaring a State of Emergency (2008) 193
 Ministry of Information 186–187, 192
 Ministry of Transport and Communications 192
 National Center for Statistics and Information 183, 194
 Penal Code (1974) 193

Press and Publications Law (1984) 187, 193
Public Authority for Radio and Television 185, 187, 192
Radio and Television Private Establishments Law (2004) 193
Telecommunications Regulatory Authority (TRA) 190
Telecommunications Regulatory Law (2002) 187
Trade Law (1990) 193
Oman Cultural Channel 187
Omani Institution for Press, Printing, Publishing and Distribution 188
Omani Journalists Association 185
Oman News Agency (ONA) 185, 187, 192
Oman Radio 187
OmanTel 190
Oman Tribune 188
Oman TV 187
Oman Youth Radio 187
Omran, Abdalla 111
Omran, Taryam 111
On E 226
Online Bahrain 158
Ooredoo 278, 298
Orange 67, 229, 315
Orange Morocco 315
Orange Tunisie 278
Orascom Telecom, Media and Technology (OTMT) 13
Orbit xxxv, 156
Orbit Showtime Network (OSN) 156
Organization of Syrian Arab Radio and Television (ORTAS) 26
Orient News TV 28
Oslo Accords 42–43, 47, 49
Ottoman Empire xii, xxiii, 3, 19, 21–22, 37, 39–40, 45, 55, 73–74, 76, 127, 164, 199–200, 218–219, 235, 251, 268–269
OTV Lebanon 9

Pakistan xxvi, 135, 167, 182
Palestine xiii, xix, xxvi, xxxi, xxxiii, xxxv, xxxvii, 1, 4, 22, 37–52, 55–56, 58–59, 128, 138, 216, 325, 327, 330–332, 335, 337, 339
Basic Law (2003) 46–47
Electronic Crimes Law 47
Law 3 (2009) 47
Ministry of Information 42–43, 46, 48, 51
Ministry of Women Affairs 48
Press and Publications Law (1995) 46
Press Law (1995) 46
Palestine Broadcasting Service (PBS) 40
Palestinian Authority (PA) 42–44, 46–47, 50–51
Palestinian Broadcasting Company (PBC) 42–43, 49
Good Morning Palestine 42
Palestinian Satellite Channel 43
Voice of Palestine 42, 49
Palestinian Business Women Forum 48
Palestinian Legislative Council 39, 43, 46
Palestinian Liberation Organization (PLO) 41, 56
Palestinian National Authority 39
PALTEL 47
Pan-Arabism 58
parallelism, political xvi, xvii, xviii, xix, xxxii, xxxiii, xxxiv, xxxvi, 7, 11, 13, 215, 219, 325
Paris, France 28, 272
Pasha, Jamal 3
Pasha, Midhat 76
patronage xxxi, 6, 230
Peninsula 132, 137
Persian Gulf (Arabian Gulf) xix, 66, 109, 127, 145, 163–164, 168
Persian (language) 146–147
Peterson, Theodore xv, xviii, xx, 323
Petra 64
Philippines, the xxvi, 146
platforms xxxvi, 12–13, 15–16, 32, 44, 50, 67, 69, 98–99, 104–105, 118–119, 123, 135, 138, 140–141, 155, 158–160, 163, 170, 172, 174, 178, 191, 210, 224, 235, 245, 270–273, 275, 278–282, 291, 298, 304, 306, 309, 313, 316–319, 337

Polisario 304
Popular Mobilization Forces 85
Press Association, the 8, 62
press, the xxxiv, 4, 8, 23, 39, 46, 50, 58, 60, 61, 62, 63, 73, 76, 81, 82, 94, 95, 98, 104, 111, 133, 134, 140, 151, 152, 163, 165, 171, 175, 177, 178, 205, 208, 218, 223, 235, 236, 237, 238, 239, 240, 241, 244, 245, 246, 252, 253, 257, 258, 270, 271, 275, 276, 291, 292, 294, 307, 311, 315. *See also* media
   freedom of 46, 58, 60, 62–63, 73, 81, 134, 140, 151–153, 165, 177–178, 206, 212, 221, 237–239, 245, 253, 271, 275–276, 292, 311–312, 315
prison 4, 8, 39, 42, 47, 51, 81, 95, 134, 139, 150–151, 171, 177, 204, 206, 217, 228, 253, 272–273, 293, 307
Progressive Socialist Party 11. *See also Al-Anba'*
protest 5, 7, 15, 22, 25, 27, 68, 82, 86, 88, 137, 205, 219, 223, 229, 290–291, 304–305, 309

Qadhafi, Mu'ammar. *See* Al-Qadhafi, Mu'ammar
Qatar xiii, xxiii, xxvii, xxix, xxxiii, xxxv, xxxvii, 8, 12, 28, 30, 82, 91, 96, 100–101, 104, 119, 121, 127–141, 145, 159, 189, 229, 256, 259–260, 278, 298, 326, 329, 332, 334, 337, 340
   Al-Shura Council 132
   Central Municipal Council 132
   Ministry of Defense 130
   Ministry of Education 130
   Ministry of Foreign Affairs 132
   Ministry of Information 133
   Ministry of Information and Culture 133
   National Council for Culture, Arts and Heritage 133
Qatar Broadcasting Service 130
Qatar Cablevision (QCV) 139
Qatar General Broadcasting and Television Corporation 133
Qatar Media Corporation 133
Qatar Public Telecommunications Corporation (Q-Tel) 139
Qatar Radio 130
Qatar Tribune 132
Qatar TV 131, 137, 139
   Channel 2 131
Quds News Network 44, 47
Qur'an 119, 130, 201, 234, 259
Qur'an Radio 112, 130
Quryna 254

Rabat, Morocco 307, 316
Rabrab, Issad 293
Radio Aden 200
Radio Al-Balad 64
Radio Algiers 297
Radio Al-Hisen 184
Radio Al-Rabiaa 238
Radio Baghdad 166
Radio Bahrain 149
Radio Berlin 148
Radio Cairo 166
Radio Corporation of America (RCA) 167
Radiodiffusion et Télévision Marocaine (RTM) 307, 311
Radio Free Palestine 50, 52
Radio M 296
Radio Mirchi 119
Radio Monte Carlo Middle East 95
Radio Muscat 184
Radio Nisaa FM 48
Radio Orient 13
radio stations xxiv, xxvii, xxxii, xxxiii, xxxiv, 4, 13, 22, 23, 26, 27, 28, 29, 30, 33, 40, 41, 42, 43, 44, 45, 46, 48, 49, 50, 58, 59, 60, 63, 64, 65, 66, 77, 81, 83, 85, 86, 95, 103, 112, 117, 118, 119, 121, 129, 130, 133, 137, 145, 157, 163, 166, 167, 168, 172, 183, 184, 185, 187, 188, 192, 200, 201, 202, 205, 206, 208, 209, 211, 219, 220, 227, 233, 236, 238, 241, 242, 243, 250, 251, 252, 253, 254, 257, 258, 259, 260, 263, 267, 269, 270, 271, 274, 275, 276, 277, 280, 281, 282, 288, 289, 296, 297, 300, 305, 306, 307,

308, 309, 311, 313, 314, 330, 332, 339, 340. *See also* community radio
Rajab, Sameera 153, 156
Ramadan 97
Ramallah, West Bank 40, 43, 49, 58
Raqqa, Syria 26–27
Ras Al-Khaimah, UAE 109
Rassemblement Constitutionnel Démocratique (RCD) 270, 272
Red Sea 55, 95, 197–198, 215, 234
refugees 1, 19, 22, 34, 38, 56, 332. *See also* migrants
regulation xvi, xxviii, xxix, 10, 22, 46–47, 61, 64, 77, 98, 109, 113–115, 122, 141, 154, 156, 163, 173, 178, 197, 205, 221–222, 225, 229, 256, 262–263, 268, 276–277, 280, 307, 319, 324, 326, 335, 340
Reporters Without Borders xxviii, 26, 153, 224, 312
Republic of Iraq 80–81
Republic of South Sudan xxv, 233–234, 236
Reuters 118
revolution xvi, 23, 39, 74, 76–78, 92, 96, 113, 120, 131, 147, 155, 158, 197, 200–201, 203–204, 207, 217, 222, 228, 234–238, 240, 244, 250, 252–253, 267, 269–270, 275–276, 278–281, 288, 291, 327
Riyadh, Saudi Arabia 93, 95, 98, 103, 199, 206–207
Rojava 25, 27
Roman Empire 268
Ronahi 27
Rotana xxxv, 13, 99–100, 329
Roya TV 64–66
RTV International 150
Rugh, William xix, xx, xxix, xxxii, 23, 43, 61, 94–95, 100–101, 113, 249, 324, 329
  The Arab Mass Media xix
  The Arab Press xix
Russian Federation xviii, xxii, 183
Ruwudaw 85
Ruz Al-Youssef 219

Saba'a Net 205–206
Saba'a Yemeni News 202
Sabafon 210
Sabahiyat 317
Sabha, Libya 250
Sabilurashad 270
Sabour, Salah Abdel 166
Sada Al-Usbu 155
Sada El-Balad TV 226
Sahara Desert 268
Salafi Madkhali movement 259–260
Salahud-Din, Iraq 75, 79
Salalah, Oman 184
Salamah, Raif 32
Salam family 11
Saleh, Ali Abdallah 199
Salman, Talal 12
Sama Al-Fan (SAPI) 29
Sama TV 29
Sana'a 199–200
Sana'a TV 202
Sana'a, Yemen 202, 206–209
Sanafir Island, Saudi Arabia 216
San Remo conference 76
Sanussiya Brotherhood 252
Sarajevo, Bosnia and Herzegovina 136
Sarkis, Elias 4
satellite 138, 250, 305. *See* television: satellite
satellite boom, the 100
Saudi Arabia xxiii, xxiv, xxvi, xxvii, xxx, xxxii, xxxiii, xxxv, xxxvii, 8, 11–13, 19, 55, 68, 74, 82–83, 91–105, 111, 119, 127, 129, 135, 139–141, 145, 147, 152, 154–156, 159–160, 163, 168, 182, 188, 197, 199, 206, 216, 226, 256, 258–259, 325, 329, 332, 334, 337, 340
  Anti-Cyber Crime Law (2006) 102
  Higher Media Council 95
  Khobar 145
  Ministry of Communications and Information Technology 101–102
  Ministry of Culture and Information 97, 103
  Ministry of Information 94, 97

Ministry of Media 97
Press Code (1964) 97
Saudi News Agency 97
Saudi Broadcasting Corporation 96–97
SBC 96
Saudi Channel 1 103
Saudi Channel 2 96, 103
Saudi Research and Marketing Company 100
Saudi Telecommunications Corporation (STC) 102
Sawiris, Naguib xxxvi
Sawt Al-Aqsa 43
Sawt Al-Falestin 40
Sawt Al-Jazeera Aden 200
Sawt Al-Kuwait 168
Sawt Al-Yemen 208
Sawt Attalib Al-Zaytouni 270
Schramm, Wilbur xv, xviii, xx, 323
sectarianism 2, 6, 7, 9, 11, 13, 20, 25, 79, 81, 87, 113, 115, 146, 152, 154, 206, 236. *See also* confessionalism
Senegal 140
Sfax, Tunisia 269
Shabiba Radio 188
Sham FM 29
Shar'ia law 128, 130, 198, 236
Sharjah-24 123
Sharjah Media Corporation 117, 119
Sharjah Press Club 116
Sharjah, UAE 109, 111–112, 116
Sharm El-Sheikh, Egypt 216
Sheba 202, 205
Shi'a Islam xxv, 6, 11, 20, 75, 84–85, 87, 92–93, 128, 146–147, 152, 154–155, 198
  Ismaili 198
  Zaydi 198
Shihi (language) 183
Shi'ite Endowment 85
Shousha, Farouk 166
Sidi Ali 305
Sidi Bouzid, Tunisia 269
Siebert, Fred xv, xviii, xx, xxii, xxiii, xxviii, xxxi, 323–324

Sinai Peninsula 215–216
Sinan Al-Qalam 306
Sindhi (language) 183
Sisi, Abdelfattah 223, 226
Siwa Oasis, Egypt 216
Six-Day War 38, 42
Skhirat Agreement 256
Sky News Arabia 118
smartphones. *See* mobile phones
Snapchat 278
Socialist Party of Yemen 201
social media xii, 15–16, 32–33, 44–45, 49–52, 62–63, 84, 86–87, 97, 102, 104–105, 114, 121, 123, 145, 154, 158, 160, 169–171, 173–178, 191, 209–211, 224, 227, 230, 244–246, 261, 278–280, 282, 298, 304–305, 309, 317–319, 340
Somalia xiii, xxxv
Sousse, Tunisia 269
Sout Al-Omma 226
South Africa 31
South Asian Hindi 157
Southern Transitional Council 211
South Sudan xxv
Soviet Union (USSR) xvi, xxiii, 20, 23
Spain xxiii, 303–304, 306, 315
Spanish (language) 288
Star FM 119
St. Helena 148
Sudan xix, xxi, xxiii, xxiv, xxv, xxvi, xxvii, xxxi, xxxv, xxxvii, 135, 216, 233–239, 241–246, 326–327, 329, 332, 335–336
  National Security Bureau 241
  Press Act (1930) 239
  Press and Press Publications Law (2004) 240
  Press and Press Publications Law (2009) 241
  Press and Publication Act (1993) 240
  Press and Publication Act (1999) 240
  Press Council 241
  Press Court 241
  Radio and Television Corporation 241

Transitional Military Council (TMA) 245
Sudan Defense Force (SDF) 236
Sudaniya 24 239
Sudan Socialist Union (SSU) 237
Sudan TV 243
Suez Canal xxxi, 218, 220
Suhail 203, 206
Sulaymaniya, Iraq 75
Suleiman, Bahjat 29
Suleiman, Majd 24, 29
Suleiman, Michel 6
Sultan, Aysha 122
Sunni Endowment 85
Sunni Islam xxv, 6, 11, 20, 75, 84–85, 87, 92–93, 128, 146, 156, 169, 198, 251
   Shafi'i School 198
Super-station 172
Sureth language 75
Swahili (language) 183, 220
Sweden xvi, 245
Switzerland 298
Sykes-Picot Agreement 40, 55
Synergy Production 226
Syria xiii, xviii, xix, xxi, xxiii, xxiv, xxv, xxvi, xxx, xxxv, xxxvii, 1–2, 5–6, 11, 19–26, 28–34, 38, 41–42, 55–56, 66, 74–76, 79, 88, 94, 128, 131, 149, 251, 274, 326–327, 330–331, 335, 338–339
   Counterterrorism Laws (2012) 26
   Cybercrime Law (2012) 32
   Higher Council for Media 27
   Information Law (2015) 26
   Journalism Syndicate 23
   Law No. 10 (1991) 23
   Ministry of Information 25
   Press Law (1949) 22
Syriac language 75, 78
Syrian Journalists Association (SJA) 28
Syrian Socialist Nationalist Party 11. *See also Al-Bina'*
Syrian Telecommunication Establishment (STE) 31
Syria TV 28, 30, 138

Tagalog (language) 146
Tahkout, Mahieddine 295
Taiba TV 243
Ta'if Accord 2
Taliban 137
Tamazight xiii, 286, 288–289
Tangiers, Morocco 306, 316
Taqla brothers 3
Tarabulus Al-Gharb 251
Tartus, Syria 24
Tatour, Dareen 51
Tazi, Abdel Hadi 166
telecommunications xxxv, xxxvi, 13–14, 29, 31, 33, 44, 47, 49, 67, 101–102, 120, 157–158, 187, 191, 193, 228, 261, 278, 281, 297–298, 316, 329, 334–335
Telecommunications Regulatory Authority of Bahrain 157–158
Telegram 210
Télé Liban (TL) 4, 6–8, 16
Télé Lumière 9, 11
television xiii, xx, xxi, xxvi, xxvii, xxx, xxxii, xxxiv, xxxv, 3–7, 9, 11, 13–14, 16, 23, 26–30, 33, 41–46, 48–50, 59–60, 63–64, 66, 77–78, 81, 83–87, 93–101, 103, 112–113, 117–121, 123, 129, 131–133, 135–136, 138, 140, 145, 150, 154, 156, 159, 163, 167–168, 170, 172–173, 178, 185, 187–188, 192, 202, 205–207, 209, 211, 220, 226–227, 233, 238–239, 241–243, 249–250, 252, 254–262, 267, 269–271, 274–277, 279–282, 288–289, 291, 293, 295–300, 305, 307–309, 311, 313–314, 329, 332, 336–337, 340
   pay-television (subscription television) 103, 138, 307
   satellite xx, 27, 43, 60, 83–87, 96, 99–100, 113, 129, 135, 138, 173, 202, 227, 254, 261, 275, 279, 297, 340
Telma 307
Telvsa TV 275
terrorism xxx, 26, 63, 79, 88, 96, 104, 134, 140, 171, 216, 236, 292, 304, 312
Tetouan, Morocco 306
The Arab Echo 57
The Arab Peninsula 57

The Daily Star (Lebanon) 12
The Electronic Intifada 44
The Financial Times 131
The Guardian 244
The New Arab 28
The New York Times 131
The Official Gazette of the Hashemite Kingdom of Jordan 57
The Old Arabic Singing 172
The Palestine Chronicle 44
The Times 148
The Voice of Women 297
The Washington Post 99, 155
Tibdawi (language) 234
Time Magazine 131
Time of Algeria 293
Times of Oman 186, 188
Tiran Island 216
Tobruk, Libya 255
Traditional Station 172
Transparency International 79
Treaty of Lausanne 251
tribes 21, 93, 101, 133, 146–147, 164–165, 169, 198, 203, 234–235, 250, 255, 285, 332
Tripoli, Libya 250, 252, 254, 256–257, 259–260, 262
Trucial States 109
Tuareg xxv, 250
Tufekci, Zeynep xxxvi
Tumblr 139
Tunisia xiii, xix, xxi, xxiii, xxiv, xxix, xxxii, xxxiii, xxxv, xxxvii, 41, 131, 139, 259, 267–282, 285, 327, 329–330, 332, 335, 337
    1975 Press Code 275
    Communication Control Council 270
    Decree-Law No. 115 (2011) 275
    Decree-Law No. 116 275
    External Communication Agency (ATCE) 272, 275
    Institut de Presse et des Sciences de l'Information (IPSI) 271
    Ministry of Information 272, 275
    Ministry of Interior 271
    National Journalism Syndicate 276
    Office of State Media 271
    Press Council 275
    Tunisian and African Press Agency (TAP) 271
    Tunisian Communist Party 271
    Tunisian General Labour Union 274
    Tunisian Movement for Liberty and Dignity 277
    Tunisian Radio and Television Corporation 270
Tunisna TV 275
Tunis News 273
Tunis, Tunisia 269
Turkey 19, 21, 24, 28, 31, 34, 39, 55, 74–76, 78, 83, 94, 98, 102, 136, 138, 140, 200, 229, 251, 285
Turkmens 75
TV218 259
Twitter 84, 103–104, 121, 139, 154, 158, 170, 174, 210, 278–279, 318
twofour54 115, 118

UAE-24 123
UAE Journalists Association (UAEJA) 115–116
Umm Al-Quwwain, UAE 109
Umniah 67
UNESCO 63
United Arab Emirates xxiii, xxvii, xxx, xxxii, xxxiii, xxxv, xxxvii, 30, 91, 100–102, 109–124, 128, 135, 139–140, 159, 168, 173, 182, 188–189, 206, 229, 256, 259, 315, 329, 332, 334, 337, 340
    Cybercrime Law 114
    Federal National Council 110
    Ministry of Information 112
    Ministry of Information and Culture 111
    Ministry of State for Artificial Intelligence 120
    Ministry of Tolerance 110
    National Media Council 114, 122
    Press and Publications Law (1980) 112–114
    UAE Supreme Council 110

United Group (UG) 29–30
United Kingdom 181
United Nations 21, 37–39, 50, 56, 60, 120, 182, 252–253, 256, 262
 Economic and Social Commission for West Asia (UN-ESCWA) 39
 International Covenant on Civil and Political Rights 60
 United Nations Convention for the Rights of the Child 60
 United Nations Development Programme 128
  Human Development Index 128
 United Nations General Assembly 37
 United Nations High Commissioner for Refugees (UNHCR) 21
 United Nations Relief and Works Agency (UNRWA) 38
 United Nations Security Council
  P5+1 countries 183
United States of America xvi, xviii, xix, xxiii, 8, 20, 23, 27, 29–30, 44–45, 74–75, 78–80, 88, 98–99, 135–137, 145, 147, 150, 152, 157, 183, 200, 218, 236, 252–253, 261, 272, 327, 339
 CIA 150
Ur 84
Urdu (language) 130, 146
US Air Force 95

Vision 2021 110
Vision 2030 96, 98, 101, 131, 138
Viva Bahrain 158
Vivendi 315
Vodafone Egypt 229
Vodafone Group 229
Voice of Bahrain 148
Voice of Fighting Algeria 288. *See also* National Liberation Front (FLN)
Voice of Libya 252
Voice of the Island 200
Voice of Tunisia People 277
Voltmer, Katrin xxviii

WAFA 44

Wahag Al-Khaleej 191
wahhabiyya 93, 128
WAM (*Emirates News Agency*) 111–112
Watts, Edward 31
 For Sama 31
We 229
Wejhatt 191
West Bank 38–41, 44, 47, 56, 58
Western Sahara conflict 304, 312
Western world xvii, xxii, xxviii, xxxii, 28, 38, 47, 56, 132, 215, 218, 313
WhatsApp 15, 139, 244
Wheelus Air Base, Libya 252
WiMAX 67
women xxvi, 41–42, 48, 97, 110, 113, 128, 131–133, 152, 158, 164, 175, 217, 222, 251, 286, 304, 308, 317
Women Media and Development (TAM) 48
World Press Freedom Day 224
World War I 3, 19, 22, 40, 74, 76, 127, 218
World War II xxiii, 145, 148, 166, 200, 236, 269–270

Yas 119
Yazidism 75–76
Yemen 200
Yemen xix, xxi, xxiv, xxvi, xxx, xxxv, xxxvii, 88, 91, 131, 140, 182, 197–212, 325–327, 330–331, 335–337, 339
 Council of Ministers 198
 Ministry of Information 201, 204, 211
 National Dialogue Conference (NDC) 199
 Northern 198, 200–202
 Press Law No. 25 (1990) 203–205
 Public Prosecutor's Office for Press and Publications 204
 Southern 197–198, 200–202
 Yemeni Constitution 198, 203
Yemen FM 208
Yemen General Corporation for Radio & Television 202
 First Channel 202
 Public Radio Program 202

Second Channel 202
Second Radio Program 202
Yemen Satellite Channel 202
Yemeni Journalists' Syndicate 204, 206, 212
Yemeni Network for Community Radio 206
Yemeni News Agency 202, 205
Yemen Mobile 210
Yemen Shabab 203
Yemen Times 206, 208–209
Yemen Today 203, 206
Young Turk Revolution 39
Your FM 157
youth ix, xxvi, 38, 41, 105, 121, 169, 175, 202–203, 205, 208, 211, 217, 279, 285, 287–288, 305
YouTube 15, 84, 139, 158, 169–170, 210, 229, 273, 306

Y Telecom 210

Zadjali (language) 183
Zagros 85
Zahrat Al-Khaleej 118
Zaidan, Ali 255
Zain 13, 67, 86, 102, 200, 243, 270
Zain Bahrain 158
Zaman Al-Wasl 28
Zamirli, Bachir Ould 295
Zanzibar 183–185
Zaydi Imamate 197
Zaydi Shi'a. *See* Shi'a Islam: Zaydi
Zayed Digital TV 119
Zionism 37–40
Zitouna TV 277
Ziyad, Um 273
Zoroastrianism 76

About the Team

Alessandra Tosi was the managing editor for this book.

Melissa Purkiss performed the copy-editing, proofreading and indexing.

Melissa Purkiss typeset the book in InDesign and produced the paperback and hardback editions. The text font is Tex Gyre Pagella; the heading font is Californian FB.

Luca Baffa produced the EPUB, MOBI, PDF, HTML, and XML editions — the conversion is performed with open source software freely available on our GitHub page (https://github.com/OpenBookPublishers).

Anna Gatti designed the cover using InDesign. The cover was produced using the Fontin font.

This book need not end here...

Share

All our books — including the one you have just read — are free to access online so that students, researchers and members of the public who can't afford a printed edition will have access to the same ideas. This title will be accessed online by hundreds of readers each month across the globe: why not share the link so that someone you know is one of them?

This book and additional content is available at:

https://doi.org/10.11647/OBP.0238

Customise

Personalise your copy of this book or design new books using OBP and third-party material. Take chapters or whole books from our published list and make a special edition, a new anthology or an illuminating coursepack. Each customised edition will be produced as a paperback and a downloadable PDF.

Find out more at:

https://www.openbookpublishers.com/section/59/1

Like Open Book Publishers

Follow @OpenBookPublish

Read more at the Open Book Publishers BLOG

You may also be interested in:

The Image of Africa in Ghana's Press
The Influence of Global News Organisations
Michael Serwornoo

https://doi.org/10.11647/OBP.0227

Global Warming in Local Discourses
How Communities around the World Make Sense of Climate Change
Michael Brüggemann and Simone Rödder (eds)

https://doi.org/10.11647/OBP.0212

Introducing Vigilant Audiences
Daniel Trottier, Rashid Gabdulhakov and Qian Hang (eds)

https://doi.org/10.11647/OBP.0200

www.ingramcontent.com/pod-product-compliance
Lightning Source LLC
Chambersburg PA
CBHW040746020526
44116CB00036B/2965